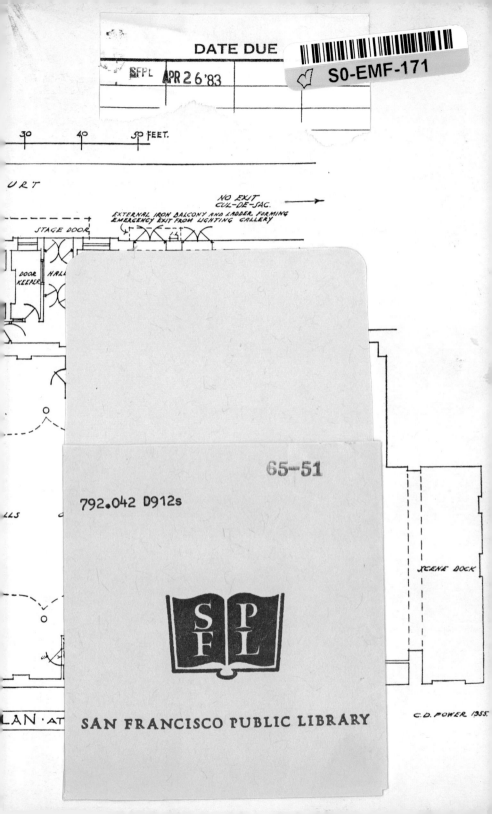

30   40   50 FEET.

URT

NO EXIT
CUL-DE-SAC.

EXTERNAL IRON BALCONY AND LADDER FORMING
EMERGENCY EXIT FROM LIGHTING GALLERY

STAGE DOOR

DOOR
KEEPER

HALL

LLS

SCENE DOCK

LAN · AT

C.D. POWER 1955.

ST JAMES'S THEATRE

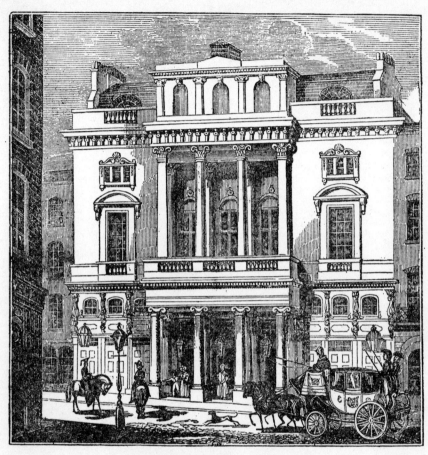

THE ST. JAMES'S THEATRE.

THE
ST JAMES'S THEATRE

Its Strange & Complete History

1835-1957

By

BARRY DUNCAN

with a foreword by
Allardyce Nicoll

BARRIE AND ROCKLIFF
LONDON

© 1964 by Barry Duncan
First published 1964 by
Barrie & Rockliff (Barrie Books Ltd)
2 Clement's Inn London WC2
Printed in Great Britain by
Robert Cunningham and Sons Ltd, Alva

TO
SINCLAIR, ERIC, ROBERT:
*other literary amateurs of my family,
octogenarians the first two before
publication of their second books*

CONTENTS

All illustrations are from my own collection. Grateful acknowledge-
ment follows appropriately, except for photographs which are not
marked and consequently cannot be given credits. The end-papers
are after an excellent plan by Charles D. Power, Esq.

LIST OF PLATES

Between pages 48 and 49

ILLUSTRATIONS IN TEXT

FOREWORD

EVERY theatre has a life of its own; and it is fitting that Barry Duncan's account of the fortunes of The St James's should start with a paragraph written as though he were about to present the public with a biographical study. On the fourteenth of December 1835, a cold and cloudy Monday, The St James's was born, its parents John Braham and his wife Fanny. Throughout his spirited chapters Mr Duncan never loses this sense of the livingness of the playhouse whose fortunes he is describing, and consequently we are given the impression, as we trace its varying managements and its numerous productions, that we are in contact with something warm and vital—not simply a building, but a personality. And when we reach the close of the book, with its movement from life to death, we feel that Mr Duncan is concerned with a story of manslaughter by insensitive committees.

He, of course, is not alone in looking upon the demise of The St James's in this way. If he had been alone, we might perhaps, hard-heartedly, have said that his approach was that of the sentimentalist; in fact, he is expressing in this volume what hundreds and thousands of people felt in 1957. Despite the efforts of almost all those associated with London's theatrical world, despite Sir Winston Churchill's offer to start a fund for the saving of the playhouse, the curtain dropped for the last time on July 29th: 'the house was full, but subdued,' writes Mr Duncan, 'they went away as from a funeral.'

The St James's has gone, beyond recall; and it is doubly excellent that we should have this volume. It tells us entertainingly of the great days enjoyed by this house during its span of a hundred and twenty-two years, indeed a noble record;

and it serves as a terrible warning. During that last sombre performance, John Gregson declared that the killing of The St James's 'should never have been allowed to happen', and he asked all the spectators 'to make a resolution' in their hearts 'that such a thing shall never happen again'. What Mr Duncan has done is to give us a volume in which full justification is provided for John Gregson's words and which may be of force in the hands of those who, in the future, are prepared to stand up against the power of modern barbarism.

ALLARDYCE NICOLL

PREFACE

SOURCES of information have been programmes issued by the theatre; published versions of pieces performed; contemporary periodicals from dailies to annuals; certain reference books; some memoirs and similar works; manuscripts and other documents in the British Museum, the Public Record Office and in my own possession. These have been augmented by the personal recollections of friends and other kindly persons whilst the account of the final thirty-odd years is naturally amplified by my own knowledge. John Braham's diaries, unfortunately brief and sometimes cryptic, were enlightening. By kind permission of Lord Strachie, I saw these by courtesy of the Historical Manuscripts Commission. For awareness of their existence I am indebted to Mr Wyndham Hewett whose *Strawberry Fair* on the life of Braham's daughter Fanny was of considerable service.

I have provided a list of most of the material used but to such I seldom specifically refer: otherwise my pages would have looked 'like a series of problems in algebra' to use Malcolm Elwin's words, in *The Times* of 4th November 1958, in a letter against the exasperating tendency to litter pages with little numbers. When quotations are obviously from playbills I omit identification but otherwise they should be easily checkable. Sources then have been included in the text whenever possible. Sometimes I may have relied too much on the perspicacity of readers, as for example when on page 2 I say 'Lockhart relates'. I feel sure though that there all will realise I mean the Scott memoirs edited by Lockhart. Most editions of these are all well indexed so no difficulty will be experienced in looking up the story about Braham which incidentally has been told in part many times since but never with any attribution.

I hope that know-alls will be patient when I elucidate what may seem obvious: things like London locations or even terms like 'Boxing Day' which recently I was asked to explain by two quite cultured persons from west of the Atlantic. My innovation of the capital letter for the definite article before the names of London theatres is for the sake of clarity since so many are topographical.

I have used the term 'director' throughout in its logical and original sense for so it is now common in America and in most fields of entertainment here. To say 'original sense' will surprise some of those 'college boys' who have become quite a feature of the mid-twentieth-century London theatre, since some of them appear to think that they invented both word and position. (Of course the university-trained entrant to the theatre is not resented, as long as he knows his own worth and earns a standing.) In a book of his reprinted lectures one of the 'new establishment' stated: 'But the director is a comparative newcomer to the theatre. Up to the end of the 19th century no such functionary appears on the playbills or is known for certain to have existed behind the scenes.'

Maybe such stupid remarks merit only laughter. They are certainly refuted many times in the following pages from the inaugural playbill onwards. Quotations from three other bills in my own collection will however prove that The St James's was not unique in the matter of directors, even if one from each couple mentioned was a one-time St James's man. The Princess's playbill for 23rd May 1844 carries the credit line: 'Stage Director, Mr EMDEN. Stage Manager, Mr WALTON.' The Windsor Castle Command Performance programme for *Hamlet* on 11th January 1849 has the credits: 'Director, MR CHARLES KEAN' and 'Assistant Director, MR GEORGE ELLIS.' Then when Henry Irving's Lyceum company appeared at the same castle to perform Tennyson's *Becket*, also by command of the Queen, on 18th March 1893, the programme included the lines:

'DIRECTOR . . . *Mr Irving.* | ASSISTANT DIRECTOR . . . *Mr Love-day.*' Furthermore it is also ridiculous to say as some do that nineteenth-century stage directors—whatever their title—were merely stage managers attending to props and scenery. Anyone who has read much about Sheridan, Macready, Phelps and Irving well knows differently.

Benefits, I might explain, were of two kinds. Except for any in aid of charities, those organised specially by beneficiary or friends went out of vogue with the Great War. Those which were part of the wages system had been almost totally discontinued thirty years before that. At The St James's in 1836 J. P. Harley was engaged as star comedian and director at £20 a week plus 'a divided benefit' at the end of the season. Normally only more junior players would share a night; even heads of departments or impresarios often had theirs. Expenses had to be met and ticket sales encouraged however. Two old actors met one day. 'Hullo—why so happy? Wasn't it your Benefit last night?' 'Yes indeed. Jolly good. Only had to make up ten bob!'

I have stayed strictly chronological throughout and have digressed only when I felt that to be essential. The diversity of entertainments have been treated fairly, except perhaps for concerts in the early days because I felt details would interest such a small minority and I am also musically unqualified to fully discuss them.

In my own younger days I had practical and varied experiences in different branches of the entertainment world whilst my past twenty-one years as a dealer in theatrical books and ephemera in the West End have certainly not been unenlightening. Consequently my viewpoint throughout this project has been that of the limelight man rather than of the galleryite; of knowledgeable and objective reporter and sometimes of critic rather than of glamour-dazzled seat-holder; of practical worker as well as student.

I must conclude by making apology to the many—especially

to those who are in varying degree aware of me—for neglecting to ask for their recollections. My excuse is simply that I came to dread more details. As it is, this finished version is considerably shorter than earlier ones, but then the historian, if I may so call myself, must discard as well as delve. Here now I offer my grateful thanks to Professor Nicoll for commenting in some detail upon my penultimate manuscript and for advising me to do the whole thing over again! As well as to those mentioned above and in my main text, I also offer my thanks to the following for having helped me in different ways; I hope no face or name has slipped my mind as I type. A third may not read my tribute for they have already taken their final curtain.

Richard Ainley, Allan Aynesworth, Leslie Bloom, J. B. Booth, Jevan Brandon-Thomas, Alec Clunes, F. Renad Cooper, Gladys Cooper, Rhys Davies, Valentine Dyall, Malcolm Elwin, Mrs Leigh Fermor, Jimmy Findlay, Gerald Forsyth, Michael Gough, Sir Denys Grayson, Nicholas Hannen, Lyn Harding, Rupert Hart-Davis, R. Hill of the Lord Chamberlain's department, William Hunter, Ann Lascelles, Prof. Dan Laurence, Charles Lefeaux, Moira Lister, Jimmy Lynton, Duncan Macarthur, A. E. (Matty) Matthews O.B.E., Eric Maturin, Donovan Maule, Malcolm Morley, Gilbert Miller, George Nash, Peter Noble, John Parker, Mr Parrish, Frank Pettingell, Mr Roberts (Lyric Theatre), Mr Rudd and others of Ashton & Mitchell, Leonard Sachs, Athene Seyler, Prof. Shattuck, Hannen Swaffer, Jessica Tandy, Ernest Thesiger, Sir St Vincent Troubridge, Horace A. Vachell, Harcourt Williams, of my publishers, John Bunting and Richard Wadleigh and to Professor Nicoll I must extend extra thanks for his Foreword.

A NOTE ON THE SOURCES

T HE following is a list of *major* sources of information. Some mentioned in the text are not listed. Many other books and periodicals have been consulted. My thanks to authors, editors and publishers.

Dictionary of Drama (A-G), Adams, 1904. *Dramatic List*, 1879. *Dramatic Peerage*, 1892. *Era Annuals and Almanacks*, 1868 *et seq*. *Green Room Book*, 1906, *et seq*. *Grove's Dictionary of Music*, 5 vols, 1922. *Representative Actors*, W. C. Russell, 1880. *Stage Cyclopaedia*, 1909. Stage *Year Books*, 1908 *et seq*. *Who's Who in the Theatre*, 1912 *et seq*.

A History of Nineteenth Century Drama, Allardyce Nicoll, C.U.P., 4 vols, 1930 etc. Without the help of this invaluable work my chronology up to 1878 could hardly have been completed.

The Athenaeum, Daily Telegraph, Daily Mail, Daily Express, The Era, The Examiner, Evening News, Evening Standard, Figaro in London 1835-9, *Figaro* 1874, *Gentleman's Magazine* 1835 *et seq.* (weather reports), *The Hornet* 1875, *Illustrated London News* 1842 *et seq.*, *The Players* 1860, *The Playgoer* 1902-4, *Play Pictorial* 1902-39, *The Observer, The Mirror* 1836, *The Sketch* 1879 etc., *The Spectator* 1835 *et seq.*, *The Stage, Sunday Times, The Theatre* 1878-97, *Theatrical Times* 1846-8, *Theatrical Journal* 1862-9, *The Times* 1835 *et seq.*, *The Town* 1837-41, *Theatre World* 1925 *et seq.*, *Touchstone* 1878, *Vanity Fair* 1874-5, *World's Fair*.

The Kendals, T. E. Pemberton, 1900. *Madge Kendal by Herself*, 1933. *The Days I Knew*, Mrs Langtry, 1921. *My Life and Some Letters*, Mrs Patrick Campbell, 1922. These have sections on the theatre. *Sir George Alexander and The St James's Theatre*, A. E. W. Mason, 1935. This is excellent in details but is not comprehensive. *The St James's Theatre*, anon., 1900. This souvenir was published by Alexander to celebrate the new century and his renovation of the building. He had commissioned Adair Fitzgerald to write the text which contains a number of errors but the portraits and view are interesting. Macqueen Pope's book under the name of the theatre, published 1958, ought to be mentioned here also if only as a warning to the unwary for it contains over a hundred errors of fact. Were it not for that and for its countless omissions it would of course have made my own work unnecessary. However I am indebted to it for the short speech, made by John Gregson on the last public night of the theatre, which *The Stage* also printed. I was not in front myself on that occasion but Mr Gregson told me the words are close enough to what he did say and so may be taken as authentic. Alexander also issued a few other souvenirs including a delightful illustrated one on *Much Ado About Nothing, Paolo and Francesca, The Prisoner of Zenda, His House in Order, The Importance of Being Earnest, Bella Donna, Liberty Hall.* Illustrated souvenirs of productions were also published from 1902 until the closing years by *Theatre World, Playgoer and Society* and *Play Pictorial.* Special programmes were also issued at times for charity matinees.

Les Acteurs et les Actrices de Paris, É. Abraham, Paris, 1859.
Dictionnaire Lyrique, Clément et Larouse, Paris, c 1869.
The Theatres of Paris, C. Hervey, London & Paris, 1846.
My Autobiography, Madame Judith, London, 1912.
Sixty Years Recollections, M. E. Legouvé, London, 1893.
Offenbach and the Paris of his time, S. Kracauer, 1937.
Offenbach, L. Schneider, Paris, 1923.
Naissance et Vie de la Comédie-Française, J. Valmy-Baysse, Paris, 1945.

Blanchard, E. Leman. *Life*, etc., edited by Scott and Howard, 1891.

Brandon-Thomas, Jevan. *Charley's Aunt's Father*, 1955.

Elwin, Malcolm. *Charles Reade*, 1931.

Lancelyn-Green, R. *Fifty Years Peter Pan*, 1954.

Macready, W. C. *Diaries* edited by W. Toynbee, 1912.

Morley, Henry. *Journal of a London Playgoer* (1851-66), 1891.

Planche, J. R. *Recollections*, 1872.

Robertson, W. Graham. *Time Was*, 1931.

Scott, Clement. *Drama of Yesterday and Today*, 1899.

Shaw, G. B. *Theatre in the Nineties*, 1932.

Wilde, Oscar. St John Ervine, 1951.

Wilde, Oscar. Life and Confessions, F. Harris, New York, 1930.

Wilde, Oscar. Letters of, edited by R. Hart-Davis, 1962.

Book I

CHAPTER I

JOHN BRAHAM'S OVERTURE

1835-1838

THE fourteenth of December in 1835 was a cold and cloudy Monday. Snow was in the offing and the ice on the Serpentine in Hyde Park and on the lake in St James's Park was already thickening so that on Christmas Day it could break and douse many a foolhardy skater. William IV, least obnoxious of the German kings, was on the throne, the succession of his teen-age niece Victoria still eighteen months away.

John Braham was in a quite natural fever of excitement for a new London theatre—his theatre, The St James's—was to open her doors to the public that night for the first time, a week later than originally planned. Yet workmen and women were still in a flurry of hammering, scrubbing, polishing; oblivious of other noises the orchestra rehearsed under the baton of George Stansbury; scene painters put finishing touches to the canvas walls of a fifteenth-century chateau; groups of players heard each other's lines in odd corners. The tang of varnish, wet paint and new-sawn wood mingled with the acrid smell of charred timber in the vestibule for already a fire there had baptised the building—though maybe in doing so it had cast some saving spell since the theatre, unlike many others, was never so attacked again. Agitating and superintending the maelstrom of players and staff were Braham, his beautiful wife Fanny and the director William Mitchell.

Almost sixty yet still acknowledged the finest tenor in the land, John Braham had been an idol for over thirty years. Early orphaned, he had been kept and tutored by the singer Leoni for whose Benefit he had appeared at Covent Garden before he was twelve. Dropping the alpha from his surname (originally that of the Patriarch) he had become a Christian and eventually one of the greatest and most powerful vocalists ever born in England. His popularity was immense, with his range of about twenty notes and a falsetto quite exquisite to some. He was too floridly flamboyant to please entirely the more fastidious colleague or critic. Wyndham Hewett quotes Miss Mitford's delight, which was in harmony generally with the populace here and in Italy. The Earl of Mount Edgcumbe, however, in his *Musical Reminiscences*, fourth edition, 1834, pp. 94-6, both praises him and analyses his faults, one of which he says was that to 'gain applause he condescends to sing as ill at the playhouse as he has done well at the opera' and regrets 'that he should ever quit the natural register of his voice by raising it to an unpleasant falsetto, or force it by too violent exertion'. The fact that as Chief of the Banditti he might find an organ in a cave and sit down to sing 'The Death of Nelson' or 'Scots Wha Hae' was accepted as a normal operatic idiosyncrasy. Small, and not exactly handsome with racial characteristics strong in face and speaking voice, he was welcomed for his charm and wit in quite good society. Composer of operatic music and of most of the songs he sang, in 1795 he had had as a pupil Lady Nelson, and had even dined with her famous hero husband when on a triumphant tour of the opera houses of Italy. As Lockhart relates, however, he was no player for when Dan Terry suggested him for a part in *The Doom of Devorgoil* (Edinburgh, 1830) Sir Walter Scott had demurred and though admitting Braham to be an angel of a singer he dubbed him a beast of an actor! Many singers have a pet sustainer, Braham's was porter of which he drank copiously, eating only when his performance was over for the day. He had all the self-confidence and love of ostentation common to his race. In his hey-day he travelled in his own gilded four-in-hand instead of by stage-coach—though that was of course for comfort not show.

At an age when most men with the capital he had saved would at least have been thinking of retirement, he embarked on this project of a new theatre. Earlier in the same year he had also joined Frederick Yates in the not very successful place of entertainment and exhibition called The Colosseum, on the south-east side of the Regent's Park. Surprisingly enough at a Parliamentary enquiry in 1832 Braham had said in effect that any player starting a theatre would be a fool. Behind him, however, was his wife Fanny Bolton, a Lancashire beauty more than twenty years his junior, as graceful and tall as he was tiny and unprepossessing and as powered by an insatiable urge to shine in high society for her own and her family's sake as he was to take it easy with his feet up and only a few cronies and a drink for relaxation. Before Fanny he had had a twenty-year liaison with the singer Nancy Storace which had been graced by one son, Spencer, who as Canon Meadows remained friendly and helpful. He had changed his surname after his half-sister Trotty caused a minor (to modern ears) scandal by running away from her husband. Storace had retired from the stage before the marriage and she died, aged fifty-one, only a few months after it.

The Braham's home in 1835 was not that more famous Fulham Grange, neglect-destroyed about 1960, but an older house of the same name, demolished in 1877 (*vide* Addenda, p. 213). The family was complete at the time of the new theatre and comprised Hamilton, Augustus, Frances, Charles, Ward and Josephine whose pet-name was Trotty. Their ages ranged from seventeen to six. The fifteen-year-old third child Fanny was a brilliant and beautiful blonde who was to marry four times and become a remarkably influential political hostess. Her career as Lady Waldegrave may be studied with interest in Wyndham Hewett's *Strawberry Fair*. The wealth she acquired she used generously. Her father and his other progeny would often have been in sorry state without her. The three eldest boys never amounted to much, each for a while became a singer, none of their father's stature. Ward, intended like Spencer for the Church, developed into nothing more than a useless though likeable waster.

Mrs Braham had not been brought up lavishly but her society expenses rose so enormously that even her husband's reputed income of £10,000 was insufficient. (A letter in my possession which he wrote in November 1816 when 'on the point of marriage' to her, agreed to £2,000 for twenty-seven nights.) The idea of a theatre emanated from her when she realised that his earning powers as a singer must eventually diminish. Aided by the minor dramatist and theatre architect Samuel Beazley, the still young and fascinating wife got the better of the old man's judgement. A decrepit hotel in King Street to the south of Piccadilly was bought for £8,000 and about £18,000 more spent on the new building.

The frontage and box-office were finished later, but ninety days after the workmen started The St James's was ready to open, even though heavy rain had delayed them for a week. Once completed, the exterior remained much the same until the end but auditorium and stage alterations, office and dressing-room additions were to be several times effected. In the beginning three- and two-guinea private boxes adorned the proscenium, behind a three-shilling pit was a promenade which was surmounted by two circles of five-shilling boxes underneath a one-and-sixpenny gallery. Almost a thousand could be seated. Two refreshment saloons were provided. Beazley was said to have taken as model the royal theatre of Versailles. Builders were Grissell & Peto. Interior decorations were in charge of Frederick Crace, the same whose magnificent collection of London views is now housed in the British Museum. Panels and carvings in the style of Watteau ornamented the crimson and gold with background of white that was the colour scheme.

Braham's first company was bright and young with a leavening of more experienced players in their thirties. Conductor and musical director was George F. Stansbury, who, born in Bristol in 1800, had been quite a prodigy on the flute, piano and violin before Catalani chose him to be her accompanist on tour. In Dublin he gained experience as musical director and though a better composer than singer, at The Haymarket in August 1828 he was cast as Macheath opposite Madame Vestris' sister Miss Bartolozzi as Polly in her first season.

Stage director was William Mitchell. Born in County Durham in 1798 he was already becoming known both as a droll light comedian and as a director since his London début at The Strand in 1832. He sailed for New York in 1836 to become an important innovator as actor-manager of the Broadway Olympic.

Companies at this time were normally engaged for the season with the London theatre year divided into a winter season beginning at or just after Michaelmas (29th September) and running to the end of Lent (devoted mainly to concerts), followed by an after-season from Easter Monday into the summer. Drury Lane, for example, opened on Saturday 1st October 1831, closed for Easter holidays on Saturday 14th April and finally after the Saturday performance of 26th May, about a month earlier than usual. The Lord Chamberlain's rules for the minor theatres will be dealt with further on. Scottish and Irish as well as provincial circuits benefited from the consequent influx of London players. New productions would be run for some weeks as patronage warranted and then alternated with other recent pieces. Revivals, fresh curtain-raisers and after-pieces would be introduced now and again as fillips. Until the 1880s the public would have felt cheated without a plurality of pieces but they could usually go in at about half-time at 'second-price' and still enjoy a couple of hours entertainment.

First vocalist of The St James's inaugural company was of course Braham himself. Seconding him was a pleasing light tenor from the Edinburgh Theatre Royal called George Barker who was said to have been once a page to Lord Byron's friend the Lady Caroline Lamb. Robert Strickland and Morris Barnett shared with Mitchell the chief character and comic roles. Charles Selby, Forester, Gardner, Hollingsworth and Stretton were the main light support. A junior was Alfred Sidney, not quite eighteen, who used his second name as surname until he reverted to his correct one of Wigan in 1839. His speaking voice was particularly melodious and his future career as actor-manager, including a spell here in 1860, and as a dramatist, was notable.

Soprano was Miss Glossop, a pupil of Braham's and daughter of the 'Old Vic' founder. Lacking the necessary power to sustain a position opposite Braham, her contract was not renewed after the first season during which she was cast mostly in revivals. Most brilliant of the girls was Priscilla Horton, a delightfully gay and sylphlike sprite of eighteen. At twelve she had joined her sister in Kemble's Covent Garden company and since then had often been on the same bill as Braham. When Charles Kemble took his daughter Fanny on her American tour, which resulted in her marriage, Abbott and Egerton took with them a number of other Covent Garden players, including Priscilla, when they took over The Victoria. She was at The Strand before being engaged by Braham and after leaving him she joined the Edinburgh Royal. Macready signed her up in 1837 and cast her as the Fool to his King Lear in the following January. The part was important since it had long been out of the hashed-up versions of Cibber and Garrick. Macready tells in his diary of their despair at finding a suitable actor. He thought of it as 'a fragile, hectic, beautiful-faced, half-idiot-looking boy'. Then Bartley had said 'A woman should play it.' Macready was 'delighted at the thought' and exclaimed 'Miss P. Horton is the very person!' Other parts she was to play opposite the great tragedian were Ariel and Ophelia. Her popularity increased with the years (so too did her weight—but we'll let that pass as said the wife in *The Shoemaker's Holiday*). After marriage to German Reid, The Haymarket conductor, she and her husband began the series of entertainments at The Gallery of Illustration in Lower Regent Street which continued after they moved north to the upper end at St George's Hall until 1895 in which year she died, as did her son and partner Alfred and their partner the large and chuckling Corney Grain. Her husband predeceased her. Their show of songs, monologues, burlesques and musical interludes was a counterpart to the rowdier music-hall, and many to whom the theatre itself was taboo delighted to patronise them.

Second to Priscilla was sixteen-year-old Laura Allison with about a year on the stage behind her. A singularly beautiful Celtic-type brunette, she had just finished a summer season at the Edinburgh Adelphi after having been at the Dublin Royal to which she had been introduced by Macready. The tragedian wrote in his diary that he thought she showed promise and when his starring visit was over she was kept on. But manager Calcraft's high opinion of her was shattered later when she stuck two long hat-pins into the calf-padding of a bumptious little actor just before he took a curtain-call one night. The pins glittered and the riot of laughter and cat-calls increased to pandemonium when he moved forward to bow for the pins entangled and brought him sprawling down to the footlights outside the fall of the curtain! In 1854 Laura, as Mrs Seymour, returned to The St James's as manageress in association with Charles Reade.

One of the older women was Mrs Garrick whose husband had been of the great actor's family. Her daughter was in the crowd from which, like some others, she later gained promotion. Another was Clara, Mrs Charles Selby, now thirty-eight and chosen to speak the opening address. Her husband, a couple of years younger, was tall, elegant and gentlemanly, a useful actor and the author eventually of over eighty widely varying dramatic pieces. Both had long careers and were much in demand at the major as well as the minor theatres. Miss Melton from the York theatre and Elizabeth Honner were among others to have parts in the first season. The girls Anderson, Josephine and Frood led the ballet.

Nearly fifty more names were on the opening bill but apart from the technical staff most of these were supers. Already mentioned was Robert Strickland, a large-faced droll little man in his late thirties who had been 'articled' to a barrister at thirteen. Wigs appealing less to him when alone than when supported by grease-paint, he was soon after that to be seen in a barn in Buckinghamshire making his dramatic début with sixpence as top admission. Since then he had played up at York and down at Margate, across at Ballyshannon and north at Edinburgh as well as at many London houses before his St James's engagement. He died in 1845 whilst in The Haymarket company.

Morris Barnett signed a three-year contract with Braham in November. Like Stansbury the conductor, he was as old as the century but had been brought up mostly on the Continent. As actor his forte was old Jews and foreigners but he was also to be author or adaptor of some two score dramatic pieces and to be music critic of *The Era* and *Morning Post*. At one time he helped to run and was doubtless therefore a voice at the Marionette Theatre in the Lowther Arcade. Mrs Barnett let rooms later in her house in Brompton Square for when newly-married George Augustus Sala called there to take apartments she assured him that she was 'the widow of that celebrated and gifted but misguided man'! The Barnetts however had separated long before his death in 1856. In the winter of 1835 he lived with his mother and once a week the ex-wife would call to collect her allowance. One evening most of that had gone on gin and she returned to Morris's home late at night, bent on making trouble. The police were eventually sent for but she clung to the bannisters and defied them to touch her. So they asked Morris to loosen her grip so they could swirl her outside. Successful, when the police got back to their station they found that she had forestalled them by rushing round ahead to lodge a charge of assault against her husband and the two officers!

Just after the contract between Braham and Barnett had been signed in November, the case was heard at the Middlesex Sessions, Clerkenwell Green, before Sir William Curtis and others. Mrs Barnett did not appear to give evidence for by then she had recovered from her spleen. The policemen were found not guilty but unfortunate Barnett was fined £10, bound over not to molest his wife for a year, and sent to prison for three months! Such an extraordinary example of English justice must surprise all except students of that side of London life. Beazley, being an architect of repute, was consequently a gentleman acceptable in City circles. He contacted Mrs Barnett to make sure that she regretted the affair, and then hunted up to explain the position to two other magistrates who promised to attend the court. The architect then called on Sir William Curtis in his City office and prevailed upon him to return to the court. With the actor again before him the noble knight made no mention of the penalties he had earlier imposed but with bad grace merely said that in the case before him the sentence would be a fine of £10. So, thanks to Beazley, Barnett appeared in Braham's first company after all.

A new opera was planned as star attraction for the new theatre. The soprano's sister Mary Ann Glossop was a minor composer, capable if not brilliant, and she was commissioned to compose the music for one, becoming, incidentally, the first woman to do so. The libretto, probably based on an earlier French work of the same name, *Agnes Sorel*, was by her husband, Gilbert Abbot à Beckett.

A custom of the time was the retention of a stock dramatist by a theatre. Fees ranged from little more than beer-money to a few guineas a week for which had to be provided new pieces, adaptations from the French or new novels or after successful pieces at other theatres. Sometimes additional fees could be earned by production elsewhere or when someone like Cumberland, Lacy or, much later, French, considered their work worth publishing. I am unable to reproduce any St James's

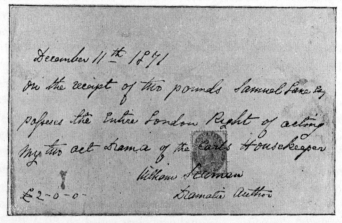

A Dramatist's Receipt

receipt but one of the famous Brittania's will perhaps interestingly suffice. With such returns, the dearth of living drama from the first half of the nineteenth century is understandably meagre. The period however was quite rich in unique literary characters and one such youngster was Gilbert à Beckett. His father was a well-known stern strict crabbit solicitor of Golden Square whose three other sons emigrated to Australia, the eldest, as Sir William, becoming inaugural Chief Justice of the new state of Victoria. Gilbert himself was called to the Bar in 1841 and eight years later became a metropolitan magistrate. As such he earned respect and affection, one of the few in such a position to do so. He was entirely self-made and owed none of his success to his father from whose home he ran away after refusal to withdraw him from Westminster School[1] when brutality there proved unbearable. Almost a hundred dramatic pieces are credited to him as well as the burlesque Comic Histories of England and of Rome which were illustrated by Leech. The Comic [legal] Blackstone was another successful effort and in company with Henry Mayhew he was founder-editor of the weekly *Figaro in London*. He started other mostly short-lived satirical journals but also contributed regularly to *The Times* and *Illustrated London News* and, from the beginning, to *Punch*. Born ten days less than a year before Charles Dickens, on 11th February 1811, they were to meet in the same journalistic-theatrical circles and become friends. Gilbert's experiences at (?) Westminster helped Dickens when he wrote about Dotheboys Hall, whilst Nicholas Nickleby was partly based on him and old Ralph Nickleby upon his father although the elder à Beckett neither ended up nor was he as bad as the fictional character. According to Forster the novelist's own father was the model for Micawber who it will be remembered however became an Australian magistrate.

Before his engagement by Braham, à Beckett had had a dozen or more farces and burlesques produced at four of the minor theatres. His first had been in January 1834 at the theatre in Tottenham Street called then The Royal Fitzroy but which was to be renamed many times. The original portico of it still exists at the stage door of The Scala. Quite a number of St James's early players were familiars there, including the ballerina Josephine and Clara Selby whose husband with Mitchell, Sydney, Barnett, Mrs Honey and the Mordaunt sisters were all there immediately before the rehearsing at the new theatre.

Now until the Theatres Act of 1843 the minor theatres were at the mercy or whim of whichever Lord Chamberlain might be in office. They could not open without his licence, only

---

[1] The school is said to have denied his having been a pupil.

when he permitted, only with what he permitted. Opera and classic drama were quite forbidden. However, licences usually allowed burlettas which meant minor musical pieces with any words sung and in rhyme. In the course of time such pieces 'evolved' so that eventually the description covered any one- or two-act piece which had not previously been licensed. Appropriate adjectives such as 'operatic' were sometimes prefixed on the playbills but even when manuscripts began to be submitted without songs the Lord Chamberlain normally licensed them without question. Fees collected by his Reader from the managers (not the dramatists) may have helped.

When it came to new theatres he could be quite unreasonable. When Rayner proposed rebuilding The Strand he was warned that no licence would be granted because his lordship said a new theatre was unwanted. Rayner defied him, got the local magistrates' licence for minor entertainments instead, and opened in the beginning of 1832 with ventriloquists, jugglers and the like. A month or so later Mrs Waylett, with Mitchell as her stage manager, offered proper theatrical performances. In her company were Forester, Selby, Strickland, Harley, Oxberry and the Garricks. They were still running at the end of June but perhaps only on sufferance in case anything resulted from the Parliamentary Committee then sitting and to which Braham made the statement already mentioned. Nothing resulted. Subterfuges included selling sweets next door at inflated prices so that lozenges at 4/- gave entrance to the boxes and peppermints at 2/- to the pit!

Because of the Lord Chamberlain's emphatic reaction their final season has a bearing on The St James's. Mrs Waylett tried again in November 1834. Her company included Mitchell, Forester, Oxberry, Priscilla Horton, Mlle Josephine, and in the bill was à Beckett's burlesque *Figaro in London*. The tickets they sold and accepted at the doors gave admission to The Victoria on the other side of the river! That was too blatant for the Lord Chamberlain who sent two spies in January to get evidence and then summoned the company to appear at Bow Street. Mitchell and Forester were fined £50 each. Mrs Waylett had fled to Brighton so the case against her and possibly others was adjourned. The theatre could not continue at the risk of such penalty and consequently closed as the weekly *Figaro in London* reported, with the loss of their subsistence by eighty-six families.

The King's Signature

Bearing in mind the twenty year association of the actress Mrs Jordan and the king, when Duke of Clarence, the royal friendship for Braham may be more readily understood. Mrs Braham also had many friends in court circles. The Strand Theatre case warned Braham not to risk building until assured he could open. So he went to the Top. Consequently, not long after Lord Devonshire's successful Bow Street foray to back his wish that no more theatres be allowed in the West End, he received a command from King William to licence one still in the planning stage. By July 1835 the Brahams had still heard nothing officially, so strings were again pulled and their friend Lord Duncannon was sent a letter, dated 22nd July, from Lord Conyngham, who had recently been made the new Lord Chamberlain, to say that His Majesty had commanded him to sign a licence for Braham without delay. The licence was signed three days later and permitted 'Burlettas, Music and Dancing, Spectacle and Pantomime' from Michaelmas (29th September) to Easter 1836.

The persistence of the Brahams was understandable for, apart from The Strand affair, a Memorial had been sent in protesting against the proposed theatre by the managers of Covent Garden, Drury Lane, The English Opera House and The Haymarket. In August the Lord Chamberlain received a similar petition from local parishioners. But the King's Edict had gone forth. Probably because of it John Braham became inclined to take chances for he blatantly referred on his opening bills to the new opera as an opera as well as an operatic burletta, and to one of the after-pieces as a farce, though that he later billed as a 'vaudeville'. In the following January his request for an extension of the licence for after Easter was refused. He then petitioned the King, asking for three months extra 'playing time'. Grumbling noises from officials may by then have reached royal ears since the answer received said that the licence terminated at Easter and that the King did not intend to extend it. Rebukes from the Lord Chamberlain's office were afterwards not slow to arrive. As late as 1842, for example, the annual sanction was delayed because of the 'uneasiness suffered' the previous season and when granted, it was with a caution to avoid offence in future.

1835

The first playbills went out early to the Press, the larger private mansions, the shops and hotels. Apology was made about the vestibule not being quite ready and the box-office under Mr Warne being temporarily opposite at No. 14. The three productions were detailed completely on a double sheet. After *Agnes Sorel* came the National Anthem, then *A Clear Case* and finally *The French Company*, both these being farces. The opening address was by J. Smith who, with his brother Horace, had been joint author of the famous parodies, *Rejected Addresses*. Every player and technician was mentioned except the dramatist of all three pieces offered! That was however quite customary whenever the author was the stock dramatist. Otherwise the writer, especially if well known, might be announced but by

St. James's THE Theatre.

Mr. BRAHAM

Has the honour to inform the Nobility, Gentry, and the Public, that his

NEW THEATRE

(KING STREET, St. JAMES'S SQUARE)

Will OPEN on MONDAY, Dec. the 14th, 1835,

WHEN, AND DURING THE WEEK,

An Opening Address

(Written by J. SMITH. Esq.)

Will be Spoken by Mrs. SELBY.

After which will be presented, FOR THE FIRST TIME,

With entirely new and extensive SCENERY, DRESSES, and DECORATIONS,

A NEW GRAND ORIGINAL OPERATIC BURLETTA,

Which has been some time in preparation, to be called

AGNES SOREL !

The **OVERTURE** and the whole of the **MUSIC** composed by Mrs G. A. a'BECKETT.
The DRESSES by Mr BRETT & Mrs BALDING.—The MACHINERY by Mr B. SLOMAN.—The PROPERTIES by Messrs. PURVIS & PHILLIPS
The SCENERY, by Messrs. ANDREWS, HILLYARD, NICHOLLS, and TOMKINS.
The PIECE produced under the Direction of Mr. MITCHELL.

Charles VII. ..... (under the assumed name of Edmund) .... Mr BARKER
(From the Theatre Royal, Edinburgh—his first appearance in London)
Baron de Lindon .... Mr STRETTON
(From the Theatre Royal, English Opera)
Count Dunois ...... (Minister of Charles VII.) ...... Mr BRAHAM
De la Grotte .... Mr BARNETT
Adolph .... (a Page) .... Miss MELTON
(From the Theatre Royal, York—her first appearance in London)
Agnes Sorel .... (Niece to the Baron) .... Miss GLOSSOP
(Her first appearance on any Stage)
Louise ...... (her Attendant) ...... Miss P. HORTON

Peasants—Mesds. Stuart, Parl, Willis. Walker, Honnor, Pope, Garrick, Penson, Johnson, Evanduke, Leslie, Gower, Jones, Smith, Brady, Thompson
Messrs. Phillips, Peart, Gill, Ellins, Willis, Richardson, Allison, Wilson, Hexham, Selkirk, Cummins, Fisher.
Vassals—Messrs. Williamson, Davis, Bishop, Guichard, Moore, Beale, Hart, Gray, Carlton, Robinson, Heslop, Scott, Alexander, Slack, Yates.
Soldiers—Messrs. Britton, Flemming, Hermon, Romney, Wright, Searle Randall, Powell, Stowell, Steel, Happ, Ravenscroft, Robins, Millan, Allen,
Swan, Andrews, Jefson, Williams, Thomas, Monkhouse, Kempshead, Green, Doyne, George, Hays, Vice, Mosley, Downey, King, Bedford.

In the course of the Piece the following Music will be sung.—

ACT I.

INTRODUCTION and CHORUS—**Nature thus smiling.**
CHORUS—**Prepare the way,** and CAVATINA—**In Camps abroad,** Mr BRAHAM
BACCAROLLE—**When Day is going,** Miss P. HORTON.
SONG—**The Sun and the Wind,** Mr BARNETT.
CHORUS and CAVATINA—**Peacefully pass away the hours,** Miss GLOSSOP,
SONG—**Oh ! breathe no word,** Miss GLOSSOP.
TRIO—**Who is yon presumptuous Youth,** Mr BRAHAM. Mr BARKER, and Miss GLOSSOP.
DUET—**It is decided,** Mr BRAHAM and Mr BARKER
RECITATIVE and AIR—**Agnes to thee,** Mr BRAHAM.
GRAND FINALE, with **Tyrolien Dance** and **Chorus,** The Solo Parts by Messrs. BRAHAM, BARKER, STRETTON,
BARNETT, Miss GLOSSOP, Miss P. HORTON, and Miss MELTON.

ACT II.

CHORUS—**Fill the sparkling Glass.**
DUET—**Vainly to me of Love you speak,** Miss P. HORTON and Miss MELTON.
AIR—**My Native Land, what pain to see thee,** Mr STRETTON.
DUET—**Ah ! yes, on my advice relying,** Mr BRAHAM and Miss GLOSSOP.
SONG—**Yes, if it's rightly understood,** Mr BRAHAM.
TRIO—**He takes her hand,** Mr BRAHAM, Mr BARKER, and Miss GLOSSOP.
DUET—**Boldly to me your caution speak,** Mr BARKER and Mr STRETTON.
SONG—**Triumph all my schemes attending,** Mr BRAHAM.
CHORUS and AIR—**To Battle is the cry,** Mr BARKER.
RECITATIVE—**Accept this Scarf,** and AIR—**Forth to the Contest,** Miss GLOSSOP.
FINALE and CHORUS:

no means always, and sometimes only indirectly as 'by the author of . . .'.

The London crowd gathered early outside on that chilly December evening. Four-wheelers lined the pavements of King Street, so that champing of horses and jingling of harness mingled with the din of the assembling throng against the faint background accompaniment of last-minute hammering as carpenters hastened their finishing touches within. Grooms and footmen slapped hands under oxters whilst ladies and their escorts gossiped amidst warm fur wraps and rugs, as *The Times* afterwards indicated.

When at last the doors flourished open, agog with exhilarating anticipatory excitement, the brilliantly costumed fashionable first-nighters hurried into the auditorium in such a rush at the side doors that the still damp distemper transferred itself from corridor wall to costume and jacket! The crush was so tremendous at the pit and gallery doors that not only did many get past without paying but attendant Golding was knocked down and his first night ended in St George's Hospital with a broken leg. A gorgeous chandelier in the centre and girandoles and stage lamps shed a glittering light upon the sparkling jewels of the ladies and orders of the men, the golden ornaments of boxes and balconies, the soft white of the walls, the deep crimson of the draperies.

Braham, Mitchell and Mrs Selby watched through the curtain peep-holes from the stage and thrilled as delighted viewers greeted the theatre and its decorations with repeated rounds of applause. Mrs Selby was charmingly gowned in white and gold and when all seemed seated and settled she parted the curtains to slip between and curtsy deeply before welcoming her auditors:

> Hovering 'twixt hope and fear, I come in haste
> To know if what you look on meets your taste?
> Survey our carving, ponder on our gilding,

And use your hands—thus—if you like our building!
You seem well seated in our Muses's bowers—
Crowded perhaps, but that's your fault, not ours!
Those girandoles ensure us from the dark,
Medallions, Watteau—à la grande Monarque.
Pit comfortable, rounded to a tittle,
And not too large, perhaps, tonight, too little!
Those tall white ladies who uphold the frieze
Are named Car—what? Caryatides
Perhaps (if here I'm out, suspend your laughter)
So called because they carry roof and rafter!
A petticoat police on rising salary,
To cry out 'Order! Order' in the gallery.
We've risen upon you like a rampant lion,
As Thebes of old was stung by Amphion.
All's not quite done, we're still in deep committee,
We mean to start a railroad to the city,
With branches well secured by bolts and hooks,
To join St James's parish with St Luke's.
Critics may cast that burden from their shoulders,
Railing is now confined to joint-stock holders.
Here ends my tune as trumpeter; what follows
Seems an affair exclusively Apollo's.
That God of Song, at sixes and at sevens,
With mighty Jupiter, who rules the Heavens,
Too weak with Jove's red thunderbolts to battle,
Dropped down on earth to tend Admetus' cattle.
He struck the light guitar for nine long years,
And when called upwards by the House of Peers—
Take down my words, reporters, while I say 'em—
He left a son on earth and called him Braham.
From infant years he now has tuned his lay,
How well, it ill becomes not *him* to say:
Grant tit for tat—excuse my woman's whim—
He gave his voice to you, give yours to him!

SJT B

Here, in St James's, now he wakes his lyre,
And rears an altar to his radiant sire,
Who views, well pleased, this temple to his praise,
And gilds our pillars with his parting rays.
Aid then our offering, sanctify our cause,
And grant us, gods, one thunder of applause!

Curtsying her thanks as the plaudits duly broke out she
slipped back between the curtains which a moment later swung
open to reveal an interior scene of a French castle, and the
action of the two-act *Agnes Sorel* began. It was dreary rather
than funny, its only dramatic interest revolving around the
mild ousting stratagems of rival lovers in the persons of
Charles VII (George Barker) and Count Dunois (Braham) for
Agnes Sorel (Miss Glossop). Stretton as the girl's uncle Baron
de Lindon, Priscilla as her attendant, Barnett as de la Grotte
and Miss Melton as a page completed the main cast. Mitchell
directed. *The Times* commented favourably on Braham,
Barker and Miss Glossop who took a call together, but the
warm applause which greeted them was for performance
rather than material since the critic thought the opera remarkably dull in book and score.

After the opera the girls Glossop, Hope and Horton sang
the National Anthem and the farce *A Clear Case* then followed.
Laura Allison romped through this as a vivacious young
hoyden eager to get married and freed from parental and school
restraint. She was supported by Mitchell as Josiah, Selby as
Captain Cramwall, Sidney as Mr Snap. Mrs Selby was Mrs
Loosely, Miss Hope was Signora Speranza, Mrs Garrick was
Flora and Miss Booth was Rose. *The French Company* concluded
the evening and was amusing enough to send the audience
away fairly happily. The setting was an inn kept by Hollingsworth with Gardner as his waiter. Priscilla Horton was a run-
away daughter and Strickland a stolid John Bull. Barnett took
the part of a touring star of the Théâtre Français with Mrs

Garrick as his prima donna and Josephine appropriately a ballerina. Mitchell played a 'barber who spoke for himself and everyone else'.

Two Saturdays later was the 26th, the traditional English holiday called Boxing Day because on the first secular day after Christmas the servants, messengers and tradesmen would solicit annual presents in decorated boxes and the squire's good lady, for example, would take around boxes of provender to retainers. On this day in town it had become customary to open the theatres with a spectacular musical or pantomime. The great Dr Johnson was exploited for The St James's when à Beckett adapted *Rasselas or The Happy Valley* for which Stansbury composed and arranged melodies.

Mitchell directed and took a part, that of 'an unhappy inmate of the Happy Valley' called Jimcrack after Johnson's Imlac. Only the original idea of a happy valley utopia was used in the one-act piece. A real Aerial Ship was invented (arranged by B. Sloman) to transport some of the inhabitants to a Fancy Fair near Kennington. Priscilla Horton was 'principal boy' Prince Rasselas, and Elizabeth Honner was his sister Princess Nekayah whose attendant Pekuah was played by Miss Melton. Characters mostly owed little to Dr Johnson however. Mrs Selby was 'a female philosopher in search of the greatest happiness principle' called Miss McDrawley. Selby was Philander Philpotts, 'a warm philanthropist', Strickland was Stilterton, 'a patron of literature', Gardner was a Gentle Shepherd and Hollingsworth was the Emperor of Abyssina (*sic*). The novelty concluded the evening which had opened with the opera which preceded *The French Company*.

1836

In the new year the opera was offered thrice weekly and on the first Monday a new two-act play was added to the repertoire. This was *A House Divided* by John Haines who was given the credit indirectly as 'by the author of' others of his works, for he was a popular dramatist who in twenty years was to have twice as many pieces produced, mostly at The Surrey or Victoria. In the new piece, styled a 'vaudeville' and played each night, Strickland was Oliver Ormond, captain of an Indian merchantman; Selby was Wilfred Worry, a married man; Forester was Frank Fearly, a single man; Mitchell was Corney Callaghan, the married man's man; Barnett was Sambo Simpkin, the merchantman's man and Gardner was the family's man Giles Gentle. They disported themselves with Mrs Selby as Mrs Worry in married fidgetiness, Laura Allison as Olivia Ormond in single blessedness and Miss Melton as Jane Jenkins in maiden doubtfulness. Then followed Dibdin's musical classic *The Waterman* with Braham as Tom Tug, Plumer as Dick, Strickland and Gardner as Bundle and Robin and Mrs Garrick and Priscilla as Mrs Bundle and Wilhelmina.

The sailor frolic was an opportunity for Braham's virtuosity. His three solos were 'The Bay of Biscay, O!' 'Farewell, my trim-built Wherry!' and 'Did you ne'er hear of a Jolly Young Waterman?' Plumer joined him in 'All's Well!' and then all the company formed up for 'Rule Britannia! Britannia rule the Waves!' *Rasselas* concluded the evening. *Agnes Sorel* was alternated with *The Waterman*.

Tuesday 12th January saw the introduction of the first really successful new piece. This was the adaptation in one act by Morris Barnett of *Monsieur Jacques* from *Le Pauvre Jacques* (Paris, 15th September 1835) by the brothers Cogniard. It was to be revived many times; the original was to be played here in the summer by the inaugural French visitors; another version, Robert Ryan's, proved popular at other London theatres as well as here too later on.

Jacques is a poor old musician who has been exiled from Sicily because of an indiscreet love affair and has become so crazed by misery that his rascally landlord can wheedle his compositions from him without due payment. Then his daughter of whose existence he had never even known, arrives on the scene to thwart the villain and save her poor old father. The curtain falls on the touching spectacle of the old maestro's gradual recognition of his long-dead love whose image he sees in their child. Barnett himself played the old man and Priscilla the daughter Nina. Both gave admirably sympathetic performances and were ably supported by Strickland, Selby and Hollingsworth. It stayed in the repertory until the end of the season and in later ones proved a useful stop-gap.

Covent Garden's counterblast on the inaugural night of The St James's had been Fitzball's version of Scribe and Auber's opera *Le Cheval de Bronze*. On 5th January Bunn had brought out his own rival but reported as more correct adaptation at Drury Lane as *The Bronze Horse*. Á Beckett burlesqued Bunn's version and produced this on Monday 18th January. The Parisian original had been done nine months earlier so Drury Lane and Covent Garden rivalry will be realised. The St James's burlesque was of course quite legitimate; the emphasis that it was based on Bunn's could have been because of hissing at that first night, though à Beckett's known personal prejudice against Bunn doubtless influenced his choice. As *Brown's Horse*, however, it lasted only a couple of performances.

The author slashed out at the end of the week in his *Figaro in London*.

> The piece was received throughout [he said] with a great deal of applause, but was hissed at the end by some of the same dirty gang whom we noticed at Drury Lane on the first night of the original opera. There is a gang of these dirty hands who get in with orders from some of the small Sunday newspaper and cheap press who all fancy they can write better themselves and consequently make a point of hissing whenever they can find an opportunity. We told Bunn this a fortnight ago. These hissers should be stopped at the doors and kicked on to the nearest station-

house. They may generally be discovered by their evidently recent indulgence of a penny shave, which by making the chin clean, brings it out in most frightful relief from the dirty cheeks and faded black cravat highly stiffened up to conceal the dirty shirt collar. These filthy beasts, fresh from the pot-house and redolent of the offensive weed, come free into a house affecting the air of savants and breathing their pestilential vapours in a foetid and truly oxygen hiss over the more respectable part of an audience.[1]

The review continued to show that the writer was not as pleased with Priscilla Horton as with Mitchell but then *The Spectator* on the same day said:

There are some things too absurd even for caricature and *The Bronze Horse* is one, so that the burlesque of that compound of noise, nonsense and tinsel produced at The St James's is a failure . . . and though less tedious and more amusing than the original, has already been withdrawn for its dullness. Mitchell's acting is capital—the perfection of burlesque, he seems quite in earnest and unconscious of the ridicule he is throwing on the character and the actor he parodies. The music is in one or two instances unsuited to the purposes of drollery and Miss P. Horton's execution of these airs is so good that it makes the audience lose sight of the fun.

A week later another new farce was substituted for the burlesque. This was *My Wife and Child* in which Strickland was Veto (averse to the nuptial knot), Selby was Plotwell (his nephew—not averse to it), Mitchell was Puny (a gross man

[1] In 1903 à Beckett's son Arthur published his *The à Beckett's of Punch* with the reservation that he did so without factual notes to hand. He then said his father ceased connection with *Figaro* in 1834 but took it up again some years later. A study of the theatrical notices, however, makes it evident that Gilbert did not drop all association at the time his son says he did and the above quotation is fairly obviously from his own penning.

and by trade a grocer), Mrs Garrick was Mrs Puny (married incog, averse to publicity), Miss Horton was Clare St Ives (a widow lady, eager for a second Lord) and Mrs Penson was Martha (nursing in secret and paid for secrecy). That Monday *The Waterman* followed the novelty, then came *Monsieur Jacques* and then *The Man with the Carpet Bag.*

The latter was one of à Beckett's better farces and had already been proved at The Victoria and The Strand where Mitchell and Forester had played Grimes and Wrangle as they now did again. In one act, the four scenes were set in the London office of wicked Lawyer Grab (Strickland), in a coaching inn, in the home of the heroine's father Pluckwell (Hollingsworth) and in the coffee-room of a country inn. Wrangle was a struggling young barrister who earned extras as a free-lance journalist inventing stories whenever at a loss for true ones. He was in love with Harriet Pluckwell (Miss Garrick) whose father was a local magistrate and defendant in an action-at-law where he risked losing his estate because property deeds could not be produced. Lawyer Grab not only had the deeds but was leading the case against Pluckwell in the town of the inn of the final scene. Afraid to let the deeds out of his proximity they are carried in a carpet bag by his man Grimes, ostensibly a stranger.

In scene 3 the Pluckwells prepared for court with Harriet snapping at her father on the defensive:

'That's all very well, my dear. But a judge is not a young woman.'

'I've heard some judges are old ones, so I'm not so very wrong after all.'

'Yes, my dear, but the decision requires a strict adherence to justice and impartiality.'

'Oh, then, I've hopes, if it depends upon justice. I thought it depended upon law.'

'Very true, my dear; but law and justice generally go together.'

'Do they? Then I suppose if they go together they don't always stay together.'

'My dear, have more veneration. Remember you are a magistrate's daughter. Law and justice are completely wedded to each other.'

'Wedded to each other! Then you'll allow that like married couples they don't always agree.'

'Your sex shouldn't interfere with these things. Females are getting as wise as men. Why, you young women will some day be wanting representatives in Parliament!'

'And why not?'

'Hold your tongue, my dear! I insist!'

All the parties eventually met in the country inn where one of Wrangle's fictitious stories brought about the dénouement. From the morning paper the landlord had read the warning to his staff that a thief was travelling the country with a carpet bag into which he stowed whatever valuables he could purloin. So when Grimes and Grab arrived the former, with the carpet bag, immediately became the butt of the suspicious staff who variously refused to serve him, whilst their ambiguous remarks would have been entirely lost were it not for the guilty consciences of the two rogues. The fun mounted hilariously until at last the bag had to be opened to prove its emptiness of silver spoons—but by that time all concerned in the case were present so the exposed deeds were recognised and the wicked discomfited, Wrangle and Harriet joined hands and Virtue triumphed. The various servants included Sidney and Gardner and Miss Stuart, who had been promoted like Miss Garrick, as well as six others.

A week later, on Monday 1st February, à Beckett's latest adaptation from the French, *The Mendicant*, was produced. This was in two acts with Mitchell as Pierre in the title-role and Mrs Selby as his wife Marie. Hollingsworth was Clement, a sanctimonious and evil old steward of an estate around a

Swiss village. Selby played the local marquis at whose coming-of-age party Clement stole a valuable cross but made Pierre think Marie was the thief. In turn Clement made Marie think her husband the guilty one so they took his advice and fled their home.

Act II opens twelve years later with the unhappy couple, now destitute mendicants, still believing each other guilty, home again for a last look at their native village. They are seen by Clement who, fearing the truth may out, sets fire to the factory and arranges that the wanderers shall be accused. They are saved at the trial by an old peasant who arrives in time to testify that he has seen Clement firing the factory, so from Pierre's neck the halter is whipped to tie instead the hands of his wicked enemy.

Strickland played pompous Mayor Grosnez and made much of his speech of welcome to the irreverent and facetiously inter-rupting marquis at the opening soirée, and then again as he conducted dictatorially the later incendiary enquiry. All action took place in the village square but admirable change of effect was contrived by Andrews and Nicholls who set Act I in summer time but the final scenes in the dead of winter with snow on the house-tops, on bushes and on the market cross, which effectively off-set the stealthy creeping of the villain across the darkened stage with his blazing torch before the flaring up of the factory and the appearance of fire-fighting villagers. The piece was well received and stayed in the reper-toire until the next novelty was ready.

Revivals meanwhile included operas *Fra Diavolo* and *The Siege of Belgrade* for in both Braham had proved popular else-where. As special attraction he engaged Mrs Laura Honey to be Captain Macheath to Priscilla Horton's Polly. On 3rd March they played the parts, both the first time, Strickland being Peachum and the Melton girl Lucy Lockit. Laura was a roguish twenty-one-year-old who had already captured the fancy of the town and had starred at most of the minors, one of which, The City of London, she later managed. In the summer to come she was to lose her husband in a capsizing pleasure boat off Battersea; she married again and numbered Lord Chesterfield among her lovers but before another five years had passed pneumonia had swept her too away.

Rebuffed by the King in February when he had tried to get him to intervene with the Lord Chamberlain to procure extension of his licence and permit (officially!) operas and farces, Braham naturally felt himself out of favour. Fanny Braham therefore approached the Chamberlain's assistant Mr Mash about performances on the Wednesdays and Fridays of Lent. She returned with the advice that no objection would be taken providing only one person at a time was on stage. More than one singer or dancer was apparently allowed.

Mrs Selby began the programme so devised with a mono-dramatic entertainment entitled *Thalia's Sketch Book*. This involved five quite long contrasting impersonations (inter-spersed with songs) as an eccentric manageress, a female pugilist, a mayoress, a stage-struck young girl attempting the balcony scene as Juliet, and others. Mrs Honey then sang and imitated personalities such as Guilia Grisi and Mrs Waylett. There followed a *pas de trois* by the ballerinas Anderson, Josephine and Frood. Braham and Mrs Honey then sang 'Vive le Roi' after which Morris Barnett presented his *Portfolio of Etchings and Sketchings* which was another series of comic monologues. Mrs Honey sang again, Miss Allison recited, two of the girls danced a minuet and a gavotte and then Braham sang his famous song 'The Death of Nelson'.

The performances concluded with those of the ventriloquist Mr Love, who was then rising to fame and had been specially engaged. (Gaiety star Mabel Love was his granddaughter.) His imitations of machines, animals, birds, reptiles and insects were quite remarkable and deservedly acclaimed as was his main offering of 'An accoustic sketch of eight voices entitled *Love's Labour Lost*' in which he enacted an extremely irritable old gentleman called Squire Screwnerve, Mr Jenkins who had just returned from a tour abroad and thought he knew everything, Harry Bang the gamekeeper who was having a disturbed sleep having been out after poachers all the night before, Christopher Catarrh who had been out with the latter and caught a cold in consequence, Gimcrack the valet and Swill the butler who both liked 'a drop', Simon the country lout and Minimus Screwnerve the son and heir. 'The whole of the characters by Mr Love without assistance will be heard conversing together at the same moment, above, below, on every side, in all parts of the theatre and the adjoining premises!' Costume changes were effected so rapidly behind screens that no sooner had one character disappeared than another was in sight with wig, cloak or other garment, as well as voice and personality, completely changed.

Through February and March revivals and new pieces continued to be introduced on the other nights until the season ended on Saturday 26th March, when they performed *Fra Diavolo*, *The Waterman*, an à Beckett burlesque of Byron called *Man Fred* where the title-role was a sweep, and *Monsieur Jacques*. Braham made a short speech and then Mitchell was presented with a silver snuff-box memento for his services as director. He sailed for America in the summer, but before that he took part in the celebratory performances under Hammond at The Strand for that theatre had at last been granted a licence. In the autumn he was playing opposite Booth at the New York National Theatre.

Some respite would not have been unwelcome. Many of the players had also been appearing at The Colosseum as well, and on such nights a coach was engaged to gallop them from one stage door to the other. They had played in twelve entirely new pieces and quite a number of revivals fresh to most of them.

Takings on opening night had been £170. Since then a third of that figure was higher than average with Braham revivals attracting more money than did novelties. No despondency

showed in the bills, however, for they puffed 'the highly successful *Agnes Sorel*', 'the roars of laughter and thunders of applause'
which greeted *Rasselas* and the 'acclamations of a crowded and
delighted audience' after *Monsieur Jacques*. The latter was perhaps the most truthful reporting but the general standard was
not bad and quite as high as anywhere else; poor receipts were
due much more to the out of the way location and to extremely
cold weather. Public transport was not then as well organised
as even twenty-five years later. Temperature that first December
evening had been 46°F. It was just as low when the doors
opened for the last night and when they reopened for the
home-going audience it had actually fallen to freezing point.

Somewhat prophetically one of the inaugural farces had been
The French Company for the theatre was destined to become
the home of French players for many years. Braham began the
fashion himself for he sub-let it for the first Easter season to
Jenny Vertpré whose company transferred from the Tottenham
Street theatre. This was not contrary to the Lord Chamberlain's
rules because although Jenny had to have his licence her
presentations were not in competition with the major theatres.
She was an exquisite little actress in her late thirties who had
made her début in a ballet in her native Bordeaux when only
five, chosen because she was pretty, elegant, and tiny enough
to emerge from a drum! She maintained a permanent company
augmented by visiting stars engaged for a couple of weeks at a
time. Amongst these were Mmes St Amand, Cossard and
Corrège; Mlles Clarisse, Clairval, Plessis and Thierret; and
MM. l'Herie, Fabien Mars, Monrose, Vizentini and Lauteman.
French players were no novelty and a top audience was
already in being. Seats could be subscribed for the season or
taken on the night. Prices were not cheap. Jenny made the front
of the pit into stalls (perhaps the earliest to do so) at 10/6d.
Boxes were 6/-, pit 4/- and amphitheatre (gallery) 2/6d. Curtain-up was at eight o'clock.

Jenny opened on 11th April with herself as Henriette in *André* after a novel by George Sand. Her presentations included classics such as *Tartuffe*, *Figaro*, *Les Fourberies de Scapin*, and lighter pieces such as *Le Gamin de Paris* and the original *Le Pauvre Jacques* with Vizentini in the title-role, Mlle Labeaume as the daughter and Lauteman as the rascally landlord, a part which had been created in the English version by Strickland. The season ran until 8th August and concluded with some remarkable guest stars for the Benefits, amongst them being the great Norwegian patriot and virtuoso of the violin Ole Bull, Madame Vestris and Charles Mathews, the Irish composer and baritone Michael Balfe and the lovely soprano Malibran. It must have been the last London appearance of the latter for her untimely death was to occur in the provinces only a few weeks later. Braham too had been on those last country concert platforms with her.

During the recess Braham recruited a number of new members for the company. To replace Mitchell he signed on John Pritt Harley for one, two or three years at £20 a week with a shared Benefit. In the papers this sum was magnified to £30. Harley was forty-seven, a top comedian of the period, of whom it was said that he 'only had to show his teeth to raise a laugh'.[1] He and Braham were of course old stage associates and the contract was agreed after Sunday dinner out at The Grange on 15th May.[2]

An amusing tale of Harley in his teens relates how he scored off a well-known fat and miserly merchant by the name of Jeremiah Dobs. The two were in a stage coach travelling on a lonely road over the Yorkshire moors and the exasperated Harley had been suffering from the grunting and snoring of the fat old man when he heard hoofbeats rapidly overtaking

---

[1] This can happen in modern times too. I remember for instance the burst of laughter which greeted Gordon Harker as Doolittle before he had said a word, at The Embassy.
[2] Braham's diary.

them, and rightly deduced them to be of highwaymen. So, as the coach pulled up and a masked face backed by pointed pistol poked through each window, Harley screwed his own visage into a dreadful idiot grimace and grinned and chuckled with apparently lunatic joy. At a second rough demand to hand his money over his head shook violently as he pointed to the still snoring Dobs.

'Money! Bobby never no money! Nunky pays for Bobby. Nunky pays for Bobby!'

'Bah!' said one highwayman to the other. 'He's a spooney. Draw the other one!'

A slap brought the snorer quickly to reality and to the tune of Harley's 'Nunky! Nunky! Poor man wants money! Give poor man money!' the merchant lost purse, watch and pocket-book whilst wise fool Harley saved his little all and gained a wonderful story.

Another recruit was Madame Sala who lived opposite the theatre and was a teacher of singing. Her father had been a plantation owner in the West Indies but she had been educated and married in London. Her husband died a few weeks after the birth of their son, who was to become famous as George Augustus Sala the journalist. Since she was left with insufficient means to support five children she had to earn a living. Charles Kemble gave her a chance in opera at Covent Garden, but the children prevented her exploiting her success and so she turned to teaching. An accomplished pianist, she was also in demand as accompanist at the well-known Velluti's Academy.

Five novices were engaged: John Parry, jun., who progressed to become a very popular entertainer; Elizabeth Rainforth who was to win fame in the operatic world and be the first *Bohemian Girl*; Julia and Kitty Smith, the nieces of famous Kitty Stephens who had become the Countess of Essex. The fifth was the lovely and talented seventeen-year-old, Fanny Stanley whose name, however, was only two months away in St Peter's Book.

Now the green-room had quickly become quite a haunt of a circle of literary as well as dramatic folk. One of the former was the well-known music critic and editor of *The Chronicle*, George Hogarth, a Scotsman and old friend of Braham's. His daughter Kate had recently married Charles Dickens who had been a reporter on the same paper, and he too was soon a familiar at the theatre where he cemented his friendship with Gilbert à Beckett. Early this year Braham commissioned Dickens and another young man John Hullah (the composer, better remembered today for his professorship) to devise an opera between them. It had been hoped to open the new season with their work but it was realised in time that it would not be ready quickly enough. So, for £30, Dickens agreed to dramatise an earlier published story called 'The Great Winklebury Duel'.

The second season opened on Thursday 29th September with *The Sham Prince, Monsieur Jacques, The Tradesman's Ball* and this first dramatic piece by Dickens which he had made into a two-act farce and called *The Strange Gentleman*. It was quite funny, Harley had produced it in sharp and snappy style, the public were delighted and it ran for fifty nights. Set in an inn called The St James's Arms on the road to Gretna Green, it revolved around the mistaken identity of the loquacious Gentleman who was fleeing from a challenge to a duel. Harley played the lead himself and Madame Sala a rich spinster, Julia Dobbs, who arrived at the inn where she expected to meet her 'intended' who was to feign madness so that he would be confined to his room and so confound possible pursuers. Two runaway girls, Fanny and Mary Wilson, were played by the Smith sisters. Sidney took the part of one of their lovers and Forester of the other. After much bustling mishap and confusion all was eventually resolved and the travellers set off happily for Gretna Green and consummation. Mrs Penson played the landlady, Gardner was the 'boots', Miss Stuart a chambermaid, Williamson, May and Coulson were waiters and Hollingsworth was a conniving local mayor.

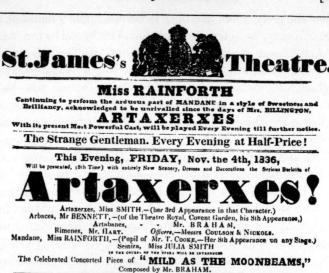

Later in the run: Half-Price at Half-Time

Later on Barnett displayed his *Etchings* again instead of *Monsieur Jacques*. On 11th October *The Miser's Daughter* was introduced to be played as well as the other three new pieces and two days later J. Lunn's new *Harmony Hall* was presented as by the author of *Fish out of Water*. The 15th was a Saturday and Braham made his first appearance this season when he sang in *The Waterman* and was 'rapturously received' as he noted in his diary. That was the third item. It had been preceded by *Harmony Hall* and *The Strange Gentleman* and was followed by *The Miser's Daughter* and *The Tradesman's Ball*.

Twelve days later came Miss Rainforth's début as Mandane in the opera *Artaxerxes* when Braham was Artabanes, Julia Smith was Semira and her elder sister Kitty sang the title-role. All were well received. On the last Thursday of November, Poole, the popular author of *Paul Pry*, saw his *Delicate Attentions* successfully presented. It was a comedy for Strickland as Mr Gingerly, an elderly bachelor on holiday in Brighton, beautifully attired in blue brass-buttoned coat, grey pantaloon and silk stocking encased legs, but bald, amorous, yet diffident. Laura Allison played his landlady's daughter with whom he fell in love, and the attentions of the title were his various quite unsuccessful attempts to attract her. John Parry was her young lover. The flowers, the latest love novel, all the gifts sent by the old fogey were unsigned and consequently attributed by her to his rival who at the end arrived just in time at her supper table to drink the first glass with a mocking gesture towards poor Mr Gingerly, who was gazing across and hoping that she would certainly attribute correctly the origin of that last gift of a bottle of wine. Even the news that someone had fought a duel on her behalf did not send her to his arms, so lugubriously he had to pack his bags and return to town and lonely bachelorhood. Audience laughter of young and old, the latter somewhat rueful, made for success.

The Dickens and Hullah ballad opera was at last ready for presentation on Tuesday 6th December. Called *The Village Coquettes*, it was a quite normally old-fashioned piece about a wicked squire and his villainous friend, both bent on seducing innocent village maidens. Strickland and Harley played two comic farmers and Braham and Forester the villains. Miss Rainforth and Julia Smith were the girls. Julia had taken over the part of Rose at short notice for Fanny Stanley had been rehearsing it and all had been charmed with her portrayal. Suddenly she became ill. On the very night of production she died, and on the Friday the unhappy company joined her family and friends to say goodbye in the tiny graveyard of the Piccadilly church of St James.

Gardner, Bennett and Forester as Maddox, Edmunds (the girls' fiancées) and the Hon. Sparkins Flam in *The Village Coquettes*

Gardner, Bennett and Parry completed the cast of the opera. At the final curtain on the first night, quite possibly for the first time ever, an author took a call which was commented upon not particularly favourably next morning by the papers. Most of them, except *The Times*, were however quite pleased with the work and the singing. Like Dickens' first piece, it had been much publicised as being by him, as Boz, for by this time he was becoming quite well known.

A clean sweep was made for Boxing Day though attendances did not improve very much for snow was falling thick. One somewhat unsuitable offering for the Christmas season was *Bletchington House or The Warning Voice* for in it the hero was condemned to death, reprieved, and then shot in error. More laughingly appropriate was *The Parish Revolution*, based on Hood's tale. The traditional musical was *The Enchanted Horn or Harlequin Prince of Persia* which was a version by à Beckett of *Oberon*. Two weeks later Braham received a demand from Planché for £20 as payment for words stolen without permission!

1837

In November the Lord Chamberlain had written to Braham to say that no extension of his licence for after Easter could possibly be granted. Now John or Fanny had since then, directly or indirectly, apparently reached the King's ear for something certainly happened to influence the Chamberlain for on 17th February The St James, The Adelphi and The Olympic were all informed by him that in future they could remain open until 31st May. Three days before the news was received officially, Lord Burghersh sent Fanny a note to say that the King had consented.

Revivals during the first five months of the year included *Guy Mannering*, *Love in a Village*, *The Siege of Belgrade* and *The Castle of Andalusia*. Nine novelties were produced. Most important new author was Anna, Mrs S. C. Hall. That remarkable literary Irishwoman's first dramatic effort topped ninety performances in its first year. Opening on 20th February and called *The French Refugee*, it gave Barnett an excellent opportunity as the aristocrat who kept his hand gloved ever since it had been touched by Marie Antoinette. On 27th March Mrs Hall's second play was presented. Called *Mabel's Curse*, it too was a period drama, this time about smugglers and roundheads after the Restoration.

Bennett, Priscilla Horton and Laura Allison as Martin,
Annie and Mad Mabel in *Mabel's Curse*

Before that, however, on Monday 6th March, Charles
Dickens' third effort was included on the same bill as *The
French Refugee* and the architect Sam Beazley's *Lottery Ticket.*
Is She His Wife? was a farce about mistaken intentions and
might have passed muster if the dialogue had been composed
with a little more thought for the players. In parts it could
almost be taken for burlesque, but Harley probably cut some
of its tongue-twisting lines which show little sign of author
tightening or polish. It ran for a week, for that matter, before
Boz's name appeared on the bills but soon after that it was
withdrawn. Laura Allison was cast as Mrs Lovetown and
two of her 'soliloquies' will suffice as example. One Tapkins

has just made exit but appears in the distance whilst she speaks:

> My mind is made up. I can bear Alfred's coldness and in-sensibility no longer, and come what may I will endeavour to remove it. From the knowledge I have of his disposition I am convinced that the only mode of doing so will be by rousing his jealousy and wounding his vanity. This thoughtless creature Tapkins will be a very good instrument for my scheme. He plumes himself on his gallantry, has no very small share of vanity, and is easily led. I see him crossing the garden.

In scene 2 she is waiting in a shrubbery:

> I cannot have been mistaken. I am certain I saw Alfred here; he must have secreted himself somewhere to avoid me. Can his assignation with Mrs Limbury have been discovered? Mr Limbury's behaviour to me just now was strange in the extreme; and after a variety of incoherent expressions he begged me to meet him here, on a subject, as he said, of great delicacy and importance to myself. Alas! I fear that my husband's neglect and unkindness are but too well known. The injured little man approaches. I summon all my fortitude to bear the disclosure.

One of the final novelties of the season was *The Eagle's Haunt* which the quaint little stock-dramatist of Covent Garden, Edward Fitzball, had written to music by Franz Glaiser founded on Bohemian national melodies. It was based on the folk-tale of a baby stolen by an eagle and ran from 5th to 31st May after which Harley made the end-of-season speech. Takings had picked up with the warmer weather which again had been late in arriving. On the last night they took £56 plus sixpence. Two days earlier, a Monday, they even had taken £62, beating the Colosseum by a tenner.

In June the old King died and the young Victoria was proclaimed. She was to become a stalwart supporter of The St James's as a frequenter of the theatre for which her late royal uncle had also done his best against the wishes of his own bureaucrats.

Some new names appeared in the bills of the third and final season, for Priscilla Horton, the Selbys and Strickland had moved on. These included Fanny Stirling, Edward Wright, J. Webster (half-brother of the famous Ben) and Arturo Giubilei the tenor and earlier Covent Garden associate of Braham's, then in his early thirties. Wright was a young low comedian from the provinces who made his London début on the first night, 29th September, as Splash in Rodwell's *The Young Widow*.

Quite a number of the successes of the previous season as well as more standard pieces and as many novelties as usual were presented during the following eight months. Eight of the latter were done before the year was out, one of the funniest perhaps being à Beckett's skit *King John* (*With the Benefit of The Act*) which was presented in October. This, according to the playbills, 'having been listened to with Breathless Interest, and the Intervals between the various stirring Incidents having been filled up with Hearty Roars of Delight . . .' was repeated every night. H. Hall, who had transferred from The Strand, was the King, Wright was Hubert, another newcomer Miss C. Booth was Prince Arthur, Madame Sala was Lady Constance and Mrs Penson the Lady Elinor.

On 19th December, a cold and rainy Tuesday, a well-known amateur billed as Mr Otway appeared for his own Benefit as Hamlet. It was a shortened version, but the Chamberlain's dispensation nevertheless had to be obtained. Laura Allison was Ophelia. The 'guest star' was actually a wealthy, long-jawed, lanky Scotsman by name Ferguson who had probably made some special arrangement to Braham's advantage. He was not

unknown in town and had appeared similarly at least eighteen
times at other theatres.

Pascal Bruno was the Christmas attraction. This à Beckett
had adapted from Theodore Hook's translation from Dumas.
Mrs Stirling, in breeches, was cast in the title-role. Mrs Hall's
The French Refugee was presented the same night with Barnett
still in the title-role and supported by Madame Sala, Laura
Allison, Julia Smith, Gardner and Webster.

1838

New productions and revivals followed each other quite as fast
in the new year. By 2nd June Haynes Bayly had had four first
nights, Wilks had had two, Mark Lemon (large and jovial
editor of *Punch*) had had one, as had Morris Barnett, Fox
Cooper, Charles Selby and Leman Rede. Three of the other
four novelties, if not all, were by à Beckett.

The first new one was Bayly's *The Culprit* in which Harley
was a naval Captain, Gardner his servant and Mrs Stirling his
wife; Madame Sala and Julia Smith supported. A fortnight
later, 17th January, Morris Barnett's *Musician of Venice* with
music by Pilati gave Braham a new title-role as Stradella when
Miss Rainforth was his wife Bianca. A week later she went
down with suspected smallpox but to her own and everyone
else's relief the diagnosis was wrong and after some days off
she was back at the theatre. Seven musical specialities were
listed in the latter piece, one of them, 'Holy Saint, my breast
inspire', was for Braham to sing, and on the organ, to accom-
pany himself.

On the 29th, à Beckett's version of *The Black Domino* was
presented with Fanny Stirling in the title-role, Madame Sala
as Jacintha, Webster, Burnett and Sidney as de Massarena,
Count Julian and Lord Elfort. Julia Smith was the 'Domino's'
companion Bridget, Miss Mears was Sister Ursula and Miss
Stuart Sister Gertrude. Some of the music was by Mrs à

Beckett. Scribe's original had been done in Paris the previous autumn. Not uniquely, and illustrative of the stupid competition in London, there were soon seven other versions running!

The next day was the anniversary of the execution of King Charles I and so no performances were permitted. This custom had been instituted by Lord Devonshire in 1832.

Fanny Stirling had already played dual roles, but Thomas Egerton Wilks' one-act farce on 6th February taxed her versatility to the utmost. This was *'Tis she! or The Maid, The Wife, and The Widow.* The scene was set in The Green Dragon on the road to Bath where Gardner was a much harried waiter by name Quickset. To the inn first of all comes a two-year a-mourning widow, Lady Eliza Blackleigh, who is half aware of her awakening love for dashing Colonel Carleton (Webster) who very soon arrives in pursuit. Before he appears, however, her elder sister Jane arrives with her husband Gabbleton (Wright) and earlier still the position has been explained in a conversation between Lady Blackleigh's servants Deborah (Mrs Penson) and Timothy (Moore). The latter tells the waiter that his mistress is travelling incognito and Quickset decides that must mean 'in an interesting condition'.

The third and youngest sister, Sophia, then arrives. After her comes her lover Charles (Sidney) and finally Sophia's guardian Admiral Triton (Brookes). The Admiral is a very tetchy nautical individual who begins to look favourably upon Charles, who is also his nephew, only after he hears he has been wounded three times and promoted to lieutenant.

All three sisters were played by Fanny Stirling, and the fun naturally mounted hilariously as in fifty minutes she appeared as Lady Blackleigh in widow's weeds, then as Mrs Gabbleton in fashionable morning dress with cap and blue ribbons, and then as young Sophia in white muslin with white satin sash; and then as the wife, as the widow, as the maid, as the widow, as the wife, as the maid, and finally as the widow who just

before the curtain fell mimicked the other two to the cheers of
the audience. Not surprisingly on the first night she had to be
shooshed back to change from widow to wife and Gardner and
Webster had to gag furiously until her re-entry properly
costumed!

Wright, J. Webster and Hart as Simmons, Brown and the
Butler in *The Spitalfields Weaver*

Four days later, Saturday, another success was added to the
bill and played with it as well as Bayly's *The Culprit* and *The
Black Domino*. This was Bayly's *The Spitalfields Weaver*, a
'satire' against the too hasty judging of a man by his clothes or
origin. Honest weaver Brown (Webster) had been bequeathed
a factory by his late employer whose niece he then married.
Laura Allison played the niece Adelle who attempted 'silk-

purse' treatment to the disgust of her wealthy no-good cousin Darville (Sidney) who almost succeeds in seducing her from her true-blue husband. Wright played the latter's comical but worthy ex-mate Simmons and Hart was butler Dawson.

One of Brown's speeches included '. . . the errors of such a man as Darville cannot render me blind to the many sterling virtues which characterise a true old English Gentleman!'

On the Holy Days of Lent this year, as also in 1837, concerts were offered with a little leavening of solo acts. Stansbury was still musical director, but Pilati, who had been conducting at The Colosseum took most of the concerts, some of which were billed as being 'after the style of Mons. Musard' the notorious musical impresario then in Paris. Star performers included the Distin family of father and four sons. Distin had been first trumpet in George IV's private band but had not had an easy time after the dissolution of that monarch's household, one of his positions being that of a retainer in a Scottish baronial castle. The family quintette, however, became famous on the Continent and they returned here with the saxophone in 1844 (*q.v.*).

The next new piece was *The Fatal Secret*, a two-act comedy by an unknown author about smugglers in the West Country. It went down well with Harley as the chief character Blaball.

Braham recorded in his diary a conference held four days later, on the last of February, when Beazley said he thought he had someone who might take over the theatre at the quite high rent of £2,500. He was told to go ahead but no deal resulted. Balfe with Beale and Addison were the prospects, for the former was very friendly with Fitzball who says in his diary for 10th and 12th March that they were planning to do this.

On St David's Day a delightful little operetta with music by Sloman and Harroway was produced. Based on a Welsh folk-tale and titled *Jenny Jones*, the book was by Fox Cooper and introduced to London a singing harpist Caulfield and his wife. She had appeared in town before; later they became regulars, mostly at The Haymarket. She was Jenny and he her lover Edward Morgan who was frowned upon by her elderly guardian and suitor Sir Watkin ap Shenkin (Brookes) with whom she lived. The scene was set in the garden of their cottage, resplendent with potted flowers ready for the local flower show. Edward, to be close to Jenny, had contrived a job as her guardian's gardener and so sported a brilliant red waistcoat and blue apron. Hollingsworth was the latter's uncle Owen Owen, and Gardner was a comic Beadle in long sweeping coat over bright yellow waistcoat with silver-buckled shoes and gold-laced tricorne. Jenny off-set them all in national costume, tall black hat and all. Seven songs had been composed and were well received, the story of course ending happily.

The author Fox Cooper would have been a good subject himself for he was more than quite a character. One son, Alfred Edgar, was a musician and the other, Harwood, a stalwart of The Adelphi under Ben Webster. Like his father the latter had literary leanings and not only wrote dramas and 'penny bloods' but edited the last 700 of Dicks' edition of plays. He had a large family, two of whom were to make their début under the Kendals here, but the most famous became known as the Renad Brothers and ran their musical show *The Swiss Express* for over twenty years at home and all over the Continent. Cecil Barrett was another, the different surnames being a normal stratagem when many of one family tour in the same company. They are today known only in the motor-racing world, with their Cooper cars.

Old Fox Cooper wrote or 'adapted' plays, contributed to and founded journals, even one of the latter, (the *Nelson Examiner*) in New Zealand though he did not succeed in going there himself as he had planned. Fox rarely had money, which did not stop him from taking over theatres. Once when he was running The Strand a wealthy Jew requested the pleasure of his company at dinner. Fox hired three cabs and on the appointed Sunday evening these arrived at the Whitechapel mansion full

of hungry actresses. 'Oi yoi yoi!' squealed the host as his large
nose quivered to the perfumes of the chattering bantering girls.
'Your company, you say! I ask the pleasure of your company,
you say. So many pleasures I didn't expect! Oi yoi yoi!' But
the joke was taken in good part and all sat down to a repast
helped out by the pie shops of the neighbourhood.

The last Tuesday of March, the 27th, was booked for à
Beckett's Benefit and though still ostensibly secret a very full
house resulted. Chief offering was the first-ever dramatisation
of *Oliver Twist*, but it was booed and never done again. There
have been twenty or more adaptations since, so because of that
and also because nobody has written about this first one
without error I will deal with it more thoroughly than one performance would otherwise justify.

Dickens had still not completed the tale in his head by the
first week of September 1838. It was published in three volumes towards the end of October although the serialisation
continued in *Bentley's* until the April 1839 issue, having begun
in February 1837. À Beckett used nothing from the previous
March or February and only the idea of Oliver being pushed
through a window to undo the door for burglars Sikes and
Crackit which was published in the January *Bentley's* (chapters
20 to 22). In the original Oliver was shot, rescued by Sikes then
abandoned in a ditch. In the play the burgled house was Mr
Brownlow's, Oliver was not shot, the accomplice of Sikes was
Fagin who was shot! The cast ('Mr' was used for the actors
where appropriate but is here dropped) and synopsis from the
playbill follow:

Oliver Twist (Master Purvis), Mr Brownlow (Halford),
Fang the magistrate (Brookes), Jones the bookseller (Hart),
Bumble (Harley), Grimwig (Hollingsworth), Old Fagin (Bar-
nett), Bill Sikes (Hall), Dodger Dawkins (Gardner), Charley
Bates (Sidney), Policeman (Moore), Officer (Alexander), Clerk
(Beal), Mrs Corney (Madame Sala), Mrs Bedwin (Mrs Penson),

Nancy (Miss Mears), Susan (Miss Harris), Peggy (Miss Stuart). The theatre property master was named Purvis so one may assume that Oliver was played by his son.

The play was in two acts of five and seven scenes:

Sc. 1. Act I. Mrs Corney's Apartment in the Workhouse. A pleasant conversation between Mr Bumble and a lady showing that even a Beadle may be susceptible on some points.

Sc. 2. A well known street. Oliver encounters on the road a strange sort of young gentleman.

Sc. 3. A room in Fagin's house. Oliver is introduced to the respectable Old Gentleman and his Pupils.

Sc. 4. The Book Stall. Oliver becomes better acquainted with the characters of his new associates and purchases experience at a high price.

Sc. 5. The Police Office. Treats of Mr Fang, the Police Magistrate and furnishes a slight specimen of his mode of administering justice.

Sc. 1. Act II. Fagin's House. Reverts to the Merry Old Gentleman and his Youthful Friends through whom a new acquaintance is introduced.

Sc. 2. Mr Brownlow's. In which Oliver is taken more care of than ever he was before. A remarkable prediction uttered concerning him.

Sc. 3. A street. Showing how very fond of Oliver the merry old Jew and Nancy were.

Sc. 4. Fagin's Domicile. Relates what became of Oliver Twist after he had been claimed by Nancy. A notable plan is discussed and determined on.

Sc. 5. Mr Brownlow's. Oliver's destiny continuing unpropitious, brings a Great Man to enquire his character.

Sc. 6. A street. Oliver is delivered over to Mr William Sikes. The Expedition.

Sc. 7. Mr Brownlow's. The Wind up. Oliver deceives more parties than one.

Plot and dialogue ran fairly true to Dickens in Act I until Oliver's arrest, for then Brownlow was forced to follow by the mob who were told to 'Bring him in!' Dickens closed the court scene with Brownlow being pushed out after his 'D—me. D—me. I'll . . .' following the magistrate's 'The boy is discharged. Clear the office.' The dramatist made the scene end:

> Brownlow: Damme! Damme! I'll . . .
>
> Fang: Fine that fellow ten shillings. And clear the office.
>
> Brownlow: Damme if this . . .
>
> Fang: Another oath! Take fifteen shillings from that fellow and clear the office.
>
> Brownlow: Here's a sovereign for you and as I think you are a d—d rascal—even if I don't say so—you'd better keep the change.
>
> *exit Brownlow, Oliver and Jones. Confusion. end of act first.*

How Halford as Brownley was expected to enounce 'd—d' one can only guess. The quotation above is from the MSS. sent to the Lord Chamberlain whose Examiner was then Charles Kemble who passed and initialed it. Did that retired actor-manager pass the 'd—d' and the more blatant oaths by error or intention? His predecessor Colman was a hypocritical renegade when Censor, but space cannot be here spared to explore Kemble's practice.

The finale was quite different from anything Dickens had published then or later. Brownlow's housekeeper Mrs Bedwin was entertaining Bumble while her master and his old friend and guest Grimwig were asleep. The latter couple are awakened by the noise of the burglars and enter the kitchen just after Oliver has appeared there, to the consternation of the loving pair. Ambush is determined upon so Oliver is sent to admit the rogues. When the police arrive Sikes draws his pistol but shoots Fagin dead in the struggle before he himself is overpowered and removed.

The play is no more badly written than others of the period

so that the audience who hissed and booed it must have been antagonised more by the deviations from Dickens than by bad dialogue, construction or acting. The appearance of Fagin as a robber and his death would have been as upsetting to the fans as to Dickens who is supposed to have been in front that night and to have become so angry that he hid below his box until it was over. The playbill announced it for repetition on the Thursday and at the curtain calls Harley attempted to repeat this but he was howled down. It was Lent so the Wednesday was concert time. One of the substitutes on the Thursday was Dickens' own *Is She His Wife?* which certainly suggests that he had been there and had protested.

Copyright did not then offer protection unless a novelist dramatised or authorised dramatisation. Braham, Harley and à Beckett certainly 'pulled a fast one' on their friend, but they doubtless excused themselves by a letter Dickens had written to Harley (as stage director) the previous year in which he said that the value of his time was then such that Braham would have to pay him £100 for a one-act or £150 for a two-act in future. Production secret had been easy to keep for the novelist was then exceptionally busy. In February he had been with 'Phiz' in Yorkshire studying schools and seeking a location for Dotheboys Hall because *Nicholas Nickleby* was begun and the printer's deadline was 15th March. *Oliver* instalments had also to be both conceived and written. The only advance publicity so far traced is the playbill and a notice in *Figaro in London* the previous Saturday.

Adair Fitzgerald in 1910 in his book *Dickens and the Drama* correctly mentions the production by date but says it 'retained its place in the bills for several weeks' which it did not. He then names six players who took part. Four of these did not. In *The Dickensian* for April 1920 the same author says Dickens 'frequently appeared' in *The Strange Gentleman* but though he writes that that 'is on record' he gives no indication of where. He further says, wrongly, that the serial 'had just finished' in

Bentley's and repeats the same erroneous names mentioned above. Again without proof he then states that Alfred Wigan 'is believed to have lent Dickens a hand in the dramatisation'.

Other mis-statements have been published but the latest in book form has so much apparent authority that I would risk running contrary to the libel laws were I to name and refute it in detail. For the benefit of Dickensians I will therefore only say that a study published since 1952 has eight errors in twelve lines devoted to this first *Oliver*!

Fitzgerald's suggestion that Wigan and Dickens collaborated hardly warrants examination. Wigan, then still known as Sidney, played the minor Bates and though certainly eventually a dramatist did not become so until about seven years later. Had the flamboyant, successful, five-years-older Dickens wanted help he would surely have approached one of the experienced frequenters of the green-room such as Selby, Barnett, Mrs Hall or à Beckett.

The original MS. (now in the British Museum) already quoted from, is no help at identification for it is a copy in three or more hands. However, apart from the fact that it was prepared for à Beckett's own Benefit, it was stated four times at least at the time that he was the author.

Alexander Forrester's weekly *The Town* named à Beckett as adaptor on 31st March and 7th April and the weekly *Actors by Daylight* on 31st March referred to him as 'The journeyman playwright of this establishment has furnished an edition of *Oliver Twist*, to enliven the public. . . . It was received with mingled cheers and hisses, and at the fall of the curtain, Harley attempted to announce it for repetition, but eventually retired.'

On 9th June 1838, when summing up The St James's season, the last-named journal continued about him: 'To what tune he must have done poor Braham for the recompense for this mass of rubbish [his recent plays] we cannot say, but judging from his improved appearance it must have been something considerable. Those that remember him hanging about the

John Braham

Below. Robert Strickland in
The Mendicant

William Mitchell

Gilbert A. à Beckett

I

Priscilla Horton

Laura Honey

Kate and Ellen Bate-
man as The Young
Couple

Fanny Kemble

Fanny Stirling

Clara Selby

J. P. Harley

Alfred Bunn

Mr Love

Mlle Plessy

Mme Albert

Mlle Rose-Chéri

Mme Doche

Rachel

Lafont

Déjazet

Bouffé

Mrs Pat

Ristori

Lily Hanbury as
Lady Windermere

Marion Terry
in *The Idler*

Miss Compton
(Mrs R. C. Carton) 1885

Schneider as
La Grande Duchesse

6

Tennyson

Tom Taylor

Miss Braddon

G. B. Shaw

Charles Reade

Oscar Wilde

7

William Brough

Charles Dickens aged twenty-seven

A. W. Pinero, 1893

Sydney Grundy, 1890

Clement Scott, 1889

Henry Arthur Jones

8

stage-door of The Victoria almost shirtless must conclude we
are no great way out. For the present we have done with this
egregious scamp, but if we again behold him thrusting his
detested person into our notice, we shall recall to his mind the
public chastisement he received from Mr Edwin of The Surrey
Theatre.' Thus perhaps was he repaid by one of the 'dirty
hands' of his tirade after the failure of his *Brown's Horse*
(*vide ante*).

On the Thursday five pieces were offered. *The Ambassadress*
was the main operatic attraction. In three acts this had been
translated by à Beckett and the music by Auber adapted by
Stansbury, first presented with Braham and Miss Rainforth
on the 5th. *The Spitalfields Weaver* and *Is She His Wife?*
followed and then a new farce by Charles Selby called *The
Valet de Sham*. In the latter Laura Allison as Miss Marchmont
(an attractive young lady) had to pretend to be her own maid
Clipper (a polished lady's lady) played by Mrs Stirling. Then
Laura had to ape an imaginary frump of an aunt, all to confuse
and confute Captain Trivet (a prejudiced young gentleman)
played by Webster who in turn had to pretend to be his own
valet. Wright played the latter and both he and Fanny Stirling
had to be rather too ready with malapropisms and execrable
French but that was to heighten the effect when they in their
turn had to impersonate their betters. It was Selby's twentieth
play but, unless any earlier unidentified ones were by him, his
first première here though both he and his wife were out of the
acting company. They also tried out *The Munich Huntsman*
without putting it in the playbill, and this strangely upset the
audience who created a disturbance in consequence!

Harley's Benefit was on 2nd April and Saturday the 7th was
the last night of the season before the Easter holidays. Webster
recited the Farewell Speech after *The Ambassadress*, *The Culprit*, *Jenny Jones* and *The Valet de Sham*. Fox Cooper was in
front and a faction unfriendly 'dreadfully hissed' him, as
Braham wrote in his diary afterwards. It was Harley's last

SJT D

night with Braham for they had quarrelled as early as 15th March when Braham recorded in his diary 'Harley by his diabolical conduct puts me in hot water'. There had been fifteen months of working time in their two seasons together.

'Gentleman' John Hooper, who had previously been treasurer to Madame Vestris at The Olympic, succeeded Harley as stage director after the recess when they reopened on the 16th, Easter Monday. Three novelties were then presented as well as *The Waterman* in which Braham was Tom Tug as usual and Miss Rainforth Wilhelmina. New members of the company were headed by Mrs Honey. Others were Jane Mordaunt and a Miss Williams, making their débuts in town, Oxberry and Mrs Frank Matthews from The English Opera House. The latter was a good heavy comedienne of thirty-one who was to return to the theatre two decades later with her husband.

The programme opened with Haynes Bayly's *My Album*, and Wilks' *The Brothers or The Wolf and The Lamb* followed, with Fanny Stirling playing the dual role of twins—Gossamer Gadfly, a cornet of the Guards, and Edward Vere Gadfly, a student. Oxberry, Hart, Mrs Matthews and the Stuart and Mordaunt girls supported. Leman Rede was author of the Easter extravaganza, *Hero and Leander* for which the music had been selected from the works of eight named composers as well as 'one or two Russian Composers with names too hard to spell'! It was a 'Celestial, Terrestial, Acquatic, Subaquan-neous' spectacle in which Jane Mordaunt was Hero to Laura Honey's Leander. Wright, Mrs Matthews, the Caulfields and many others supported.

Mark Lemon's *Love and Charity*, in which Fanny Stirling played Julia Amor, Phoebe Pop and Louis Bertrand with the support of Mrs Matthews, Miss Williams, Oxberry and Webster, and then Bayly's *The British Legion* were the only novelties of the after-season. One revival at the end of May was *The Devil's Bridge* but the Lord Chamberlain noticed this and, pointing out that it was listed as an opera, ordered them not to put it on again.

The Saturday of 2nd June was the final night of the season and it proved to be Braham's final night as actor-manager of his own theatre. That title is not really a correct one for him because although he provided the money his managers, first Mitchell then Harley then Hooper, were the real governors and his wife Fanny was no nonentity in the business. For instance, in the spring of 1837 *The Town* reported that she had been angling for Tyrone Power to star at her theatre. Normally, however, she did not figure in publicity. Power, incidentally, was not engaged though a favourite play of his was then put on but with Daly in Tyrone's usual part of the fake dominee in *The Irish Tutor*.

Braham's resources had in fact been so drained that he could not finance another season. The Colosseum was barely paying its way but must not concern us here, though without that 'investment' he would have had more free money. His partnership there with Yates, incidentally, had lasted six months and on the last day of 1835 he wrote in his diary 'Separation between Yates and me. Thank God.' St James's standards had been high as well as prolific with roughly three premières to each of the twenty months of the three full seasons. With three to five presentations each night the revivals of these and standard operas, farces, etc. had been legion and cast and stage staff had earned their money even if scenery had been mostly flats and set pieces. The more important productions, such as *Rasselas* with its Aerial Ship, had been much more extravagant and justified the individual billing of scene painters, machinery and property masters. It is also worth emphasising the importance of the director in the organisation since in the twentieth century it has often been stated that he just did not exist. Not only in Braham's time but later he was a necessary cog even if of varying competence. On the initial bill, for example, Mitchell received a separate line above the cast-list:

'The Piece produced under the Direction of Mr Mitchell'.

So the company disbanded. Braham himself was back at Drury Lane in the winter; Miss Rainforth joined The Lyceum and later Covent Garden where she was Ophelia to Macready's Hamlet; Laura Allison went to The Haymarket. Priscilla Horton and Harley were already with Macready, the one engaged to be Ariel and the other Caliban.

The theatre was advertised for sale or to let. John Hooper's appetite had been whetted by his two months as director but half a year went by before he could raise sufficient funds. Meanwhile Fanny Braham did what she could to exploit the place but she was unable to do more than arrange occasional concerts under, for example, Mme Eckerlin with conductors Curioni, Negri and Bochsa and starring pianist Döhler, the popular dramatic basso Lablache and baritone Michael Balfe. The great French ventriloquist Alexandre was once reported to be going to appear but apparently did not though, as in the past, he was at The Colosseum. Until 1842 Fanny remained in charge behind the scenes. Her name never appeared on the bills but until the Theatres Act of 1843 it was not made compulsory for the manager's name to be so printed. After that both name and private address had to appear. The rule was not always adhered to here, perhaps because the building had living accommodation.

CHAPTER 2

LIONS AND TIGERS, MONKEYS AND BALLET
1839-1841

JOHN HOOPER'S 'lesseeship' lasted four months from his first night on Monday 4th February. He recruited famous veteran septuagenarian William Dowton but his acting company of twenty-odd was not his main attraction. His stage director was George Ellis who had been at The Haymarket after four years under Murray in Edinburgh. Ellis became well known, especially in Charles Kean's famous 'antiquarian' Princess's seasons, but here too later on. Mrs Hooper, Jane Mordaunt and Miss Fortesque headed the ladies and Robert Roxby and Leman Rede the men with Alfred Sidney who from now on used his real surname as Alfred Wigan.

Animals on stage had already been introduced at Drury Lane and Hooper determined to exploit the fashion. His playbills splashed around town the 'Astonishing' features of the new management: 'The Great M. Taudevin's MATCHLESS FOREST of PERFORMING LIONS and TIGERS, LEOPARDS and PANTHERS!' Though advertised as from the Continent and under the patronage of the Prussian monarch, scandal said they were hired by the week from Wombwell's Menagerie. Their performances were certainly hardly edifying. When the curtains swung back a large den was disclosed occupying most of the stage. In one corner of it a smaller cage enclosed a lion and ledges above were adorned by a leopard and a black panther. Another leopard, two tigers, and a lioness roamed apparently loose below.

Trainer Taudevin, in traditional Roman-soldier type of costume, marched into sight, acknowledged rather feeble applause, then entered the main den. He fondled the prowling animals, kissed the lion through the bars, successfully encouraged the lioness to leap through a hoop, even placed his head between the jaws of a tiger. Then out he backed, closed the doors and clapped his hands. Flunkeys dragged on a large basket of chunks of meat and Taudevin proceeded to spear these and reward his animals. They responded to their supper with so little abandon that the audience hissed with disdain.

Half a dozen new pieces were produced by Hooper but nothing of note. His second Monday saw the first three together. Erstwhile partner of à Beckett and remembered for his massive 'London Labour and London Poor', etc. was Henry Mayhew the author of *The Young Sculptor*, a playlet about Michelangelo. Mayhew also collaborated with Baylis in *A Troublesome Lodger* which with Bayly's *Friends and Neighbours* were the other novelties.

Some publicity was later built up when it was reported that one of the tigers had killed a panther in a 'dreadful encounter' but not whilst an audience was present. Hooper was over in Paris at the time searching for more attractions, and these he later announced as 'Herrn Heinrich Schreyer's only and numerous troop of MONKEYS, DOGS and GOATS'. They supplanted Taudevin on Easter Monday, 1st April, and proved fairly successful in drawing crowds. After all, as Hooper's bills proclaimed, 'in consequence of the great sensation they had created in Paris he had been induced to visit that Capital for the purpose of witnessing their extraordinary exhibition. The incredible feats of these wonderful animals induced the Lessee, without hesitation, to secure their exclusive Performances.'

The entertainment was on a higher level than that of their predecessors. Stars were even billed by name: Little Nanine, Little Jacob, Jacotot and the 'highly trained dog Caesar'. The entertainment was divided into three parts of eleven scenas which included sword play, gun drill and such like military

ST. JAMES'S THEATRE.

Combined Attraction!!!

Notwithstanding the increasing attraction of **HERRN**
Schreyer's Veritable Troop of Monkeys & Dogs!
The Manager has the satisfaction to announce to the Public, that he
has entered into an engagement (for a limited period) with

Mr. GILBERT, Mr. WIELAND,
Miss BALLIN,
AND THE WHOLE OF THE CORPS DE BALLET
From the
THEATRE ROYAL, DRURY LANE,
who will (in consequence of the triumphant reception, from a brilliant and
overflowing audience) make their appearance every Evening in the

Daughter of the Danube.

On MONDAY, May 6, and TUESDAY, 7, 1839,
Will be performed, an entirely Original Barletta, of a peculiarly novel construction, to be called THE

Jealous Husband.

Dr. Sidney, Mr. BROOKS. Edward Mortimer, (an Artist) Mr. HOOPER.
Frederick Clifton, Mr. R. ROXBY. Frank, (Servant to Sidney) Mr. CARLTON.
Emily Mortimer, Mrs. HOOPER.

To which will be added, the Performances of

HERRN HEINRICH SCHREYER'S
Veritable Troop, 45 in Number, of
MONKEYS AND DOGS,
Which have created so great a sensation in PARIS, VIENNA, BRUSSELS, BERLIN,
HAMBURGH, and all parts of the Continent.

exercises. An 'Air with Variations' was played on the violin by The Great Mandrille who later acted the part of a deserter who was then arrested, tried, condemned and executed. Little Jacob conducted the subsequent Funeral Obsequies!

The Drury Lane ballet company under Gilbert, Wieland and Miss Ballin were engaged at the end of April. *The Devil on Two Sticks* and Adolphe Adam and Pilati's *Daughter of the Danube* were among their offerings. Benefits began in May, novelties including a troupe of Spanish dancers, Hungarian singers, and 'the English Jim Crow', John Dunn, rival of Rich

the American coon minstrel who made his English début in
1836. The varied season, reported to be quite successful, ended
as June began.

The rather notorious name of Mr Bunn appeared on the bills
as manager when the doors reopened on 5th November. Up to
the day before he was still officially lessee of Drury Lane
although steps to make him bankrupt were being set in progress
by the proprietors because of his enormous debt to them.
Fanny Braham's arrangement gave him his first ten nights rent
free but after that he was to pay a proportion of the takings.
Most of the company came from either The Lane or Covent
Garden for his policy was to present ballet, opera and burlettas.
Old-timers included Morris Barnett, Stretton and Mrs Garrick.

THEATRE ROYAL,   ST. JAMES'S.

Under the Management of Mr. BUNN.

Mr. H. PHILLIPS, Mr. ALLEN, Mr. STRETTON,
(Principal Vocalists from the Theatre Royal, Drury Lane)
Mons. SILVAIN,
Madlle. MAGDALEN YATZKOFSKA,
Mademoiselle PAULINE GUICHARD,
Mrs. GURNER,
TOGETHER WITH
A POWERFUL COMPANY AND NUMEROUS AUXILIARIES.

After which, will be performed, *(for the Fifth Time on the English Stage)* the popular French Ballet of

La Fille Mal Gardée.

Colin,
Thomas, Mr. BECKET,   Mons. SILVAIN,
Lise,   Madlle. GUICHARD,   Mr. T. MATTHEWS *(From the Theatre Royal, Drury-Lane)*
La Mere Simon, Mr. HEATH,   Alain,   *(her 4th appearance in England,)*
Peasant, Madlle. CERES, *(from the Academie Royale, Paris)*
In the course of the Ballet will be performed

Particularly interesting was his opening ballet, the comic *La
Fille Mal Gardée*, although he erroneously billed it as for the
first time on the English stage. The part of the lover Colin was
danced by Silvain and that of the farm-girl of the title, Lise,
by Mlle Guichard who was advertised as making her English
début. The wealthy farmer-mother, la Mère Simon, was interpreted by Mr Heath for it is of course a somewhat grotesque

role. Alain, the clumsy ploughman clod favoured by Simon for the hand of Lise, was given to the great clown Tom Matthews, successor to Grimaldi and grand-uncle of A. E. Matthews. Beckett was Thomas and a peasant girl Mlle Ceres from Paris, Magdalen Yatzkofska danced a *pas seul* during the ballet which concluded with a grand *Pastorale* by the entire *corps*.

John Braham sang again when *Masaniello* in the second week was presented, with Adeleine Cooper as Elvira and Pauline Guichard as Fenella the dumb girl heroine sister of the revolutionary. Three new pieces were produced amongst other revivals but after seven weeks the doors closed on Saturday 21st December. They did not reopen on Boxing Day as at first announced.

1840

Sensation of 1840 was the marriage of the young Queen Victoria to Prince Albert. Bunn and Fanny determined to exploit the consequent influx of Germans by bringing over Schumann's opera company of Mayence from Brunswick. As further sop they asked permission to change the theatre's name to 'The Prince's'. Royal sanction to do so was accompanied by Her Majesty's intimation that a box for the season would also be subscribed for.

The Germans opened under the new name on Monday 27th April with *Der Freischutz*. The repertory included Beethoven's only opera, *Fidelio*, Spohr's *Faust*, Weber's *Euryanthe* (based on the same source as Shakespeare's *Cymbeline*), Marschner's *Der Templar* (from Scott's *Ivanhoe*), Mozart's *La Clemenza di Tito* and Kreutzer's *Nachlager in Granada*. Spohr's *Jessondra* in June and Gluck's *Iphigenia in Tauris* in July were given their first London hearings.

Royalty graced The St James's, albeit as The Prince's, when the Queen with her bridegroom and suite occupied a specially prepared box in May for *Faust* and in July for the Mozart production. The season ended with July, the royal festivities having relaxed the Lord Chamberlain's regulations.

In August a French company transferred from The Olympic for a short time and an amateur club called The Thespians murdered *Macbeth* in October.

Braham and most of his family now went off to tour America. The eldest boy, Hamilton, was put in charge to make the best of his poor abilities. Young Fanny, already at nineteen a widow, married in Edinburgh to become Lady Waldegrave a few days before the family joined their ship. They sailed in October on the maiden voyage of the ill-fated *President*, an oak-built three-masted steamship, big for her day but well under 300 foot keel. Five months later she was to run into a gale three days out from New York to founder with all hands. On board was Tyrone Power, great-grandfather of the third of that name, the justly popular stage and screen star who most regrettably was to die in his early forties whilst filming in Spain in 1958. Old sailors will not be surprised to learn that on board on that final voyage was a 'sky-pilot', as there was too when the *Pegasus*, an Edinburgh to London packet, struck a rock and foundered in July 1843, amongst the drowned being a friend of Tyrone's the actor Elton.

Morris Barnett teamed up with composer John Barnett to form an English Opera Company and arranged with young Hamilton Braham to open on 26th November with *Fridolin*, the score by F. Romer, the libretto by Mark Lemon. They also produced a new sketch by T. E. Wilks, and Mrs Selby was chosen to speak the optimistic Opening Address which concluded:

> British our voices, British all our Band,
> Let but a joyous British cheer requite
> Our pleasing toil on this eventful night.
> The Gladdening boon shall prove our Cause to bless
> An Augury of long and sure Success!

Unfortunately they did not attract, and after eight bad nights they offered John Barnett's own *Mountain Sylph* on their second Saturday, 5th December. On the Monday the doors did not reopen.

1841

Except for 1889, this was the worst year in the theatre's history. It opened only for occasional amateurs or concerts such as when Allcroft arranged one to present a new young pianist Mlle Launitz.

CHAPTER 3

THE FRENCH, THE MAGICIANS, THE ETHIOPIANS UNDER JOHN MITCHELL

1842-1854

JOHN MITCHELL took over in 1842 and a successful, varied and interesting decade began. In his mid-thirties, founder of the Bond Street theatre ticket agency which still bears his name (Ashton & Mitchell), he had put on a French company at The Lyceum in 1836 and soon became the Queen's theatre agent, all her Windsor Castle and other out-of-town entertainments being left in his hands. Eventually his silk hat and meticulous appearance as he drove each morning to the Palace in his white brougham earned him the sobriquet of 'Old Silky'. Impresario of London and Paris, he had a home in both capitals for he was married to Madame Alcain, widow of a Carlist Spanish grandee. She had two children, Herminie and Pepito, by her first marriage and by Mitchell two boys, Gaston and Robert who became an eminent journalist and politician. George Mitchell the dramatist who died in 1919 was a grandson. In the Franco-Prussian war, John Mitchell, by then retired, held a semi-government post as press liaison officer to English journalists. Herminie married Offenbach (*vide* 1844).

John Mitchell established The St James's as the legitimate home of the French stage in London. Vernacularly it became known as 'the French theatre' whilst its notepaper was printed 'Théâtre Français, King Street à Londres'. Performances were on Mondays, Wednesdays and Fridays. Subscriptions were

invited except for the Wednesdays and prices were raised from
2/- to the gallery to 6/- the boxes. Other entertainments were
later arranged for the 'off-nights'.

A permanent company was engaged with Mlle Eliza Forgeot
as directrice and a succession of visiting stars from Paris

Theâtre Français heading: letter to Charles Kean's Princess's manager

arranged to follow each other: M. Perlet, Mlle Plessy, Mlle
Déjazet and M. Bouffé. Excellent light comedian Perlet opened
this first season on Monday 7th February in *Le Bourgeois
Gentilhomme* and *L'Ambassadeur*. In his repertoire were also

L'Artiste, L'Avare, Le Malade Imaginaire and *Le Comédian d'Étampes.* The latter had already been popularised in London by Charles Mathews in his own adaptation, *He would be an Actor.* Perlet proved himself an intelligent and delightful player in the original, entering as a white-trousered, open-necked youth who speedily donned a ragged wig and ancient dressing-gown to become a toothless, infirm and doddery octogenarian. Next he became a deaf and cranky gardener and finally a cold and haughty English lady most annoyed with all the 'foreigners' in Paris.

Mlle Plessy followed in April and played in *Valérie ou l'Aveugle, Le Rêve de mon mari* and *Le Misanthrope.* She was a tall and graceful girl whose forte was light comedy but her versatility was displayed when for her Benefit she played Valérie, Celemine in *Le Misanthrope* and then in English, Lady Freelove in *A Day after the Wedding.* Daughter of a strolling player, she had been a pupil of Samson at the Conservatoire in 1829 and made her début in 1834. Two years later she was created *sociétaire* but after her marriage to writer Arnould in 1845 she renounced her position when tempted by an offer of 85,000 f. a year for a decade in St Petersburg. That breach of contract cost her a fine of 100,000 f. but for appearing at the Farewell Benefit of her old master Samson she was forgiven and in 1855 welcomed back into the official fold as *pensionnaire* at 24,000 f. with three months annual furlough. In November that year Charles Dickens saw her and in writing to thank the actor Régnier for his seat he said: '. . . If I could see an English actress with but one hundredth part of the nature and art of Madame Plessy, I should believe our English theatre to be in a fair way towards its regeneration. . . .'

Tiny vivacious Virginie Déjazet arrived on May Day to play the boy husband in *Les Premières Armes de Richlieu* and in other pieces. She was the delight of Paris where she had made her début when only five in a solo dance. As singer and actress, especially in breeches parts, she was always both lucky and

popular. Now over forty, it was not until she was seventy-seven
that she was to sing in public for the last time, at her Benefit
in Paris not long before she died.

In June came Bouffé. In his early thirties, and in both
quality and visage kin to the knighted Olivier who was to
sparkle on the same stage a century later, Bouffé was far
superior to the average French or English player of the period.
Encouraged by poor stage-lighting, traditional gesture and
expression tended to become too grandiloquently exaggerated
and so drown any pretension to naturalistic portrayal. Directors
like William Mitchell, with the necessary power intelligently
wielded over a permanent company, were the exception not
the rule. Bouffé gave studied interpretations of real and individual persons in the characters allotted him, each distinctively
different no matter how close in age one might be to another.
Where less gifted actors were always themselves *in* character,
Bouffé was always *the* character, appearing to be so naturally,
not acting so.

On 6th June he opened as Grandet the miser in *La Fille de
L'Avare* (after Balzac), the closing scene reminiscent of
Shylock and Jessica, for Eugénie, played by Eliza Forgeot,
steals her father's gold but not to run away with a lover for her
action is to save a relative from ignominy. As the miser the
actor excelled, his vividness thrilling especially at the discovery
of the emptied treasure chest. He staggered back, face blank,
voice failing and husky, palsied like his hands at the shock. As
Eugénie proclaimed her guilt, the agony of the parent trembled
across the footlights. Silent, almost deprived of movement, it
was the violent yet impotent gestures of his hands, the desperate
incredulity in his features, the eventual slow sinking to the
ground, torn and worn by terrific inward passion, that showed
the intensity of the miser-father's despair and suffering.
Bouffé's second character on his opening night was in *Les Vieux
Péchés*, again an old man but an entirely different one. Here
was an ex-ballet dancer become a wealthy provincial mayor,

hating his past and fearful lest it be discovered. Yet the obvious vanity, elasticity of stride, the occasional quick tripping step involuntarily betrayed him.

Also in his repertoire was the playful and jolly sixteen-year-old of *Le Gamin de Paris*; the simple, honourable old curé in *Michel Perrin*; the decrepit though garrulous oldest inhabitant *Père Turlututu*; the young conscript Trim in *Les Enfants de Troupe*; Bossu in *Maison en Lotterie*; the poor schoolmaster in *Le Bouffin du Prince*; the cobbler who wanted to be an actor in *Les Merluchons* and the old musician *Pauvre Jacques*.

This first French season under John Mitchell closed on 8th July. It had been remarkably successful. Though many productions had been new to London, others like the last named were quite familiar in adaptation. Queen Victoria had been present with Prince Albert to enjoy Mlle Plessy in *Le Misanthrope* on 4th May and again on 13th June when Bouffé was playing the old ex-ballet dancer and *Le Gamin de Paris*. Both the French and Hungarian Ambassadors as well as many titled members of society had been frequent witnesses of the performances. Everyone connected with the theatre looked forward.

Back in April Mitchell had engaged for the off-nights one of the top conjurers of all time. This was Louis (or Ludovic) Dobler whose standing may be gauged by the many of his profession who were to use his name in after years. A handsome, blond young man, elegant in white silk blouse, black velvet tunic and tights, he made effective entrance upon a darkened stage where two hundred candles could just be discerned as they awaited ignition. At a rapid tattoo on the drums, Herr Dobler swept into sight, stopped, swirled off his cape, raised pistol, aimed, fired. Into instantaneous flame burst every one of the candles!

A magic bottle—proved empty—was filled with water before it provided glass upon glass of white wine, then red, then foaming champagne. Really empty at last, broken in two, it revealed

a large silk handkerchief. Watches borrowed were nonchalantly
flung crashing to the back of the stage. But at command of a
pistol-shot they appeared in the eyes of a goggling idol, which
later shot out its tongue ornamented with rings, borrowed too
from ladies in the audience. Purloined bunches of keys appeared
like fruit from the branches of a bush which sprouted leaves
too as the conjurer watered it. Into a stew-pot, suspended and
isolated over a fire, he placed four plucked fowls. The lid was
removed a moment later and four pigeons flapped out to circle
around the private boxes. Borrowed handkerchiefs were
plunged into a pail of water but returned clean and crisp as
from an ironing board. A lemon was passed down to the stalls.
Cut open it displayed an egg. That broken showed a walnut,
that cracked disclosed a ring borrowed a moment or two earlier
from a lady a few seats away.

A girl's straw hat was whisked from her lap with polite
apology but when examined by Dobler on the stage he dis-
dainfully crumpled it up before tossing it over his shoulder.
But hardly had the hat seemed to hit the floor of the stage
than Dobler's pistol pointed high at the proscenium arch where
the hat then dangled until the pistol blazed and floated it
down to be seized and returned unharmed with a flourish to
its owner. For finale an old battered hat of his own was produced and stamped upon to prove its emptiness. Yet from it
was squeezed bouquet after bouquet of sweet-smelling flowers
which the conjurer threw to the ladies in the stalls until the
curtain fell to save him further exploitation! This 'Natural
Magic' was well patronised by junior members of Court and
society as well as the general public who delightedly continued
to be amazed and intrigued until well into August.

On 1st July a performance of Rossini's *Stabat Mater* was
given and again on the 11th when the Duchess of Kent, mother
of the Queen, was present. Gabussi conducted. Soloists were
Mlles Pacini and Lutzer and the great tenor Mario supported
by the basso Josef Staudigl who had made his London début

SJT E

UNDER THE PATRONAGE OF

THE RIGHT HON. THE EARL FITZHARDINGE.

ST. JAMES'S **THEATRE.**

HISTRIONICS.

On THURSDAY EVENING, Feb. 26, 1846.

Will be presented Colman's admired Comedy of

JOHN BULL,

OR, AN ENGLISHMAN'S FIRESIDE.

Peregrine................MR. PALMER.
Sir Simon Rochdale...MR. SPENCER,   Frank Rochdale...MR. HARCOURT.
Job Thornberry............(*1st time,*)............MR. KIDDLE.
John Bur.........MR. COPLING,   Dan.........MR. OGILVIE.
Dennis Brulgruddery .... MR. KNIGHT.
Simon.........MR. HURLSTONE. Mr. Pennyman.........MR. SHIRLEY.
The Hon. Tom Shuffleton .... MR. VINCENT.
John...MR. HANSARD.   Robert...MR. HANNS.
Lady Caroline Braymore ....MISS HILL.
(*Her Second appearance on any Stage.*)
Mary Thornberry .... MISS BENSON.
Mrs. Brulgruddery.............MRS. DRAKE.

SONG, BY MISS TWEEDDALE.

To conclude with the Musical Piece of

THE WATERMAN.

Tom Tug.....................................MR. E. DAY.
Bundle.........MR. MORELAND,   Robin.........MR. MORTIMER,
Wilhelmina..MISS O'CONNOR.
Mrs. Bundle...................MRS. DRAKE.

DRESSES BY MR. NATHAN, TICHBORNE STREET.

DOORS OPEN AT HALF-PAST SIX, & CURTAIN TO RISE AT SEVEN PRECISELY.

Society Amateurs

with the German operatic company two years before. A society amateur group called The Histrionics appeared in October; generally offering a major classic and a modern farce, they became regulars in future years. Miss Rainforth was at Covent Garden and she returned as one of the principal singers at concerts which were arranged during the winter, when performances included the *Stabat Mater*, Beethoven's *Mount of Olives* and Barnett's *Mountain Sylph*.

Back in the summer, in May, a petition was presented to Parliament which was of great import for it helped to hasten the Act of August 1843 which wiped out the Patent Theatres monopolies. It gave freedom of presentation and defined the powers of the Lord Chamberlain even though it both increased and limited them. Managers generally have come to welcome the position created by the Act, authors to oppose it. Signatories to that petition were almost fifty dramatists including Mrs Hall, Morris Barnett, Edward Fitzball, Mark Lemon, Henry Mayhew, Leman Rede, Charles Selby and others whose works had been or were to be produced here.

Braham was still in America. In June The Grange was entered and his furniture sold against his debts by court bailiffs.

1843

A tremendous storm heralded Mitchell's second French season. Almost a hundred ships were wrecked on British coasts on the night of Thursday 12th January. The company were then rehearsing and they opened on the Monday afterwards with Mme Thérèse Albert as star in the title-roles of *La Comtesse du Barry* and *Georgette*, the latter a frolicsome peasant hoyden to contrast vividly with the courtly mannered favourite of Louis XV. Chief support was Mlle Forgeot and MM. Cartigny and Rhozevil.

Madame Albert was a versatile and accomplished Parisian

darling, as delightful a songstress as actress. She had made un-
official début when only four years old for one day for fun her
grand-mama dressed her up in her own part as a very old lady
and sent her on instead of herself. Little precocious refused to
comply until promised the reward of a dancing marionette also
in the evening's bill. Unfortunately the puppet was next on
the programme and was already pirouetting before the drapes
when Thérèse demanded immediate payment. Impatient, she
marched back on stage: 'Make haste, mademoiselle! I have
finished my turn and am waiting for you!' All had then to be
explained to the delighted audience who insisted that the
reward be paid forthwith, to the mortification perhaps of the
interrupted puppeteer.

The Queen was in front on the last Monday of February
with her mother, husband and full suite, and in March when
Mlle Plessy was the star she was in her box twice.

Upon Sylvanie Plessy's return to Paris she sent back a
turkey as a present to her manager. Mitchell invited Ebers of
Her Majesty's to dine with him. When carved, instead of the
luscious truffles with which the bird had been stuffed in Paris,
nothing was found inside except the dullest of potatoes! Irish
Mary was post-haste summoned from her kitchen.

'Truffles, is it! Bad cess to the dirthy muck. Sure an' I
dumped thim where they belong of course, into the sink they
are now!'

Ebers and Mitchell made a rush and indeed in the sink the
truffles still reposed amongst the peelings of their supplanters.
Rescued and washed, they arrived at table a day late with the
hash instead of the roast!

John Braham was back home, and in February and March
he appeared in various concerts in his own theatre with his son
Charles. His voice, said some critics, was as much improved in
melodiousness as with age it had decreased in volume.

Mme Eugenie Doche was the star for April. She was the
twenty-year-old sister of ballerina Adelina Plunkett and had

made her début six years before at Versailles. Already she was a favourite with Parisians and had created as many as thirty-four original parts. In 1852 she was the first Marguerite of *La Dame aux Camélias*, Fechter being the Armand.

Déjazet followed in May and Bouffé for the final weeks of the season which ran into July. The Queen was twice present for him.

Les Enfants Castelli, a group of children or midgets who had been presented unsuccessfully in ballet at Covent Garden in October, were given another chance here the following month. Old Braham appeared again in concerts over the winter, this time with baritone Hamilton as well as light tenor Charles, but neither of them was in the same class as his father.

1844

Adolphe Achard, a good low comedian, was the opening star when the French returned in the new year. He was supported by M. l'Herie who had been here in 1836. Mme Albert followed and then Mlle Plessy. Mlle Déjazet was the final star but towards the end of her reign Mme Albert returned as extra attraction. Déjazet's daughter Herminie was in the company also and when *Carlo et Carline* was presented she was the Columbine while her mother played the Harlequin part which disguised Columbine's lover so as to confute an old roué also in pursuit. Their last night was 13th July.

Dobler returned for his second English season on 23rd April and stayed until 1st July. His repertoire was much as previously though he had improved some of his illusions, for instance the one where a borrowed ring was discovered inside a walnut now began by firing a cartridge from his pistol and from the cartridge came a glove inside which was the lemon. . . . He also relied more upon dexterous feats of legerdemain with cards than upon mechanical devices. He was on his mettle, however, for at The Adelphi he had strong competition from the flamboyant

Professor Anderson who had graduated from the Colosseum and was quite in his own class.

The Mitchell salon in Paris under Mitchell's wife had become a rendezvous of the intellectual élite. At that time Jacques Offenbach was earning increasing renown both as 'cello soloist and as composer for that instrument, and Mitchell invited the youthful stranger to a party one afternoon. Attraction between him and Herminie Alcain was immediate and mutual; but two conditions were made by the Mitchells to a marriage: that Jacques turn Catholic and that he prove himself in London. So for his protégé the prospective-step-father-in-law arranged Musical Union concert appearances in May 1844 and also the honour of playing in Windsor Castle during the Ascot races week when the Emperor of Russia was one of the guests of the Queen. The letter the twenty-year-old Offenbach excitedly wrote on 8th June to a friend about his English successes may be read in his biographies. In August, not long after Mitchell's London French season was concluded, the pair were married.

Dobler finished on 1st July and was followed at once by Charles Kemble with a series of nine Shakespearian Readings, from *Macbeth*, *Caesar*, *Romeo*, *Othello* and other plays, though only six had been planned. It was an innovation for the long retired younger brother of Mrs Siddons who had left the stage to be its censor (*ipso facto*), but resigned in his son's favour after many bouts of illness. Mitchell had arranged a series of the Readings for him to give before the Queen. With the Palace cachet a repeat followed at Willis's Rooms a few doors down the street from the theatre and success there warranted the larger auditorium.

Concerts and other entertainments with Braham and his sons, and Distin and his sons when they played on the Sax Horn lately invented in Paris by the Belgian Adolphe Sax, kept the place open irregularly through the autumn. Two of the vocalists were the Smith girls who had made their débuts in the Charles Dickens period. The Histrionics also performed.

1845

In Paris Mitchell arranged a performance in the royal theatre in the Tuileries before Louis Philippe on 16th January. Macready was Hamlet and Helen Faucit Ophelia, for they were acting in Paris for a few weeks at the Salle Ventadour. Their impresario was Mitchell who tried to get the tragedian for the off-nights of the coming St James's season but even the offer of £40 a night—which for a house holding hardly £200 was generous—did not result in a contract. Macready mentions the offer in his diary and also his chagrin when he returned home and discovered that the poniard he had received as a royal gift was not gold at all but only silver-gilt! Mitchell had been given a snuff-box and Helen Faucit a bracelet, both jewel encrusted.

The St James's opened a week later than first advertised when on 27th January a well-filled house welcomed Mlle Nathalie and M. Lafont in the comedy *Le Mari à la Ville et la Femme à la Compagne* and a drama about the revolution, *Pierre le Rouge*, in which Lafont enacted three characters. This season Mitchell tried out a six-day week and backed the extension with a galaxy headed by the great Frédérick Lemaître himself, as well as Mlles Olga Chaplin-Rose, Clarisse and Plessy with MM. Ravel, Régnier, Achard and Arnal.

Biggest draw in the Lemaître weeks was *La Dame de St Tropez* which had run over a hundred nights when produced in Paris. Both he and Mlle Clarisse played the roles they had created, those of Maurice the husband who was poisoned and Hortense the accused wife. Clarisse was a lovely blonde, a lyrical actress and remarkably quick study with the voice of a bell whose simple charm had earned her the sobriquet 'La rose du boulevard'. Though still only twenty-five she had been here with Jenny Vertpré, having made her début long before that as a child at the Gymnase Enfantin.

The drama was vaguely based on the murder case against

Mme Lafarge and is forensically interesting for it was the first play in which poison analysis was demonstrated on stage, and discussion followed in the papers about the advisability of allowing the public to know so much!

The Queen was in front eight times during the season which closed after the middle of July. In seventy-one nights eighty-four pieces had been presented of which fifty were new to the London stage.

Mitchell's young directrice, Eliza Forgeot, whose charming supporting performances had always earned her favourable notices, returned in August from a short holiday at home to find that a £50 note as well as a bracelet and some ribbon had been stolen from her jewel box. Next month at the Old Bailey her chambermaid and male accomplice (who had tried to change the note) were sentenced to ten years transportation and twelve months hard labour in the House of Correction.

In June, by which time the six-day innovation had been dropped, the placards announced for the off-nights the *Soirées Mystérieuses* of M. Philippe. He was another new to London top-line magician but one who was proud of his traditional Merlin tall-pointed headgear and ornamental gilt and jewelled flowing costume. Nor did pistols and a single static idol satisfy him. For Philippe there was a little cannon to introduce and assist and a puppet to fire it. Instead of one bottle from which to offer a choice of wines Philippe displayed a whole little shop with two tiny assistants to serve sweetmeats or liqueurs as demanded by the audience. At the boom of the gun or whisk of his wand candlesticks became fans, flowers turned into a Columbine and a Harlequin who danced and coquetted or whistled and even smoked a pipe—so lifelike at times that no one could decide whether a child was there aping a marionette or not. For finale he waved a great shawl in the air, even threw it high from his grasp. Quickly swirling it round him as he caught it he as quickly unwrapped it to show at his feet a bowl full of swimming goldfish. Repeating the swirling, another

M. Philippe

bowl appeared—and after he had descended from the stage to the aisle, almost at the feet of the stalls—yet another. Leaving the last bowl he returned to the stage to take his bow but before he did so the shawl swirled twice more and as it swept around his feet the first time half-a-dozen ducks quacked their way into sight and marched offstage while the second swirl produced two geese who solemnly marched off in the opposite direction!

The theatre was refurbished during the autumn and Lafont with Mlle St Marc opened the French season as early as 3rd November. Announced for the future were Déjazet, Rose-Chéri, Mmes Albert and Doche and finally the great tragedienne Rachel.

'The Histrionics' were busy as usual, but more interestingly in November before Prince Albert were writer and artist amateurs headed by Charles Dickens, George Cruikshank, Douglas Jerrold, John Leech, Henry Mayhew and Mark

Lemon in Ben Jonson's *Every Man in his Humour*. Braham and his sons also sang again before the year was out.

1846

Cruikshank and Tenniel (*Alice in Wonderland's* pictorial originator) headed artists alone in January, during which month Mme Albert arrived.

Fanny Braham died on 15th February. Old John was very broken up and though he kept an engagement later to appear in Brighton he was not to sing much more in public. His daughter Fanny, Lady Waldegrave, made him an allowance so that he was never in want, and soon afterwards he made a new home in Bloomsbury's Great Ormond Street which was much more in the centre of his own world.

Towards the end of March when Mme Doche was the star the young comedian Narcisse died suddenly and for some reason unknown the star's brother, M. Plunkett, did not attend the funeral. He was hissed off the stage by the audience upon his next appearance.

Earlier, on 21st January at the Hanover Square Rooms, James A. Dumbolton's Ethiopian Serenaders had attracted notice. They were an American troupe of coon minstrels. Proud to carry a letter of recommendation from President Polk they were the second burnt-cork troupe to arrive, and they inaugurated what was to become the traditional costume—a species of evening dress instead of the 'plantation costume' of fancy jacket and striped trousers. Discounting one-man or double-act entertainers, the first troupe had been the Virginia Minstrels of 1843 in which year they had also been the first in America. Mitchell gave them a trial on 9th February. Their popularity with all types of society proved so enormous that they were kept on for a full six months, into August, after which they toured the provinces as successfully.

They were five in all: Harrington and White on banjos,

The Ethiopian Serenaders

Germon on the tambourine, Stanwood on the accordion, Pell on the bones. The entertainment comprised riddles, back-chat, burlesque lectures, sentimental and comic songs, all with much by-play of raising eyes to Heaven at sadness and loud chuckles and interpolations at comedy. Plantation and other melodies included 'Merrily the Banjo Sounding', 'Dis Young Nigger of Ohio', 'The Dandy Broadway Swell', 'A Life by the Galley Fire', 'Lucy Neal', 'Lucy Long', 'Dis Nigger's Journey to New York'. Their finale was 'The Railroad Overture' when the noise of the engine and whistle with the bustle of crowds were laughingly imitated with great spirit.

Their verve, movement and brilliantly co-ordinated vocalisations combined with the novelty of their instruments—for neither the banjo nor the accordion had been invented for more than about sixteen years—attracted enthusiasts as diverse as Gladstone and tiny 'General' Tom Thumb. The latter almost stole their thunder one night for when noticed he had to stand out upon the ledge of his box to acknowledge the audience's acclaim before they would let the Serenaders proceed!

Rose-Chéri made her London début on 4th May in *Geneviève* and *Un changement de main*. She was only twenty-one but already popular in Paris for her first appearance had been before she was six, although her stage career really only began in 1834 when her father toured with her and her sister Anna in his own company in specially chosen plays, as the young Bateman girls were to do here in 1851.

Lafont and Déjazet followed from 1st June. To the latter's dressing-room after the first night came to greet her the young Prince Louis Napoleon. Destined to be President two years later, then Emperor, then refugee in England once again, he had only just escaped from the fortress of Ham and set up an establishment in King Street hard by the theatre. On his watch-chain was an amulet Déjazet had sent him for good luck whilst he was still a prisoner of Louis Philippe.

Rachel was billed to open on 6th July but whether she was

ill as one report said or merely in a tantrum Mitchell had to
rush over to Paris and he did not return with her until the
second week of the month. She opened as Camille in Corneille's
Les Horaces and appeared later in *Andromache* and *Phèdre* and
then closed the season on 14th August with her interpretation
of Soumet's *Jeanne d'Arc*.

Two Saturdays before, on the first, a fearful freak storm had
broken over the country in the afternoon. Many people were
killed by lightning or floods or injured by hailstones reported
as large as apples. In town so much glass was smashed at
Buckingham Palace that it was estimated that £2,000 would be
needed to replace that alone. At The St James's the hail broke
800 squares of glass in the windows and skylights. (106 years
later, in the same month, lightning was to strike the roof and
flood the stage during a performance.)

Famous ballerina Carlotta Grisi danced in a mixed entertainment on 4th August for a Benefit to her cousin Ernestine who
was the wife of Gautier. On the 19th the Duchess of Somerset
and the Duchess of Leinster took the theatre between them to
present three little protégées from the former county. They
were the Turner sisters, four-year-old violinist Sophia, and
Rosina and Caroline of six and eight who were duettists on the
harp. They were delightful and had they only been earlier in
the season would have been worth presenting more than the
once, so said 'La Belle Assemblée'.

Even though a princess was born at the end of May the
Queen was fourteen times in her box over the season, the last
time when Rachel was Phèdre on 22nd July. A fortnight earlier
the Serenaders had been specially sandwiched into the French
programme for her when Déjazet and Lafont were the stars.

The French were early again in the winter for Mlle Augustine
Brohan opened on 13th November. The veteran Perlet arrived
later in support but she returned home for Christmas.

The Ethiopian Serenaders ended their tour, which had included an appearance at Arundle Castle when the Queen and

Prince were visiting, and reopened ten days before Christmas so that the House Full boards went out to welcome the new year.

1847

Lemaître and Mlle Clarisse were the stars for January, on the 18th of which the Queen was there to see them in *La Dame de St Tropez*. Lafont and Mlle Fargeuil relieved them and then Rose Chéri took over in April.

This was the time of the 'Hungry Forties' and in April a party of the nobility, aided by Fanny Kemble, Jane Mordaunt and the Vandenhoffs, performed Sheridan Knowles' *The Hunchback* in a Benefit for Scots and Irish peasantry. As after-piece they put on Planché's *Faint Heart never won Fair Lady* and the author relates that one of the gentlemen was so drunk he could only stumble about the stage but though Queen Victoria was in her box she was more amused than offended by the exhibition. Certainly any rebuke had no effect since he died of 'D.T's' a couple of years later! The Queen was in front again under the same auspices a couple of weeks later on her way home from listening to Jenny Lind at Her Majesty's Theatre in The Haymarket. Over the first seven months of the year she was in fact present at The St James's no fewer than eighteen times, four of them to see Rose-Chéri, once for the Serenaders and twice for Rachel.

Mlle Denain and M. Régnier were the stars for May, Bouffé for June and Rachel for July. One night, after having played the frisky young *Gamin de Paris*, Bouffé had just sat down to make-up for the part of the old priest in *Michel Perrin* when a stranger followed Count d'Orsay into his dressing-room. The Count was an habitué of the theatre and well known to all so when he asked Bouffé if his friend as a particular favour could watch him change his make-up from boy to kindly old curé the request was naturally granted without ado. The transformation completed, the visitors withdrew but d'Orsay whispered as he did so that the stranger preceding him was Prince Louis Napoleon. Years afterwards the courtesy was repaid as Bouffé explained to Jules Janin who tells the story. It was time for the actor to retire and arrange his Farewell Benefit. At his own Variétés, or Gymnase where he had won his spurs, he might have got 7,000 f. To everyone's surprise it was held at the Opera and he got three and a half times as much. The Emperor had granted a request from the actor who had delighted him in exile.

An actor who was to win world fame opened the winter season on 6th December. He was Charles Fechter, recently married to Eleanora Rabut who had made her London début on 5th July in the title-role of *Valérie* and as Sabine the wife of Horace when Rachel played her sister-in-law Camille. Fechter had appeared at the Comédie-Française in 1845 but had been born twenty years before that in London's Hanway Street (a turning that cuts the corner of Oxford Street and Tottenham Court Road) of an English milliner mother and sculptor father from Alsace. He died in 1879 in America where he had retired after a notable career playing in English the great roles. When he was running the London Lyceum he gave the Prince of Wales lessons in make-up. Shortly afterwards Queen Victoria was frightened in a corridor of her own palace when accosted by a most disreputable beggar!

1848

Bocage, actor-manager of the Odeon, was the new year star from 3rd January. On the Wednesday, two days later, he played Creon to Eleanora Rabut's *Antigone*. (The Sophocles tragedy was quite familiar to Londoners for Miss Vandenhoff at Covent Garden and Helen Faucit at The Haymarket had acted the same part relatively recently. Notably since then the celebrated Anglo-American Genevieve Ward had been Antigone at the Crystal Palace in 1875 and then seventy-five years after that Vivien Leigh and George Relph movingly interpreted the great drama at The New.) To Mendelssohn's score and with fifty singers and musicians, mostly recruited from Drury Lane, under the baton of Benedict (later Sir Julius), the action was set on a raised centre dais with chorus accommodated down front and on each side. Reports to the Queen were so favourable that she commanded a special matinée for 26th January. The only other occasion upon which she was present this season was on St Valentine's Day when Mlle Nathalie was star.

A French revolution broke out about this time which made Louis Philippe flee to England and Louis Napoleon hurry the other way, eventually to take over instead. Communications, however, were not interrupted and Lafont came over to lead the company in April.

Another Frenchman to cross over then was the conjurer Robert-Houdin whose *Soirées Fantastiques* Mitchell presented from 2nd May to 14th August. He was a remarkably slick operator but to cover the fact that most of his illusions, even if amplified and more dexterously performed, were not novelties in London he cried out the louder that all had been invented by himself, some even specially for this occasion. Even the billing as 'of the Palais-Royal' indicated that that was his own theatre, but he only used it in the off seasons of the dramatic company there, unlike Philippe who did have his own little theatre on the Boulevard Bonne-Nouvelle. Actually he had just been beaten to it by Herrmann at The Haymarket before Easter with illusions identical almost with his best. These were 'The Inexhaustible Bottle', 'The Magic Clock', 'The Suspension Etheréenne' and a second-sight act as well as a magic portfolio out of which all sorts of items were produced.

Robert-Houdin offered all the above but he called the second his 'Cabalistic Clock' which was an apparently transparent dial hanging only by a ribbon which obeyed his spoken command to show whatever time was requested. His most impressive illusion was the *Escamotage de Robert-Houdin, fils*, which was Robert-

Houdin's son 'suspended in equilibrium by atmospheric air, through the action of concentrated Ether' which concluded by showing the boy horizontal in the air and apparently supported

Robert-Houdin

by nothing except his elbow on the top of a walking stick. The bottle act was better than Dobler's for he produced any of a dozen different liqueurs at command instead of just three wines. Other illusions were called 'The Wonderful Orange Tree',

SJT F

'The Safety Casket', 'The Fans and Cannon-balls' and 'Auriol and Dudureau' which was a little puppet scena ostensibly free from any manipulation.

As well as on the three off-nights he appeared on Wednesday matinées also as soon as the public began to clamour for seats. On the evening of 19th July the Queen commanded him to the Palace to entertain her guests and children.

The Parisians were still fighting each other in their streets so Mitchell brought over the entire Palais-Royal under Ravel for a fortnight in June. Lafont had been followed in May by Achard who wound up the regular company earlier than usual.

Also in June, over at Drury Lane, another exiled company, Dumas' Théâtre Historique, had attempted to present *Monte Cristo*. English actors however, feeling that it was all right for foreigners to appear at The St James's but not anywhere else, filled Drury Lane with themselves and their supporters, be-hatted and overcoated, and created such a disturbance on two nights running that the French gave up. All were not on the side of the ruffians of course, and Macready not only called personally to apologise but a letter of his to that effect was published in *The Times*.

Mitchell gave the visitors sanctuary and they opened on 21st June but *Monte Cristo* was so long that it took two days to perform. The author himself was 'on the barricades' in Paris so made no personal appearance.

Grisi and Perrot danced at Mitchell's own Benefit, and on the last night of July and final one of the French season amongst the usual distinguished persons in the audience were the Countess of Blessington accompanied of course by d'Orsay.

In the winter the Histrionics enjoyed themselves and on 6th December Dumbolton presented a new troupe of six Serenaders, prefixing his own name instead of the ethnological one. Robert-Houdin returned shortly afterwards for their off-nights to have quite as successful a season as his first one.

1849

A comic opera company without visiting stars supplanted the Serenaders on 15th January. Mlles Charton, Guichard and MM. Couderc and Octave sang the chief roles. The first named was commanded to sing at a concert in the Palace in the spring. Robert-Houdin, who concluded his engagement at the end of April, twice appeared at the Palace. The Queen was, however, also in her box fourteen times including the night of 20th June which was Mitchell's Benefit. Prince Albert and many British and foreign nobility were also there and as a testimonial Mitchell was presented with a magnificent silver-gilt candelabrum and richly chased cup and salver by the Duke of Beaufort and Dr Daniel on behalf of the subscribers.

1850

The Opéra-Comique reopened on 7th January with the same feminine leads but new men in Chollet, Nathan and from Brussels the tenor Lac. Halévy's *Val d'Andorre*, which had run a hundred nights in Paris, was the première, other presentations including Herold's *Zampa*, Ambrose Thomas's *Caïd*, Adolphe Adam's *Le Roi d'Yvetôt* and *Postilion de Longjumeau*. Though the Queen was only there four times their three months were still quite successful.

Alfred Bunn was experiencing one of his bad periods but though fifty-four he was as resilient as ever, and the announcement towards the end of February that he would appear personally three nights a week until Easter encouraged quite a run on the box-office by a public agog for scandal, slander and back-stage revelations from the much admired, hated, notorious, extraordinary impresario. The stage was set as his own study and his 'Literary and Dramatic Monologue' was divided into the History of the Stage; Shakespeare; his own opinions and reminiscences. Magic-lantern slides and paintings illustrated the talks.

The dramatic company engaged after Easter were led by two couples and then Rachel, all from the Comédie-Française, the latter being preceded by Lafont from the Variétés. Opening pair were Mlle Denain and Samson, the twenty-fifth *doyen*, who surely held the honour longer than anyone else for he had done so for twenty-one years when he retired in 1863. Mlle Nathalie and Régnier (twenty-seventh *doyen* to be) relieved them in May.

The Queen was present only once this season, on 19th June, for Mitchell's own Benefit. On some of the off-nights artists and other amateurs occupied the stage.

FRENCH PLAYS.
ST. JAMES'S THEATRE, KING STREET.
Lessee, Mr. JOHN MITCHELL, 33, Old Bond Street.

☞ NOT AN ORDER WILL BE GIVEN.

FIRST APPEARANCE
THIS SEASON
OF
THE EMINENT TRAGEDIENNE,
MADEMOISELLE
RACHEL,
WHO IS ENGAGED FOR
A LIMITED NUMBER OF REPRESENTATIONS.

Rachel made the first of twelve appearances on 1st July. As usual her parts included Phèdre and Camille as well as Marie Stuart, and for the first time in England Adrienne Lecouvreur. Scribe and Legouvé had written the latter part, in the tragedy which they titled after the chief character, almost as a commission from the actress. Though based upon the great eighteenth-century player, the story was fictional. Now plays could not be produced at the Comédie-Française until accepted by a committee. During the writing of the play Rachel turned against the idea of it and news of her reaction having circulated, when the five acts came to be read by Scribe, an enormous roomful sat mute throughout. Legouvé, however, was determined that Rachel should play the part and on the same boards which had been trod by Lecouvreur herself. Six months later she capitulated after another reading, this time by the junior collaborator and in front of only half a dozen including Jules Janin.

Rachel was of course magnificent in the play, particularly in the last act where the young actress dies through the poisoned bouquet. Rachel's original antipathy had had some psychic reason, and the play always affected her strangely for she associated it with herself and her own early death. Even at the first rehearsal this was so, as Legouvé tells us. So emotionally taut was she when she played Adrienne that here on the last Monday of July 1851, just as she stretched out her hands to take the poisoned bouquet of flowers, in the tense and silent house a dog suddenly barked in the auditorium entrance and Rachel dropped unconscious as though she had been struck on the heart. It was the last part she was ever to play on a stage, on 17th December 1856, in Charleston, U.S.A.

Under Mitchell's management since 1848 Fanny Kemble had been giving Shakespearian Readings. She opened here when the French season ended towards the close of July and continued well into August, using the versions her father had adapted for his two-hour Readings here six years earlier.

Dramatically, her entrance was preceded by a footman bearing an enormous tome which he reverently placed between two immense candlesticks upon a mahogany table down centre of the stage. Fanny then made stately entrance, bowed, lowered herself upon the high-backed chair the flunkey positioned for her and opened the volume. Though Henry Irving heard her *Hamlet* at a later series than this and thought her dreadfully out-dated, other judges at various times were more than pleased as long quotations from Longfellow, Anne Thackeray, Henry James (sen.) testify in Bobbé's book on Fanny.

1851

Mr Love the ventriloquist on 24th February returned to open a year of remarkable diversity with a series of his 'Polyphonics', which included imitations of the sounds of kitchen utensils as well as other sketches and impersonations as before.

Tyrolese singers entertained for a week when Love went off on a long tour which began in the minor halls of the suburbs. Then from 24th March to 15th April Fanny Kemble returned to continue her Readings until she was transferred down the street to Willis's Rooms.

On Easter Monday J. H. Anderson, 'Professor of Natural Philosophy, the originator and inventor of Modern Scientific Magic, Great Wizard of The North and World Renowned', performed his 'Royal Entertainment of Natural Magic, the same as performed by him, at the express command of Her Majesty at Balmoral Castle, when the late Mr Anson, by command of The Queen, presented the following letter of approval to Professor Anderson—"Balmoral Castle, 17th August, 1849. Mr Anson is commanded by her Majesty to express to Mr Anderson the great satisfaction which her Majesty has derived from his Entertainment of Natural Magic this day, at Balmoral. To Professor J. H. Anderson." '

The Aberdonian, equally good as showman, conjurer or—in national parts such as Macbeth or Rob Roy—as actor, thrilled and baffled his audiences quite as successfully as any visitors from the Continent. As his advertisements, from which come my quotations, emphasised, whether he called them 'astounding wonders in Natural Magic' or 'Séances Fantastiques, Anglaises et Etrangères' the London press pronounced them to be the 'NE PLUS ULTRA of all Magic, Ancient or Modern, Native or Foreign'.

Anderson's main illusion was his answer to his French rivals with the suspension of his son in the 'Magic Laboratory', which he called 'the incredible Feat of the Invulnerable Child, Wonder of the Mystic World, but seven years of age'. Otherwise he 'illustrated scientifically the fallacy of Witchcraft, Necromancy, Demonology' every night for a week from 21st April and then twice daily thrice a week until 17th May. Two days later, on Monday, he began a long tour at Bath Theatre Royal.

A strong French company had started on his off-nights from the 28th led by Régnier and Lafont and Mlles St Marc and Judith. The latter was that fine handsome Jewess who was to be elected *Sociétaire* the following year. Though no relation to Rachel as sometimes stated, they were the best of friends, and it was for Judith's Benefit that the other made her final bow to Parisians just before that tour to the States which was to prove a fatal strain to her spirit-driven, over-taut physique.

On 19th May a change of stars was effected when an infusion from the Palais Royal including MM. Amant, Dernal and Levassor began to arrive. Rachel arrived on 2nd June. Fanny Kemble returned the following week to give matinée readings and Levassor gave occasional matinée solo entertainments for as well as being a good actor he was a delightfully articulate singer of French narrative songs. Donna Petra Camara, whose troupe of Spanish Dancers had enthralled audiences at Her Majesty's, took over on 22nd July for their own Benefit. Bouffé was the final star and he held the fort until August was well in, for the season had been specially extended because of the crowds in town for the great Crystal Palace Exhibition which the Queen had officially opened on May Day. She had been three times here in May when the stars had been variously MM. Régnier, Lafont, Levassor, Mlles Judith and St Marc; and twice in July specially to see Rachel.

London was almost surfeited with the bizarre and extra-ordinary this year because of the Exhibition. As well as the normal plays and operas at the theatres there were galloping horses not just at Astley's and Batty's but at Drury Lane. There was a 'Locomotive Aerial Machine', passengers paid to ascend in balloons, Magician Robins in Piccadilly passed his 300th performance, Love ventriloquised in Chelsea, Diaramas and the like slowly turned to show painted pictures of the world in Leicester Square where also Lapland Giantesses were being exhibited, 'uran utans' and a hippopotamus were novelties at the zoo, 'small-footed Chinese Ladies' were in Knightsbridge and a mandarin held court in his ornamental junk (managed by Fox Cooper) on the Thames whilst Red Indians sold curios from wigwams in Pall Mall.

Phineas T. Barnum in New York was late in finding something to vie with his fellow showmen but then he heard of two child actresses touring the deep south swamps and river townships in the minor company of their father Hezekiah L. Bateman. Barnum reached out and Kate and Ellen Bateman starred here from Monday 25th August until 18th October.

Their repertoire included the fight scene from *Richard III* when eight-year-old Kate was Richmond and Ellen, her junior by two years, was Richard; the trial scene between Shylock and Portia; the dagger and other excerpts from *Macbeth*. In *Old and Young* Ellen played an old gardener and Kate acted four different mischievous children. In that they were quite delightful as were they too in *The Young Couple* which had originally been written by Scribe for Léontine Fay when a child star.

Barnum's sagacity had far-reaching results since it is unlikely otherwise that the father would ever have arrived in England. He it was who was running The Lyceum when Henry Irving persuaded him to present that famous *The Bells*. It was his youngest daughter Virginia who married Edward Compton and gave birth to (Sir) Compton Mackenzie, Viola, Frank, Ellen and Fay. Many chorus girls and others still remember, and later ones have reason to bless, the sometimes fierce-seeming but kindly 'Old Mother Compton' of the Stage Girls Club who was Virginia. Sidney Crowe was a daughter of Kate and Francis Greppo (who married Irene Rooke) a son of little Ellen.

1852

Fanny Kemble's Readings ran this year from 3rd February until 3rd April. They included *Richard III, Henry VIII* and *King John* but began with *A Midsummer Night's Dream* when a chorus of sixteen under the baton of Mr Grice also sang Mendelssohn's music. That melody was strangely moving to Fanny for the composer had been a lifelong friend ever since 1829 when both of them, charming and beautiful twenty-year-olds, had become the fêted darlings of London, she for her Covent Garden Juliet, he for his pianoforte playing of the songs and music he was then composing. He had died in November 1847 and though their lives had gone their separate ways she felt his loss so much that when commanded to read the *Dream* to the accompaniment of his music at a memoriam performance at Buckingham Palace she had actually begged to be excused —an incredible thing to do which earned her heavy disfavour at Court until it was explained to the Queen that Fanny knew the ordeal would be more than she could stand without breaking down. In fact, a few weeks after the funeral in Berlin, Fanny had been present here at The St James's for that *Antigone* in January 1848 when his music had been played, and at the well known strains she had burst out crying and had had to withdraw behind the curtains of her box to hide her grief.

Déjazet and Lafont opened the French season on the off-nights from 16th February. The former had not been over for some time so she was greeted vociferously for even though the years were creeping up on her she seemed as full of life as ever. In the comedy *Le Marquis de Lauzan* to confuse lawyers she had to assume various 'breeches parts', and she was also the Duke in *Les Premières Armes de Richlieu*. Lemaître and Clarisse followed from 8th March with *Don Caesar de Bazan*, d'Ennery's *Paillasse*, Victor Hugo's *Ruy Blas*, and others.

Régnier and Roger came in April with Mlles Denain and Marquet. The latter was Delphine, daughter of the old tragedian and sister of dancer Louise. Of another generation is Mary Marquet who was sponsored by Sarah Bernhardt when her parents wanted to keep her out of the family profession and who at the time of writing is still an honoured *Sociétaire*. Rose-Chéri and MM. Levassor and Numa were the stars when the season ended on 14th July. The Queen had been ten times in front.

Fanny's Readings were only at matinées in March, for in the evenings a Hungarian Band under Kolozdy gave a series of concerts. The latter were followed by the Tyrolese Singers who had returned, and then from 2nd June for four weeks Mitchell presented Emil Devrient's German dramatic company. Both the Queen and the Prince were there to welcome them on their first night when they performed Goethe's *Egmont* about the hero of the Netherlands when under Spain. Schiller's *Don Karlos*, Lessing's *Emilia Galotti* and Schlegel's adaptation of *Hamlet* were in their repertoire but interested readers may find a full review in Professor Morley's *Journal of a London Playgoer*. The Queen honoured them five times more and would have done so on the final night too had news of the death of a relative of her husband's not prevented her.

Under the patronage of the Ambassadors of Turkey and Austria and the Duchess of Somerset a Benefit was given for the Bateman children on 9th August. The players, who gave their services free (perhaps to make sure that the precocious ones got their passage money!) included Walter Lacy who was to be in The Lyceum company with them two decades later, Fanny Wyndham who was subsequently to be a directrice here and Sam Cowell (grandfather of Sydney Fairbrother), comic singer and half-brother of Mrs (Sydney Francis) Bateman.

The Tyrolese Singers appeared again for two weeks from

13th September. Their advertisements could now boast that they had entertained the Queen at her holiday home in the Isle of Wight and also her mother in Clarence House. They and their chief attraction, the zither, were followed by a dozen Germans calling themselves an 'Organophonic Band' who had had the somewhat original idea of turning themselves into an orchestra of musical instrument imitators. Their novelty attracted enough money to keep them going throughout October.

A lecturer held the stage for a couple of weeks from 8th November. He was Henry Smith who had been travelling in Australia, even then still a land of mystery, of gold, sheep and strange mammals. With enormous painted panoramas of the scenes of his far-off experiences he thrilled his hearers with tales of giant nuggets lying for the picking in the unpaved streets and tripping up drunken diggers as they stumbled homewards; of leaping kangaroos and of black-bearded bushrangers murdering and shooting at lonely stations. Between the panorama changes he sang songs like 'The Miner's dream of Home'.

A marionette theatre was in the Lowther Arcade which ran diagonally from the Strand to Adelaide Street inside a delightful Georgian block which mostly still remains. The puppets had let their theatre to the entertainer Woodin whilst they went on tour. Returning to find him unwilling to close down, they took over the vacant St James's for a holiday season from 6th December and ran well into the new year. Delighting both children and parents, they presented specially written new plays, burlesques and adaptations of popular melodramas, etc. *Ali Baba*, *Don Giovanni or The Spectre on Horseback*, *Romeo and Juliet*, *Guy Mannering* in varying form were offered and, particularly apt here, with newly created puppets, *The Ebony Marionettes*, with which they burlesqued the Serenaders. Apparently about two feet tall, their lip movements, action and brilliant costuming were all favourably commented upon.

1853

A full five-month French season began on the last day of January with Ravel holding the fort until Lafont came in March, on the 4th of which Queen Victoria occupied her box, having done so also a week before. She intended being present ten days later too, but the date clashed with Ben Webster's final night at The Haymarket so she went there instead and postponed her next visit until the 16th. She was in front again on 4th April and three days later gave birth to Prince Leopold, Duke of Albany, an accouchement of particular interest since to aid it Dr Snow administered chloroform, the royal example naturally doing much to fight prejudice. Appropriately, since the drug was first used as an anaesthetic in Edinburgh, the Prince[1] grew up to be quite a Scotophile as was his predecessor in the dukedom, the eighteenth-century *soi-disant* Charles III, erstwhile Bonnie Prince Charlie.

Mitchell gave the players a holiday at Easter and put on again Robert-Houdin who subsequently performed on twice-weekly matinées as well as the off-nights to the French. Feminine leads variously included Mlles Fleury, Luther, Lambert, Claire Berton, Page and Brohan. Régnier arrived in May and Rachel in June. The latter opened as Phèdre. She also acted two recently created parts, the title-roles of Augier's *Diane* and Mme de Girardine's *Lady Tartuffe*. In the last she was a powerful dual-charactered beautiful and fiercely loving woman though withal cruel, treacherous and hypocritical.

The Queen saw Rachel in both her new parts as well as in *Adrienne Lecouvreur*. At a matinée concert in aid of the German Hospital on 20th June she attended with her husband and cousin the blind King of Hanover—son of her unpleasant Uncle Ernest, Duke of Cumberland, who had been hastily 'banished' to become that king when his brother William was about to die. Rachel's last performance was as Camille on

[1] Full name: Leopold George Duncan Albert.

29th June when some of the royal children were in front
though their mother was that night at The Princess's in
Oxford Street.

Devrient's company followed the French for a month with
Teutonic versions of *Hamlet* and *The Taming of the Shrew* as
well as other dramas including Schiller's *William Tell*. The
Queen went twice to see them.

A very poor English opera company began a season on 29th
October with *La Sonnambula* and a ballet. Tatty scenery, in-
adequate voices and a weak and inefficient orchestra aroused
contemptuous demonstration from their first-night audience.
They opened on a Saturday and a week later a fairly full house
resulted upon the announcement that a new operetta *Pierre* by
a young composer Duggan would be presented. There were
only two characters in it, however, sung by Miss Lowe and
Drayton, and after the curtain fell it stayed down for fully two
hours.

It was soon whispered around that the band were refusing
to return to the pit until they were paid for their first week's
work. The gallery enjoyed themselves by singing, whistling
and making loud and ribald jokes about the affair, but the rest
of the house merely got thinner and thinner as the night wore
on. Drayton eventually appeared to apologise 'for a slight
accident behind the scenes' which produced a spate of cat-calls
from the 'gods' and more acid comments from the few still
sitting lower down. Then a few of the orchestra slipped back
into their places and the last act of *Sonnambula* was laboured
through. The ballet girls had wisely gone home long before so
that terminated the evening's entertainment as well as the life
of the company.

1854

Except for amateur shows the theatre remained closed through
another cold and snowy winter. It reopened on 28th April with

a dramatic company under Lafont. The Queen with her husband and mother was there on their second night and encouraged them another six times up to 3rd June, as well as having been present at an amateur entertainment on 2nd May in aid of the dependants 'of soldiers ordered to the East'. The 'East' was the Crimea, for war had begun at the end of March. An amusing sidelight on that peculiarly 'gentlemanly' war (not that the cannon-fodder had reason to agree with the adjective) was the edict published at the outbreak that Russian ships were to be allowed to unload and have six weeks' grace whilst no ship was to be taken at sea if she had left port after war had been declared.

One of the French plays, under its English title *David Garrick*, was to become the enormously successful comedy in the repertory of Sothern and later in that of Sir Charles Wyndham. The original was supposed to be based upon an incident in Garrick's life though it was called *Sullivan, comédien de Drury Lane*. M. Brindeau, *Sociétaire* of a decade's standing, made his English début in it to an enthusiastic house which included the royal family. The plot relates how Garrick was invited to a merchant's dinner party under instructions to display atrocious drunken habits so as to deflate the desire of the host's daughter who was enamoured of the actor. The stratagem fails for the actor returns in Act III, enamoured in his turn, to marry the girl.

Others in the company were Mlles Luther, Fix, St George and M. Régnier. All went home about the beginning of June and were replaced until 2nd August by a light opera company headed by Marie Cabel.

The King of Portugal was a guest of the Queen this summer and she took him three times to see them, going herself six times in all, being so delighted with Donizetti's *La Fille du Regiment* that she saw it three times with Marie Cabel in the title-role. This was to be almost the Queen's final year of theatre-going. Though only in her thirties the cares and enor-

mous amount of work which the State more and more demanded
of her began to weary her and take their toll upon her energy
and time. This year she was here fourteen times. Only twice
more was she to be in front, once in 1857 and again in 1861.

John Mitchell too was getting tired. His regular active
management was now concluded.

CHAPTER 4

A POT-POURRI OF MANAGERESSES

1854-1878

AN interesting but hardly successful venture lasting five months began this autumn when one of Braham's inaugural girls returned as manageress in association with the well-known novelist Charles Reade. She was Laura Allison, now about thirty-five and billed since the forties as Mrs Seymour, for she had married following her Haymarket engagement after the Braham seasons ended. He was some kind of financier, probably sephardic in origin, and older than her. They lived now in a house in Jermyn Street which they shared with a friend of her husband's, a dapper little swell with no money called Curling, and Braham's great big basso-profundo son Augustus. The famous platonic friendship between her and Reade matured after the death of Seymour so need not be here explored. Their theatrical partnership and companies operated in town or on the road to advantage in after times. Forbes-Robertson, Tom Robertson and Ellen Terry were amongst those who gained valuable experience under them.

Reade was quite a character. Ellen Terry in her memoirs called him 'dear, kind, unjust, generous, cautious, impulsive, passionate, gentle, placid and turbulent but always majestic, a stupid old dear and as wise as Solomon!' Laura and he lie in the same grave in Willesden churchyard under the epitaph he composed: 'Here lies the great heart of Laura Seymour, a brilliant artist, a humble Christian, a charitable woman, a

loving daughter, sister, friend, who lived for others from her
childhood. Tenderly pitiful of all God's creatures, even to some
that are frequently destroyed or neglected, she wiped away the
tears from many faces, helping the poor with her savings and

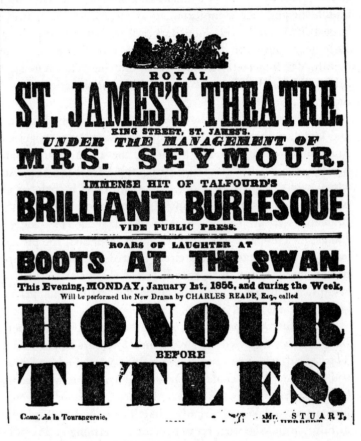

soothing the sorrowful with her earnest pity . . . her face was
sunshine, her voice was melody, her heart was sympathy. . . .'
She had died in 1879, Reade five years afterwards.

The poet Robert Buchanan knew them well and said she
'deserved every word of the passionate eulogy which Reade

SJT G

composed and had engraved upon her tombstone'. He himself described her as 'bright, intelligent, noble-minded and generous to a fault . . . vivacious and altogether charming . . . impulsive and occasionally wrong-headed, but with the finest of all virtues, charity'. John Coleman said she was 'a trifle over middle height, fair complexion, oval face, frank open brow, large bright hazel eyes, long dark lashes, light brown glossy curly hair, pure yet delicate acqueline nose, exquisitely cut mouth, dazzling teeth, slender waist and magnificent bust, a bright ringing laugh and a crisp clear sympathetic voice at times soft, gentle, low'.

These were the two who opened the theatre on Monday, 2nd October, though her name only was billed as manageress. Annoyingly enough to the historian, the Lord Chamberlain was lax and was not enforcing paragraph VII of the 1843 Act which said that place of abode of licensee must be printed on playbills. Perhaps because living quarters, used by some of the Brahams, were part of the building he considered its address sufficient. The place was cleaned and redecorated, the pit and gallery enlarged and a dress circle created instead of the first tier of boxes. Prices were even below Braham's at 1/- gallery, 2/- pit, 3/- upper boxes, 5/- circle, 6/- stalls. The private boxes were 1½, 2 and 2½ gns.

The acting company numbered thirty-four, plus supers. Isabella Glyn and George Vandenhoff with Mrs Seymour and Tom Mead, who was also stage manager, were the best known and the leads. J. L. Toole, famous comedian to be, was making his London début as were others including Eleanor Bufton, a fifteen-year-old Welsh girl who, like Toole, had been playing in Edinburgh. She went on to become a charming and popular actress but Toole very soon returned north for a while. Others included the Misses Robertson, St Clair and Lydia Thompson another who was just beginning a notable career.

Opening attraction was a five-act drama by Tom Taylor and Charles Reade called *The King's Rival*. The plot turned around

the marriage of Miss Stewart (Miss Glyn) to the Duke of
Richmond (Mead) which was hindered by her ex-lover King
Charles II who was played by Vandenhoff. Mrs Seymour was
Nell Gwynne and Toole was Samuel Pepys. Though this was
Reade's ninth play and third joint effort with his even more
experienced collaborator it ran for four hours. Cut by half it
might have been perfectly successful and enjoyable.

Charles Selby was the author of the supporting farce which
ended the evening. Called *My Friend, the Major*, it proved a
starring vehicle for Toole as a bailiff, Weazle, who enjoyed
himself when taken to a dance disguised as a Major by one of
his gentlemen 'clients'. Toole really saved the night for he sent
the audience away much happier than they otherwise would
have been.

It was again an exceptionally severe winter, so cold that the
Thames froze over at Richmond and the Queen changed her
carriage for a sledge for her airings in Hyde Park. War news
combined with the weather in hitting the box-office.

A burlesque inspired by Perea Nena, who was drawing
crowds to The Haymarket, was produced a couple of weeks
later. This was Selby's *The Spanish Dancers* which successfully
featured Lydia Thompson and Toole. At the end of the month
an adaptation from the French in three acts by Reade, *Honour
before Titles*, was introduced without success. Lydia's dancing
in a ballet, *Beauties of the Harem*, helped to retrieve matters
and the house filled for a Benefit for St Mark's Hospital in
December when amateurs supported Miss Glyn as Lady
Macbeth.

The Christmas extravaganza was by Francis Talfourd, an
experienced and successful author who had worked with
Reade two years before at The Strand. *Abon Hassan* was this
vehicle, well spiced with puns and parodies, for Toole as Al
Rascid and Miss Marshall in the title-role with Miss Elsworthy
as Hassan's young lady.

1855

Well-tried favourites such as *The Lady of Lyons*, *The Stranger*, *The Wonder* and *The School for Scandal* were other features of the season. In the latter Mrs Seymour was Lady Teazle, Miss Bulmer was Maria and Mrs Stanley took the part of Mrs Candour. Vandenhoff was Charles Surface.

ROYAL

ST. JAMES'S   **THEATRE.**

ADMIT TWO TO DRESS CIRCLE.

_____ day, _____ 1855.

Not Admitted after Seven o'clock.

M _____

⁎⁎ *The Name of the Party presenting this Order must be inserted.*

'paper' for a 'deadhead'

The new year novelty delighted most of the critics but they were unable to influence enough of the public to make *Alcestis* worth while to the box-office. It was a lyrical play adapted from the French by Henry Spicer. Barry Sullivan and Miss Vandenhoff were specially engaged to be Admetus and his wife Alcestis. A chorus of sixty was recruited and the orchestra en-larged with Sir Henry Bishop to conduct. One of the scene painters was Telbin who was to become, after years for The Lyceum with Irving, a *doyen* in that department. The playbill carried a long explanation of the fable, which was signed Laura Seymour though Reade was probably the actual originator of it. It proved to be Sir Henry's final public appearance for he was very ill even as he conducted and at the end of April he died.

A month later, on 17th February, after the theatre had been shut for a few days, they presented *Clarisse or The Foster Sister*, an adaptation of Robertson's *Noemi* which itself was from the French. It was the after-piece to Reade's own *Art*, in which Laura was Nance Oldfield in this play about old-time stage folk like his more successful *Masks and Faces* which the Bancrofts made famous at The Haymarket.

By the time March was in the doors had closed on the venture. Reade was to remember it only with bitterness, and even fifteen years later when Mrs Wood was being a success here with *She Stoops to Conquer* he made a note about the 'double and treble attractions of Bishop, woman of genius, Barry Sullivan . . . could not attract to that beastly theatre'. Perhaps if Laura Seymour had been sufficiently objective as well as bold and strong enough to have forced Reade to drastically cut his dialogues, for example, the season might have proved a sounder attraction.

In June Levassor with Julie Tessiere took over to give monologue and duologue entertainments.

Rachel appeared in August for a limited season which was to be her final one in this country. She was only thirty-five yet the brilliant flame was to be snuffed out in just over two years. One of her last performances was at Drury Lane at a special Benefit for the French Charitable Association. As if people presaged something, every night she was at The St James's the house was crowded out even though her supporting company was disgracefully weak. She acted *Les Horaces*, *Phèdre*, *Andromache*, *Adrienne Lecouvreur*, *Lady Tartuffe*.

1856

In February there was talk that Priscilla, Mrs German Reed, was taking over with her husband but instead they leased the smaller Gallery in lower Regent Street for their entertainments already mentioned. She did, however, appear on 16th April for a Benefit *Othello* with Louisa Vinning and child pianist Mlle d'Herbie.

Old John Braham died on 17th February. He was eighty-two. Strangely, this same year, the three men who had been his strongest support in the opening days of the theatre also died: Morris Barnett in Montreal in March, Mitchell in New York in May, à Beckett in Boulogne in August.

In the spring Alfred Mellon conducted an orchestra of forty in a series of well-attended concerts. The star was Picco, a blind Sardinian virtuoso on a tiny flute. Peace in the Crimea had brightened the West End, but had it not been for occasional amateurs and musicians the theatre would hardly have been open at all though Grunfeld's German dramatic company did try a run for a little while in the winter.

1857

Over £70 was raised by amateurs in February for dependants of the Margate and Broadstairs lifeboatmen who had been lost in rescue work.

In March Sam Emery and Sir William Don transferred from The Marylebone. Don was an ex-Guards officer, a six-foot-seven Scot who had run through a fortune before he took to acting, which he did too late perhaps to be able to rise above mediocrity. Most of his acting career was wisely spent in America and the Antipodes. Their season here lasted two months during which they produced one new comedy, *The Belle and the Boor*. Revivals included *Frankenstein*.

For a couple of months from May Offenbach presented his brilliant little company and delighted critics and public alike with his gay and merry melodies in the witty and enchantingly played *Les Deux Aveugles*, *Dragonnette*, *Croquefer*, *M'sieur Landry*, *La Nuit Blanche*, *La Bonne d'Enfant*, *Les Pantins de Violette*, *Le Duel de Benjamin* and *Ba-ta-clan*. In the company

were Mlles Dalmont, Coraly Guffroy, Mareschall and MM.
Gertpré, Guyot, Pradeau and Tajan.

Queen Victoria paid one visit to the theatre on 8th June, and
one night the company travelled to Claremont to perform the
first three pieces above enumerated before their own exiled
Queen Marie-Amélie and the two young princes whose father
had died in 1850.

Coon minstrels returned with the début on 3rd August of
J. W. Raynor's Christy Minstrels. Raynor had been in the
original troupe founded by E. P. Christy in New York in 1846.
They played to good houses for a week, extended to two, before
transferring to The Surrey to continue their many years of
success in England, their popularity causing many to copy their
name.

An Italian *opera buffa* company under Ronzani started a
rather unsuccessful season from 3rd November, running only
into December. Alberto Randegger was conductor.

Professor Wiljalba Frikell, with his 'Two Hours of Illusions',
transferred on Wednesday 9th December from Willis's Rooms
where he had been since 23rd November after making his
London début on the 12th at the Hanover Square Rooms. He
was to run almost every night with at least one matinée a week
until his 200th performance next May Day. German, though
supposed to be Finnish and advertised as physician to the Czar
and Czarina, his 'Physical and Natural Magic' was claimed to
happen without the aid of any apparatus at all and he certainly
used as little equipment as possible. The crimson curtains
swung back to reveal only a couple of chairs and a table in front
of a small screen on the otherwise empty stage. Frikell made
his bow in evening dress, his cuffs pushed back and his coat-
tails slapped to prove them empty. Then from his large silk
handkerchief he began to pull one ostrich feather after another
until it seemed that hundreds lay around his feet. From the
same source there came four glass globes each swimming with
gold or silver fish. Followed another hundred ostrich feathers.

Then he borrowed a wedding ring, bent it, broke it with a hammer, wrapped it in paper, fired it from a pistol. A large envelope was presented to a spectator who then produced

Professor Frikell

eleven more, each inside another, until the last displayed the missing ring, still broken. Breathing on it Frikell then ostentatiously sealed it into twelve more envelopes before handing that package to the owner who of course found her ring inside the twelfth, perfect again.

To a lady spectator he gave a canary to hold. No matter how lightly she did so she crushed it, so the Professor cut off its head, rubbed its body in his hands until it disappeared, then offered the lady a choice of two lemons and from out of hers, when peeled, flew the canary.

Using a tumbler of coins he combined a ventriloquial with a second-sight act. From a bottle of old port there flapped a pigeon. Three small flags rubbed between his fingers kept producing more and more little flags until there was almost one for each of his audience. An egg, crushed in his hand, was found instead inside a lemon.

From a borrowed hat he produced 124 half-pint cups and then a hundred or so scent sachets which were distributed. Then playing cards in profusion came out but as he laid the hat down on the table there was a loud explosion from it so he pushed it off and jumped upon it, then tore it up, wrapped the bits in paper and gave it back to its still startled owner. Whereupon there was another bang and inside the parcel was found a baby! But at last the hat came sailing down from the proscenium arch, completely restored.

The most startling illusion was the loading of his pistol by spectators with six silver bullets and the subsequent shooting by one of them at Frikell who protected himself with a silver salver which each bullet invariably struck before it fell to the stage! An orchestra played during the intervals. He himself talked in German, Russian and broken English.

1858

Mitchell had presented the supposed Finn, and in March he arranged a 'séance' before the Queen in Windsor Castle. Frikell's astonishing run ended on 1st May, a Saturday, and on the Monday Carlo Andreoletti, who said he was physician to the King of Sardinia, was presented in 'Soirées of Mystical Illusions', also with no apparatus.

Mitchell announced that Carlo had been the sensation of the Parisian winter season but whether or not that was so, London was satiated and neither he nor another Italian, Antonio Poletti, at the end of the month in Hanover Square, was able to attract at all. The professional paper *The Era* would have none of

Carlo of whom it said: 'a more poor, trite, uninteresting exhibition was never placed before a London audience'. All the same Mitchell put him on before the Queen in Buckingham Palace for his manipulative skill and dexterity were worth exploiting in an intimate atmosphere if not in a theatre.

Ristori, Italian claimant for the mantle of world tragedienne, was presented on 16th June, her third English visit. *Macbeth*, *Phèdre*, *Ottavio*, *Lecouvreur*, *Falso Confidenze*, *Medea*, *Maria Stuarda* and Giacometti's *Elizabetta* were all performed in Italian and on the whole magnificently, though often the gestures were somewhat too grandiloquent. Interested readers are again referred to Professor Morley, who said during the controversy which soon raged over the respective merits of Rachel and the Italian: 'The two actresses differ widely from each other. Rachel dazzled and startled us by flashing an electric life into words and lines, unrivalled in giving an intensity of meaning to a single phrase. Ristori has this power, but in less degree, her excellence lies in a clear conception of the part she represents, a subordination of detail to the just working out of the central thought. . . . In *Phèdre*, where Rachel inspired terror, Ristori awakens pity.'

Ristori's season ended on 15th July. On Monday the 17th she had a Benefit at Covent Garden.

In the winter amateurs appeared, often for charity, and on 1st November a Benefit was arranged for Fox Cooper. Towards the end of December Remusat's French lyric company opened with Mlles Faure, Céline Mathieu, MM. Fougères, Montclar, Berger and Emon, etc. Before that a crooked M.P. for Greenwich called Townsend played Shylock and other parts.

1859

Remusat closed in February. In May Jules Samson arrived with his dramatic company. He was a son of the old master and his offerings included many plays familiar in translation

such as *Le Courier de Lyons* and *Le Perle de Savoie*. He had
hoped to present Dumas' *La Dame aux Camélias* but the censor
refused to pass it.

Augustus Braham now formed an English opera company
with his brother Hamilton, Susan Pyne and Mme Rudersdoff.
They opened in June with a Spanish ballet and produced half
a dozen pieces including *The Pearl of Savoy* and *Raymond and
Agnes*, the latter an opera based on the famous melodrama *The
Monk*. They did not open again after the week commencing
4th July.

An English manager of twenty-five, who was later to become
well known, now decided he would see what he could do and
leased the theatre for a year. He was F. B. Chatterton, and on
1st October he opened with prices even lower than Laura
Seymour's, but with no second-price except for the private
boxes: 6d. gallery, 1/- pit, 2/- upper circle, 3/- circle and
5/- stalls. His company was quite strong and included Lydia
Thompson, Clara St Casse, Nelly Moore, Miss Murray (who
married Sam Brandram), Katherine Hickson, Eliza Arden,
Mrs Frank Matthews and his directrice Fanny Wyndham.
Among the men were Sam Emery, Leigh Murray, Australian
Charles Young, H. B. Loraine (who played here under Alex-
ander when eighty), H. T. Craven the actor-dramatist who
was home after four years in the Antipodes, Dewar and George
Barrett who was also stage manager.

Lydia Thompson was the merry sprite who had danced her
way into London's heart as Little Silver-hair in The Haymarket pantomime of 1853 before she was fourteen, and who
had been one of the Seymour/Reade attractions the following
year. She became such a rage that the students of Moscow as
well as Berlin would unharness her horses and substitute
themselves, but one critic in Chicago disliked her professionally,
and then personally after she had waylaid him with a fiercely
wielded whip!

Clara St Casse was more than a year younger though she

had tasted public adulation longer than had Lydia for her début had been at the Newcastle Royal before she was eleven, singing songs between the acts when Miss Glyn was Lady Macbeth there in 1852. Later she was one of the first Little Eva's in *Uncle Tom's Cabin* and made her London début at The Brittania in 1854.

Nelly Moore was a moving wee emotional sixteen-year-old who was soon showing such promise that everyone predicted a great future. But her flame burnt too brightly and she died in January 1869 whilst at The Haymarket.

The first-night after-piece was a popular farce, *A Dead Shot*. Preceding it were two novelties, Fitzball's comedy *The Widow's Wedding* and a Leicester Buckingham burlesque on the Sheridan Knowles tragedy the title of which was amplified to *Virginius, or The Trials of a Fond Papa*. 'Produced under the direction of Mr Barrett' who was Appius Claudius, it was quite amusing and stayed on into December. Charles Young was Virginius, Cecilia Ranoe, whose mother with Sam May designed and saw to the costumes, was Caius Claudius and 'ripe for any villany', Clara St Casse was Icilius and Eliza Arden the latter's 'brother' Lucius. Mrs Frank Matthews, who was actually no particular beauty and in the company was first character or 'heavy', played Virginia ('a gem of loveliness, styled on account of her youth and beauty, The Early Pearl of Rome, with a general penchant for admiration, a particular weakness for Icilius, and an eager desire to become a person about to marry'). Lydia Thompson was a Mysterious Stranger. There were ten other speaking parts and the ballet.

The National Anthem was sung every night for the first week and later bills quoted from nine different papers the most eulogistic phrases about the redecorated house, plays and audience reactions.

They had opened on a Saturday, and on the Wednesday produced a new ballet farce by the *Times* critic John Oxenford called *Magic Toys*. In this Lydia danced a hornpipe and other

solos as well as a *pas demon* for she was Valentine the son of
Merlin a magician who was played by Mr Robins. Clara was
Ergandula and sang a new song specially composed by F.
Kinsbury, 'Oh, give me back my pretty Toy'. Mr Francis was
Mother Goose and Miss Denvil completed the cast as an Imp.
It ran for 103 performances, the first piece here to touch a
century.

Half a dozen other new pieces were produced in the first
three months and then on Christmas Eve three novelties began.
Mark Lemon's *Garibaldi's Englishmen* was a skit on a drama by
Tom Taylor at Astley's. *The Household Fairy* by Francis
Talfourd was for two players only: H. T. Craven as a ruined
aristocrat saved from suicide by the timely arrival of a strange
visitor in the person of Fanny Wyndham. The pantomime was
by J. C. Collins, its full title: *Punch and Judy or Harlequin and
the Fairy of the Crystal Caves*, the music by Hayward. There
were two clowns, one, Paul Herring, well known as such; the
other was Alfred Glanville, nineteen at the time and unknown
but destined to win fame as 'The Great Vance' of the music-
halls. (Many readers may remember a wonderful impersonation
of Vance by Stanley Holloway in the film *Champagne Charlie*.)

1860

A young author really began his career on 11th February when
Frank Burnand saw his classical burlesque *Dido* produced.
Though just down from Cambridge he already had had four
pieces accepted by the publisher Lacy to whom he showed
Dido. Lacy passed it to Miss Wyndham who with Charles
Young's backing influenced Chatterton. £25 down and £1 for
every night after twenty-five was the offer made and delightedly
accepted by Burnand, destined to be author of 150 pieces, to
be knighted, to be editor of *Punch*. It ran eighty times to the end
of the season. Burnand married the teen-aged Cecilia Ranoe
who was King of the Winds.

For the Eastertide Benefits the great tragedian Charles Dillon was engaged to play d'Artagnan in *The King's Musketeers*, etc.

Immediately afterwards Adrien Talexy opened with an excellent company, many of them already familiar, including Mlles Delphine Fix, Adèle Page, Maria Basta, Duverger and Mme Doche. The men were led by Brindeau and the young Got who had been *Sociétaire* for ten years and was twenty-ninth *doyen* from 1873 to 1894.

As an extra summer season Chatterton presented another of the great ones, Barry Sullivan, in a round of his favourite parts, *Hamlet*, *Richard III*, *Macbeth* and *Richelieu*. Sullivan, who had been here for Mrs Seymour, had just returned from the United States. Katherine Hickson was Ophelia and Lady Macbeth. Support was mostly specially recruited but Clara St Casse was Hecate, Victoria Vokes being Fleance and as well as the usual three male ones there were twenty-five singing witches! The score was Locke's. In September (the star's engagement was for a fortnight at the end of August) when *The Beggar's Opera* was presented Clara was Polly Peachum, F. Charles being Macheath. On 3rd September Mrs Charles Young made her first appearance here when she was Pauline and Leigh Murray was Claude Melnotte in *The Lady of Lyons*. Soon afterwards the season ended.

A new lessee opened the winter season on 29th October. He was Alfred Wigan who had progressed into a popular actor-manager and dramatist since his early days with Braham. After a long illness he had made a come-back to a tumultuous welcome at The Adelphi early in 1859 and was to run here for just over a year. He added a shilling to most of the prices but reintroduced the second-price except for the gallery which he kept at sixpence.

Wigan's painstaking stage director was his wife Leonora Pincott, no beauty but an admirable and intelligent actress. Leading girl was Louisa Herbert the beautiful slim blonde who became heroine of the Rossetti circle and later successful

manageress here. Supporting her were Nelly Moore, Clara St
Casse and an exquisite little spark of quicksilver the Serbian
Albina de Rhona. Male leads were George Belmore, Sam
Emery, Charles Young and Ben Terry. The latter was an
Irishman whose wife Sarah had chosen the more worldly re-
warding rigours of stock and touring stage instead of those of
her father's Scottish manse. They had been with the Keans at
The Princess's where their eldest girls had made their débuts,
for these were the first of the famous Terrys. Kate had played
Prince Arthur in 1852 and Ellen had been Mamillius in 1856.
Kate, now sixteen, was engaged with her father.

The season began with a new drama commissioned from
Tom Taylor about life in India, *Up at the Hills*, and a re-
polished fairy piece by Planché called *King of the Peacocks*.
On 19th November the bill was changed to three old pieces
including *Still Waters Run Deep* and that hardy favourite back
again, *Monsieur Jacques*, in which Wigan played the title-role
of the old musician. On the 26th Albina made her début (she
had come via St Petersburg) in Palgrave Simpson's *Smack for
a Smack*, after which she delighted everyone with her dancing
of the Highland Fling and Spanish and Polish dances. It was
she who later took over and rebuilt the Soho Theatre which
she renamed The Royalty.

An extravaganza by William Brough called *Endymion or The
Naughty Boy who Called for the Moon* was 'Produced under the
Direction of Mrs Alfred Wigan' as the Christmas piece. Miss
Herbert was Diana or the Moon, Clara was Cupid, George
Belmore took the part of Pan, Marion Taylor of Endymion
and Mr Terry 'his' father. Kate Terry and Nelly Moore were
among the nymphs, Dewar was 'Putaplasteron—the Family
Doctor, an M.D. by diploma but an A.S.S. by nature'. Score
was by the musical director Wallerstein. Costumes were by
Mrs Curl and Nathan. Properties were credited to Turtle and
mechanical effects to Garnett. Scenery was by F. Lloyd and
Walter Hann. The latter was just twenty-two and was to do

much work here in the future even into the new century for
Alexander.

The author, who was to write the following Christmas piece
also, was the prolific and successful progenitor of more than
sixty often similar pieces, alone and with his brother Robert.
Lionel the actor was their brother, whose son Sydney married
Lizzie Webster, granddaughter of the great Ben who was to
take over here at the end of 1863.

The other Boxing Day offering was *The Isle of St Tropez*.
Burnand and Montague Williams had adapted this from the
original which had been a *tour de force* for Lemaître here in
1845. Miss Herbert played the innocent wife Amelia who was
accused of poisoning her husband Henri (Alfred Wigan) by
the real villain Antoine (Emery). Dewar was the wife's ex-lover
Charles and Mrs Buckingham White and George Belmore her
friends the Dumerys. Terry was Gerfaut the doctor, Elizabeth
Romer was Margot and Dawson the sailor Louis.

1861

Queen Victoria made her last ever visit to The St James's when
on 7th February she arrived specially to see the poison drama
in English of which she had seen the original so long before.
The Easter extravaganza was Maddison Morton's *Pasha of
Pimlico* and before the season ended about the beginning of
May they also produced Palgrave Simpson's *A Scrap of Paper*
from the French *Les Pattes de Mouche*. The latter had already
been otherwise adapted but it was an excellent vehicle for the
Wigans in the central characters Prosper and Suzanne. Belmore
was Brisemouche the naturalist. (The Kendals were twice to
revive it here, *vide* 1883/7.)

Lambert Dennery brought a French musical company over
for a short summer season. He had been conductor the previous
year.

Wigan reopened in October with a series of revivals including

St Tropez. His only novelty was a comedy, *The Poor Nobleman*, by Charles Selby, which Mrs Wigan again as usual directed.

George Vining was stage manager for the new winter season and at Christmas the Wigans withdrew and his name went on the bills as manager. Most of the company were the same but newcomers now or since October included Frank Matthews and another from Braham's time, Miss Rainforth. Vining himself was one of an extensive stage family. Now in his mid-thirties, he was first cousin to Mrs Wood who was to have a much longer run here in the future than he had.

Charles Dance's comedietta *A Wonderful Woman* was the curtain raiser on Vining's first night which was Boxing Day, and W. B. Bernard's farce *The Boarding School* was the concluding item. Between these was Brough's new extravaganza *Perseus and Andromeda, or The Maid and the Monster*. Catherine Lucette was Perseus and Louisa Herbert filled the other title-role as 'a little duck who nearly met a fowl end, through the pultry conduct of her parents'. Mrs Matthews was Danae 'dwelling with her son Perseus at the court of Polydectes where she finds herself bored as well as lodging, vainly woo'd by the King: in fact the more he woo'd the more she woo'dn' '. Nelly Moore was Kautatarta, 'a strong minded female citizen'. Kate Terry was Dictys, Frank Matthews was Polydectes 'king . . . of a little spot of Greece—oily in speech, unctuous in manner, in*fat*uated by Danae . . .', J. Robins was Hyloesaurus 'a monster crooked in shape . . . remarkable for his awful twist'. There were nine other speaking parts and a large crowd.

Back-stage credits were as fulsome. 'The new and extensive scenery designed by Mr Lloyds and painted by himself, Mr Hann and numerous talented assistants. . . . Costumes, entirely new though unmistakenly ancient, by Mr Nathan aided by at least nine tailors, equal to any one man in power; and Mrs Curl whose numerous assistants, spite of their sewing vocations, cannot be looked upon as mere sew-sew people. The properties by Mr Turtle, who will provide the genuine style of thing and

SJT H

no attempt to put us off with mock-turtle. Machinery by Mr Garnett. Music by Mr Wallerstein. The Piece produced under the Direction of Mr George Vining.'

1862

Three weeks later the manager's own *Self-Made* replaced one of the minor pieces, and on 8th March Alfred Wigan's brother Horace saw his name on the programme as author of *Friends or Foes* which he had adapted from Sardou's original *Nos Intimes*. On the 24th a new dramatist was given his first chance when *Under The Rose* was produced. He was George Roberts (G. Walters) who was to write some thirty successful pieces in the future. A couple of days later Kate Terry had to take over from Miss Herbert in *Friends or Foes*. She was hardly eighteen though she had been on the stage intermittently since her Prince Arthur at The Princess's in 1852. She proved so excellent in the part that she was kept on in it and won press mention as well. Her chance came because she had studied every part in the play.

The next big production was on 5th May when another Willy Brough spectacular, *Prince Amabel or The Fairy Roses*, was presented and then ran well into July. Sisters Carry and Sarah Nelson made their débuts in it, the former as the Prince and Sarah as Princess Violet, a Cinderella with two ugly sisters Tartarella and Dragonetta played by Elizabeth Rainforth and Mrs Frank Matthews. Their father was King Turko the Terrible, a *bad sovereign* of the Author's *own coining* but which he hopes may *pass*, the inherent *baseness* of the metal being so thickly covered with *g(u)ilt*. Frank Matthews played Turko and Belmore was his 'Prime Minister Gruffangrimio, a villain of the deepest *die*, in fact a *dire* villain'. Ashley was Amabel's father, King of Hearts Buonocore, and W. H. Stephens Lord Kootoo their Chamberlain.

Many other princesses and others supported and with the

large corps de ballet delighted. The choreography was by
Oscar Byrne, the dancer whose father had been chief panto-
mimist in Garrick's company. George Belmore had married
Alice Cooke, of the still existing circus family, in April and
for a while his Christian name appeared as Garstin which was
in fact his real surname. He was a very likeable and popular
fellow and a character actor capable of creating the most
diverse roles. He died after a long illness in New York thirteen
years later, his funeral being attended by almost all the theatrical
fraternity of that city; the Vokes family sent $1,000 to help
defray the expenses incurred in his illness.

Vining did not close for the summer and produced a fresh
piece every four weeks or so, his last being J. M. Morton's
two-act *She Would and He Wouldn't* for 6th September. Soon
after he wound up his company because Charles Fechter had
taken over The Lyceum and asked both Vining and Kate
Terry to join him there, which they did.

It was not until Boxing Day that the theatre reopened under
the sole management of Frank Matthews. The company was
a fresh one except for his own wife, Miss Herbert and the conductor Wallerstein. E. Chatterton was still in the box-office
where he had been since F. B. Chatterton had taken over.
George Ellis returned as stage manager and director of productions. Newcomers included Ada Dyas, Adeline Cottrell, Patti
Josephs, Charles Harcourt, Gaston Murray and Sam Johnson.
After training on his father's Ayrshire circuit the latter had
been at the Edinburgh Royal for a couple of years and was well
known in the north, though he had also played at The Lyceum.
He was to return there in the days of Irving with whom he had
acted in Sunderland when the latter made his début.

Planché's *Faint Heart Never Won Fair Lady* and two new
productions began the new season. Burnand and Williams
were the authors of the farce *Carte de Visite*, which was about
a husband hiding in an ottoman and a photographer thought to
be an assassin. The extravaganza was by H. J. Byron, surely

the most prolific punster of the century. Before he died in 1885 his successful productions amounted to almost 150 panto-mimes and plays, etc. *Goldenhair the Good* was his present one, his twenty-fourth in five years, four of which were being produced in London this 26th December for the first time! For Burnand it was only a double-first, for he had a burlesque coming out at The Olympic.

Louisa Herbert was Goldenhair, banished from fairyland for falling in love with a demon and told she must live on earth as punishment until she could win a human husband and bring him back with her. Her choice fell on grumpy old Gruntz (Frank Matthews) but when she eventually allowed his loving housekeeper to have him instead she was welcomed back to fairyland as reward for magnaminity.

1863

On Saturday 3rd January *The Dark Cloud* was presented successfully. It was a heavy drama by Arthur Sketchley under his real though lesser known name of George Rose. Arthur Stirling had been many years on the Bath and Bristol circuit and he now made his metropolitan début as Philip the villain who had ruined and sent to transportation and death the young husband of Miss Herbert who later remarries. Eventually the villain himself comes back from the Australian goldfields with a forged death certificate to blackmail the family, but he is defeated by the Frank Matthews's who played a Scots medical couple who had settled in the village after having been in Australia too. They proved that the certificate date was forged, so the heroine had not married again before the death of her innocent, wrongly convicted first husband, and all ended happily.

An anonymous farce *The Smiths at Norwood*, and then a tragi-comedy called *The Merry Widow* by Leicester Bucking-ham were in turn added, and then on Saturday 28th February was created the classic *Lady Audley's Secret* by George Roberts from the popular novel by Miss Braddon. Play and players won plaudits. Miss Herbert was the beautiful, dramatic and villainous bigamist who pushed her first husband Talboys (Gaston Murray) down a well, set glorious fire to the inn where the suspicious nephew of her new husband Sir Michael was lodging, and finished with spectacular insanity when the undrowned

THEATRE ROYAL,
ST. JAMES'S
KING STREET, ST. JAMES'S STREET.

UNDER THE SOLE MANAGEMENT OF
MR. FRANK MATTHEWS

All Complimentary and other Free Admissions Entirely Suspended—the Press Exempted.

LAST NIGHTS of the PRESENT SEASON

After which, **COMMENCING AT EIGHT O'CLOCK,** (26th, 27th, 28th, 29th and 30th times) the New Drama, in Two Acts, with Entirely New Scenery, Music, Appointments, &c., &c,, founded on Miss Braddon's popular Novel of the same name, and adapted expressly for this Theatre, with her sanction, by George Roberts, Esq., entitled

LADY AUDLEY'S
SECRET

THE MUSIC BY Mr. WALLERSTEIN.
The Dresses by Mr. Nathan and Mrs. Curl.   The Appointments, Decorations, &c., by Mr. Phillips.   The Scenery Painted by
MR. WILLIAM BEVERLEY

Talboys rose like a wraith to confront her. Frank Matthews was Luke the gamekeeper who saved the husband from the well; Arthur Stirling created the part of Robert Audley but Charles Harcourt, making his London début, took over from 30th March. J. W. Simpson played Sir Michael Audley and the Misses Lavenu, Ada Dyas, Adeline Cottrell with Messrs Norman, Wilson, Taylor and auxiliaries supported.

The drama was quite a sensational success and ran for 104 nights to the end of the season. Miss Braddon's name was not missed from the programme which announced 'adapted specially for this Theatre, with her sanction, by George Roberts, Esq.'. Largest type on the playbill other than the title, which was one inch taller, was five-eighths inch for 'Mr William Beverley' and for the two scenes he painted and designed: the library in Act I and the lime-tree walk in Act II. Three other scenes, however, were painted by Fenhoulhet and two by Fenton. The music was 'by Mr Wallerstein. The Dresses by Mr Nathan and Mrs Curl. The Appointments, Decorations, etc., by Mr Phillips' and 'The Drama produced under the Direction of Mr George Ellis'.

From Easter Monday there appeared a burlesque by Willie Brough upon Dion Boucicault's *Effie Deans* (which had been based on Scott's *Heart of Midlothian*) called *The Great Sensation Trial or Circumstantial Effie-Deans!* Roguish darling Marie Wilton (Lady Bancroft to be) and Jimmy Rogers were specially engaged for it and led the laughter which suddenly clouded when some days later, on 14th April, the popular comedian Jimmy died a few hours after his performance when he was only forty-two years old. A Benefit for his widow was given to a full Drury Lane on 18th May at which many St James's players appeared as well as other top names including Ben Webster, Toole and Bedford.

Frank Matthews' last night was on 4th July when he took his own Benefit. After redecorating during the recess it was confidently expected in town that his management would continue, but he had not been well and at the last moment he approached Ben Webster of The Adelphi to ask him to take over instead. Ben agreed to the responsibility and opened on Boxing Day. As stage manager he appointed his brother Fred (maternal great-grandfather of Barry Lupino sen.), took on as many of the old company as he could—many had already been rehearsing anyway—changed over a little with his Adelphi people, in future using some there and some here, and was ready only a week after his arrangements began.

The leading company announced for the season comprised Wallerstein still as musical director, but scenic artists Danson and Sons; Ben Webster himself, Toole, Paul Bedford, Mr and Mrs Charles Mathews, Mrs Frank Matthews, Mrs Stirling, Miss Cottrell, Fanny Josephs and Miss Wentworth. In addition there were H. J. Montague, James Johnstone, Frederick Robinson, J. Clarke and the Misses Dalton, Percival, Henrietta Sims, Mrs Stoker and others not all immediately.

Ben opened with Hollingshead's popular farce *The Birthplace of Podgers* and his own son's *Hen and Chickens*. The new piece was the 'Comical Conglomerative Absurdity, *1863 or The Sensations of the Past Season with a Shameful Revelation of Lady Somebody's Secret*', which was by H. J. Byron who again had three other pieces produced on the same night for the first time. It was much more in the nature of a revue than burlesques had normally been in the past, for in it Toole parodied Fechter's Lyceum *Hamlet* and Miss Percival, as 'an Alluring Lady from The Adelphi', made fun of Kate Batemen's melodramatic Jewess *Leah* which was to pass its 100th night in January. Highlight of the evening was little Toole's pushing great big lugubrious Paul Bedford, as the unwanted husband, down the well into which he was too fat completely to disappear.

1864

The famous light comedian Charles Mathews and his second

wife, Lizzie Davenport, appeared on 11th January in the former's own *Adventures of a Love Letter* and Blanchard Jerrold's *Cool as a Cucumber*. The first was dropped at the end of the month in favour of a new Leicester Buckingham comedy called *The Silver Lining* and several revivals were introduced, but the Christmas piece stayed on well into March. Then the Easter extravaganza, Planché's *The Golden Fleece*, was produced; Miss Herbert was re-engaged on 11th April for a revival of *A Day after the Wedding* when *The Silver Lining*, *Cool as a Cucumber* and *Under the Rose* were in the programme.

The first new play by the argumentative and somewhat obstreperous Irishman Dion Boucicault to be produced here was *The Fox Chase* on 11th May. It, or something called *The Fox Hunt*, had been done originally in New York eleven years before. Unfortunately it had similarities to that French play *Sullivan* which in English as *David Garrick* had only ten days earlier arrived at The Haymarket with Sothern. Tom Robertson's play had only two acts and there were five in Dion's who, according to some of the critics, had used half a dozen French plays to make his one. Ben Webster issued a statement saying the play had been sold to him as being entirely new, and that started a public controversy in *The Era* where Dion and Ben slanged each other and raked up whatever history suited them. I.O.U.s of as much as £200 which Ben still held unpaid, and the twenty-year-old *Fox and Goose* containing the same idea which they had collaborated upon and which Ben had then produced at The Adelphi, were among the points raised. However, the latest version ran, with three other pieces, until 25th June and in the future Ben did not refuse to produce other pieces by Boucicault.

In fact on the Monday, 27th June, when four fresh pieces were presented, one of them was the result of an old collaboration between Dion and Mathews who starred in it. Authors were credited with the others, Tom Taylor's *Sheep in Wolf's Clothing*, Charles Mathews' *Little Toddlekins*, and John Oxen-

ford's *Bristol Diamonds*, but *Used Up* had no author mention!
Gossip, it is true, had suggested in 1844 when it was first
presented, that Lord Ranelagh was the one who had made the
original translation from the French *Le Blasé*.

The title was current slang for being bored or blasé, which
was the mood of Mathews as Sir Charles who was about to
marry Lady Clutterbuck (Mrs Frank Matthews) when into
their compartment rushed blacksmith Ironbrace (Henry
Ashley) with the news that the lady was his run-away wife.
The hero proved a match for the brawny one in the fight which
followed, but in the end they crashed locked together through
a window into the river below. Singly, each saved himself,
thought himself a murderer, lived such a virtuous life in future
that all ended well, and the baronet lost his ennui in the delight
of honest toil and the love of a simple maid, Mary (Patti
Josephs). Other parts were taken by Walton Chamberlaine,
James Johnstone, Smithson and Branscombe.

Faust and Marguerite was the title of the next burlesque to be
produced, on Saturday 9th July. By Burnand, it ran to the end
of the season on Friday 12th August. Oscar Byrne was again
engaged as ballet master; while the scenery, music, etc. were
by the house men. Ashley and Lizzie Mathews were in the
title-roles and the latter's husband Charles was Mephistopheles,
'who on Metropolitan Railway descriptive line might be
termed one of the Underground authorities'. Chamberlaine
was Wagner, assistant to Faust, H. J. Montague was Valentine
in the costume of a German policeman and John Clarke was
Dame Martha, a fat Teutonic innkeeper.

Webster started his winter season on 19th September, a
week later than first advertised, with Arthur Sketchley's *How
will they get out of it?* a bright little comedy which had been
first done for Mathews' Benefit on the last night of the summer
season; the *Faust* travesty, and *Under the Rose* by G. Roberts,
for four players and described as a 'comic scene'. Constance
Roden and Fanny Hunt were new girls and Frank Matthews

was back. Webster put on three new plays before the end of the year but by the beginning of December announced 'Last week but two of the present management'.

On Boxing Day Miss Herbert's name went up as manageress. W. S. Emden was her acting or general manager, Telbin and his sons H. and W. were the scenic people, Milano, who was best known as a harlequin, was engaged as ballet master, Mrs Curl for the costumes, McKenzie was kept on for the mechanics (transformations etc.) and Wallerstein was still conductor and musical director. Mr Larttice was specially engaged to arrange a cabinet rope trick for Miss Herbert's big production which she backed by pieces from the recent repertoire.

Her attraction was another Willy Brough burlesque, *Hercules and Omphale; or The Power of Love*. For Hercules she engaged the brilliant Charlotte Saunders, who had been a child actress under Alexander in Glasgow and the first Oliver Twist in Edinburgh before making quite a sensation in the York circuit when she was about nine as an Infant Roscius enacting Hamlet, Macbeth, etc. Her first London appearance was at The Marylebone in 1848. She was quite a remarkable character actress who combined, one might say, the powers of the Baddeley sisters of the twentieth century, having all the droll impersonating capabilities of Hermione as well as the pregnant acting strength of Angela. With a fine forehead, large expressive eyes and mouth, her personality was strong yet charming.

The opening scene showed the council hall of the palace of Eurystheus, King of Mycenae (Frank Matthews) where the assembled throng were grandiloquently informed by the King that he had got rid of that strong-man nuisance Hercules for at least a year by giving him some paltry jobs that would take even him that time to do. But as he spoke a frightened messenger arrived to say that Hercules had finished all his tasks and waited without. After a flurry of orders to shut all doors and bar the windows, the King was about to flee to his tower for safety when everything shuddered to a standstill at a thundering crash, while the enormous brazen doors that filled the up-stage wall shattered to fragments and Charlotte Saunders appeared, black bearded and tremendously muscled.

Sweetly she apologised that she had not meant to knock so loudly, but a moment after when one of the courtiers offended he received a kick that sent him swishing through the air to disappear into the flies! For losing his temper Hercules was then punished by the gods by being sold into slavery. Miss Herbert, as Queen Omphale of Lydia, was soon languishing for him, since after purchasing Hercules she had fallen in love with him and with her maidens had taught him the new-fangled sewing machine and other household chores. But the jealous King soon heard of her passion and sent an army to capture her prospective lover who, only because he had been found asleep, was brought back in chains. Then, well tied with ropes and chains, the captive was locked inside a cabinet brought to the centre of the stage and all relaxed knowing him to be well secured. But Hercules had watched the conjurers and spiritualists of the day, so hardly had the keys been turned than the cabinet doors swung open and Hercules took his bow, all chains and ropes neatly piled beside him!

1865

Miss Herbert planned and brought out a new piece monthly and for Easter another classical burlesque, this time *Ulysses* by Frank Burnand. For the title-role she engaged young Fred Robson whose father, the famous 'Little Robson', had died when only forty-three on 12th August last, the night that the season here had ended. The subsidiary title was *The Iron-clad Warrior and The Little Tug of War*. This after-season was her first free of commitments made by her predecessor, so although the acting company remained much the same she changed scene painters to the Grieves, father and son, and took on Frank Musgrave as musical director.

Charlotte Saunders made a very funny Jupiter, Montague was Mercury and Felix Rogers was Minerva, goddess of Wisdom. Miss Weber was Cupid, Bessie Alleyne, who had made her début in January, was Telemachus 'aged one month in scene 2, aged seventeen in scene 5—in both cases a very fine boy for her age'. Her elder sister was Palamedes, Captain of Zouaves in the Grecian army. The Misses Marion and Cardinal were two suitors of Penelope the wife of Ulysses, played by Eleanor Bufton. Miss A. Colinson was Calypso and Mr Smithson was a Black Nurse. More suitors, coloured soldiers, nymphs and the like completed the cast.

John Oxenford's four-act adaptation from Miss Braddon, *Eleanor's Victory*, was produced to run with *Ulysses* from 29th May. Miss Herbert was the heroine Eleanor Vane, Mr and Mrs Frank Matthews were Major and Mrs Lennard, Arthur Stirling was Richard Thornton as well as being the new stage manager, J. Johnstone was Mr Vane, Frederick Robinson was Bourdon, Montague was Launcelot Darrell, Gaston Murray was Mr Monkton, Brown and Barker were Baptiste and John and the Misses Weber and Marion were Laura Mason and Susan while Mlle Cardinal was Georgette.

The drama followed the original very well considering the long and quite complicated story of how Eleanor eventually vanquished the villain Darrell and his accomplice Bourdon, who had ruined her father and sent him to his suicide. Miss Braddon was in a box on the first night, but according to *The Era* was unaccountably ignored at the end when the leading lights were called for individually by the audience. Miss Herbert impressed everyone so much that she was called for between the acts and received a tremendous ovation at the final curtain.

Miss Braddon was not unnoticed, however, after the finale of the novelty which opened the winter season on 14th October. It was a wet and miserable Saturday and John Brougham this time was the adapter of her *Only a Clod* which was presented

as *Caught in the Toils*. Miss Herbert had a new stage manager
in Mr Belton who had been in the provinces for a decade. He,
Walter Lacy and F. Charles were the most important new
names. Though well enough received, it was replaced on 20th
November by a revival of *Lady Audley's Secret* which ran into
December with *The St James's Ladies Club* which had been
the second piece from the end of October. By Mark Lemon, the
latter was an earlier comedietta he had brought up to date
with topical allusions.

   Lady Audley was replaced on 16th December by a revival
of *The School for Scandal* in which Miss Herbert made a
decided hit as Lady Teazle. This success encouraged her to
revive six other classics in the next twelve months or so. On
Boxing Day Oxenford revised the old Tom Dibdin *Harlequin
Hoax* as *Please to Remember or The Manageress in a Fix* which
ran over the holidays.

                               1866

She Stoops to Conquer appeared on 27th February with some
success. John Clayton (first of the Calthrops who later married
Dion Boucicault's daughter Eva) made his début as Hastings.
Miss Herbert was of course Kate. On 4th April the Goldsmith
was replaced by *Much Ado About Nothing*, which in turn was
followed on 10th May by *The Rivals* when Miss Herbert was
Lydia Languish, Mrs Frank Matthews was Mrs Malaprop and
Eleanor Bufton and Ellen McDonnell were Julia and Lucy.
Frank Matthews and F. Charles were Sir Anthony and Captain
Absolute, Gaston Murray was Faulkland. Walter Lacy played
Bob Acres, Fourness Rolfe was Sir Lucius O'Trigger and
John Clayton was Fag. Robson, Dyas, White, France and Miss
Graham made up the cast.

   It was still 'essential' to have more than one piece in a programme, but Miss Herbert was sensible and did not swamp
things as had been done too much in the past. One curtain-

raiser or after-piece was her sole sop to fashion. In one of these, *The Rear Admiral* in April, Ellen McDonnell made her début and in June in *Jack in a Box* Rachel Sanger appeared.

For her own Benefit on 27th June Miss Herbert played Lady Teazle again and William Creswick made his first appearance here, as Joseph Surface. He then played Oakley when she was Mrs Oakley, and Walter Lacy was Lord Trinket on 16th July when Colman's *The Jealous Wife* was revived.

Miss Herbert's new winter season was particularly notable because it introduced the word-spinning genius W. S. Gilbert to the play-going public and Henry Irving made his first successful metropolitan appearance.

John Oxenford's farce, *Professor of What*, opened the season on 6th October with Mrs Cowley's *The Belle's Stratagem*. The curtain-raiser was about the mistaken identities of a circus acrobat and a schoolteacher and the jealousy of a country-bumpkin waiter. Miss Herbert and Irving won favourable mentions, the *Illustrated London News* reporting on him as 'a new actor of great talent'. As Lady Touchwood, Carlotta Addison made her first adult appearance. Her sister Fanny, two years older at nineteen, was to make her London début in November at Her Majesty's. Their father was the comedian E. P. Addison.

Irving's engagement (at £3 a week) was due to the three-act drama, *Hunted Down or The Two Lives of Mary Leigh*, presented on 5th November. The author, Dion Boucicault, had previously directed Irving and Kate Terry in it in Manchester where Charles Reade saw it and advised Miss Herbert to get the London rights. Dion agreed when she applied, but stipulated Irving's engagement as director and as actor of the part he had created.

The plot revolved around the blackmailing machinations of reprobate Scudamore (Irving) who had run away with heroine Mary Leigh's money after bigamously marrying and then deserting her at the church door. Miss Herbert played Mary who eventually remarried, thinking the villain dead. That of course was the signal for his evil reappearance, but 'the dark shadow was dissolved' from over Mary's distracted head when in the end Rawdon Scudamore's real wife Clara (Ada Dyas) arrived to save the innocent and confront the guilty. Walter Lacy was the new husband John Leigh and Mrs Frank Matthews a comforting friend of the family. The play had been long in rehearsal for it had been planned to open the season. It became an immediate success and ran a good three months into February.

Early in the winter Miss Herbert had asked Tom W. Robertson to write a play for her, but that by then famous author had just seen his *Ours* produced at Marie Wilton's Tottenham Street theatre and he was in the middle of another for The Princess's. He suggested that a witty friend of his on the same comic paper *Fun*, might well be worth encouraging. The friend was Gilbert of future Savoy Opera fame, but, as one paper said after his first night, at this time known as 'the caricature artist in *Fun*'. After a chat at the theatre Gilbert promised to bring something round in a dozen or so days. He was back in ten with what he called an 'eccentricity', a skit on Donizetti's *L'Elisir d'Amore* (the elixir of love) which he titled *Dulcamara or The Little Duck and the Great Quack*.

The burlesque was put into immediate rehearsal and presented on the Saturday of Christmas week. Only after its successful reception were author's terms mentioned.

'How much do you expect us to pay you, Mr Gilbert?' asked Emden.

Gilbert had no idea how to answer such a direct question so he quickly computed ten days at £2 a day, a week's rehearsals, say £10. They'd put 'Esq.' after his name in the programme and this was Miss Herbert's St James's so he couldn't very well ask for plebeian pounds.

'Thirty guineas, Mr Emden.'

'Oh, no! We never pay in guineas, Mr Gilbert. Make it pounds.'

'Done!' said Gilbert.

Gilbert, in telling the story many years later (in *The Theatre*, April 1883), said Emden looked a little disappointed throughout, but then after the cheque had been signed and passed over he said:

'Now take a bit of advice from an old stager who knows what he is talking about: never sell so good a piece as this for £30 again.'

Robertson's sister, Madge Kendal, told the same story nearly seventy years afterwards about Gilbert and Buckstone at The Haymarket but, as I shall have reason to point out later, her memory was sometimes at fault.

Frank Matthews was quack doctor Dulcamara who sold love philtres in the market square and J. D. Stoyle was his assistant Beppo. Carlotta Addison was Adina the Little Duck. Ellen McDonnell was Nemorino and Eleanor Bufton was the pretty little peasant girl Gianetta who attracted lawyer Tomaso (Gaston Murray). Belcore the Infantry Sergeant was played by F. Charles who also 'arranged the dances and action'. Catarina (an exquisite villager) was played by Miss Marion and afterwards by Miss Gunness. Later Miss Conway was Maria, a part which Miss Gunness had created. The scenery was by John Gray, the score by Van Hamme who this season was musical director, costumes by Mrs Curl, props and decorations by J. Lightfoot and machinery by Mathews. It was in five scenes beginning with the exterior of Adina's farm and then the interior of Nemorino's house. The market-place was the setting for the third scene for which the dancers Mmes Austin and Amy Thompson had been specially engaged. Scene four was set inside Adina's farm and the finale was on the village green. It proved a draw up to Easter.

Jimmy Rogers

Rachel Sanger

Tom W. Craven

Mark Lemon

Laura Seymour

George Vining

9

F. C. Burnand

J. L. Toole

John Oxenford

Alfred Wigan

Arthur Williams

Charles J. Mathews

Lillie Langtry

Mrs John Wood

E. S. Willard

Left. Marie Litton

Right. Henry Irving

Left. Marie Wilton

Right. Nellie Moore

H. J. Byron

Frank Matt

Mrs Frank Matthews

Charlotte Saunders

Lionel Brough

Charles Fechter

Sam Johnson

Walter Lacy

Frédérick Lemaître

Left. Ben Webster
(the first)

Right. Laura Allison
(Mrs Seymour)

Victorien
Șardou

Dion
Boucicault

Left
Hermann Vezin

Right
H. J. Montague

Ada Cavendish

Kate Bishop

Marie Tempest

Kate Terry

Carlotta Addison

Henrietta Hodson

Lydia Thompson

Charles Wyndham

Left
William Terriss

Right Jane Vezin

16

1867

Holcroft's *Road to Ruin* replaced the Boucicault from 9th February and that was replaced in March by *A Rapid Thaw* which Tom Robertson had adapted from the French (and had the honesty to say so on the programme) for Miss Herbert, as he had promised to do when recommending Gilbert.

It was not a good choice as it happened, because it was another terribly cold winter though the ice in the Regent's Park was not strong enough to hold the skaters who crowded there, for it broke and forty were drowned. Miss Herbert had been ill so Eleanor Bufton had played the lead as Sophia to Henry Irving's Harry Dornton in the Holcroft play, but she was better for the commissioned piece or else it would have been postponed. It was in two acts after Sardou's *Le Dégel* and was a play within a play, the first scene opening with royal pages disporting themselves in a snowball game in a park, and concluded inside a chateau with a rehearsal of a play about Venus and Adonis. In the original Déjazet created the part of Hector which Miss Herbert took. Irving played The O'Hoolaghan and Ada Cavendish and Millie Jones made their first appearances here as Clarisse and Gabrielle. Scenery was by Frederick Fenton.

Audiences justifiably objected, perhaps, to snow inside the theatre as well as outside, but anyway during Lent a clean sweep was made and *The School for Scandal* revived again as well as the little comedy *The Merry Widow*.

The Easter Monday novelty was an adaptation from the popular novelist Ouida by George Roberts which he called *Idalia*. In this exciting drama Miss Herbert was a beautiful spy and Irving her co-conspirator Count Falcon. The dispatches they coveted were carried by Charles Wyndham. It was almost the London professional début of that future knight and builder of two of London's theatres. He had, however, appeared at The Royalty in Soho when he and Ellen Terry were students

SJT I

there of that Albina di Rhona who had danced at The St James's in 1860. He had also acted under the future St James's manageress Mrs Wood in New York before he became a surgeon in the Civil War, for he had qualified in Dublin in 1861.

Idalia opened in a Parisian café with the conspirators eavesdropping as they watched the dispatches handed furtively to Charles Wyndham. Scene 2 was a rocky pass high among desolate mountains. A bridge spanned the centre of the stage over a tumbling, splashing torrent which was fed by a real waterfall. The waterfall was magnificent! High from a point in the back-cloth it gushed over the papier-mâché rocks and down into the channel to run under the bridge and then off-stage. Frederick Fenton had done the décor again and as the curtain rose to the otherwise empty stage the scene was greeted with a quite spontaneous round of applause. Unfortunately there was just too much water. A trickle spread from the rocks to the path and over the planks of the bridge and from there down over the gently sloping boards of the stage towards the footlights and orchestra pit. Outside in London it was still freezing cold and as the water spread inside it froze there too.

Then into sight came Count Falcon's assistant (F. Charles), pistol in hand as he gazed about before essaying the crossing of the bridge to the opposite rocks where ambush had been planned. Alas! As his feet touched the slippery planks of the bridge his arms shot high, the pistol flew through the air, and down he went with a plomp and a slither into the stream below. Immediately after came Irving, also stealthily creeping on his long spindly legs and all unaware of the disaster ahead or the reason for the strangely tumultuous applause in what ought to have been a tense and silent scene. Irving too went flying as he reached the treacherous spot on the bridge and then slithered to join his accomplice just emerging below, to the delight of the spectators now all agog for the next victim.

But Wyndham cheated them for he was next on, and had had time to peek around to speir the cause of the unplanned merriment and so most carefully had picked his way and avoided, for the moment, all slippery patches and unexpected tumbles. Waiting then until the first two could take up their allotted positions, Wyndham crossed without mishap until the pistols fired and he retreated backwards to an ordered fall on the bridge as the shots rang out again to hit him, though not before the dispatches had been flung from the enemies' reach into the torrent below.

Now, most unprofessionally, the beautiful spy had fallen in love with the handsome courier and so had followed after her chief gunmen in an attempt to save him, should he prove foolish and gallant enough to protect his papers with his life. So Miss Herbert appeared then in the rocky defile and ran to raise Wyndham's wounded body where it lay. She too, almost as she stooped, slipped and lost her balance so that she fell, spread-eagled over the object of her affection, her voluminous skirts and petticoats swirling up so that all that the hysterical audience could see were her lovely long legs convulsively kicking!

The next scene was an interior one, and though the waterfall had gone the ice on the stage had not, for carpets hurriedly spread were not large enough by far. Soon in progress was a wordy battle between Miss Herbert and Irving about her most incorrect love for the enemy courier, when the door opened and the latter entered. The lovers rushed to meet, their arms outstretched. Alas, again! Their outflung arms went high as slippers touched a frozen spot and down they both went to slither forward on their bottoms until their legs instead of fingers clasped.

Rowdier and funnier still was the final scene of all for in a mountain glen soldiers and villains had to fight, and as they did so and chased each other they fell and slipped and slid, while boulders which appeared huge enough to have stayed still even in an avalanche went bouncing and rolling about the stage. Never had an audience at The St James's enjoyed themselves so much. By the time all was nearly over the players were holding their sides and tears of merriment dimmed their eyes as they tried to shout their author's blood-curdling lines of curses and death threats. In the final tableau, where Irving in the centre clasped his chest in dying agony as his life blood seeped crimson between his fingers, a gurgling grin appeared on his face until all the company joined with the audience in the laughter that could no longer be contained!

Both *Lady Audley* and *Hunted Down* were revived for the Benefits in May and June and Sothern came over from The Haymarket as extra support before the company went off on a summer tour.

Raphael Felix (Rachel's brother) brought over a dramatic company which opened on 24th June. Headed by Mlle Deschamps and Ravel they were booked for a month but, after opening auspiciously before the Prince of Wales and the French Ambassador, their success warranted an extra dozen days. For Ravel's Benefit of 30th July Charles Mathews appeared in the original French of what he had adapted as *Cool as a Cucumber* which he played the same evening at The Olympic.

When the doors reopened on 16th October it was upon what proved to be Miss Herbert's final managerial season. Fenton and Van Hamme were in their old departments with George Ellis as stage manager. Willy Clarkson's father appeared as perruquier on the bills for the first time as did the 'Gas Inspector, Mr Pepall'. The acting company included Ada Cavendish, Kate Kearney, Sophie Larkin, Eleanor Bufton and Miss Love. The latter was the daughter of the great ventriloquist who had died in April in poor circumstances because of long ill-health. Friends and admirers had rallied at the last moment to the family's aid when the facts became known.

Newcomer to the company and England was John Sleeper Clarke. He was, in fact, in flight from repercussions in the northern American states because he was the brother-in-law of John Wilkes Booth who had assassinated President Lincoln

two years before—or so one story had it. He had been married
to Asia Booth, much to her later regret and sorrow for, though
a strong broad comedian, according to her he was a mean and
nasty man.

In the States he had built up the part of Major Wellington
de Boots in J. S. Coyne's *Everybody's Friend* into a more
prominent character than originally written. Coyne now re-
wrote the whole play from that point of view and, as *A Widow
Hunt*, it became the main new offering and ran to the end of
the year. As soon as the actor learned to tone down his rather
loud backwoods style he became quite popular in the West End.

1868

Miss Herbert had not appeared at her own theatre because she
had accepted an engagement to star at The Adelphi in the early
winter, but she returned on New Year's Day for Tom Craven's
one-act comedy *The Needful*. The author himself took part as
well as most of the company. Clarke had left at Christmas, as
had Irving who joined The Queen's in Long Acre where one
of the interesting characters he was to play was Bill Sikes to
Nelly Moore's Nancy, when Toole was the Artful Dodger and
that delightful sprite Henrietta Hodson was Oliver Twist. The
latter was the only one of those three not yet familiar here.

Among revivals was Stirling's *The Skyrockets of Her Majesty's
Service*, which was his refurbished *Bluejackets* originally done
at The Adelphi in 1838 when Laura Honey had played Fanny
the daughter of Port-Admiral Trunnion. Evans now played the
Admiral, which had been created by Frank Matthews who
was now out of the company otherwise naturally he would have
been cast again in his old part. Eleanor Bufton was the new
Fanny and Nelly Nisbett was her maid Betsy Bodkin, originally
Mrs Keeley's part. Fanny's lover Charles (Allen) was too
gentlemanly for her old shellback of a father, so he shanghaied
him aboard *The Bombshell* at anchor in the bay, but foolishly

left on guard only a coloured sailor Jacko (Brown) and antique master-at-arms Chaser (Bridgeford). Fanny gathered her girl friends, dressed them up in sailor suits, manned her father's Barge and led her crew to the rescue.

No sooner had they captured the almost unmanned ship, however, than they too were attacked, for the Admiral soon gathered his 'liberty' men and sailed in pursuit. Though Fanny was a real Admiral's daughter who'd keelhaul the first lubber who looked askance at her, her crew proved neither bold nor shipshape enough, so that even the gun they aimed at the Admiral and his marines got turned the wrong way round and as the charge exploded they all went flopping on their bottoms with their legs in the air, easy targets for the 'enemy' who sprang aboard to kiss and cuddle instead of cut and thrust!

William Farren joined the company in the spring and on Easter Monday Madame Celeste, who was not long back after a five-year tour mostly in the Antipodes, appeared for a Farewell Season of twelve performances commencing with Coyne's *Woman in Red* in which little Miss Love earned favourable mention amongst the plaudits to the veteran. Miss Herbert took her own Benefit on Monday 27th April when she was Lady Teazle, and on the Saturday her season and managership ended. She was to return the following year under Mrs Wood, but soon she married and retired though for a while she ran the tiny Bayswater Bijou Theatre for pupils in dramatic art with whom she sometimes did appear at prize performances.

Felix arrived again on 11th May with a dramatic company headed by Ravel, and on 22nd June came the Offenbach troupe who were heralded by a blare of trumpets for Hortense Schneider making her London début as *La Grande-Duchesse de Gérolstein*. Libretto was by Meilhac and Halévy, the score by Offenbach, the Variété being the scene of the first production on 12th April 1867.

Hortense Schneider was acknowledged in Paris to have donned the cloak and dancing shoes which Mlle Mars had worn in the beginning of the century. Of delicate features under reddish-tinted golden hair, she was a vivacious dancer and actress with a sparkling, strong and gay singing voice, a charmingly graceful creature personally. Offenbach himself had been the first to recognise her talents and potentiality.

As a girl she had run away to join a travelling troupe. At one time after too long a series of supperless evenings resulting from poor attendances, they had struck a lucky patch in the little town of Agen near Bordeaux when the house had actually filled and the audience cheered and applauded in excellent humour. Reacting as any company does when an audience is in perfect rapport, they all sang and danced and acted with more brilliance than they had ever done before. Hortense, completely carried away by suddenly fed high spirits, in the excitement of the moment picked up backstage an old pair of boots just as she made entrance. Gracefully she handed these to the first actor she passed upon the stage who, taking his unexpected cue with aplomb, as carefully accepted them and then laid them gently upon a handy nearby table. Another, as he made exit, took them up and carried them off to hand to the next one coming on. So it went on until everyone, even the King in the play, had handled the boots in turn!

The mystified audience nevertheless enjoyed the subtlety of what they certainly could not understand, and applauded more fiercely than ever when at the final curtain the boots were carried on by their 'inventor' Hortense. The tragi-comic sequel was not so happy. The next year another fit-up was on the road and the same play produced. Alas, the Agen audience would not settle down. The company sang their sweetest, they laughed and jollied along to their utmost but nothing but groans and restlessness rewarded them. Long before the final curtain the strange murmurings had developed into shouts and then the seats were being smashed, the tumult crazy, the mayor and military sent for.

'Nothing but yourselves to blame!' shouted the irate mayor

to the huddled and uncomprehending players. 'Mutilating a masterpiece of French literature! Taking money under false pretences! The boots! Where were they? Where were the boots? Disgraceful to miss them out!'

In 1855 Schneider reached Paris, and after auditions ending with 'We'll let you know' she came to the tiny Bouffes-Parisiens, where Offenbach only had to play the accompaniment half-way through her first song before he recognised her quality and engaged her.

Now, so long after, the Prince of Wales and the Duke of Edinburgh led the brilliant assembly that nightly thronged The St James's. The thirty-five-year-old was still a girl and her vivacious brilliance, the delirious gaiety of Offenbach's music, the abandonment of the dancing, the risqué songs and asides and sparkle of the complete ensemble captivated London as it had done Paris.

The exhilarating *Can-Can* became again the talk and scandal of the town, for *La Grande-Duchesse* revived its popularity though it had been known on the stage for the past couple of years. During the late sixties and early seventies the more sedate journalist often raised hypocritical eyes and hands to heaven at the 'depravity' of the dance. For example, some six years after Schneider first danced it at The St James's, the critic of *The Penny Paper* let off steam one day in a diatribe: '... the evil is spreading ... with the most libidinous gestures ... wanton wriggling and posturing which panders to the brute in man. ...'

The *Can-Can* was of Spanish-Moroccan genesis introduced to Paris in the late thirties or forties by that tempestuous little pock-marked Musard who held satanic sway over his orchestra and the dance world of Paris for many years. The high-kicking speciality of the dance really originated because of the police! These gentry, by order of the authorities, were stationed in the smaller dance halls to keep decorum within bounds. (A Lord Chamberlain tried to do the same with police in London theatres once but he failed so we'll let that diversion pass.) The officials would move about amongst the dancing throng and whilst their backs were turned the professional entertainers and hostesses would then vie with each other to see how many of the hats of the patrons sitting drinking at the tables they could kick off as they danced around the tight-packed rooms. Eventually the high-kicking became part of the routine of the 'number'.

Begun as a quadrille, the dance was performed by pairs of girls in male and female attire. In the opening movement the bodies met close together, slowly swaying yet full of gesture and voluptuous undulation, pressing and easing until the beat of the music quickened and the girls vibrated more aggressively violent, until their bodies swung apart at arms length before swirling back to clinging contact and then animated repetition until eventual termination after a wild gallop around the floor with the dancers throwing themselves, exhausted, upon the surrounding couches. Afterwards adapted to the stage, the scintillating music created by Offenbach, and others like Hervé and Lecocq, particularly fitted the gaiety of the dance and they in fact wrote specially to incorporate variations of it into their operettas.

At The St James's the programme was changed on 13th July to Offenbach's *La Belle Hélène* and a fortnight later the season ended.

In August as anticlimax a certain Walter St John took over with one Don Edgardo Colona, all the way from Mexico to play Shakespeare so they said. Cibber's bastardised version of *Richard III* was their chosen opening but that, even more than the genuine, requires an actor of outstanding merit. The Mexican Don was dreadfully weak and in any case he was recognised by many to be ex-crowd actor Edward Chalmers. His ideas and ambition were grandiose far above his proper station, and long before his first night was due to end his unkind audience were cat-calling and laughing at him.

A week later, on Saturday 22nd August, the actors, few of

whom were any better than their star, were seen to be arguing under their breath between their lines. Then in the interval after the second act an apology was made from the stage which included intimation that there was not enough money in the kitty to pay stage hands or actors. So the gallery, most unreasonably but delighted at an excuse to misbehave, began to tear up the benches. The actors and stage hands, well aware that if damages too were to be deducted from the receipts there would be still less for themselves, rushed through the pass doors to subdue with no ungentle hands the rioting objectors, and with the help of others of the audience eventually ejected them. The curtain rose no more that night, the theatre emptied and did not reopen under that management.

Miss Herbert's old general manager W. S. Emden was the next to hold the licence of the theatre, but actual lessee and directrice was Mlle de la Ferté. She was a young French girl with English aspirations who had recently had a minor part in *La Grande-Duchesse* at The Olympic. Emden engaged the same staff except for a new musical director in W. Corri and ballet master Imri Kiralfi. Acting company included Lucy Rushton, Maria Simpson, Mrs Poynter, Gaston Murray, Charles Coghlan, George Jordan and Arthur Williams.

Williams was billed as from the Manchester Theatre Royal though he had actually been playing at the old Richmond Royal near London. There he had been noticed by a friend of Emden's named Henry L. Cohen who recommended him 'in very flattering terms', as he said in a letter to Williams himself at a later date. Then about twenty-three, the actor of course developed into one of the country's most popular comedians, albeit sometimes annoying to authors for his penchant for gagging. In fact he really won his spurs by so doing, and by building up his minor part as Lurcher in the comic opera *Dorothy* until he and it became the hit and made it run its famous 900-odd times. Before joining Carl Rosa Williams had been one of Hollingshead's stalwarts at the old Gaiety, to which he later returned to be a leading light under George Edwardes. Biographers have boasted that Irving played over 670 parts in his lifetime but Williams beat that total easily, for before his final curtain in 1915 when he was seventy he could reckon on having played more than a thousand parts! He became a great collector and much of the material upon which this present history is based, as well as many of the illustrations, were only saved from destruction by the sagacity and delight of Arthur Williams in keeping relics of his own and earlier theatrical times. His collection passed in part to the late George Black and then to me through his impresario sons, George and Alfred.

Mademoiselle's season began on Boxing Day with a farce called *The Secret Panel* and then a new comedy by Gilbert à Beckett, son of the inaugural dramatist. The extravaganza which followed was an old one of Planché's which he had polished up specially.

Arthur Williams appeared in all three, Gaston Murray in the first two, the manageress only in the last one. *Glitter*, the comedy proved hardly up to West End standards. It contrasted, somewhat weakly, a happy country life with a crooked city one, but the stock-comedy part of a parvenu manufacturer earned Arthur Williams favourable mentions and Lucy Rushton gained applause several times during the action. Coghlan was also very funny in it as a young 'swell' because he parodied Squire Bancroft of The Prince of Wales's.

The Sleeping Beauty had originally been written for Madame Vestris at Covent Garden in 1840 when Harley and Miss Rainforth had been in it. Mlle de la Ferté now played the Vestris part of Princess Is-a-belle, but mostly in French to everyone else's English, so amusingly and sweetly as to be delightful. Arthur Williams played Harley's old role of Baron Factotum the Great Grand Lord High Everything. Florence Eveleigh was the Lady Aurora Abigail which had been created by Miss Rainforth. Maria Simpson was the Prince Perfect who

arrived through the Magic Forest in Part III to undo the
wicked sleeping 'gift' that Fairy Baneful (Mrs Poynter) had
bestowed in the opening banquet scene. Thomas (surnamed
Noddy) King of Noland was played by Flockton supported by
Miss Hill, making her début, as Queen Serena. Fairy guests
were the Misses Mierabell (from Liverpool), Duval, Gordon,
Howard, Fortesque, Shelley and Myles. As well as a large
ballet and crowd, others were Master Flight, Mrs Caudle,
Miss R. Lea and Allen, Speedy and Valentine Hayes.

Though a parrot which had been 'engaged' from a tavern
in one of the adjacent alleys was very naughty and had to be
hastily removed from the Princess's boudoir, the rollicking,
running, rhyming and amusing singing kept the house happy
even if it did get a bit noisy when the pauses between the scenes
dragged on too long. Planché had composed a new 'cats' duet'
for Miss Eveleigh and Williams and that was encored every
night. Kiralfi, whose famous Earls Court shows are still remembered, with four others of his family had created a delightful
ballet which they danced with fans to great effect.

In the Covent Garden finale the visiting fairies had been
drawn up to the skies in their own magic chairs, but there had
been hitches even there which were not risked now and all
departed in one magnificent illuminated galley. All the same,
preparations had been rushed and Fenton's eight scenes
proved less wonderful than advertisements had claimed, whilst
the scene-shifters were so dilatory that the first night was not
over until half an hour into the Sunday morning although it
had begun at seven! On the whole the house was quite good-
humoured about it all, and up in the gallery they revived what
was reported to be the old custom of singing popular songs
during the intervals.

1869

Business was not good even though press notices had been

more favourable because of the players than the pieces and scenery apparently justified. On Saturday 9th January, therefore, the two main pieces were scrapped and, after the farce, *The School for Scandal* was substituted as well as a new ballet, *The Amazon's Farewell*. Lucy Rushton, who had been in Canada and the United States for some time, made an interesting Lady Teazle, Edmund Phelps was engaged to be Joseph Surface, Coghlan was Charles and Mrs Poynter was Mrs Candour. Flockton was Sir Peter, Gaston Murray was Backbite, Williams was Moses, Celia Logan (again specially engaged) was Lady Sneerwell and Miss Bruce was Maria.

They closed on Friday the 29th for the final rehearsal of a new drama *Red Hands*, by à Beckett again, but since the *Illustrated London News*, for example, called it a 'dreadful melodrama' perhaps they need not have bothered. Shortly afterwards the company was disbanded. They had introduced Arthur Williams earlier than might have been and had given a few weeks work to a small acting and a large ballet company of at least sixty as well as to the ordinary back and front staff, otherwise ... Probably an 'angel' was backstage somewhere and dropped anything up to £2,000 for the privilege but, whether it was the girl's own money or other people's, Emden had fifty years experience behind him and ought to have done better.

Felix returned as impresario from 26th April with his dramatic company headed by Brindeau and Léonide Leblanc who were reinforced by Lafont in the middle of May. One of the presentations was *Le Marquis de Villemer* which was by George Sand alone, and another was *Ces Beaux Messieurs de Bois-doré* which she had written in collaboration with Paul Maurice.

In June Felix presented Schneider again in the operettas *La Grande-Duchesse*, *Barbe-Bleue* and *Orphée aux Enfers*. All Offenbach's, the libretti of the first two were by Meilhac and

Halévy, the last, first done in Paris in 1858, by Crémieux. Dupuis was with them to take the part of Fritz which he had created in the first-named, and the season, though short, was eminently successful and well attended by young Society headed by the Prince and Princess of Wales and the latter's kinsman the Crown Prince of Denmark, who several times took a party to the theatre before the final night on the last of July. Albert Vizentini of the Paris Porte-Saint-Martin was conductor.

The next lessee was a woman who did not need to depend on others for anything. Matilda, Mrs John Wood, had arrived. Daughter of Henry Vining and cousin of George who had been manager here at Christmas 1861, she was now in her late thirties and had made her town début only three years before at The Princess's—three years after the death of her husband whose name, however, she retained and by it she was always publicly known. Another of her cousins, Fanny, married E. L. Davenport and their grandchild Doris Rankin was the first wife of Lionel Barrymore. Southampton had been the theatre of her first appearance but for many years after that her name was a popular one in New York. Like Miller fifty years later, she was to introduce both American plays and players. There the parallel ends for she was actress as well as manageress and brisk innovator.

Mrs Wood took possession in the late summer and immediately started a tremendous bustle. Neither short of money nor mean about the spending of it, she engaged the Queen's own decorator James Macintosh and the two set to. The original plans were hunted out and followed when suitable. An extra entrance was made to the stalls. The pit was abolished and its benches replaced by extra stalls. Wide passageways were made along the sides, down the centre and at the back, so that again as in Braham's time a promenade divided the rear seats and the entrances to the stalls bar.

The upper walls were distempered in pink but a rich paper

of similar hue was chosen for the walls of the dress circle and stalls. The time-tarnished cupids and other ornaments were freshly gilded and the circles painted in pastel blue. Blue satin valances and white lace curtains dressed the private boxes and around the grand tier was run a broad band of scarlet velvet to offset the background. All seating was renewed or re-covered in blue damask relieved by ruby edgings held by brass pins. A delightfully charming ensemble was re-created.

A new green stage curtain ornamented with the royal arms was hung between the repainted proscenium arch, and on a new act-drop John O'Connor depicted the Merry Monarch Charles II setting out for the play from St James's Palace, whilst in the foreground D. White had painted the gay noble dramatist Lord Rochester in company with Pepys and his wife.

Private boxes cost from 2 to 4 gns., stalls 7/- with a few rear rows at 5/- 'reserved for ladies and gentlemen arriving from the suburbs not in evening dress'. Grand circle was 5/-, upper circle 2/6d. and gallery 1/-. Prices compared more than favourably because Mrs Wood inaugurated 'no tips and no charges for cloakrooms or programmes'. As she herself said: 'I would most certainly object to being charged for the bill of fare at my favourite restaurant, so why should I expect my patrons to pay extra for what is precisely the same thing in a theatre?'

The free programmes were not skimpy slips but four 9 × 12-inch pages pleasantly printed in blue and (except for some small ones later) without advertisements. As well as the bill of the play they provided snippets of gossip, details of items lost and found in the theatre, reprints of reviews, etc. The back page was devoted to cab and railway fares, the various omnibus routes and refreshment prices. The latter department she let out to Spiers & Pond. Champagne cost 2/- to 5/6d. a pint; spirits, wines, beers were 6d. per glass and so was lemonade. As well as the stalls bar there was the large one above the vestibule and adjoining that a smaller one for the upper parts of the theatre (all as it was in the end).

She engaged W. H. Montgomery as musical director and American Barton Hill as stage manager. Mme Collier was ballet-mistress. In advisory capacity she signed up J. R. Planché, who as well as being author of extravaganzas and other shows was an authority, still today recognised, on costume, and the proud holder of the office of Somerset Herald. He had had long experience of a similar nature both with Charles Kean and Madame Vestris. Probably recommended by the great American showman Artemus Ward, for whom he had been manager, the writer E. P. Hingston was made her general or acting manager. He had also worked for 'Wizard of the North' Professor Anderson. A popular descendant of Hingston is the well-known manager of Glyndebourne opera, Moran Caplat.

Grand Opening Night was Saturday 16th October with the curtain billed to rise at seven on Offenbach's *Treasure Trove*, at eight on Goldsmith's *She Stoops to Conquer* and at a quarter to eleven on a new ballet *The Magic Waltz*, with choreography by Mme Collier and score by Montgomery. None of Offenbach's hundred-odd pieces have a similar title to the first of these but I have not followed the clue of the five characters. Susan Pyne and Henrietta Everard were Mmes Catherine and Franchette; Bessie Lovell was Denise; Frank Crellin and Henry Broughton were Farmer Guilot and Cartouche.

The five-act comedy was in three scenes: the alehouse where Tony Lumpkin sets the pace, the Hardcastle dining-parlour and then their drawing-room. These had been variously painted by Grieve, Lloyds and O'Connor. (Some action would have been in front of the drop.) Costumes were by Sam May and Mme Ridler. Three Americans were in it: Barton Hill as young Marlow, tall and burly Mark Smith as old Mr Hardcastle and round and fat A. W. Young as his comic servant Diggory. Miss Herbert played Kate Hardcastle and Miss Henrade was her friend Miss Neville. Sallie Turner was the maid and Sophie Larkin her mistress Mrs Hardcastle whose son by her first marriage, Tony Lumpkin, was romped through by Lionel Brough who was reckoned by all to be one of the best exponents ever of that part. J. G. Shore was Miss Neville's lover and young Marlow's friend Hastings. G. P. Grainger was Sir Charles Marlow, Gaston Murray was Stingo the innkeeper. As well as supers, other servants and tavern drinkers were led by Naylor, Barrier, Jefferson, Otley and Broughton. The whole comedy was rollicked through like a country carousal as it ought to be. The house rose and roared its approval at the final curtain.

The ballet afterwards was really unnecessary but most of the audience waited for it or returned to their seats from the saloons when the warning bells rang. (The latter were another innovation of Mrs Wood's.) A Russian ballerina called Antonia Gospoja Ribet was cast as Beauty, Frank Lacey (billed as The American Harlequin but reported as British born) was Mischief and Miss Osborne Armstrong was Hippolyte. Happy peasants dancing were interrupted by Mischief who sowed discord amongst them until Content appeared to defeat and make him vanish in flames of coloured fire.

No hitch marred the performances and the audience happily left to the strains of 'The St James's Gallop', composed by the conductor in honour of the new venture. Before the season ended the comedy was to be performed 160 times, its longest run to date and a remarkably long run for any piece at that time. Perfection had been aimed at and very nearly achieved, for Mrs Wood's spirit of purpose had inspired the new group with such a happy faith in her and in themselves that they had been well cemented into an excellent unit.

Six weeks later the minor pieces were dropped. The classic then began at seven and was over at a quarter past nine, there having been one fifteen-minute interval. At half-past the curtain went up on the first of five scenes (by Grieve, Callcott and J. Galt) of *La Belle Sauvage*. This was a burlesque by the Dubliner John Brougham of his own *Pocahontas* which had

SJT K

Mrs. Wood, Lal Brough, Mark Smith and A. W. Young in La Belle Sauvage

first been produced in New York in 1855 and in London in
1861 at The Princess's. The plot was told in the programme
in a burlesque of Longfellow's epic 'Hiawatha': how John
Smith and his friends were captured by King Powhatan, who
later decided to 'terminate' them, especially since he had
promised his daughter 'To Count Rolff, a German baron,
With immense estates in Rhineland, And a broken English
accent, And a Tyrolean warble, Who had courted Pocahontas,
With a low Dutch boorish fashion, That was anything but
charming To Powhatan's lovely daughter!'

Princess Pocahontas gathered all her lovely schoolfriends and
they rushed to the rescue of her lover John Smith lying bound
at the feet of the King, who waved his club in the air and orated
until rudely stopped by the girls: 'With a spear at his breast
pointed, With an arrow at his eye aimed, With a pistol his head
threatening!'

So the King surrendered and then agreed to play cards with
Smith for Pocahontas, was blatantly cheated and gave in after
exacting a promise to be taught how to cheat so well.

Mark Smith made an enormous and most impressive King
Powhatan. Very tubby Young was the lugubrious long-pipe-
smoking Count Rolff and Lionel Brough a comic John Smith.
Star of the evening, however, was Mrs Wood making her first
appearance at her own theatre. She made a charming roguish
Pocahontas. She was a comedienne with such a broad sense of
fun that to very respectable ears she verged upon the vulgar.
She vivaciously spiced her almost masculine style of droll
urbanity with occasional fire and eyes opened wide for in-
nuendo—something of a George Robey at times but really
more of a Ronald Frankau (who resembled her facially also)
with a touch of Hermione Gingold.

It was a musical with the score arranged by Montgomery
and the dances by Mme Collier. A fairly large crowd was led
by seven others of the men in the company and nine of the
girls: Bessie Lovell, Carrie Wright, Everard, White, Ellis,

Ramsey, Varcoe and Collins as Dahlinduk, Krosascanbe, Lumpasuga, Luvlicreeta, etc. At least one of the songs became so popular that it was pirated and stayed in the country's repertoire even half-way through the next century. This was 'The Dutchman's Little Wee Dog' which Young sang, the words being by Barton Hill.

The after-piece was a revival of Theyer Smith's two-character farce *A Happy Pair* which had been first produced here the previous year. Miss Herbert and Farren played their old parts of newly-weds he becoming obnoxious towards her because of her adoring sugar-sweetness, which later (upon advice) changed to a get-it-yourself attitude which brought him back to his senses and true love.

1870

No changes had been necessary at Christmas and Mrs Wood topped her January programmes with 'A Happy New Year'. *School for Scandal* was put in rehearsal and the cast announced, but booking for the Goldsmith stepped up so much that the Sheridan was shelved. The 100th night was 10th February, and after the show there was a party on the stage for the ballet and minor members but the others, together with leading critics and friends, were entertained at Verrey's. In the chair was Hingston the manager, supported by Lord William Lennox and John Oxenford (of *The Times*) because Mrs Wood unfortunately was ill. She sent a basket of bouquets and button-holes for all with her letter of thanks and apologies. Another of her guests was Palmer of Niblo's, New York.

Emily Thorne took over for Mrs Wood, who was not really better until May although she was able to return sometimes before that. Emily was a sister of Sarah who is well remembered for her famous 'school' at the Margate Royal. Emily had not long returned from America where she had been popular mostly as a ballad singer for about seven years. It was over there in Chicago, by the way, that Lydia Thompson and her 'Blondes' hit the headlines in February when she and Pauline Markham waylaid Storey of the *Chicago Times* outside his home and lashed him with cowhide whips because of the slanderous things he had been writing about her and the company. He fought back with his cane and hands, but her manager Henderson (they were married then or later) and another local journalist Gordon were there to see 'fair play', so Storey only managed to damage Pauline's hat and neckwear. The fines they cheerfully paid for their public behaviour—which in court they exulted in—were the cheapest and best advertisement they ever had.

Ash Wednesday was 2nd March this year and, theatres still having to close by order of the Lord Chamberlain, Mrs Wood took the opportunity to give a party at the Red Lion off Drury Lane to all thirty-four of the staff of the theatre. Stage-carpenter Cawderey represented her in the chair with chief gas-man Pepall as deputy.

When *La Belle Sauvage* reached its 152nd night it was dropped temporarily in favour of the famous French play *Frou-Frou* by Meilhac and Halévy, which had been a success after the 30th October production the previous year at The Gymnase. Adaptation was by Ben Webster, jun. and the direction by Alfred Wigan's brother Horace. Mlle Beatrice was engaged to play Gilberte, the frivolous wife whose rustling frou-frouing silk skirts gave the play its name. Miss Henrade was the self-sacrificing sister and William Farren the old roué their father. Barton Hill was the husband. (Many readers will remember the delightful Gilberte by Jean Kent in the revival eighty years later.)

The play was successful but it was the cause of no little worry and trouble. Tried out at Brighton three weeks earlier, it would never have reached The St James's on 14th April had a court action gone against them. Music publisher Cramer sought an injunction, saying he owned the English rights. He lost, so it opened as planned on the Thursday and he opened his version, which had been done by Sutherland Edwards, at The Olympic on the Saturday. Then on 2nd May the original French one was presented at The Princess's by Raphael Felix. As if that were not variety enough Mrs Wood changed hers on 25th May for a version done by her old friend Augustine Daly of New York. Miss Hazlewood then played Gilberte and Sarah Thorne her sister Louise, otherwise the cast remained unaltered.

The scenery too remained the same but the original costumes by Worth, Alexandrine and Poole were augmented by still more from Paris. Delighted comment on these had already appeared in feminine journals, but in *The Graphic* sounded a carping voice, that of the editor Sutherland Edwards, who sneered at the 'old and faded scenery'. His biased jibes were discounted by partisan John Oxenford in *The Times* whose adjectives included 'rich and elaborate', whilst the *Morning Post* spoke of the 'splendour and elegance of the *mise-en-scène* ... marvels of millinery, dresses costly in material and fanciful beyond all precedent in design!' These remarks were reprinted in the programmes.

She Stoops to Conquer was then played alternately with *Frou-Frou*, but eventually old comedies like *Paul Pry* and *The Spitalfields Weaver* replaced the latter. J. L. Toole played for some of the Benefits as did W. H. Kendal, whilst manager Hingston got the Hanlon Midgets as special attraction for his night. The classic was played in all 160 times and the burlesque reached its 200th performance on the last night of the season, Saturday 16th July. Mrs Wood made a pretty speech at the final curtain and retired, as *The Era* reported, 'amid cheering, waving of handkerchiefs and numberless bouquets'.

Mrs Wood took the main attractions on tour and left a minor company headed by specially recruited John Clarke (the English comedian not the American), Maggie Brennan and Kate Bishop (mother of Marie Lohr). They were beaten by a heat wave, 90 in the shade, which closed down all theatres still open in town.

In Manchester Mrs Wood saw sixteen-year-old Fanny Brough playing in Mrs Calvert's company where she had been for a couple of years and had won plaudits, especially for her Ophelia to Barry Sullivan's Hamlet. Mrs Wood signed her up, so Fanny joined the company in which her uncle Lionel had been re-engaged as chief comedian. Others were G. P. Grainger, Gaston Murray, A. W. Young, Charles Otley, William Farren, Lin Rayne, Dan Leeson, Harry Cox and Fred Mervin. Henrietta Everard, Sophie Larkin and Sallie Turner were joined by Lilian Adair, Marion Inch and by Mrs Hermann Vezin. Rehearsals started early in September under new stage manager Harry Egerton and conductor King Hall. (*v.* Addenda, p. 183.)

Saturday 15th October was first night of the new season. Tom Taylor's curtain-raiser *To Oblige Benson* began it and Oxenford's farce *Only a Halfpenny* ended the evening. Main attraction was Sardou's *Fernande* which had run a hundred nights when produced at the Gymnase earlier in the year. Mrs Wood had hoped to use her friend Daly's version, which was already on in New York, but she found herself properly forestalled this time for Sutherland Edwards had bought the rights personally from Sardou so she had no option but to do his. Sardou's name as author was followed by Edwards as 'revised by' him on the bills. It will have been remarked upon that dramatists in England seemed no longer to be stealing. This was mainly true but the subject is too long to be explored now. Daly's MSS., production notes and advice were also utilised by Mrs Wood.

All trace of immorality had been removed said the hand outs to the press, and much certainly had been cut from the original but all the same it was so full of intrigue, jealousies and gambling crooks around the innocent daughter of a gambling-hell proprietor, with an attempted suicide, a duel, a lost letter and an anonymous one, that there was still sufficient dramatic

Lin Rayne, Fanny Brough, and Jane Vezin as the Marquis Fernardo and Cladtlio in Fernard.

interest to give the company fine acting parts and to draw the crowds until well into the next year.

Fanny Brough played the innocent Fernande, Farren was the turned-respectable solicitor Pomerol married to Mrs Wood as Georgette. Lal Brough was the wonderful Brazilian mulatto Commander Jarbi who, studded with diamonds, worsted the crooks at their own game. Gaston Murray was the suave gambler Bracassin and Dan Leeson was the gangster Roqueville. Acting gem was Jane Vezin as jealous Clotilde, who sought to marry Fernande to Lin Rayne as the aristocratic Marquis des Arcis only so that she could later debase him by exposing the gambling-saloon origin of his bride; but all ended happily.

The Princess of Wales took a party on the second night, and though members of Society were frequent visitors they had been more often for *La Belle Sauvage* following the Prince and Princess's example who went at least five times.

After that first ballet Frank Lacey had been engaged at Astley's. On 17th February, still under thirty, he died. Five days before that so too had George Hogarth, aged eighty-six, and the son-in-law Charles Dickens he had introduced to Braham died on 9th June. It was a strange year in that way for St James's people; others were Levassor and Leigh Murray in January, William Brough in March, Edmund Phelps at thirty-two and Mrs Burnand at twenty-seven in April. She had been Cecilia Ranae, one of the young girls in the company when Miss Wyndham was manageress (*vide* 1859). In May there were Mark Lemon and William Willott who had put on concerts sometimes in the early days. Mrs Caulfield who had been Jenny Jones in 1838, and Balfe the composer who had sung here for Jenny Vertpré, died, the first in September and the other in October.

In 1871 only four folk of major St James's interest took their final calls: Paul Bedford in January, T. W. Robertson in February, Robert-Houdin in June and Frank Matthews in July. Mrs Wood's Uncle Fred Vining died in June and the year

before in the same month her Uncle James, the father of George
who had been manager here after Wigan.

1871

A play before its time replaced *Fernande* on 16th January. This
was *War*, Tom W. Robertson's final work. Finished and then
rehearsed as he lay on his deathbed, though only forty-two, it
was also his major philosophical drama, designed to show the
futility and stupidity of war.

Unfortunately he had set it during an earlier 'affair' between
France and Germany, but at this time the Franco-Prussian
war was drawing disastrously towards its end with Paris lying
under the siege guns of the Hun. He had made a French
colonel exponent of the glory and an elderly 'good' German
see the aftermath even before the beginning. Londoners were
too pro-French to accept such a thesis then, even if it had been
Louis Napoleon who had thrown down the gauntlet and was
ready to follow it with his broken sword and run out on the
battle very soon.

The play was in three acts. In the first, news of war between
France and Germany broke up the betrothal party of Fanny
Brough as Lotte whose father Herr Hartman (A. W. Young)
was 'a perfect gentleman, with a touch of the scholar and
pedant in his manner'. They were in the English home of
Lionel Brough as Captain Sound, R.N., 'hearty but not rough;
in every respect a captain of a man-of-war, not the master of a
halfpenny steamboat'. The Captain's daughters were friends
of Lotte's and were played by Alice Barrie, Jenny Mori,
Marion Inch and Lilian Adair. Her fiancé was handsome Oscar
de Rochevannes (Fred Mervin) whose father the Colonel
(Henri Nertann) was a professional of the old school: 'with a
slight French accent, not to pronounce his words absurdly, or
shrug his shoulders, or duck his head towards his stomach,
like the conventional stage Frenchman . . . knightly courtesy,

with a mixture of ceremony and *bonhomie'*. The above quotations from Robertson's stage directions tend to show why he was the milestone credited with the influence he did exert.

Act I ended with departure to join up. Before that the French Colonel proclaimed: '. . . above arts, science, literature —above the base thing you call commerce, there is glory! Glory to a nation is as honour to a man; without glory a nation is valueless, as without honour a man is beneath contempt.'

'And I tell you that glory is a delusion, a snare, a cruel lie,' replied the elderly Hartman. 'It means burnt homesteads, ruined villages, abandoned homes, desolation and despair! What say you, Captain?'

The sensible Britisher answered: 'I say I hate war; but when once you begin to fight, fight it out—you're better friends after.'

Act II was set at night outside a shell-hit church. Guns in the distance sounded nearer as the scene ended with the battle coming up again. Oscar and his father the Colonel as wounded prisoners lay in the lee of the shattered walls. Tending them were Lotte and her father, both in the Red Cross. Lotte and Oscar were married when it was thought that he could not live and he had to be abandoned when the fighting got too close.

The still essential happy ending was contrived at the end of the last act with Oscar returning from the dead, for he had been rescued and taken to Spandau hospital by another 'good' German field doctor.

On Friday 3rd February the dramatist died, in his forty-third year. Reaction to the play had not improved and had he not been so ill Mrs Wood would have taken it off sooner than she did. On the 4th it was replaced by an old comedy, *Naval Engagements* by Charles Dance.

Supporting pieces in the first and this season have not always been mentioned. One of these, on 28th January, was a refurbished skit called *Jenny Lind at Last*. Mrs Wood was Jenny

Leatherlungs and she parodied not only the famous Swedish Nightingale but Titiens, Patti, Mario and Formes. Lal Brough was Manager Bunn. Mrs Wood, one of the papers reported, 'whose animal buoyancy is naturally in excess, gave the audience a rare treat for she was in high spirits and played her best'.

A burlesque about love in ancient Rome called *Vesta!* became the main item from 9th February and proved sufficiently funny, and extravagantly dressed by Sam May with scenery by Hann, score by Frank Musgrave and choreography by Milano, to attract fairly good houses. Book was by H. B. Farnie, a big Scotsman with a penchant for enormous collars and flowing ties, a little 'Billy Coke' hat and thick short reefer jacket, who considered himself a tremendous hit with the ladies. Many libretti are credited to him but most of his work was in collaboration or taken outright from the French. He would run over to Paris, do the rounds, choose his fancy and write the libretto on the way home in train and ship. Banal rather than witty, he was the butt of the critics but other people's music helped his stuff to pass muster.

The Two Thorns was added to the bill on 4th March. This was a comedy which had been tried out in Liverpool as *The Coquettes*, by James Albery (father of Sir Bronson), and though witty was not up to his *Two Roses* or later plays. Jane Vezin played an actress who had married above her station and dreaded the bottle-loving propensities of her old actor father. Veteran Henry Marston played the latter character who turned the tables on his daughter when it transpired that he was a member of an ancient noble family himself!

On Easter Saturday, 8th April, were produced Farnie's *Rival Romeos* and *An Actress by Daylight* which William Cowell had adapted either from Charles Reade's *Art* or from the original by Fournier, *Tiridate ou Comédie et Tragèdie*. Mrs Wood played Anne Bracegirdle which in Reade's version had been Ann Oldfield played by Mrs Seymour. A new nautical burlesque by Burnand called *Poll and Partner Joe* was introduced in May and the usual variety of pieces for the Benefits in June. Last night was 22nd July.

It proved to be Mrs Wood's last active season for some years but she continued as head lessee. She was in the Burnand burlesque but, like the year before, she had not been well and the strain of managing everything as well as the strenuous parts she played were not improving her health. Her final company comprised Fanny Brough, Sallie Turner, Nelly Bligh, Marion Inch, Lilian Adair, Caroline Parkes, Emma Chambers and Henrietta Everard; Lionel Brough, Gaston Murray, H. T. Craven, Alfred W. Young, Harry Cox, F. Mervyn, William Arthur, W. J. Hurlstone, John Barrier and George P. Grainger. Conductor was T. Hermann. Five of the men had been with her from the beginning, and two of the girls though some of the others may have won promotion from chorus or ballet.

Stanley Dust's name as secretary had replaced Hingston's as manager on the bills for the second season. Without a major assistant even just to see to deputies, no one, certainly not a widow in imperfect health, could run a big theatre properly. Whether she had anyone of either sex in her personal entourage with whom she could discuss problems I do not know, but some such person is usually necessary to get the best out of one if only to encourage and do chores. Mrs Wood soon after returned to America, leaving the letting to an agent, and was not seen on the London stage again until the end of 1873 when she appeared for Charles Reade and Laura Seymour at the Long Acre Queen's.

On Saturday 30th September a new Royal National Opera Company opened the doors of The St James's and Rose Hersee as Elvira in Balfe's *Rose of Castile* made her rentrée after two years in America. Prices stayed the same but a fortnight later the pit was restored at 2/6d. with 'crimson velvet chairs'.

Swedish tenor Nordbloom, Florence Lancia and Mr Maybrick made their London débuts. *Il Trovatore, Bohemian Girl, Lucy of Lammermoor* were in the repertoire. A stage version of

Sterndale Bennett's cantata *The May Queen* was announced
but objection by either the librettist or composer forced can-
cellation. After 21st October they moved to the East End
Standard as start of a provincial tour. Afterwards Rose Hersee
returned to the States at £100 a week before coming home
again to join Carl Rosa. In 1872 she was singing for that famous
company in Nottingham, swathed in bandages, as were others,
a couple of hours after their train had been in a smash.

Raphael Felix opened on 6th November for a long, but for
him, final season.

1872

The French were in occupation for nine months, some of the
most important players being Ravel, Brindeau, Parade, and
Mlles Adele Page, Julie Riel, Fargeuil, Thierret, Schneider
and at the end of May the vivacious pupil of Déjazet, Cécine
Chaumont.

Ravel was retiring and for his Farewell Benefit on 4th April
the London theatres honoured him with official groups from
five of their number. There were ten playlets etc. and then the
Cerémonie d'Adieux. From The Adelphi came Ben Webster,
Harwood Cooper, Miss Furtado and others, from The Gaiety
came Constance Loseby with four others; Kate Bishop and
four from The Court; from The Philharmonic came Sara and
three other girls to dance the Drogan Quadrille and from The
Haymarket Buckstone brought five to play *A Rough Diamond*.

The dreadful shadow of murder hung over the theatre later
that month. Pretty Julie Riel was living at 13 Park Lane in a
house (Hitler bombed it away) lent her by a noble admirer,
with her mother and two servants. Julie returned from a
week-end in Paris to find that the cook had murdered her
mother and then fled. The sentence, after capture in Paris, was
later commuted to life imprisonment.

Felix died in his forty-seventh year on 10th July but they

kept going until the end of the month and during the last week arranged a Benefit for his family. Plays presented over the long season included *Adrienne Lecouvreur* with Adèle Page in the title part written for and created by Rachel. Other plays in-

M. Ravel

cluded *Frou-Frou* and Sardou's *Rabagas* which was to be done here in English soon, and *Les Pauvres de Paris* which several times had been adapted by Boucicault and others.

Richard Mansell, one of two Irish brothers whose real name was Maitland, took over in the late autumn. (Lauderdale Maitland was his nephew.) He was a happy-go-lucky fellow, more notorious than successful and usually in the midst of money or other trouble. His twenty-year-old gay compatriot George Moore remembered in his *Confessions* years later 'the good times behind the scenes of The St James's and it was not till the backers refused to supply any more money and the theatre had to be closed . . .'. Had it not been for that tightening of the purse strings Moore would have seen his name on the bills as a dramatist for they were planning something. As it happened, fifty years were to go by before his name was so printed.

Operettas and other light pieces with plenty of girls were Mansell's bait for public and backer. Alfred Cellier was his musical director and Offenbach's *The Bridge of Sighs*, the English libretto by H. S. Leigh, was his main attraction when he opened on 18th November, a Monday. *The Virginian Mummy*, a farce, preceded it.

First performed in 1861, *Le Pont des Soupirs* had twice failed to draw in Paris. Twice Mansell had to postpone opening before he actually did. A skit against republican government in Venice, the funniest passage was between two rival Doges settling political differences by seeing who first could reach the end of long greasy poles stuck out over a dirty canal! The first night did not go smoothly and long waits between the changes could have disturbed the audience, but they were good-humoured and nothing untoward occurred.

Everything happened to Mansell! On 3rd December the gas workers in London went on strike, quite without warning apparently and not long before curtain-up. Except for The Gaiety and some which had candles or old-time oil lamps, all the theatres had to return money or, as with Dick Mansell, tell the audience to come back the next night.

As extra attraction for Christmas Mansell announced a very naughty quadrille by a new troupe of French girls just arrived. On Boxing Day no orchestra filed into sight for the overture. The farce went through without a hitch but then the interval lengthened inordinately. At last Mansell slipped on in front of

the curtain and began 'Through some misunderstanding . . .'
to be interrupted by a gallery shout 'Why haven't you paid
them?' 'That is not it at all', responded the manager. 'Will you
hear me out? They have been paid their money to the last halfpenny but the larger portion of the orchestra has not turned up.'
He then asked them to permit the operetta to proceed accompanied by two violins, the double-bass and a harmonium!
Luckily the audience were in kindly mood so *The Bridge of
Sighs* was got through somehow without disturbance but,
money paid or no, the doors remained shut the following night!

1873

With a new manager and backer, perhaps combined, in the
American Stephen Fiske, Mansell reopened on 8th February
with the same operetta but cut and tightened up. Fiske had
done a version of Sardou's *Rabagas* and that was ready on the
25th for Emily Duncan to make her début as the little ragged
boy. Charles Wyndham, who had come back from the United
States again, was in the title-role. The Prince and Princess of
Wales were present on the first night, but soon after the company closed down.

Humbert's Belgian light opera company began a fairly
successful season in May. They were honoured by the presence
of their own King and Queen who were over on a visit, and
by the Prince and Princess of Wales and other frequenters.
Mlles Fonti and Desclauzas were the leading ladies, the former
taking the part she had created in the inaugural Brussels
production the previous December of *La Fille de Madame
Angot*.

Amongst amateurs in the winter was a young clerk called
Samson. Nearly twenty years later, as George Alexander, he
began the theatre's longest and most successful period.

1874

Francis Fairlie was the next manager. He was an ex-army man,
his real name F. C. Phillips, who had paid for his experience
as a manager in Liverpool before reaching town. R. P. Emery
was acting-manager and H. Gilmer-Greville, whose name and
position as assistant stage manager smells suspiciously like
money, with conductor Dubois were supported by George
Barrett and Dick Mansell as directors.

Opening night was Saturday 2nd May, with a revival of Tom
Robertson's *Progress* in three acts and Offenbach's *Vert-Vert*
for which H. Herman and Richard Mansell provided the
libretto after Meilhac and Nuitter.

George Barrett played the part of Dr Brown and directed
the comedy. He had been here as stage manager for Chatterton.
His elder brother was the more famous Wilson, whose grandson
of the same name is known less in the south than in Edinburgh
where he ran his famous company for many years. Fairlie
collaborated in the direction and played Mr Bunnythorne (a
vulgar retired contractor) for he was quite a good comedian.
Leonard Boyne played John Fenne, Rose Coghlan was Eva
and Mrs Buckingham White was Miss Myrnie. Knight, Boleyn,
Greville and Palmer supported.

Trouble back-stage held up the second act and for the delay
the orchestra suffered, deservedly so for they were dreadfully
incompetent, though the spate of cat-calls and ribald chaffing
from the impatient if skimpy audience did not help the conductor. Luckily the curtain rose before the onlookers got out
of hand and their good humour was soon restored—but a mood
had been created.

Vert-Vert had originally been presented in Paris in 1869.
The title was the name of a parrot in a school for young ladies.
When it died they transferred the name to their shy young
boot-boy who was played by Mlle Manetti. Barrett was the

gardener and Boyne the ballet-master. Greville and Mansell
were two Hussars who with three more were the only other
men amongst over thirty named girls including Elisa Savelli
from the Naples San Carlo, Lilian Adair, Rose Roberts and
Clara Douglas. Two of the young ladies were married to the
Hussars and another to the ballet-master. Vert-Vert fell in love,
officers were smuggled into the school, they visited the local
tavern and fun and frolic was the order of the day.

Unfortunately the order was not apparent to the audience
because apart from a speciality act, The Orpheon Troupe of
four girls who danced *The Riperelle*, and a few of the others
besides those named above, the rest had been chosen only for
their looks. Costumes had been provided (scanty as ordered)
by Auguste and scenery of the three acts painted by Julian
Hicks.

Mansell was announced as director of the production, but
he was of the type who say it will be all right on the day without
realising that that necessitates planning and hard work. Even
experienced girls must have a routine worked out for them
which must then be rehearsed and rehearsed until it becomes
automatic. The girls were therefore not to blame for the
dreadful fiasco this first night became for they had not had the
direction or rehearsals they were entitled to get.

Even so, they were opening a week later than first planned.
Some six months later co-librettist Herman wrote to *The Era*
admitting or implying that everyone had been in a state of
panic behind the scenes, that there had never been a full
rehearsal or run-through, that the music had been chosen from
half-a-dozen Offenbach scores (that would have been because
they were stealing them and could not get the full original),
that the words had been rushed together in forty-eight hours
(why that was so is anybody's guess since they had advertised
to open a week earlier than they did—they might have used the
extra time to polish at least!). Herman finished his explanation to the profession by complaining that nobody did what

they had been told to do at such rehearsals as they did have.

The house had been emptyish for the first play *Progress*, but as nine o'clock drew nigh it began to fill up with groups of white-fronted, empty-headed young bloods from the pubs and clubs of the neighbourhood, who strolled in lackadaisically wielding silver toothpicks as they audibly commented upon the charms they expected soon to thrill them. The comedy was slow to end and the interval afterwards interminable with the band execrable. Ably seconded by impudent youth in the stalls, the gallery soon worked itself back into its former cat-calling mood, so that when the curtain did at last rise on the operetta it would have needed something very brilliant indeed to counteract the prevailing atmosphere.

The hotch-potch had little vitality and before long the company were stumbling over their lines and missing cues. Mansell and Gilmer-Greville appeared in glorious uniform and began what seemed to be a duet but their voices were so weak they merely pantomimed and their gestures were so broad and ludicrous it appeared as if they realised the fact! Roars of laughter and cries of advice showered upon them until they fled the scene. Three girls then entered, also resplendent but with more revealing jackets and tights. They flopped upon a table and got fairly well through a naughty drinking song as they waved their beer-mugs in time with themselves if not with the band. After that Mansell appeared again but as soon as he heard the first chords he shook his head at the conductor who then tried something else. His choice was wrong again so Mansell bent down over the footlights and started quite an altercation with poor Dubois. They spoke too softly for many to overhear, however, and the house became suddenly quiet and expectant.

'Say *something*, guvnor!' cried at last a voice from the pit, and the house hooted with laughter. Mansell fled again and the stage remained empty with not a sound except for a worried whispering from the musicians. Then slowly into sight came

Mansell, most unwillingly but pushed by two brawny arms.

'Here he is again!' shouted a delighted galleryite and Mansell wriggled free and fled out of sight once more.

The Orpheon Troupe were then put on for their much publicised *Riperelle Dance* in vain attempt to save the show, but the house was by then in such a turmoil that not even a Patti or a Grisi could have broken through.

At the finale all the girls lined up in two curving lines beginning at the arms of the proscenium arch until they met up-stage centre. As the orchestra increased the tempo and the girls marked time, Mansell and Greville as the leading Hussars ought to have marched into sight, left and right up-stage, met in the centre, marched forward to the footlights and then taken up position as heads of each column. No officers made such entrance and the girls began one after the other to twist around looking for them.

'Mansell! Mansell!' shouted the audience but the pair had lost courage and neither showed his face again that night. Eventually the girls did a bit of a marching routine and as *Figaro* reported later: '. . . after a wild impromptu chorus the curtain came down at last early on Sunday morning, ending as it had begun, in chaos.'

That night (or early morning!) Fairlie sent round a letter to all the papers asking the editors to give them a second hearing before printing reviews because 'everybody on the stage was paralysed in consequence of the abominable behaviour of the gallery'. Some complied by ignoring the affair altogether and most of those who covered it made amends later by reporting, for example, 'an incredible improvement'. *Vanity Fair* had little but harsh words for it, but of that more anon.

The company strenuously rehearsed all day Monday and throughout the week. Dubois, who had been heard counting the time out loud to the band on the first night, threw down his baton in despair on the Wednesday. It was picked up by C. Vandenbouche with a firmer grip, so that after a week of daytime rehearsals and nightly public performances the show took shape and began to play to quite appreciative audiences. Miss Norrie Jordan and a Mr Russell supplanted the two disastrous Hussars, the cast was changed around slightly, and the routines and lyrics were polished up. A new Love Waltz song was introduced for Savelli which was encored nightly, and their advertisements almost truthfully proclaimed that 'the new brilliant bachanalian finale the Piff-Paff' and 'the astounding Terpsichorean Revel the Riperelle' were 'rapturously now received'.

The *Riperelle* helped to swell the houses and became the talk of the town with its gay abandon and scanty costumes. The Lord Chamberlain was complained to, he inspected the performance, ordered the skirts to be lengthened, advised Mansell about the length when humbly asked how long he thought they ought to be but missed seeing the tongue in Mansell's cheek. Mansell added the required couple of inches and advertised the alterations as designed by the Lord Chamberlain! The Marquis made him pay dearly for that impudence for he left a permanent ban in the office against his ever being granted a manager's licence again. Consequently in after years Mansell ran shows on the Continent and at minor places outside the Chamberlain's jurisdiction. In 1889 he was manager of the Liverpool New Empire and in 1902 of the Bayswater Coronet. He died in 1907, before which he was a familiar figure, tall and fur-coated and very much an 'old pro' on the 'Poverty Corner' of the day.

The next difficulty was caused by Boosey the music publisher who sought an injunction to stop the show for he said he owned the London rights. Boosey lost, so he actually helped them with even more publicity, and before they closed on 4th July the fiasco had become a smash-hit! They then went on tour to see queues stretching all round the Liverpool and Manchester theatres to the accompaniment of spinsterish squeals in the local papers about the infamous dregs of London and Paris flaunting their long legs in the faces of respectable northern citizens.

On 12th June they had substituted for *Progress* John Oxenford's *East Lynne*, the only authorised version. Barrett directed this and played Bullock the policeman. Leonard Boyne was the wicked Sir Francis Levison, Boleyn was Archibald Carlyle, Rose Coghlan was Lady Isabel and Ada Allcroft played poor Little Willie who died. Lilian Adair was Joyce and Miss Reid was Wilson. J. Swift was Earl Mount Severn, J. Everard was Mr Justice Hare and A. Knight the suspected murderer Richard Hare. F. Wood was Lawyer Dill, Mrs White was the elderly Cornelia Carlyle and Bessie Hollingshead was Barbara Hare the second wife of Archibald. Marie Ferrara took the part of Susanne.

The tour was a successful riot, and upon their return to town they took the old Globe (near the Strand end of Kingsway before that highway was created) and ran there until the beginning of December.

The sequel was quite amusing in its own way and gained as much publicity if not reward. After Fairlie's circular most editors ignored the show entirely. Mortimer's *Figaro* castigated it but gave it a good notice when it had been polished. Bowles's *Vanity Fair* not only slated it but cast innuendos about 'philanthropic young and old rich men seen behind the scenes and being ogled by some of the girls from the stage' without mentioning any changes for the better other than, for example, on 23rd May: '. . . improved and the singing less flat but the dance uncalled for and indecent', and on 13th June: 'brilliant dresses, pretty music, indifferent singing and a rather improper dance'.

The last quotation was in Bowles's regular 'Plays to See' feature, but in the same issue in his 'At the Play' column he gave a fairly favourable review of *East Lynne* which he concluded with more about *Vert-Vert*: '. . . . [being] one of the most indecent dances on the stage it is very likely to take with the public'.

Fairlie briefed famous Serjeant Ballantyne and issued a writ for libel against Bowles and the publisher Blenkinsop. They, through Mr Day, Q.C., pleaded 'justifiable comment for the public good' and reaffirmed that the dances had been indecent, the actors unrehearsed and that the prompter had been heard throughout! The case was heard before Mr Justice Keating and a jury on 7th and 8th December.

Interesting facts were elicited during the proceedings. Twenty-one performers were in the orchestra. They were paid 'about £40' ($200.00) a week between them. Two of the artistes got £15 and £12 but the total artistes' salaries amounted to no more than 'about £150'. (About fifty were named in the bills.) The *Riperelle* girls of the Orpheon Troupe, who had danced on the Continent but were all English, received £10 a week between the four of them. Small parts were paid 21/- a week. One girl worked free to gain experience but later was put on the sheet at 15/-. All the same, explained Fairlie in the witness box, at some theatres girls only got 10/- a week and pantomime chorus were usually paid one shilling (25c.) a night.

Fairlie was emphatic that the actors in *Progress* were word-perfect because most of them had been with him on a preliminary tour. He refused to admit that there had been anything indecent in the *Vert-Vert* dances. As has often been said by other managers at other times, he declared that everything that went wrong was the fault of the gallery who obviously had been organised beforehand because they even had accordions with them. Naturally the cast were upset but it was the behaviour of the audience that was the sole cause of the 'snowball'.

Many theatre folk spoke to much the same effect for the plaintiff. The costumier said that the dresses of the Orpheon Troupe were 31½ inches—1½ inches longer than the usual length in town, which had been ordered by the Lord Chamberlain (loud laughter in court). George Barrett agreed with what had so far been said and mentioned that his part in *Vert-Vert* had been unimportant until he built it up with gags.

'With what?' interposed the judge.

'Gags, my Lord' repeated Barrett and Serjeant Ballantyne hastened to explain:

'He means, my Lord, that he added words which had not been written by the author.'

'Ah! I see. Did you get promotion then, Mr Barrett?'

'My part went much better but I didn't get any extra pay, my Lord.' (Loud laughter.)

Much merriment was caused by artist John Soden who also had seen nothing indecent in the dancing, for he admitted writing articles for journals by then defunct. He had written a farce called *Wanted, a Wife and Child*.

'Was that before you saw *Vert-Vert* and the *Riperelle*, Mr Soden?' asked his lordship, enjoying his field-day.

Eventually Bowles entered the box and swore he had several times gone to watch the dancers and each time they were most indecent in their gestures and movements. The case for the defence was clinched when the Marquis of Hertford, the Lord Chamberlain himself, was called to the box. Several times he had received letters of protest about the dance and consequently he himself went to The St James's to see it. The only reason, he said, that he had not banned it forthwith was because he knew the season was ending and the show going on tour to places where he had no jurisdiction. He had no desire to furnish excellent advertisement by banning it in town.

Two of the *Riperelle* girls themselves arrived in court then for they had had to travel down from Birmingham and their train was late. Plaintiff's case was closed but the judge with gracious alacrity allowed them to give their evidence. So Emily White who had danced as a boy, and then Rose Rippington, testified that they had never intended anything indecent nor had they had the least idea of anything indecent any time they were dancing or even rehearsing the *Riperelle*.

D'Oyly Carte, then with four or five years experience behind him, said he thought *Vert-Vert* such a poor piece that the artistes did not have a chance. He was such a fair witness that both sides were apparently afraid to ask him if he thought the dance indecent! Musician Alfred Raimo said that once half the band played one tune and the rest another and that conductor Dubois lost his head and just laid down his baton! Raimo had been disgusted at the dance. Another well-known name and one which was to appear on future St James's bills was that of the next witness, the Hon. Lewis Wingfield, who said it had all been so bad that he had hurried away without waiting to see the dance!

Laugh of the day was reserved for income-tax man Vaughan who demonstrated to judge and jury with his coat-tails just how the dancers' skirts had swirled and so shown that underneath they didn't wear a lot of underskirts as in the ballet at the opera. All the Orpheon girls had on underneath were 'swimming drawers!' He had complained to the Lord Chamberlain.

After Day's closing speech Ballantyne replied to the accompaniment of much 'suppressed applause' from the public galleries, but all the same after the judge's summing up the jury found for the defence without leaving court.

Except for slurs on the girls the result was fair enough and not unexpected. They were certainly luckier than opposite numbers dancing in a similar operetta in a New York theatre which was raided a fortnight after the *Vert-Vert* case, for the police marched the dancers in their scanty costumes through the bitter winter streets before they locked them in the cells overnight. Of course England was as illogical and logical then, and just and unjust, as laws and lawyers and their myrmidons doubtless always will be. For example in this same December at Chester Mr Justice Brett, full of pity, had refused to pass judgement on a woman found guilty of killing her brutal husband. He sent her home, saying that sentence was postponed until she be called upon 'and God forbid that you should ever be so called upon'. Yet not long before, a man for forgery and a woman for theft had been publicly hanged together in the heart of London. As for post-office workers—on 'go slow' strike as I write—thirty of them had had the impertinence to ask for a rise in pay (during the *Vert-Vert* case week) and the P.M.G. replied by ordering their immediate dismissal!

Fairlie's final night had been on 4th July when for his own Benefit he had revived *The Bridge of Sighs*. M. Marye's French dramatic company followed on Monday the 6th. Mlle Agar was star in *Phèdre*, *Brittanicus*, *Horace*, and other plays but the weather was very hot so support was not good.

Stephen Fiske took over on his own from 24th October with *The Black Prince*, which he announced as by Lecocq with libretto by Farnie. Lecocq sent a letter to the papers denying ever having written such a piece, and it transpired that the Scotsman had been up to his tricks again and sold the American a hotch-potch of various tunes and words garnered from many different published works of the composer. The after-piece by Oxenford and Hatton was not new either, except for the title *The Guardian Angel*, for it was a revised *Too Clever by Half* in which Toole had appeared in February at The Gaiety. Now it fell flat and was hissed.

A great to-do had been made about a wonderful scene in the operetta when an iron-clad warship would be sunk in full view, but the movement of the ship was so jerky that the house roared with laughter and when the massive cliffs it was to be wrecked upon began to wobble and undulate in sympathy the audience went into hysterics. Emily Duncan and Nelly Bromley were in the cast, but even the brilliant dancing of Selina Dolaro, with her castanets, could not make the show a success. They kept going, however, until the second week of December and closed on the 15th.

On 11th December old John Mitchell died. Numerous private carriages and five coaches of mourners followed the hearse drawn by four black horses to the family vault in Brompton.

1875

Amateurs, supported by pro's when appearing for charities, kept the theatre from being entirely neglected over the winter months. Then on Saturday 27th March it opened under Marie Litton who had been on tour after closing her Court Theatre in February. With her came Charles Dubois (who had been musical director of *Vert-Vert*), Henrietta Hodson, Millie Cook, Rose Egan, the Clifford Coopers, Edgar Bruce (who was to build The Prince of Wales's), outsize W. J. Hill, E. W. Royce (of later Gaiety fame), Charles Wyndham and many others. Scenery was in charge of Walter Hann.

Marie Litton opened with *Brighton*, which F. A. Marshall had anglicised in four acts from Bronson Howard's American play *Saratoga*, and concluded with William Brough's burlesque *Conrad and Medora*. The comedy had already proved an excellent vehicle for Wyndham as the handsome hero with whom lots of girls fall in love, which he reciprocates until he finds himself in difficulties when too many of them congregate. In America the play had been rejected by Laura Keene and then by Selwyn because they thought the girls too fast and blatant. Daly risked it in New York. Thirty years later, when going on tour in England, the manager said, 'It's too slow. We'll have to put more ginger into the girls!' In the after-piece Henrietta Hodson was Conrad the Corsair and, as a pressman reported, 'as piquant as she was picturesque'. Miss Litton was Medora 'as arch and amusing as skilful in realising comic situations with which the burlesque abounds'.

She produced various light favourites in the season but her only new pieces were the most interesting, historically. The first was the three-act *Tom Cobb or Fortune's Toy*, a comedy by W. S. Gilbert produced on 24th April, when Clifford Cooper was Irish adventurer Colonel O'Flipp and Edith Challis his

St. James's Theatre.

Responsible Manager ... ... Miss LITTON.

THIS EVENING

The Performances will commence with CHARLES SELBY'S Celebrated Farce, the

DANCING BARBER.

Dunderhead Twaddle, Esq. - Mr. CLIFFORD COOPER   Alfred Flintfolic, Esq. - Mr. VINCENT
Lord Flitterly   -   Mr. RUSSELL   Lord Minchington   -   Mr. CHARLES STEYNE
Mr. Snapley (Russia Merchant)   Mr. DE VERE   Bailiff   -   Mr. SAUNDERS
Narcissus Flintfrizzle   (the Dancing Barber) - Mr. E. W. ROYCE
Lady Flitterly - Miss MURIELLE   Mrs. Snapley - Miss ROSE EGAN   Betty - Miss E. DOYNE

The action–of the Farce is supposed to take place in 1825.

After which, an entirely New and Original Farcical Comedy, in Three Acts, entitled

TOM COBB

OR, FORTUNE'S TOY.

BY W. S. GILBERT.

Colonel O'Fipp (*an Irish adventurer*)   Mr. CLIFFORD COOPER

Tom Cobb ⎱ (*young Surgeons*)   Mr. E. W. ROYCE
Whiffle ⎰   Mr. EDGAR BRUCE

Matilda O'Fipp (*the Colonel's daughter*)   Miss EDITH CHALLIS

Mr. Effingham ⎱   Mr. DE VERE
Mrs. Effingham ⎰ *a Romantic*   Mrs. CHIPPENDALE
Bulstrode Effingham ⎱ *Family*   Mr. W. J. HILL
Caroline Effingham ⎰   Miss LITTON
Footman   -   .   Mr. RUSSELL
Biddy   -   .   Miss E. DOYNE

ACT I.–SITTING-ROOM IN COLONEL O'FIPP'S HOUSE.
ACT II.–SAME AS ACT FIRST.   ACT III.–AT MR. EFFINGHAM'S.

Three Months are supposed to elapse between each Act.

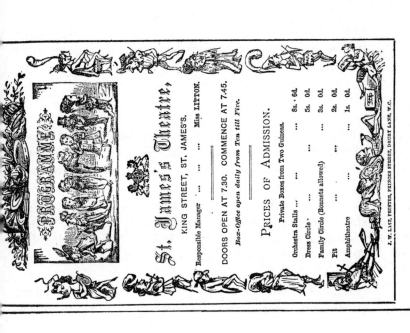

PROGRAMME

St. James's Theatre,

KING STREET, ST. JAMES'S.

Responsible Manager ... ... Miss LITTON.

DOORS OPEN AT 7.30.   COMMENCE AT 7.45.

Box-Office open daily from Ten till Five.

PRICES OF ADMISSION.

Private Boxes from Two Guineas.

Orchestra Stalls ...	...	8s. - 6d.
Dress Circle -	...	5s. 0d.
Family Circle (Bonnets allowed)	...	3s. 0d.
Pit	...	...	2s. 0d.
Amphitheatre	...	...	1s. 0d.

J. W. LAST, PRINTER, PRINCES STREET, DRURY LANE, W.C.

daughter Matilda. Royce and Bruce were Tom Cobb and Whiffle. Mrs Chippendale and de Vere were the heads of the Effingham 'romantic' family and Hill and Marie Litton their children Bulstrode and Caroline. Russell was the footman and Miss E. Doyne was Biddy.

The other piece, which ended the evening from 5th June, was *The Zoo*, 'a musical folly' by B. Rowe with music by Arthur Sullivan. The five leads in this were Henrietta Hodson and Gertrude Ashton as Eliza Smith and Letitia. Carboy, Brown and Grinder were played by Florentine, Bruce and Steyne. Twenty-four others were named for chorus and crowd. The B. Rowe credited for the words was B. C. Stephenson who was to write the long-running *Dorothy*. The second Gilbert and Sullivan joint piece, *Trial by Jury*, was then enjoying its initial run at The Royalty, but, it will be noticed, the famous partnership had not properly begun.

Miss Litton's final night was 26th June. Her season was reported to have been quite successful, but she would have been wiser to have remained at the smaller Court where, even if expenses had not been much less, audiences seemed larger and everything therefore went better.

1876

Alfred Wigan's brother Horace had been running the Holborn Mirror (where First Avenue House now stands, replacing the bombed First Avenue Hotel). He took his own Benefit there on Saturday 6th January and transferred to open at The St James's on the Monday with Merivale and Simpson's *All for Her*, a three-act drama which he had had on since October, and a new farce by Reece called *Pretty Poll*. Rose Coghlan, Caroline Hill and Constance Brabant were his leading ladies and John Clayton his chief male support.

Wigan revived various pieces, by himself and others, during the spring but after 8th April he went on tour with the company and Mrs Wood took over the management personally again after a fortnight's shut-down. Prices had been variously lowered by her managements or sub-lessees. Now she made the private boxes one to five guineas, stalls 10/-, dress circle 5/-, upper 3/-, pit 2/-, gallery 6d. Doors open at 7 p.m. Commence 7.30. Gallery 7 to 7.30, 1/-. She did not act herself until 3rd June.

Alfred Cellier was her musical director. Two years before, when he occupied that position at Manchester, his comic opera *The Sultan of Mocha* had been produced there. It now got its first London showing with Constance Loseby as Dolly, H. Corri as the Sultan, Strickland as Grand Vizier, G. W. Anson as Sneak, A. Brennir as Peter, E. Connell (later G. H. Riley) as Flint and G. Paris as Frank. Lucy and Moggy were played by the Misses Forrest and Wilmore. Making his London début as the Lord Chamberlain, was rare little comedian George Shelton but, like Irving and Toole before him, he too returned to the north afterwards even though Mrs Wood tried to persuade him to stay on. Later, after many years in Toole's company, he did return here in 1897 and then many times in his most famous role of Smee in *Peter Pan*. The composer conducted the orchestra and chorus of seventy.

The first night was 17th April when Alfred Wigan's 1845 farce, *Model of a Wife*, preceded the opera. George Shelton played Tom, F. Strickland was Stump the art teacher and Anson the Frenchman Bonnefoi. Mrs Stump and Clara were played by the Misses E. Toms and Amy Forrest. Another farce was substituted four weeks later but by June the opera had drawn its quota, so on the 3rd Mrs Wood made her reappearance in Shirley Brooks' *The Creole* as well as in an up-to-date *Jenny Lind at Last*, now called *Nilsson or Nothing*. Edmund Leathes, who had been in The Queen's company with her and had then played Laertes to Irving's first Lyceum Hamlet, was in *The Creole*, with Emily Cross in the title-role and W. H. Stephens, Mervin, Forrester and Jackson.

The building had by this time passed into the ownership of Ulsterman Viscount Newry who will be referred to as the Earl of Kilmorey from 1880 since he then succeeded his grandfather. Newry was something of a musician, song writer and impresario. The Globe in Newcastle Street was also his. The

Viscount Newry

elder Augustus Harris of Drury Lane had died before he was fifty in 1873. His widow was the theatre costumier 'Auguste et Cie', and his young son was already making his name as a stage director as well as actor. It was he who was to make Drury Lane pantomimes renowned for magnificent brilliance, and to be knighted before he died when only forty-four in 1896.

Mrs Wood and the Viscount now sent young Augustus over

to Paris to study *Les Danicheff* whilst it was in its 150-per-
formance run at the Odeon. Because of provincial engagements
he was only able to negotiate for them to cross the Channel for
a month so the original company opened on 17th June and
closed on 15th July.

The author, named as Pierre Newsky, was Pierre Corvin
Kroukoffskoi the husband of Stella Colas, who was renowned
more as a person than as actress, at least on the English stage.
The comedy-drama had been revised by Dumas and was now
staged by M. Bondois with new sets by Julian Hicks and Bruce
Smith. Apart from Mme Fargueil as the Countess instead of
Mme Picard, all had created their parts in the original on 1st
January and even though they had been playing so long the
change of country and theatre put them on their mettle.

The scene was laid in Russia before the freeing of the serfs.
Vladimir Danicheff (M. Marais) was in love with Anna (Hélène
Petit) the personal serf of his mother the Countess (Mme
Fargueil). The latter therefore sent him to Moscow to her
chosen match for him, the Princess Lydia (Mlle Antonine).
To clinch matters the slave Anna was then ordered to marry
the coachman Ossip (M. Masset) who of course has to obey,
but since he naturally knew the whole position and loved Anna
he could not bring himself to force her to share the conjugal
bed. In the end Vladimir returned from Moscow, Ossip nobly
entered the Church as the only way divorce could be brought
about, and finally as a priest officiated at the marriage of the
lovers.

The perfect characterisation of the cast of eighteen, the
smooth production and beauty of the complete ensemble left
such an impression of excellence upon audiences that it was
not until Bernhardt arrived three years later at The Gaiety
with the Comédie-Française that it was equalled or excelled.

Mrs Wood's winter season began 14th October with 'a new
eccentric comedy', *Three Millions of Money*, by Fred Lyster
and Jo. Mackay after the French of Labiche and Gille. Set in

London with scenery by Bruce Smith, Mrs Wood was fortune-hunter Florence Desmond who with the assistance of her servant John chased a mad Yankee with too much money. American George Clarke was the latter, Colonel Jefferson was C. Dexter, and John was played by George Honey the famous little comedian who had made London sit up when he created the part of Eccles in *Caste* back in 1867. Another great actor, Charles Warner, played impecunious lover Paracelsus Daffy. Others were the Misses Maria Daly, Oscar Byrne, Lavis, Wilmore and Telbin; Messrs Clifford Cooper, Fred Mervin, George Darrell, Leduc and Bauer.

In the comedy Mrs Wood and George Honey sang a comic duet *à l'italienne*. A farce had been the curtain-raiser. Stalls were dropped to 7/6d.

The Virginians by Bartley Campbell the American was produced on 20th November. Lydia Foote played an unfortunate wife who married the hero, played by S. Pierce, only to suffer the unexpected return of R. Markby as her real husband who had been missing, thought killed, after the Civil War. Mrs Wood and Honey supplied the necessary comedy to relieve the drama, but although the author was loudly called for on the first night his play had to be replaced on 2nd December by *London Assurance*, when Mrs Wood made a brilliant Lady Gay Spanker and Lydia Foote an excellent Grace Harkaway.

1877

The Danicheffs was the new year offering on 6th January in an English version by Lord Newry himself. Charles Warner was Vladimir whose mother the Countess was played by Fanny Addison. Mrs Wood was the Princess Lydia and Lydia Foote the serf Anna. John Clayton was Ossip. Among others were Hermann Vezin, F. H. Macklin and Charles Stanford the musician (who also had a part in the curtain-raiser) as a pianist to the Princess, a part apparently introduced by Newry.

George Richardson was musical director as he had been since October when he replaced Lyster the co-author then mentioned. The drama proved a draw and ran until 13th April, for the players were all first class and the authentic Russian customs, setting and dramatic story made interesting novelty.

A month earlier, 12th March, Mrs Wood put on Kate Fields in her own curtain-raiser *Extremes Meet*. Macklin (later E. J. Benbrook) was Captain Howard, a woman-hater who had been refusing to allow a younger brother to marry. To him came Kate, as Maude Stanley the sister of the girl, and she of course proved such a softening suppliant that not only did the bigot give in about his brother's marriage but he and Maude married too. Maria Daly and Ada Morgan supported.

For Passion Week they shut down to play at Brighton instead. Then on Saturday the 14th in place of the drama, Massinger's classic *A New Way to Pay Old Debts* was revived. The Hon. Lewis Wingfield designed the costumes which Mme Laly made. Hermann Vezin was Sir Giles Overreach, the Misses le Thiere, Kate Pattison and Maria Daly were Lady Alworth, Margaret and Froth.

A fortnight later Charles Reade's *Wandering Heir* was revived, trimmed and tautened, with Mrs Wood in the part she had created at The Queen's in 1873. It was that of puritanical slave-owner Philippa Chester which Ellen Terry had taken over afterwards when Reade persuaded her to make her rentrée to the stage. Edmund Leathes too played his original part of James Annesley the wandering heir. Ada Morgan, who was still the child in Kate Field's piece, played the heir when ten years old. Maude Milton made her début as Maria Surefoot, a puritan maiden. The idea had been suggested to Reade by the Tichbourne case but was not based on it. The large cast also included Clifford and Charles Cooper, Beveridge, C. Winstanley.

A new comedy by Hamilton Aide was later announced as in preparation, but he was unlucky for the *Heir* and the farce proved sufficient attraction until Saturday 26th May when the season ended.

Eight years had passed since Mrs Wood first signed a lease for the theatre and she did not now renew. In the late eighties she ventured again into management very successfully at the rebuilt Court. Whenever she had been personally in control here she had proved success possible but the others in between, most if not all of whom had been sub-lessees though appearing on the bills as managers, had often failed to give evidence of the necessary 'touch' entailing perspicacity rather than money.

Shakespearian lecturer Morlande Clarke organised an evening in November in aid of an Indian famine fund and then on 29th December, a Saturday, Ada Cavendish opened what was called a Farewell Season prior to her departure for America. Lessee and manager was Sam Hayes who ran his ticket agency in Regent Street. He said he would make the theatre the home of Shakespearian and old English comedy and, if he could get the plays, of modern comedy as well.

Ada's farewell lasted five months and a plan to change the programme fortnightly was generally carried out but the company Hayes recruited were almost too experienced in their own individual ways. Under a strong director they might not have set the Thames (or temse) on fire but W. H. Stephens combined acting with his position as stage manager. Though he had forty years on stage behind him—which included world tours and the building and running of the Sydney Queen's—he did not manage to cement the others into a team: and for the classics a unified style is one of the essentials.

The company all the same was not a poor one and certainly many of them were on familiar terms with the boards and each other. *The School for Scandal* was the first presentation when Ada Cavendish was Lady Teazle, Mrs Bernard Beere was Sneerwell and Sallie Turner Mrs Candour. Others included

Stephens (Sir Peter), Henry Forrester (Joseph Surface), W. Herbert (Charles Surface) and Lin Rayne (Backbite).

1878

Lord Lytton's *Lady of Lyons* appeared on 12th January with Ada as Pauline, Mrs Chippendale as Mme Deschappelles and Kate Rivers as the Widow Melnotte. Forrester played Claude Melnotte, Stephens was Damas and amongst the others was W. H. Selby as Gervais.

As You Like It was introduced for a month from 5th February. Some matinées, from the Saturday three days before that, of *The Rivals* were also offered, when the regular company was augmented by Farren as Sir Anthony Absolute and Charles Warner as Captain Absolute. Forrester played Faulkland and Righton was Bob Acres. Maclean was Sir Lucius O'Trigger. Helen Barry made her first appearance in the part of Languish whilst Mrs Chippendale played Malaprop and Mrs Bernard Beere was Julia. Miss Chetwynd was Lucy. On the 23rd, also a matinée, Miss Herbert returned to play Lydia Languish.

The first new play of the season, presented on Saturday 9th March, was Palgrave Simpson and Claude Templar's *The Scar on the Wrist*. This, like the others except the Shakespeare, was a single play innovation without support. Scenery for the prologue and three acts was by H. Potts. It was an exciting drama full of incident which began with old recluse Sir Leonard Marsden (A. Beaumont) making a will in favour of his only daughter Alice (Ada Cavendish) and scorning his nephews Reginald (Titheradge) and Aubrey (H. Vaughan). Alice interrupts two masked men stealing the will but fails to prevent them murdering her father. They throw her over the balcony but one of them is scarred on the wrist by Alice in the struggle.

Four years elapse after that prologue. Reginald has succeeded to the title and let the old manor to another recluse, Lord Snowbery (Stephens). Emily Fowler played the latter's beautiful daughter the Hon. Ethel, who has befriended the orphaned and now mentally deranged Alice. Secret doors and panels and attempted poisonings are followed by the exposure and suicide of villain Aubrey, the betrothal of heroine Alice, now sane again, to Sir Reginald, and of the Hon. Ethel to a gallant Captain Onslow (Edmund Leathes). Henry Forrester and Kate Rivers were Robert and Martha Claypole and Mrs Leigh Murray was Mrs Sweetapple. Except that it was out of harmony with the previous plays of the season and so did not bring in the audience it might otherwise have done, it was quite successful and well played by all. The Titheradge, incidentally, was George, father of Madge.

Sam Hayes stuck to his resolve to change the bill frequently and so on 27th March Tom Taylor's *Lady Clancarty* was revived, both Ada Cavendish and Emily Fowler playing the parts they had created four years earlier at The Olympic. Henry Forrester was Othello to Titheradge's Iago from 8th April. Miss Emerson was Desdemona and Mrs Bernard Beere the Emilia. Forrester had been Iago to Irving's Othello some time before and most critics thought he would have been better to have enacted that role again, though his pathos was generally remarked upon and his final burst of indignation against Iago magnificent.

Twelve days later Tom Taylor and Paul Merritt's *Such is the Law* was produced. This was a drama about the law which laid down that a man must not marry his sister-in-law, but the authors begged the question by later making the girl in the play no actual relation after all. The cast was strong: Ada Cavendish, Kate Compton (aunt of Fay) and her husband R. C. Carton, Charles Kelly who stole the play as a comic Yorkshire servant, Leonard Boyne, Titheradge and others.

Mrs Wood returned to play Lady Gay Spanker in *London Assurance* which was put on among the Benefit specials in the final weeks of the season in May. Ada Cavendish finally departed to America where she appeared in August.

Sam Hayes opened up again on 17th June when with Charles Head he presented the operetta *The Little Duke* which had been adapted from the original of Meilhac, Halévy and Lecocq by Saville-Rowe and Bolton-Rowe. It was a transfer from the Islington Philharmonic. The adapters were actually the critic Clement Scott and B. C. Stephenson. They themselves directed, G. B. Allen conducted, Potts did the scenery, Mrs May the costumes and Clarkson the wigs. Leads were Alice May, Ethel Pierson, Emma Chambers, Edward Wingrove, Stanley Potter and J. D. Stoyle. For the first time the actresses were listed ahead of the actors on the programme.

Sometimes in the following months amateurs appeared for Benefits, etc. as they had done at earlier matinées, but Sam Hayes did not continue here as impresario.

ADDENDA

JANE VEZIN (p. 151, &c) had married the American tragedian in 1863, three years after her appearance here in Chatterton's autumn season when she was thirty-two and still Mrs Charles Young. Though really English, she had been hailed then, like her husband, as Australian. Born in Bath, a niece of Leman Rede the actor-dramatist, she had starred as Jane Thompson in juvenile roles, when only eight, in Sydney where her actress mother had immigrated. As dancer and actress she had progressed in stature and popularity, especially in Hobart and Melbourne. Two years before the Youngs decided to sail for England, G. V. Brooke highly commended her for her support on his 1855 star tour. The Melbourne Garrick Club arranged her Farewell Benefit for which an Address in her honour was composed by Sir William à Beckett—that Chief Justice brother of The St James's inaugural dramatist. She was seventy-four when she died in 1902 after a very successful London career.

CHAPTER 5

JOHN HARE AND THE KENDALS
NINE YEARS OF STEADY SUCCESS

1879-1888

IN the summer of 1878 Mrs Kate (Bateman) Crowe, baby
Richmond of 1851, gave a party in her Brook Green west
London home at which many theatre folk were present,
Taglioni, the Charles Keans, Irving and Toole, the Bancrofts
and Lord Newry amongst them.

News was current that Squire and Marie (Wilton) Bancroft
were thinking of vacating the Tottenham Street Prince of
Wales's which they had made, over many years, the most con-
sistently successful small London theatre. So Newry asked
Mrs Bancroft, at this party, if she would take over his St
James's. She had, she told him, been pondering just such an
idea but had rejected it in favour of The Haymarket which was
also in the wind if not yet in the market. Some years earlier,
when he knew Mrs Wood did not want to continue, Newry
had suggested to Kendal that he run it, but even after promising
to spend £2,000 on it he had not persuaded Kendal to risk the
project.

So Lord Newry successfully turned to John Hare who had
proved himself an able actor-manager since 1875 at The Court,
after ten years under the Bancrofts with whom he had made his
début. Madge (Robertson) Kendal and her bridegroom had
joined his company after many years under Buckstone at The
Haymarket. Another Hare recruit had been Charles Kelly, and

Ellen Terry later left the Bancrofts too to join him and incidentally to marry Kelly. Had she not left, two years later in
December 1878, to begin her famous partnership with Irving
at The Lyceum, she would doubtless have followed in the steps
of her elder sister Kate to The St James's.

John Hare would not take on the larger theatre by himself
but the Kendals were already in semi-secret partnership so it
was decided to continue the association openly in King Street.

Their Court last night was on 19th July 1879 and at the final
curtain Hare outlined plans for comedy and comedy-drama, as
he had been doing, and hoped that he would 'be able to successfully conduct The St James's which up to the present had
laboured under the stigma of being unfortunate'. Charles
Santley then led cast and audience in the National Anthem.

With minor exceptions only, the entire company transferred,
including the acting or general manager John Huy and musical
director Schoening. Assistant stage manager was Rowley
Cathcart who, although under fifty, had about forty years experience behind him for he had appeared many times as a child
in the same company as his father. He had been with Charles
Kean throughout the famous Shakespearian Princess's period.
Other members of the company were Mrs Gaston Murray,
Kate Phillips, Cissy Grahame and William Mackintosh, T. N.
Wenman, Draycott, Rowley, Chevalier, de Verney and T.
Brandon. The last was to be famous as the author of *Charley's
Aunt*, and later reverted correctly to Brandon Thomas.

The only recruit was debonair but ill-fated[1] William Terriss.
He had led an adventurous life: in the Royal Navy, as a tea-
planter, twice shipwrecked, a sheep-farmer in the Falkland
Islands (where Ellaline was born) and an actor in between.
Now he settled down to become—tall, handsome, personally
charming—the matinée idol of London, beloved too by
fellow-players.

Harford was scene-painter throughout, in the beginning

[1] In 1897 he was murdered by the insane actor Prince.

with Gordon and a couple of times with Walter Hann. As
since Mrs Wood, no tips or charges were allowed. Prices were
the same as at The Court: stalls 10/6d., circles 6/- (6/6d. after
1881) and 4/-, pit 2/6d. and gallery 1/-.

The theatre glittered again for the opening night of Saturday
4th October so that the *Sporting & Dramatic News* could
report it 'the most sumptuous and magnificent theatre yet
erected in this country'. To Lord Newry the credit. The foyer
was utilised as a gallery and showed seventy or so paintings by
Corot, Fantin-Latour, Alma Tadema, Val Prinsep, Luke
Fildes (grandfather of Audrey), G. F. Watts (Ellen Terry's
first husband), Frederick Barnard, du Maurier (father of Sir
Gerald) and others.

Val Prinsep, whose paintings hung in the front, was author
of the curtain-raiser *Monsieur le Duc*. Characters as well as title
were French so probably it was an adaptation, or this might
have been because it was about a libertine confronted with the
news that the girl he had been trying to seduce was his own
daughter! It had been tried out in the provinces and had a
happy ending.

The main play was G. W. Godfrey's adaptation from the
French, *The Queen's Shilling*, in three acts. Tested at matinées
at The Court, it had an army background with Mrs Murray as
Mrs Major Ironsides, the very military sister of peppery little
Colonel Daunt (Hare) who had just been appointed to the
19th Lancers. Kendal played wealthy Private Maitland whose
discharge was in the mail and who broke barracks to attend a
ball where after a quarrel he was wounded in the arm in a duel,
of course in mufti, by his unknown new Colonel. The discharge
arrived in time so the Colonel could forgive him, especially
after having proved his courage by gripping the wounded arm
next morning: for the only effect was that Kendal's face became
'so white that women in the audience used to faint', as Madge
related later in her memoirs.

The baritone Charles Santley was engaged specially to lead

the singing of the National Anthem between the two plays. An indirect association of his was his marriage twenty years before to Gertrude, the niece of Fanny and granddaughter of Charles Kemble.

John Hare directed, and did so throughout his lesseeship, whether he was acting or not. He was a slight little man in the mid-thirties with a remarkable stage presence and sense of comedy best brought out in old-man parts. Strict, peppery and apt to be sarcastic when directing, he was, for all that, both respected and loved by the profession quite as much as by the public. Knighted by King Edward, he died in 1921 when he was seventy-seven.

Madge Kendal, young sister of the famous playwright Tom W. Robertson, was four years Hare's junior and was with us until she was eighty-seven in 1935. George V created her Dame of the Order of the British Empire in 1926. She beat all the French girls mentioned earlier, for her first appearances had been before she was five. That was at The Marylebone, one of them being a blind child in *Seven Poor Travellers*. When she was ten she played Little Eva in *Uncle Tom's Cabin* at the old Bristol Royal, before she was sixteen she was Ophelia to Samuel Phelps and Desdemona to the first great coloured actor Ira Aldridge. To quote William Archer, she was an actress 'of rich endowment and rare accomplishment, the ideal incarnation of English womanhood, her beauty of expression rather than of form, at her finger-ends all methods of modern comedy and drama, excelling in unsophisticated unidealised everyday emotion, of fresh and delicate humour'. As a woman she was very much a no-nonsense person; certainly to some she seemed a martinet for she would brook neither vulgarity nor incompetence and could be caustic. But added to the finest Victorian virtues she possessed a gracious queenly charm apparent in later years, and a sense of fun so that even when bitingly sarcastic the onlooker, if not the recipient, could see a twinkle in her eye! Though the real guv'nor of her company from its inception, she was always a comrade and good trouper—witness, for example, her donation of £50 to the Actors Association Fighting Fund when the predecessor of Equity was in trouble in 1919. As a director—which she was of most productions after they parted with Hare—she was particularly meticulous and inspired admiring respect as well as love in those she trained. She and her husband were in love until he died in 1917. They lived a kind of dual life, for outside the theatre they used his real surname so that there were people who knew them as Mr and Mrs Grimston but not as the Kendals for all their fame.

William Hunter Kendal was the same age as John Hare and had trained in his teens at the old Royalty and then in the provinces before he joined Buckstone and met his wife-to-be at The Haymarket in 1866. Outshone by Madge's brilliance, he was for all that a sound actor and excellent comedian who played to perfection either fops or nincompoops as well as characters from the most ordinary way of life with veracity and understanding. As Eric Maturin related in a radio talk in 1950, Kendal was adept at character emphasis by makeup not with grease-paint but with water-colour for which he used a brush (a relic of pre-grease-paint-days in fact). He could create an almost automatic bond of sympathy with his audience as in *The Queen's Shilling* incident.

In the latter play Miss C. Nott took over from Mrs Murray for a while and Denny succeeded Mackintosh as Sam who was one of the Lancers. There were three others of these, Sergeant Sabretache by T. N. Wenman, Mickey Doolan by Cathcart and Sandy McPibroch by Brandon Thomas. William Mackintosh was born in 1855 in Melbourne, but he made his stage début not far from his clan country in Elgin in 1872. Three years later he appeared for Mrs John Wood in Dublin. The Court company he joined not long before the transfer here. He was an intelligent character actor who became much in demand as his work got known, and was appreciated by Irving, the latter's son Laurence and Beerbohm Tree.

The one-act play was changed on 18th December for another by Alfred (later Lord) Tennyson. Based on a Boccaccio tale, it was in Italy in the thirteenth-century mountain home of an impoverished Count (Kendal). Mrs Kendal played the Lady Giovanna, a wealthy widow for whom he cherished a love kept secret by his poverty. Mrs Gaston Murray was back to play the Lady's attendant and Denny was the Count's. The Count divided his love between his falcon and the widow, so when one morning she passed by his door and then invited herself to breakfast, what could he do but order his falcon to be served up since his larder was bare? After eating, she declared the purpose of her visit. Her child was ill. She had promised her the falcon as a pet.

Tennyson lived in the country so a special dress rehearsal was called at his request. Accompanied by his son and protected by a screen, with a rug over his legs and a hot-water bottle at his feet, he heard the playlet through. At the end, without sign or word, the two arose and stalked to the doors. Before the son followed his father into the cab he paused with one foot on the step to turn to John Huy and say 'My father liked the play!' Such behaviour, so it was explained, was because of the poet's shyness.

A real falcon was imported from Germany, but on the night the Prince of Wales was coming it strangled itself with its chain. They used a dummy for a while and then bought another from a French sailor which frightened Madge as much as the first had done.

The printed version differs somewhat from the acted one which ended with the curtain falling after a long pause which succeeded a lengthy speech by the Count to the effect that his falcon and his heart had just been eaten. As the poet wrote it, it ended with the pair plighting their troth after all. (Perhaps the cutting of his lines for the more dramatic curtain was what made him stalk out so silently.) As printed the instruction to kill and serve the falcon was given off-stage. Some critics

reported that the order was given aloud but in such an under-
tone that most of the audience missed it. Whether because the
horror was therefore not fully established until the end, or just
because of the unpleasant motif which after the first night
would have been no secret, the piece was not particularly well
received by either critic or public.

1880

Theyre Smith's duologue *Old Cronies*, for Mackintosh and
Wenman, replaced the Tennyson on 6th March. In it one old
friend visited another to seek advice and tell of falling in love.
On the 13th the main item was changed to Tom Taylor's crook
drama, *Still Waters Run Deep*, until May; *The Queen's Shilling*
was after that put on again for a few weeks; Maddison Morton's
farce, *A Regular Fix*, was revived with T. W. Robertson's *The
Ladies' Battle*. The latter was from the French of Squire and
Legouvé and was about an Austrian Countess who shelters a
handsome Bonapartist in her castle. The theme had been
used before and has been since. On 10th July their first season
ended. It had been quite encouragingly successful.

They began the winter on 9th October with *Old Cronies* as
curtain-raiser to *William and Susan*, which was Douglas
Jerrold's famous *Black-Eyed Susan*, rewritten and with an
extra act, by W. G. Wills. In December Coghlan's *Good Fortune* from the French of Feuillet replaced *Susan* which had
been variously received. Coghlan's ran until 7th January without anything else on the bill.

1881

Arthur Wing Pinero, three generations British of Portuguese
origin, was an actor in Irving's Lyceum company. He had
begun when nineteen, about six years earlier, with the Edinburgh Wyndhams. Six minor pieces by him had been produced

but nothing of importance until in November *The Money-Spinner* created a sensation in Manchester. Hare put it on from 8th January between *Old Cronies* and the old *Sheep in Wolf's Clothing*.

Of continental setting if not origin, it was in two acts and gave John Hare a chance which he eagerly and successfully took to portray the 'hero', a delightfully disreputable old reprobate of a card-swindler called 'Baron' Croodle. Two daughters used to help him by attracting victims and by cheating, Dorinda the younger (Kate Phillips) and Milly (Madge Kendal). The action began when Milly had turned respectable by marrying provincial clerk Harold (John Clayton) who, however, had been 'borrowing' from his firm and both were at their wits' end since the accountants were expected. To their lodgings then came her father and sister, with Lord Kingussie who had fallen for Dorinda and stipulated that Croodle should live an honest life with the prospect of an allowance in the offing. Kendal played the wealthy m'Lord and Mackintosh was Detective Faubert who arrived to shadow Harold. Milly suggested a game of cards and cheated to get the money to save her husband, but the detective saw the manipulation, clever though she was. Revelations followed recriminations but all in the end was forgiven, the detective bribed and the money loaned to save the clerk from prison.

Well written and produced with much by-play, the acting glossed the morals for there wasn't one law-abiding citizen amongst the lot. The public were delighted enough but most of the critics were chary about its being suitable for the company or theatre. None had anything against the acting and all praised Hare as the brandy-swigging-on-the-sly old scoundrel.

From 22nd February to 12th March Mrs Gaston Murray in the Tom Taylor after-piece and Kate Pattison in the Pinero played Mrs Kendal's parts. The Kendals were living in Harley Street and hardly had her cab started off to the theatre one night when the horse stumbled. Madge thrust her head out of the window to see why, just as they were at a lamp-post, and her head crashed against it. The cabby pulled up, the door swung open and Madge crumpled to the pavement with 'blood pouring from my forehead'. The rest of the story is from her account also, but amusingly enough when she came to write her memoirs 'misallusive' thinking made her post-date it by five years to the run of *The Hobby Horse*. Surgeon Alfred Cooper was stepping from his own door hard by. He pulled a hair from the cab-horse's tail and sewed up the wound on the spot! He wouldn't allow her to be moved even back the twenty doors or so to her own house: so into the nearest she was carried to disturb her hostess when she found out she was succouring an actress. Madge repaid her by introducing her to a parson whom she married. When news circulated that she was again well enough to go to the theatre she was offered the private carriages of eleven admirers. She chose the Duke of Fife's since he was first to offer.

After Easter *The Lady of Lyons* ran alternately with *The Money-Spinner* until at the end of May another Godfrey adaptation, *Coralie*, was introduced. Winifred Emery joined for this on her way up the ladder on which she had stepped when only eight. She was a daughter of Sam who had been here before she was born. She married Cyril Maude in 1888. The season ended 16th July.

Mrs Kendal was unwell when they were due to reopen, so they waited until 27th October when they put on her late brother's *Home* and Clement Scott's *The Cape Mail*. The critic acknowledged the latter as 'from the French'; actually it was from the same *Jeanne qui pleure et Jeanne qui rit* which had been done here long before as *The Merry Widow*. In it Madge proved her worth as the young wife who thought she had become a war widow and read fictitious letters to her blind mother-in-law, ostensibly from the missing soldier, who appeared in the doorway when she was in the middle of one. The original title of course referred to the young wife's pretending, not to any joy at her husband returning 'from the dead' for that happened only at the end of the one-act.

Madge's nephew Tom appeared in his father's play. Rowley Cathcart's daughter Maud was also in it, as was Kate Bishop the mother-to-be of our own and Australia's darling, Marie Lohr.

Boxing Day was a Monday and Hare then put on Val Prinsep's *Cousin Dick* (which he had done at The Court) instead of *The Cape Mail*. On the Thursday, instead of *Home*, Pinero's *The Squire* was presented in three acts with incidental music by Frederic Clay and 'Mr Stedman's Choir' for a 'Chorus of Villagers'.

Madge Kendal played Kate Verity who was the Squire of the title. Kate had married Lieutenant Thorndyke but kept it secret at his request until finding herself *enceinte*. Faced by her demand to proclaim their true relationship, Thorndyke (Kendal) disclosed to her that his first wife was not dead as he had thought. The two were discussing their problem when Wenman, as her rejected suitor Gilbert Hythe, sprang through her window, shotgun in hand, to demand explanation why—so late at night—she entertained a strange man in her room. In a vain attempt to pacify the jealous intruder, all was explained to him. Unappeased, he raised his gun and was only stopped from shooting his rival dead by the heroine's prayers for her unborn child as she knelt before him.

Young Tom Robertson and Ada Murray played Izod and Christiana Haggerston, a gipsy lad and his sister. Steyne was the local reporter, Mackintosh and Miss Brereton were the Squire's manager and his daughter, Gunnion and Felicity. Two comic rustics called Fell and Robjohns Junior were amusingly played by Martin and Brandon Thomas. Hare himself was a weird mad parson, the Rev. Paul Dormer. (Those who notice that the cast in Hamilton Fyfe's 1902 book on Pinero differs from the above may care to note that Fyfe's cast is of the 1888 revival.)

SJT N

The play was without doubt the young dramatist's most promising, though he had been unable to conceive any climax equal to the strength of his dialogue, for all ended in a happy prospect with news of the death of the first wife. Audiences, however, were perfectly satisfied.

1882

As the new year began the charge of plagiarism by playwright and managers was quite openly being made. The plot was too similar to Thomas Hardy's *Far From The Madding Crowd*, and as it became known that Comyns Carr and Hardy had not only dramatised the latter's novel but had had difficulty about getting their MSS. back again from John Hare, there appeared to be no defence at all.

Thomas Hardy, Carr and famous lawyer George Lewis sat ominously in a box one night but no writ arrived afterwards. Hare had already returned the mislaid MSS. with the remark that Mrs Kendal had not liked it. Madge admitted that this had been said, but only as an excuse, for she denied ever seeing the MSS. Pinero denied seeing it too but did admit to reading the novel, but only after he had nearly finished his play.

Mrs Carr in her memoirs bluntly used Hardy nomenclature for Pinero characters. Her husband asked point-blank questions about similarities. Critic Dutton Cook in the February *Theatre* sided reluctantly against Pinero. Publicity was enormous. If anyone was to blame, the guilty one must have been Hare who had had the MSS in the summer. Perhaps he had passed on the gist of it to Pinero but he could hardly have done that honestly with Comyns Carr's ink hardly dry.

Hardy and Carr produced their play under the original title of the novel in February 1882 in Liverpool. Marion Terry was their heroine Bathsheba and her brother-in-law Kelly played Gabriel Oak. J. H. Barnes was the Sergeant. After a tour they opened at The Globe when Mrs Bernard Beere took over as

Bathsheba, but notwithstanding the controversy they were not successful.

Suspicious similarities certainly existed but *The Squire* proved the better play and ran 170 times until the end of the season on 15th July. Both pieces were set in the country and included a gipsy with a sister, both second acts closed with the heroine saving her husband from a jealous yokel—in the one a sergeant from being beaten up and in the other a lieutenant from being shot. Though Pinero had a parson and a reporter who were not in the Hardy-cum-Carr play and the pieces ran to different endings, the characters otherwise balanced perfectly.

In the summer Pinero played in his own *Daisy's Escape* when Mrs Bancroft, Jessie Milward, Toole and others appeared at a special matinée in aid of the Jews of Russia.

The tour of *The Squire*, after holidays, was so long and successful that a winter season did not begin until 9th December when B. C. Stephenson's *Impulse*, after *La Maison du Mari*, started the fourth season. In five acts it told the story of a grass widow (Linda Dietz) who ran away to Paris with a gigolo (Arthur Dacre) but whose husband (Wenman) arrived there to save her before her virtue had been lost. Madge Kendal played an elder sister but Hare did not take a part though Kendal and six others did.

1883

Impulse was sole piece on the bill and reached 200 performances by the last night of the season, 20th July. The autumn tour was now an institution, but since Wenman and Dacre dropped out two recruits had to be raised. From Madge's family *Caste* Company, which toured the north mainly with her brother's plays in repertory and which her nephew Tom now ran, she picked Herbert Waring after seeing him in Southport. He became a loyal stalwart of The St James's for forty years. George Alexander had been signed up at ten guineas a week for the tour and twelve in town afterwards. He too had been in the Robertson company but since then had been with Irving for over six months up to July 1882, after which he had toured and played in town as is detailed later.

The fifth season opened on Monday 17th September following a week at the Liverpool Court. They ran *Impulse* for four weeks as toured except for newcomers Ada Murray and J. Maclean.

The theatre shut for the week ending 20th October, on which night they presented *Young Folks' Ways* which was founded on *Esmeralda*, a tale by Mrs Burnett of *Little Lord Fauntleroy* fame. It had been dramatised by American actor William H. Gillette whose English fame rests on his writing and acting the first stage Sherlock Holmes.

John Hare reappeared to play decrepit Old Rogers, a North Carolina farmer, and father of beautiful Esmeralda who was played by one of old Ben Webster's granddaughters, Annie. Jane Vezin, by now a *grand dame* carrying great respect, was hen-pecking termagant Mrs Rogers. George Alexander was Esmeralda's hill-billy lover Dave Hardy, owner of as poverty-stricken a farm as their own. Act I showed the log cabin and Act II a Paris studio, for a mining discovery gave the Rogers sudden wealth and the mother dragged them off to buy a titled husband for young Es'. Madge Kendal, Linda Dietz and Maclean played a nice English family, the Desmonds, who worked to stop Ma Rogers from forcing a marriage with the Marquis (Brian Darley). Kendal played artist Estabrook who in Act I told Dave that George Drew (Waring) was really a prospector and so stopped the Rogers being swindled, for they had been about to sell for very little. Dave's warning made them sell for a deposit and annual payments, but this did not help his suit with Esmeralda so he was left behind.

Dave followed to Paris all the same and starved outside her window. Eventually the mineral vein was found to run through Dave's land, not the Rogers', and happy marriage took place in the end. Two more acts set in Paris dragged the play out just that much too far. Hare and Mrs Vezin were much more in their element in the log-cabin opening than in Paris. She as a nagging, ragged old virago and he as an easy-going, tobacco-chewing, sitting-in-the-sun old wastrel were delightful, but when transported, their material was not enough for three acts. Alexander was too gentle for the hill-billy, Waring 'looked more like a thief than a horse' but didn't work his part up strongly enough as *The Times* said. It was Miss Webster's début and the *Standard* in commenting on this was surprised that she 'acted so gracefully and naturally' on her first appearance, and complemented her and her teachers especially over the passionate scene in Act III where she had to repudiate 'her cruel mother's authority'.

However, the play ran on its own fifty times until 20th December when *A Scrap of Paper* was revived with curtain-raiser *A Case for Eviction* by Theyre Smith. In the latter George Alexander was a young doctor, Frank, and Linda Dietz was his wife Dora. Young May Whitty played the important part of Mary, their maid. It was her third appearance in London; in 1918 she was created a D.B.E. She married Ben Webster, who joined the company here after she left, and both of them were making films and playing on the New York stage, she more often than Ben, in their late seventies. Each was eighty-two at their final call, May a year after him, in 1948.

The playlet the three began the evening with was a remarkable little piece. The main character never appeared. He was an Irish major, lazing in bed upstairs, around whom everything revolved as Mary attended to his repeated requests for brandy and soda and whisky until Frank went up to really get rid of his guest but returned laughing at the jokes he'd been told. When Dora went to chase him out she returned sobbing because of the major's poor old mother back in Ireland. But then his wife arrived (unseen) and the major fled with the wife after him and peace returned. It was delightful.

Though still Palgrave Simpson's *A Scrap of Paper*, the play now presented was a little different to that of the Wigans in 1861 who used Sardou's nomenclature. The elderly entomologist Brisemouche then had a sister Zenobie (Miss Rainforth) who rather fancied the young lover Anatole, now Archie. In this production she was the wife instead of sister. The *Scrap* was a letter hidden in a lover's cache by Lady Ingram (Linda Dietz) long before her marriage. Never collected because of a duel, it was later found by Colonel Blake (Kendal) and most of the play was around the cut and thrust between him and Lady Ingram's friend Susan Hartley (Mrs Kendal) in her efforts to regain it, and his attempts for various reasons to hold. Misapprehensions, jealousies and other love affairs held the attention by the acting of Waring as husband Sir John, Hare as unworldly host Dr Penguin, an entomologist, and Mrs Gaston Murray as his wife. Annie Webster, her future sister-in-law May Whitty, Ada Murray with Rowley Cathcart and his son, de Verney and young Dion G. (Dot) Boucicault completed the cast.

1884

George Alexander, being only in the curtain-raiser, allowed them to 'lend' him every night to American Mary Anderson who was playing Gilbert's *Pygmalion and Galatea* at The Lyceum. (Irving was touring America.) Alexander played in the one-act *Comedy and Tragedy*. It had been author W. S. Gilbert who had asked for him. Madge Kendal had of course created Galatea at The Haymarket in 1871. An amusing 'prophecy' is worth noting here. The writer in *Figaro*, after mentioning Alexander's nightly journey, etc., went on: 'at some not very distant day, by a development of apparatus which will do for sight what the telephone and audiophone do for sound, a company of star actors performing on some central stage will be seen and heard, not only at a dozen theatres in London, but at the chief provincial play-houses as well.'

Another story of him was in *Life* at this time too. A policeman chasing a burglar entered the studio of Julia Folkard and, seeing a reflection of Alexander's portrait in a mirror by the light of his little lantern, shouted 'There he is!' and sprang with truncheon raised; luckily at the mirror not the portrait!

No change proved necessary until on 17th April Pinero's adaptation of G. Ohnet's *Le Maître de Forges* was presented as *The Ironmaster*. John Hare took no part but for the first time the programme announced 'The Play Produced under the Direction of Mr Hare'. It was a strong drama in four acts with nineteen parts, and ran 200 times in town until 21st January with the usual break from the middle of July until 2nd October. During the tour the theatre was redecorated and alterations required by the Ministry of Works carried out. Alexander left them then to rejoin Irving who had engaged him for his next American tour which began in Quebec on 30th September.

Lovell and then Herbert Waring took over Alexander's part of Octave. Brandon had been playing de Pontac, a general. After the tour he played Waring's part of Baron de Prefont and used his full name Brandon Thomas for the first time.

1885

The 200th and last night of *The Ironmaster* fell on the third Wednesday of the new year and on the Saturday, the 24th, the curtain went up on *As You Like It*. Hermann Vezin was engaged to play Jaques and a young countrywoman of his, Marion Lea, made her début as Audrey. They were both from Philadelphia in fact, though he had left there in 1850 when he was twenty to make his name as a great actor. She lived, now or later, with her half-sister Mrs Lea Merritt whose famous painting 'Love Locked Out' hangs in the Tate Gallery. When Elizabeth Robins reached England three years later they became friends and teamed up to present Ibsen who was taboo to the commercial leaders.

In the Shakespeare Madge Kendal played Rosalind, Linda Dietz was Celia and Miss Webster Phoebe. 'Auguste' made the costumes which the Hon. Lewis Wingfield designed. Stedman's choir was back and Alfred Cellier composed the songs as well as the overture and incidental music. Only John Hare as Touchstone and Hermann Vezin were really properly in key; the others mostly were too schooled in modern comedy to spring back so easily.

They closed for the end of Lent on 28th March and re-opened on Easter Monday, the 6th, with *The Queen's Shilling* and C. F. Coghlan's *A Quiet Rubber*. In the former their original parts were played by Mrs Kendal, Mrs Gaston Murray, Hare, Kendal, Cathcart and Rowley.

In June they changed to a triple bill: *The Goose with the Golden Eggs* by Augustus Mayhew and Sutherland Edwards; Pinero's *The Money-Spinner*; Theyre Smith's *The Castaways* who were Juan Larkspur and Lilian Selkirk on a desert island, played by the Kendals. The first piece was a farce about lawyers. Mackintosh returned to the company to be one of these, Mrs Paget played his wife and Miss Webster their daughter Clara Turby. E. Hendrie was another called Flickster, Lovell was Bonser a clerk and May Whitty was Mary. In the Pinero six of them played the parts they had created including de Verney as a porter. Herbert Waring now played Clayton's part as the 'borrowing' clerk Harold and Lydia Cowell was the younger sister Dorinda who had been created by Kate Phillips.

The winter novelty was Pinero's *Mayfair* after Sardou's *Maison Neuve*. A number of newcomers were in this, the best known perhaps being the unpleasant Charles Brookfield. The dress rehearsal went rousingly well—unlucky signal! The play fell flat on the first night and was slated by most of the critics.

1886

As omened, Pinero was good enough for only two months, so

on 4th January they revived *Impulse*. Arthur Dacre returned
to play the gigolo Victor de Riel. Linda Dietz, de Verney, the
Kendals and Mrs Murray also played their old parts. Mrs
Paget, Brookfield, Waring, Cathcart and Lovell filled the
others.

A new comedy by Deslandes, *Antoinette Rigaud*, translated
by E. Warren, ran from February into May. It was preceded
by Henry Arthur Jones' curtain-raiser *Bed of Roses*. Smith's
Uncle's Will was added later. On 25th May these were dropped
for *The Wife's Sacrifice* from d'Ennery and Tarbé's *Martyre* by
Sydney Grundy and Sutherland Edwards. The Kendals with
Mrs Pauncefort, Misses Vane and Webster, Hare, Clifford
Cooper, Brookfield, Waring, Cathcart, Hendrie and Paget were
the company.

Long runs were now usual in London and to combat ennui
and widen experience enthusiastic young players banded together as 'The Dramatic Students' for special matinées. This
summer their fifth, for example, was *Love's Labour Lost* here
on 2nd July. The Misses Webster, Mary Dickens, Ada Ferrar,
Lillie Belmore, Eric Lewis and Fuller Mellish were among
them.

Pinero was again the dramatist when the ninth season opened
with his original *The Hobby Horse* on 23rd October. Madge
played Mrs Spencer Jermyn, a society lady with a penchant
for saving the souls of waifs and strays. To do so she took up
residence in the lodgings of an East End curate, the Rev. Noel
Brice (Herbert Waring), who thought her a maiden and so was
declaring his passion on his knees at the moment her husband
looked in to see her. John Hare played the latter who was a
sporting gentleman with an establishment near Newmarket.
His philanthropic gesture had been the founding of a home for
decayed jockeys, such as two old rogues Mr Shattock and Mr
Pews, interpreted delightfully by Mackintosh and Hendrie.

Maud Tree joined them to play Miss Moxon. She had
married Beerbohm two years before when she was twenty-four

and since then had started making a name for herself at The Gaiety and elsewhere though she was in fact a classical scholar. Miss Webster, Mrs Murray and Miss B. Huntley with Brandon Thomas, W. M. Cathcart, Fuller Mellish, Albert Sims, C. W. Somerset, Hendrie and young Master Reed completed the cast of a comedy which was better acted and more deeply written than most of the convention-bound audience appreciated, for there was actually some hissing on the opening night, but it ran, with fifteen-minute *Case for Eviction* added before Christmas for 110 performances.

1887

On 1st February the theatre closed because on that night the Kendals and Rowley Cathcart were appearing at Osborne in the Isle of Wight before the Queen. Theyre Smith's *Uncle's Will* and Gilbert's *Sweethearts* were the chosen pieces. Cathcart was one of the three by express wish of Her Majesty who remembered him from back in the Charles Kean days. An extra five guineas for him was included when the cheque covering all expenses arrived later. It was the first Command by the Queen since the John Mitchell days.

Tom Taylor's historical drama, *Lady Clancarty*, was revived on 3rd March with Mackintosh as an admirable William III, Herbert Waring as Lord Charles Spencer and the Kendals as the Clancartys. Ben Webster made his official début as Lord Woodstock. Mrs Murray was Mother Hunt, Mrs Tree was Lady Betty Noel, Miss B. Huntley and Miss Stanton were Susannah and the Princess Anne.

They were again mostly not quite in period but the play ran well enough and opened the winter season on 8th December.

Before then, on 5th November, Mrs Marsham Rae had taken the theatre for a month to present her husband's adaptation from the German of *The Witch*, with Sir Charles Young's *Petticoat Perfidy*. Maud Cathcart, Grace Arnold and Alexes

Leighton were in the latter, the first two also in the main drama.
Henry Neville, S. Charteris and A. E. Aynesworth were the
most notable of the men. It was Allan Aynesworth's first
speaking part in town and earned him an engagement here later.
He went on to delight playgoers for sixty years and, born in
1865, did not die until 1959.

The drama, although in it too a young girl denounces herself
at a church door and is torn to pieces by the mob, bears little
resemblance to that adapted by John Masefield from the
Norwegian, produced here in 1913, other than in the horror of
both. Mrs Rae played the Lady Alma and Sophie Eyre the
Lady Thalea.

1888

New year gossip was confirmed when the first of a series of
Farewell Revivals, *A Scrap of Paper*, was announced for 16th
January. Maud Tree played Lady Ingram instead of Linda
Dietz as the wife who had lost the love letter but the other
main parts were again played by the Kendals, Hare and Waring.
Old Cronies, with Mackintosh in his old part Dr Jacks, but now
with Hendrie as the other old man Captain Pigeon, was the
curtain-raiser.

On 9th April they presented Lovell's *The Wife's Secret*
which they had not done before. Lewis Waller joined them to
play Lord Arden and Fanny Brough to be Maud. For the
second time only the programme carried the note: 'The Play
produced under the Direction of Mr Hare'.

The Ironmaster followed from the 28th with Waller as the
Duc de Bligny and Aynesworth as de Pontac, parts which had
been created by Henley and Brandon Thomas. Henry Kemble,
Rose Murray and Fanny Brough were in it as well as the
Kendals, Waring and Mrs Murray who had been in the original.

Final revival was *The Squire* from 16th June. John Hare, the
Kendals and Mackintosh played their old parts of the Rev.

Paul Dormer, Lieutenant Thorndike, Kate Verity and Gunnion. Charles Burleigh and Rose Murray played the gipsy couple, Blanche Horlock was Felicity Gunnion, Sims and Hendrie were Fell and Robjohns Junior and Branscombe was the reporter. Waring was the pugnacious Gilbert Hythe.

On Saturday night, 21st July, a particularly brilliant audience gathered to bid farewell at the end of the tenth season of the most successful management the theatre had known. The stage was afterwards piled high with baskets and bouquets of flowers. John Huy was presented with a diamond tie-pin as token of his admirable front-of-house co-ordination. The speeches by John Hare and W. H. Kendal acknowledged the loyalty of audiences, professional players, production and front staff whose co-operation had made the overall success of the venture.

Though Mackintosh was the only one besides the Three who had been in first and last plays, Huy, Cathcart, Harford and Schoening had been with them throughout. Nothing epoch making marked the lesseeship, encouragement of Pinero maybe their most important contribution to the advancement of the theatre; but they showed, as first the Bancrofts at The Prince of Wales' and then Irving at The Lyceum had already proved, that happy and contented staff, back and front, properly encouraged, were an essential part of success.

The principals had welded their players into a team and though there was a certain amount of change as plays or seasons ended, the spirit of a first-class company was even strengthened by its very flexibility and all were creditably affected. Most were there for several seasons running, while some, like Mrs Gaston Murray, Brandon Thomas and de Verney, only missed acting throughout by one or two plays. All became familiar with each other's idiosyncrasies and the resulting smooth, beautifully costumed and mounted productions did really become a byword in the profession and outside. To have played in the company gave a cachet of which players became quite proud. There had also been many juniors un-named in the programmes.

The Kendals, after a holiday, took a company on a tour of America. Hare joined Mrs John Wood for the opening of the rebuilt Court Theatre pending the completion of The Garrick which was being built for him.

CHAPTER 6

BARRINGTON, MRS LANGTRY AND OTHERS

1888-1890

RUTLAND BARRINGTON, famous Savoyard, 'had developed a very bad attack of ambition', as he says in his autobiography. With the promise of money behind him he signed a lease, but as soon as he did so his backer withdrew and Rutland carried on with his own savings and much misgiving.

First night was 13th October with a new drama by Sydney Grundy and F. C. Phillips called *The Dean's Daughter*. Statuesque and beautiful Olga Nethersole played Miriam of the title. Barrington was her father, the Rev. Augustus St Aubyn, a poverty-stricken, bailiff-besieged country vicar hoping to become a dean through the good offices of his prospective son-in-law, Sir Henry Craven (John Beauchamp). Barrington's well-endowed figure admirably suited the odious, beautifully sanctimonious, canting rogue conceived by the dramatists and he exploited the character almost too well. As he fobbed off the dunning tradesmen Chetwynd (Duncan Fleet) and Twentyman (Charles Dodsworth) the audience were put wise to the position. Against her will Miriam was married to the libertine Sir Henry who became Ambassador to Turkey and deserted her for another.

Lewis Waller played handsome hero George Sabine who had been repulsed by her father's wish, and still was, for honour's sake, even when Miriam had been abandoned. But when attacked by lascivious Prince Balanikoff (Ed. Sass)

St. James'
Theatre

Sole Lessee
&
Manager,
Mr
Rutland
Barrington.

Notice,

Any Attendant accepting a
Fee being liable to instant dismissal the
Management earnestly requests that
NO FEES shall be offered.

J. Bernard Partridge.

The Dean's Daughter Programme

George was close enough to burst into the room and save her. Divorced, Miriam was about to marry good young Lord Ashwell when her nasty father arrived to denounce her as a divorced woman. Sir Henry came on the scene too to back her father, so Miriam turned weeping and scorned towards the river. Noble George was quickly there to chase and clasp her to his bosom and the curtain fell on her accepting him at last.

Others in the cast were Caroline Hill, Adrienne Dairolles, Mary Barton and Emily Cross; Allan Aynesworth, Newall, Dixon, Trent and Montague. Décor was by Walter Johnstone and Julian Hicks. Carl Armbruster was conductor. Prices were still as in 1879 with no tips or fees. For the first time (other than decorations) an illustration, by Bernard Partridge, appeared on the programme, and Barrington listed ladies first and his own name at the very end, both the reverse of normal. The innovations did not bring luck or discount the omen of the opening date.

Excellently cast and played though it had been, the drama failed for really no other reason than that society and suburbia could not face parsons, who ought to have been pillars of respectability and honour, floodlit as swindling schemers and libertines. Critics afterwards feigned shock at the 'incarnate selfish meanness', 'contemptible unnatural conduct of a church dignatory', 'utterly untrue to life and false art' etc.

Those who did go, applauded, but they were radicals and not the family suburbanites who keep the box-office happy. An unfortunate and outrageous demonstration on the first night was naturally distressing but had nothing to do with the presentation. Clement Scott was by now well on his way to becoming Lord High Reactionary Critic Pooh Bah. His last review had annoyed gallery and pittites, who also were getting a little above themselves, as has happened since. When Scott arrived in the theatre they rose as one man and booed him. The play was in four acts. Each time the curtain fell they repeated their expression of dislike and even at the very end they were rude enough to begin again and would not even let the players take their calls. Eventually George Edwardes rose up in his stall and shouted to them to behave themselves, that they were not giving Barrington a chance, that they ought to go home quietly and say what they wanted to to Scott outside. 'Don't forget my first night next week!' he ended.

Curtain-raiser *A Patron Saint* was added on the Wednesday and then on 29th November W. S. Gilbert's first non-musical for some years was produced. As *Brantingham Hall*, this proved as unpalatable as Barrington's first offering: it was a most involved melodrama bearing no semblance to what was becoming expected of Gilbert. The play opened in Australia on a sheep-farm where the heroine Ruth (Julia Neilson), a very pure wife of the Hon. Arthur, was soon the subject of fisticuffs between her husband and villain Crampton (Lewis Waller). She stayed behind to nurse her sick ex-convict father when Arthur returned home to claim his inheritance but when she got news that he had been shipwrecked she sailed to make the claim instead.

Reaching home she found Crampton there before her and already holding a mortgage over her father-in-law Lord Sax-mundham (Nutcombe Gould). Pride prevented the latter accepting aid from a convict's daughter. Crampton refused to sell her the mortgage since he wanted her body not her purse. Ruth then proclaimed that she had never been married so automatically the money she had claimed went instead to Saxmundham. The Hon. Arthur then returned from the wilds to which he had escaped from his watery grave and the curtain fell to tears of joy.

Acting honours went to Lewis Waller for his handsome and boldly played villain, and to Julia Neilson in her first year on the stage, of whom Clement Scott said 'this beautiful and sweet-voiced actress showed of what she is capable'. Norman Forbes played Ross, a missionary. W. Herbert was the Hon. Arthur. Mrs Gaston Murray and Miss Norreys and four other men besides some of those in the former play were in the cast. Barrington himself played Mr Thursby, a quite minor role.

The righteous ones objected strongly to the idea of a woman renouncing such a sacred thing as marriage, no matter how noble her reason. Five weeks later Barrington had to shut the doors and soon stood in the bankruptcy court even though Gilbert, in a vain attempt to help, had refused to claim for royalties. Soon after he returned to the comic-opera world where he belonged.

1889

Lord Newry was now the Earl of Kilmorey and on 14th May he lent the theatre free for a Benefit for John Huy. Old friends who rallied to perform included the Kendals, Hare, Lionel and Sydney Brough, Wyndham, Waring, Aynesworth, Cathcart, Kate Phillips, Mrs Gaston Murray. John le Hay the ventriloquist also performed.

1890

Lillie Langtry, famous 'Jersey Lily', was the next lessee. She appeared as Rosalind on 24th February with Arthur Bourchier making his London début as Jaques. Marion Lea was engaged to be Audrey again. Norman Forbes, Charles Fulton and Walter Gay were in the list and the Hon. Lewis Wingfield superintended. Once casting was over Lillie crossed to Paris leaving Wingfield to conduct rehearsals which he did with such good will and imagination that when she returned she found the company on strike! The final dress rehearsal was called at last and all went well. Next morning Mrs Langtry woke with red spots of measles decorating her beautiful face, for the microbes had been incubating ever since a dinner in Paris. 'Postponed' slips were hurriedly pasted on the bills.

A month later the Prince and Princess of Wales headed the

brilliant audience gathering for the first night. The classic was perhaps better received than acted but as well as the principals mentioned, Laurence Cautley for his Orlando and Amy McNeil for her 'fresh and sparkling' Celia won mention. Violet Armsbruster was Hymen.

Lillie tells the story in her autobiography of how one night at a party on stage for players and society friends she ordered a race down the street, round St James's Square and back again. A large policeman brought the cavalcade to a sudden halt.

'Now, now. What's going on here!'

'Only fun, officer.'

'Fun! And the Bishop in his nightshirt looking on from his window over there!' [The Bishop of London's town house was then at No. 22.] Then the policeman recognised one of the guests.

'O dear, my lord! Really! You must stop this you know.'

'Not for nuts!' said the young peer. 'When's the police sports this year?'

'July 6th, my lord.'

'And I hope you're the treasurer?'

'I am, my lord!!'

'Well, put these in your notebook instead of your scribbling!' A few pound notes and the policeman obsequiously faded away.

Sydney Grundy's drama *Esther Sandraz* from Belot's *Femme de Glace* changed the bill on 3rd May. Burnand's musical one-act *The Tiger* preceded it. Clement Scott was always glad to be able to stick his knife into Grundy. He had done so over *The Dean's Daughter*. This time he started on Lillie by commenting about people only going these days to see beautiful faces and expensive costumes and sets. Then he told of Grundy's sharp practice in selling his play. It had gone the usual rounds which included Mrs Langtry who had rejected it. In America she heard that Amy Roselle had agreed to play it at a trial matinée and immediately cables passed and Lillie bought all other rights.

So Scott wrote, but he was a scented[1] rogue who would amplify a grain of truth or invent a story to suit himself. His gibe about beautiful faces was half justified perhaps, but Lillie had been acting for nine years and had been very successful, and when she was it meant that a company of players was also successful and in work. The way she bought Grundy's play was outrageous if true, but he was more at fault than she was for even if Amy had been stupid enough to go to the expense and trouble of trying out the play without an option he ought to have been decent enough to have told her about Mrs Langtry's proposals and given her an option.

Mrs Langtry went down with pleurisy in June and Bourchier took over. On the 26th he presented Justin McCarthy's *Your Wife* and Lady Violet Greville's *Old Friends*. Annie Irish and Adrienne Dairolles were engaged but he was unable to get things going. Doubtless the reason for that was his inexperience for though he was to run The Garrick successfully from 1903 that was after he had been partner with Wyndham, and at this time he had only been on tour with Lillie since leaving Oxford where he had been a founder of O.U.D.S.

Frou-Frou was presented again at a charity matinée on 10th July with Bourchier, Henry Neville, Fred Terry, Gertrude Kingston, Fanny Brough and Edith Woodworth who was Gilberte. Soon afterwards the doors closed.

The final French company to play here in this century, in fact for forty years, began a short season on 3rd November under M. L. Mayer who had followed Mitchell as impresario to the French (with Felix in between). It was Mayer's twenty-third London season.

Mme Chaumont starred in the first week in three one-acts. She was supported by Mlle Stuart who the following week starred as Jane de Simerose opposite M. Valbel as de Ryons in Dumas' *L'Ami des Femmes*.

[1] It was J. B. Booth who told me of Scott's penchant for scent.

Mrs Langtry was still lessee but already a new lease had been signed and she in fact opened a season at The Princess's on 2nd December with *Antony and Cleopatra.*

ADDENDA

JOHN BRAHAM'S HOME (p. 3) The Grange, formerly Copt Hall, stood, with fields and farm adjoining, on the North End Road near where the Fulham Road touches Walham Green. A thousand yards north in the same road, nearer Hammersmith, was the other Grange where lived Samuel Richardson, Burne-Jones and other famous folk including in 1881 (Sir) Henry Irving. Bought by the local Socialist council, this beautiful house was demolished, despite many protests, and flats built on the site. Certainly one would rather see homes instead of offices as have supplanted The St James's but in Fulham there are countless slummy properties which surely could have been cleared instead of a charming house of long romantic associations.

Laura Allison, nee Tucker, Mrs Seymour (p. 7 &c). In his book *Charles Reade,* 1903, the actor-manager John Coleman relates rather fanciful tales of Laura's early days. Now Coleman was as notorious as was Macqueen-Pope sixty years on. For example, Dibden in his *Annals of the Edinburgh Stage,* 1888, says on p. 394 that he was 'the author of several very inaccurate theatrical works'. Coleman wanted a romantic story so kind-hearted Laura supplied one—but she blended her own adventures with some of her old associate Priscilla Horton as well as maybe others. Coleman was too enamoured to check.

Mitchell's family (p. 60). There was also a daughter from his marriage to the Carlist refugee widow Mme d'Alcain. She became Mme Lentz and was mother of the dramatist Georges Mitchell.

Fox Cooper (p. 43). A biography by his great grandson F. Renad Cooper has now been published by Barrie & Rockliff, 1964, as *Nothing Extenuate.*

A Page of Souvenirs

Book II

CHAPTER I

THE DAYS OF GEORGE ALEXANDER

PART I: 1891-1899

TERMS were agreed between the Earl of Kilmorey and thirty-two-year-old Scotsman George Alexander who was in full possession of the theatre before the end of 1890. Electricity was installed to supersede the old hot and dangerous gas, soft and mellowing though that had been. The brisk ambitious spirit of the new lessee and his wife animated a flurry of painters, upholsterers and cleaners, the whilst a new one-act was rehearsed and play continued at The Avenue of which Alexander was then actor-manager.

George Alexander Gibb Samson had dropped his last two names when he turned professional on 7th September 1879 at the Nottingham Theatre Royal with the stock touring company of Swanborough and Vernon. Afterwards he had been with the Robertson company and in April 1881 made his London début at the East End Standard. From 26th December to July 1882 he was with Irving at The Lyceum where he made a hit as the blind Caleb Deecie in *The Two Roses* and then was Paris in *Romeo*.

On 8th August at St Mark's he married Florence Théleur.

She was French and the couple made the perfect pair such unions so often do. Florence was a charming and practical person whose companionship, good taste and intelligence helped her husband gain the success he did. She did not die until 1946, so many will remember her persevering urge as organiser of charity collectors especially at Benefits. In their early St James's days she made all the hats, and usually all the dressing of the stage was in her hands as well as the 'housekeeping' until the formidable Mrs Evans took over the latter department. Many have paid tribute to her in their memoirs. Ernest Thesiger made his début under her and her husband and says Alexander was a wonderful producer who really took trouble to teach the youthful novice the rudiments of acting. Of Florence: 'she would flit from one member of the cast to another, whispering "you were the *making* of the play", and though none really believed her flattery they still felt all the better for her kindly insincerity!'

Madge Kendal, on the platform at their St James's silver jubilee, said: 'And what a wife you have been . . . your magic touch . . . is the tenth wonder of the world!' Dame Irene Vanbrugh acknowledged her as being at the heart of their theatre; Cyril Maude that she was accountable for a great deal of the success of her husband. Graham Robertson, who had a lot to do with productions and who with his mother shared a summer house with them at one time, honoured her: 'She posed as the charming, pretty, empty-headed butterfly . . . beneath this innocent mask lurked a strong personality, clear headed, long sighted, infinitely patient and tactful, an untiring worker and firm friend, wise, brave and generous . . . of the greatest use to her husband both at home and in the theatre and her marriage to him was one of the best of his many good strokes of fortune.' Also in his *Time Was* Robertson quotes from a letter Alexander wrote not long before he died: 'Florence has been simply an angel through it all.' She was on the 1884/5 Irving United States tour when one night some gauze at the back in the *Hamlet* play scene suddenly blazed up. The whole audience rose and cried 'Fire!' Florence shrieked 'This always happens. It's part of the play!' Everyone sat down, said 'part of the play' and Irving kept on without a break—so she herself related in the appendix to Mason's book on Alexander. There too she tells of making the hats, choosing the gowns to suit the sets, acting as assistant stage manager generally and being paid £5 a week for her work. Most important too were her appearances at the final rehearsals which she viewed with such a fresh critical eye that they called her 'the sledge-hammer'.

Alexander had finished his education at Stirling High School under an old-time dominie of modern outlook who had instilled in him those talents of tenacity, sense of order and rather puritanical rigidity then common to his nation. The training stood him in good stead and was not abused in later life. Not until he was twenty-one and so could honourably refuse to continue in commerce as his father desired, did he do so. Experiences as an amateur fixed his ambition and though that was not to be a *great* tragedian or comedian, his worth may be gauged by the £45 a week which Irving was paying him in 1889.

I will subsequently refer to Alexander as 'Alec' for as such he was known to his intimates and so did Florence refer to him. The honeymoon had not been a long one for before the end of August he took over Forbes-Robertson's part in *The Parvenue* (Court, 8th April 1882) for the tour beginning then at Liverpool. They returned to The Court on 14th November and in December he began to tour opposite Miss Wallis as Romeo, Maurice de Saxe in *Adrienne Lecouvreur* and other top roles. By then he had been signed up six months in advance, for he appeared 'by permission of Hare and Kendal'. At The Opéra-Comique he was in *Bondage* from 31st March 1883. In April at The Gaiety with Miss Wallis he was in a series of matinées as they had toured. On 23rd April he was Armand to Miss Lingard's Camille at The Imperial and on 9th June appeared in Wilkie

Collins' unsuccessful *Rank and Riches* at The Adelphi. In May and June he earned good notices as director of distinguished amateurs and professionals in Greek and English tableaux at Cromwell House in aid of King's College (Ladies) Building Fund.

The Hare and Kendal tour and St James's seasons followed and with his subsequent career are fully documented as the previous details are not. With Irving from 1884 to 1889, he was at The Adelphi until he took over The Avenue in February 1890. His success there as actor-manager encouraged him to sign up the larger St James's, even though just before he did so his manager ran away with about £700. Such a loss was no laughing matter but although Irving typically said he would be welcome back at The Lyceum Alec was not deterred and carried on undaunted.

Alexander profited from his varied experiences. Hit-or-miss methods were not for him and the Hare and Kendal régime was the example he followed more than any other. Ten years later his fellow-countryman the critic and Ibsenite William Archer interviewed him for the *Pall Mall Gazette* and quoted him as saying: '. . . luck is knowledge, instinct, organising ability. . . . I have succeeded partly because I have been my own master but mainly because I have loved my art, not acting only but management, and have worked at it conscientiously, untiringly.'

His policy and organisation which developed as they progressed were based on three principles: British before foreign; well-balanced dramatic characterisation instead of centre-of-stage star actor-manager high over minor players and parts; perfectly cogged and oiled wheels back and front of the curtain.

Staff were chosen with care and so well treated that disloyalty became unthinkable and long years of service resulted. Decorum was the rule so that the chatter of staff voices never rivalled rattling crockery nor was ever heard that raucous female cry of 'bar this way' which heralded the intervals and jagged the nerves and upset the mood of sensitive mid-twentieth century patrons.

Back-stage, carpets, mostly overlaid with white drugget, lined all corridors and departments. Stage-hands were attired in white overalls, with cuffs coloured to denote their duties, cotton gloves and white soft shoes into which they had to change immediately they arrived. Visitors were banned from dressing-rooms which were at one time reached by a staircase for ladies and another for gentlemen.

A green-room was reinaugurated, known as 'the long room', where friends and the Press could be entertained. To quote the fine sporting and dramatic journalist J. B. Booth: 'when there, one found oneself in the position of the honoured guest—but not to waste time in society gossip for the play was the thing.' The theatre had its own definite atmosphere, the same writer says in his *Sporting Times* memoirs, and was run on business lines where although extravagance was taboo, accounts rigidly scrutinised and sensible economy was the rule, Alexander for all that was an intelligently generous person.

To quote actress Sydney Fairbrother, he built a 'marvellous organisation where perfection was always attained'; or Ernest Thesiger: 'the most efficiently run theatre I ever knew'. Many others have paid like and affectionate tribute. Here is Ellen Terry's: 'Conscientious, dear delightful Alec! No one ever deserved success more than he did and used it better when it came. . . . He had the good luck to marry a wife who was clever as well as charming, and who could help him.'

British dramatists were far from numerous in those days but Alec not only approached those he valued but many who had not written for the stage at all. Among the latter were Conan Doyle, Arnold Bennett, Galsworthy, Max Beerbohm, A. E. W. Mason, the poets Stephen Phillips and John Davidson and Oscar Wilde. After Alec's death his accounts showed that he had paid out as much as £7,000 as encouragement for material never used (*vide* Mason). Writers were made welcome to call to discuss ideas.

Once presentation was decided upon Alec had model sets built and all movements, positions, etc. discussed and planned (not fixed) with the dramatist and technicians. After that he himself was in control. Pinero's subsequent quarrel and refusal to write again for Alec was over this very point, for that dramatist would not allow anyone but himself to direct his own work. Even he gave in eventually to Alec.

Remembering his own hard days under Irving when rehearsals exhaustingly had gone on for as long as five or six hours, he made a set rule: Rehearsals from 11 a.m. to 2 p.m. prompt at both ends, but finals were twice daily when the theatre was shut. Another innovation was his dress rehearsals which were called long before first nights so that players and stage-hands became perfectly accustomed to costumes, sets and props. Naturally everything was not all so ordained from his first minute at the theatre.

Admission prices were 10/6d. stalls, 7/- and 5/- dress circle, 3/- upper circle, 2/- pit, 1/- gallery. In 1917, his last time of acting, the only differences were 6d. on the first rows of the dress circle and 1/- on the first rows of the upper circle and 6d. on the pit. No tips or charges for cloakrooms or programmes were allowed until 1905 when the latter were charged for.

He engaged Walter Slaughter as his musical director but Robert V. Shone and Alwyn Lewis were brought with him from The Avenue as stage and business manager respectively.

First night was 31st January when the complete cast in R. C. Carton's *Sunlight and Shadow* transferred from The Avenue where they had been running since 1st November. As afterpiece a new bright little trifle called *The Gay Lothario* by Alfred Calmour was presented with Alec, Laura Graves, Maude Millett and Ben Webster. Though of no importance it was in merry contrast with the main play and sent folk home happily

instead of sorrowfully, for before it they had seen Marion Terry
as Helen the pure unselfish daughter of hard-working country
Doctor Latimer (Nutcombe Gould), her spoilt and adored
pretty younger sister Maud (Maude Millett) who had an
empty-headed lover called Bamfield played by Ben Webster.
Yorke Stephens played Mark Denzil who was Helen's suitor,
and Alec was the local choir-master George Addis who was a
kindly cripple nursing in secret a noble love for Helen which
he would not disclose because of his infirmity. Helen's happiness was shattered when Ada Neilson made appearance as the
long thought dead and dreadful Janet, wife of Mark. Janet,
however, did conveniently die later on, and only cripple Addis
knew. His suit would have prospered had he kept that quiet
but he nobly told his news, the lovers could marry after all and
he retired again into the background. Comic relief by Alfred
Hollis as a bibulous gardener proved welcome. Clement Scott
praised the sentimental piece and urged his readers to hurry
off to see it.

From Monday 23rd February the theatre closed for final
rehearsals of a new play by the young Australian Haddon
Chambers. This, *The Idler*, was a melodrama which had already
had a three-month run in New York and which Mrs Langtry
had been going to produce in London. For her, however, it was
not enough of a one-woman play, and only the advice of Squire
Bancroft had freed it and its author for Alec and saved a long-
drawn-out quarrel.

Marion Terry, Maude Millett, Nutcombe Gould and Alfred
Hollis were joined by Herbert Waring, American John Mason,
Lady Monckton and Gertrude Kingston. They with Alec
appeared when the doors were opened on the Thursday. On
the Monday *The Gay Lothario* returned as a curtain-raiser
with Miss Granville as Letty the maid, a part which had been
created by Laura Graves who was now promoted to be her
former mistress Amanda Goldacre. Ben Webster had been the
valet Sparks and was now Sir Harry Lovell which Alec had

been. Vernon Sansbury was the new valet. Set in eighteenth-century Bath, it was a flirting flutter which might have been a contemporary piece written in that city. The costumes had been designed by Percy Anderson and the set by Joseph Harker. That famous scene-painter, father of comedian Gordon Harker, had also done the scenes in *Sunlight & Shadow* and did one for *The Idler*. All in the latter were interiors, the other two by W. Hann and W. Johnstone. It was a strange custom, still common then, to have a different designer for each set. Some even kept their colour scheme secret from the costume folk! Florence Alexander was well aware of this and acted as liaison for they were building a wardrobe for their theatre. It was then normal—except at The Lyceum mainly—for players to provide most of their costumes for themselves.

The Idler ran until the end of the season, 17th July. It was a tale of a gold-mining fugitive from a drunken brawl murder, of blackmail, an averted duel, of pure love. Clement Scott was by this time, as *Daily Telegraph* critic, the doyen defender of the sacred past. His writing in that paper and in the weekly *Illustrated London News* certainly carried weight in many quarters. Eventually his position went to his head but that is a long story, partly demonstrated in my pages. Now he praised Alec's choice of play and the acting by all, whilst at the same time showing that his dagger was still at hand for the moderns: 'I do not envy that form of intellectuality that can despise the picture of such a woman as is portrayed by Miss Marion Terry —woman in heart, woman in mind, woman to the very finger-tips—and turn her off the stage to make way for a score of Hedda Gablers, or Rebecca Wests. . . .'

On the last night the one-act was changed for Walter Frith's *Molière* which, with Alec in the title-role, showed the last hours in the life of the great dramatist. Newcomers to the company in that were Howard Russell and George Gamble whilst in the main play Wilton Lackaye had taken over from Mason.

After a holiday and short tour the theatre reopened on 28th

September with the former bill. On 7th November the curtain went up on the four-act *Lord Anerley* by Mark Quinton and Henry Hamilton, based partly on Matthey's novel *Le Duc de Kandos*. The scenery was by H. P. Hall, the wigs by Fox, the costumes by Morris Angel.

Arthur Bourchier played the title-role; E. W. Gardiner was Travers, a detective; Alec was Rupert Lee, alias José the Gaucho; Waring was Lester, known as Miguel; Nutcombe Gould was the Earl of Edgehill; Ben Webster was George Beaufort and Holles was Evans. Laura Graves was the Hon. Esmé, Gertrude Kingston was Mme de Sivori and Marion Terry was Evelyn Carew. This strong drama opened with a knife fight in a corral near Buenos Aires when renegade Anerley was vanquished by Rupert and then stabbed in the back by Lester. These two were escapees from Devil's Island. Lester pointed out Rupert's resemblance to the dead Lord Anerley and they set off to claim his inheritance. The old Earl at home was blind so that was fairly easy, but then in the end the detective proved that Rupert the supplanter was in fact really the true Lord Anerley for he was the long-lost child of a first marriage!

A comedy called *Forgiveness* by Comyns Carr replaced the drama on 30th December. Marion Terry, Fanny Coleman, Laura Graves and Dolores Drummond with Alec, Gould, Bourchier, H. H. Vincent, Gardiner, Fred Everill and H. de Lange were the cast.

1892

Alec had now been a year in occupation and things had gone more smoothly than during his first year in management at The Avenue. His first play of significance, however, took more time and gave more work and trouble than all the previous ones together.

Oscar Wilde's star had been flashing for over a decade but,

except for the minor *Vera* and *Duchess of Padua* which had been or were about to be produced in America, no play had emanated from him. Alec was as fascinated by the brilliant Irishman as anyone else in their world and he determined to net his wit for The St James's. Even before Alec had moved over from The Avenue he had given Oscar a £50 cheque, for on 2nd February 1891 Oscar wrote from Tite Street to 'My dear Aleck' saying he could not 'get a grip of the play yet', and offering to return the money (*The Letters*, p. 282). Alec let the money stay, probably doubling it later since other reports say Oscar had £100 in advance, but he had to pester Oscar regularly afterwards. Frank Harris rings true in his life of Oscar when he makes him say: 'Alec has been bothering me to write a play for him and I have an idea I rather like. I am going to shut myself up in my room and stay there till it's written. I wonder can I do it in a week, or will it take three?'

Before the end of 1891 the MS. was flourished in front of Alec and a £1,000 refused in favour of royalties. (The 'beer money and a fiver' of fifty years before had indeed vanished!)

Tentatively called *A Good Woman* (the subsequent sub-title), *Lady Windermere's Fan* was soon decided upon and re-writing and alterations begun. The original manuscript is littered with changes in the hands of Alec and Oscar, for it was at first by no means stage-worthy and all Alec's tact was needed before his practical knowledge and intuition prevailed. The production troubles are fairly well dealt with in A. E. W. Mason's book to which the reader is referred.

The three sets of the four acts were separately designed by H. P. Hall, 'the scenic artist of the theatre'; Walter Hann, who had worked here as early as 1861 though he did not die until 1922; and Harford who had been here throughout the Hare and Kendal régime. The full cast ran: Lord Windermere (Mr George Alexander), Lord Darlington (Mr Nutcombe Gould), Lord Augustus Lorton (Mr H. H. Vincent), Mr Charles Dumby (Mr A. Vane Tempest), Mr Cecil Graham (Mr Ben

Webster), Mr Hopper (Mr Alfred Hollis), Parker (Mr V.
Sansbury), Lady Windermere (Miss Lily Hanbury), The
Duchess of Berwick (Miss Fanny Coleman), Lady Plimdale
(Miss Granville), Mrs Cowper-Cowper (Miss A. de Winton),
Lady Jedbourgh (Miss B. Page), Lady Agatha Carlisle (Miss
Laura Graves), Lady Strutfield (Miss M. Girdlestone), Rosalie
(Miss W. Dolan), Mrs Erlynne (Miss Marion Terry).

Incidental music was by Slaughter, the dresses were by
Mmes Savage, Purdue and Yorke. Wigs were by Fox.

The plot of course turns upon the reaction of innocent and
righteous Lady Windermere to the latest scandal of the town
in Mrs Erlynne, since the former never learns that the latter
is her own mother who had run away twenty years before and
has returned to blackmail Lord Windermere into sponsoring
and financing her return into Society. Stirred to believe the
worst by the Duchess and cad Darlington, Lady Windermere
runs to Darlington's flat to throw herself into his arms but
drops her fan as she hides behind a curtain when all the men
arrive. She is then saved from disgrace when the fan is found
by the self-sacrifice of Mrs Erlynne, who nevertheless captures
Lord Augustus as a husband and exits abroad with a large
annuity from Windermere as extra solace.

The minor parts were all attractively played with Fanny
Coleman making an amusingly talkative middle-class duchess,
Laura Graves a delightful 'yes mamma' daughter and Vincent
a laughable slightly caricatured Augustus. Gould was hardly
at home as the cynical Darlington and Lily Hanbury was really
miscast in the title-role for she was a buxom hearty tennis and
swimming girl. Marion Terry was agreed by most to be superb
as Mrs Erlynne and Alec made a charming gentleman in his
part which called for little more.

The critics were not unanimous. The *Athenaeum* said 'Mr
Wilde shows himself a revolutionary and an iconoclast,' but
suggested he had waited too long before disclosing the relation-
ships. The dramatist's intention was honoured by refraining

SJT P

from further explanation but the termination was thought somewhat curious; '. . . the whole construction is neat and ingenious . . . the chief attraction the dialogue, smart, epigrammatic, flippant, cynical . . . not a few of the diamonds paste . . . the audience only ceased to laugh to applaud . . . not a dull moment . . . perfectly mounted and well played. Mr Alexander has little to do and does it well; Mr Gould is excellent; Miss Hanbury plays better than she has previously played and may very possibly become an actress; and Miss Marion Terry, though a little perplexed with the character she takes, seems likely [in future] to realise it. . . .'

Now though that writer thought the secret disclosed too late, Wilde had not wanted to do so until the very end and it was with great difficulty that Alec persuaded him to change it from the second night. Oscar later in a letter to the *St James's Gazette* admitted this, and that he and his young friends agreed with Alec. Certainly audiences cannot appreciate the reactions of the ignorant Lady Windermere nor those of her husband and Mrs Erlynne unless they understand why he allows himself to be blackmailed.

As he tells in his *Time Was*, the painter and author of *Pinkie*, etc., Graham Robertson, met Oscar in the street on the day before the first night. Oscar made sure Graham had a seat and then told him to go to a certain florists.

'Order a green carnation button-hole for tomorrow night. No, I know there's no such thing, but they arrange them somehow at that shop; dye them I suppose. I want a good many men to wear them tomorrow—it will annoy the public!'

'But why annoy the public?'

'It likes to be annoyed. A young man on the stage will wear a green carnation. People will stare at it and wonder. Then they will look around the house and see every here and there more and more little specks of mystic green. "This must be some secret symbol" they will say, "what on earth can it mean?" '

'And what does it mean Oscar?'

'Nothing whatever, but that is just what nobody will guess!'

Whatever the reaction of most of them to the green carnations, the brilliant first-nighters were almost entirely delighted with the play and the cry of 'Author!' was not long delayed.

Oscar strolled into sight, once the tumult had reached crescendo, and leaned languidly against the proscenium arch, a gold-tipped cigarette dangling from his lips, its smoke lazily enhancing his nonchalant stance, green carnation in his button-hole.

The house hushed. Then a sibilant gasp of horror issued from the lips of young Mrs Clement Scott and from all within her hearing, so she wrote later, 'at the insolent effrontery of the dramatist' and the 'hideous emblem in his button-hole'.

The tension tightened, Oscar languidly removed the cigarette, puffed out a long stream of smoke, then drawled:

'I am so glad, Ladies and Gentlemen, that you like my play. I feel sure you estimate the merits of it almost as highly as I do myself!'

The house rocked with laughter and renewed applause.

If the cigarette smoke had been puffed directly into his own face Clement Scott could not have been more horrified. Ironically he suggested in the *Illustrated London News* (after similar remarks in the *Daily Telegraph*) in a long rigmarole, that Oscar perhaps was a cynic of deep significance intending to 'reform society by sublime self-sacrifice, that the curious attitude adopted on his first night was so extraordinary that he must have said to himself "I will show to what extent bad manners are endorsed in this unrestrained age. I will do on the stage of a public theatre what I would not dare to do at a mass meeting in the Park. I will uncover my head in the presence of refined women but I refuse to put down my cigarette. I will show no humility and I will stand unrebuked. I will take greater liberties with the public than any author who has preceded me. The society that allows boys to puff cigarette smoke in the faces of ladies in theatre corridors will condone the originality of a smoking author on the stage." '

After more in the same theme Scott mentioned Oscar's complimenting the 'audience on its good sense in liking what he himself has condescended to admire' and eventually came to the play itself. Again he put Oscar's imagined thoughts into words:

'. . . I will prove . . . that the very instinct of maternity—that holiest and purest instinct with women—is deadened in the breasts of our English mothers. . . . You have seen how the good mother can desert her new-born infant without a pang. . . . I will show you a mother who leaves her daughter for ever, unkissed, and goes downstairs to accept the hand of a roué. . . .' Scott concluded with a prophecy which was to be fulfilled: 'Meanwhile, society at large will rush to see his play.'

Oscar's curtain 'speech' quoted above is from Frank Harris, who admitted that Robert Ross only recalled Oscar saying that he had enjoyed the evening immensely. Oscar, however, re-enacted the whole scene at a party some days later, with natural elaboration, and Frank pointed out that consequently it was difficult for anyone present on both occasions to differentiate. Frank's version tallies with Scott who would certainly not have been at the party. Others say the speech was longer still.

Winifred Emery, who had been here in 1881 and since had been acclaimed as quite a genius, took over soon after from Lily Hanbury and a couple of minor changes were later made. In March Walter Frith's *Midsummer Day* was introduced as curtain-raiser.

The summer tour was as successful as the first run. As the fame of the theatre spread the annual tours became such important events that local mayors met the trains with full civic pomp and ceremony. Complete coaches were hired, baggage ones for the scenery and props, saloon ones for the company. Such consideration paid dividends in publicity but primarily in happier, easier artistes, for even in those days of private enterprise journeys could be fatiguing. Alec had begun the

system even before his St James's days. In his year at The
Avenue, for as short a run as the thirty miles to Reading he
hired a whole saloon for the company. Reading was his natal
town where still lived his father whom he introduced to Fanny
Brough and Elizabeth Robins, the latter much impressed by
the old man's 'good looks and distinguished manners'. For
two years after his début, Alec told her, his father would have
nothing to do with him!

The winter season opened on 31st October with the company
as before except for Edith Chester as Lady Agatha, and a new
curtain-raiser in W. L. Courtney's *Kit Marlowe* with Alec as
that poet.

A sentimental comedy, on Saturday 3rd December, followed
the brilliant but melodramatic Oscar Wilde play. This was
Liberty Hall by R. C. Carton, the author of the transfer from
The Avenue. His real name was Critchett; he was married to
Fay Compton's aunt who acted always as Miss Compton. The
new play told the story of two sisters, Amy and Blanche, played
by Maude Millett and Marion Terry, who had taken refuge
with an elderly cousin, William Todman (Edward Righton),
an impecunious bookseller. Their father had died and rather
than wait to meet an unknown cousin who inherited the en-
tailed estate they tried to earn a livelihood from Blanche's
amateurish paintings. Fanny Coleman played their aristocratic
old servant Crafer who accompanied them as chaperone. Shop-
boy Robert Binks was played by Master Richard Saker,
youngest representative of a very old theatrical family still
active. Alec played Mr Owen, the heir in disguise, who became
a lodger and influenced the household and their friends in the
same way though not so strongly as Jerome's Stranger sixteen
years later.

Others in the cast were Ailsa Craig, Ben Webster, Gould,
Vincent, Vernon Sansbury and Alfred Hollis. Ailsa of course
was Edy, daughter of Ellen Terry and niece of the leading lady.
Hathorn and Norbury took over minor roles from Gould and

Sansbury before the end of the successful run which lasted till the season finished.

1893

Alec's second momentous presentation was Pinero's *The Second Mrs Tanqueray* which followed from 27th May. This prodigious morality drama out-rivalled in publicity propensity anything previously done in the commercial theatre where Ibsen and Shaw were still taboo. As it was, without Pinero's name production would probably have been impossible. John Hare rejected it as too daring. Alec took the MS. to think over on his summer holiday in 1892 in the cottage they shared with the Graham Robertsons. Even when he did decide to produce it he intended to test public reaction at trial matinées first. Eventually full-scale presentation was determined upon.

That inevitable punishment must visit associate as well as sinner was the play's message, but this had never before been quite so demonstrated with such strongly drawn characters in situations so dramatically conceived. It tells of Aubrey Tanqueray marrying Paula, woman of many scarlet pasts; of his convent-trained daughter Ellean refusing to satisfy Paula's heart-cry for love and sympathy until too late, for when softened herself by love her lover proved to be one of Paula's past protectors! Captain Ardale implored his former mistress to keep their secret, but Paula refused to so purchase happiness for all and confessed as preliminary to ending life by making exit through her bedroom window.

Almost a year elapsed between acceptance and presentation, mainly in search of a Paula. Pinero had thought of Olga Nethersole when conceiving the part but Hare refused to release her from contract. Second choice was Janet Achurch who had been the first Nora in Ibsen's *A Doll's House* in 1889. Julia Neilson, Lily Hanbury and Winifred Emery were also considered and rejected, the last only when they heard she was

expecting a baby. Mrs Alexander and Graham Robertson were
sent on a tour of the theatres to size up possibles. First on their
list was Evelyn Millard at The Adelphi. Evelyn was to be
engaged later by Alexander and did play Paula but now, at
twenty, gentle and beautiful, she did not seem to the two
seekers to have the inner fire they sought. Practically unknown
Mrs Patrick Campbell was second-lead. She had been ill, was
working out a fortnight's notice, unhappiness and low spirits
showed in an unimpressive performance. Until she made an
exit. To quote Graham: '. . . she was thin, with great eyes and
slow haunting utterance . . . had to leave the stage laughing:
the laugh was wonderful, low and sweet, yet utterly mocking
and heartless. Florence and I both realised that there was the
ideal Paula.'

Pinero went to watch upon their advice and agreed. Mrs Pat
—as she will always be called by those who knew and loved or
hated her—was sent for and engaged. The Gatti brothers then
meanly withdrew their notice and said she must stay on to the
end of the run of their melodrama as contracted.

The *Tanqueray* cast was otherwise complete. No one could
say when Mrs Pat might be free. Alec engaged for Paula the
girl who had been his second-lead when he began at The
Avenue, the beautiful American Elizabeth Robins who in 1891
had been the first Hedda Gabler. As C. E. Raemond she was
to become more successful as writer and famous for her
journey into Alaska than as an actress, but she was important
in the latter capacity for her first dozen years in London after
initial experience in America where she had played opposite
Booth. Had it not been for Beerbohm Tree's jealous 'mixing'
she would undoubtedly have been in Alec's first St James's
company also—but that is another long story which cannot be
exploited here but may be gathered from her own *Both sides of
the Curtain*.

Then the Gatti's took off their drama and Mrs Pat was free.
Alec's invidious task was made easy by Elizabeth Robins'

magnanimity. To quote from Mrs Pat's own book: '. . . with
the most remarkable and characteristic generosity [she] surrendered the role to me: "Dear Stella, . . . I congratulate you
upon your splendid fortune in having *The Second Mrs Tanqueray* to play. From what I have read of the part it is the kind
of thing that comes along once in an actress' lifetime, seldom
oftener, and that it has come to *you* is my best consolation for
having lost it myself. . . . There is to my mind no woman so
enviable at this moment, dear savage, as *you*. Keep well and
strong. Yours affectionately always, E. R. May 2nd, 1893." '

The complete cast at last could be called, and on stage they
assembled to listen to Pinero as he read to them his play. Cyril
Maude was to be Cayley Drummle, the old friend of Aubrey,
and in his autobiography says: 'We marvelled then at Alexander
having been able to get it past the censor. We started next day
with all the proper scenery and with every prop ready.'

Maude Millett was Ellean. Amy Roselle was Mrs Cortelyon
the country neighbour who had been a friend of the first wife.
Edith Chester was the horrid Lady Orreyed, slut-parallel of
Paula, whose husband Sir George, tippling and outside the pale
because of his marriage, was played by Vane Tempest, himself
a member of the aristocracy and adept, so said scandal, at
playing himself, a vapid P. G. Wodehouse type. Ben Webster
was Captain Ardale, Nutcombe Gould was Misquith the Q.C.
and M.P., Murray Hathorn was Dr Jayne and Hollis the butler
Morse. George Alexander was of course Aubrey Tanqueray.
Walter Hann and H. P. Hall created the scenery and Willy
Clarkson the wigs.

No director's name appeared on the programme but rehearsals were mainly in the hands of the author who took
immense pains with the cast, especially with the new leading
lady. Rehearsals did not go smoothly for she was still con-
valescent and had not had much experience as an actress. The
rather frigid high-society manners of The St James's were
hardly encouraging to the emotional woman suddenly trans-

planted from the green to the rarefied atmosphere of the *haute école*. For a long time it was felt that a mistake had been made, but gradually feeling altered and her piano playing in Act III certainly made the company realise that Mrs Pat was not just a 'piece from The Adelphi'. Then one day Mrs Pinero, Myra Holmes, the actress daughter of the Cheshire Cheese proprietor, looked in to watch a rehearsal and afterwards said: 'I don't know what you are talking about. I think she's very good.'

The atmosphere changed. Suddenly everything went magnificently. On the last Thursday they ran through splendidly, on the Friday flatly—lucky omen.

On Saturday 27th May the theatre filled with its usual brilliant first-night audience. At the end of the second act, which culminated with the violent scene between Aubrey and Paula over her inviting the Orreyeds for the week-end, they burst into tremendous applause and called not only for Mrs Pat but also for Pinero. Quite correctly the author waited until the finale, but from that moment waves of enthusiastic emotion poured across the footlights to inspire the players as only just such audience reaction can do.

Cyril Maude remembered the tumult at the final curtains: 'I shall never forget it. People stood up at the end and cheered and waved their handkerchiefs—the enthusiasm was overwhelming.' A riot of wildly excited congratulating friends invaded the stage but Mrs Pat slipped quietly away and was found next morning in bed with her children when Florence Alexander arrived with the news that practically every paper was as enthusiastic as had been the audience.

Clement Scott was in America else the *Daily Telegraph* would not have been amongst the number. He returned on the *Aurania* a month later and was furious to find the favourable notice his substitute had written about a play he then decided he 'loathed and despised'. Failing to counteract the increasing success which he attacked mainly on the improbability of the characters' reactions to their situations, and goaded by other critics who objected to his own too-late carping, Scott stooped on 19th August in the *Illustrated London News* to an article headed 'A Strange Coincidence: or The Second Mrs Wife'.

Scott was driving, so he said, along St John's Wood Road and as he passed the cottage in which Pinero once had lived he was hailed by a woman from a hansom. The horses were pulled up and the critic and his old friend, whose name he had forgotten and who now lived in Germany, chatted long enough for her to tell him to get Paul Lindau's *Der Schatten* and adapt it. He searched the bookshops but they 'had apparently all been sold out'. So he got a copy from Germany and found it to be a story about an officer who took as his second wife an actress who had been previously seduced by the lover of the officer's sister. When the last two refused to part the actress drowned herself. Throughout his longish article Scott mentioned 'second Mrs Wife' nine times, Tanqueray four times, Pinero six times, coincidence thrice, Alexander thrice, Mrs Patrick Campbell twice, The St James's once. He then bemoaned his misfortune in not being able to adapt the play for fear of Pinero accusing him of plagiarism. As extra emphasis he raked up the accusations which years before had been aroused by *The Squire*.

Now Mrs Clement Scott was very much younger than her husband. She had been an actress and was a darling in old age, but when she wrote her memoirs between the wars she forgot the beginning of her husband's story and said nothing about the carriages but that the article had been prompted by a letter. Scott, of course, was too cunning an old rogue to mention a letter he might be asked to produce. His story could neither be proved nor disproved.

Pinero visited Sir George Lewis. That solicitor, who has been mentioned earlier, acted also for Clement Scott, luckily for him and his proprietors. Lewis smoothed the matter over by extracting the following letter which was published by the editor of the *Illustrated London News*:

'Sir,—I desire to state that in the article written by me, and published in your paper of Aug. 19th last, I did not intend to suggest that Mr Pinero had in any way obtained his plot from Paul Lindau's *Der Schatten*, or had ever heard of that play, and I regret that my comments should have caused Mr Pinero pain.—Yours obediently, Clement Scott.'

Scott's malice never died. Seven years later he had the impudence to reiterate his original innuendoes, safe from action, in the *New York Morning Telegraph*, using phrases such as 'but is there a ghost walking about The St James's Theatre who tells plots to destitute dramatists?'

The provincial tour was a sell-out and provoked as much controversy as in town. As the Alexanders said in an interview published in *The Sketch* for 13th December, they received 'shoals of letters, to say nothing of a sermon, endless articles, and a breezy correspondence in the *Birmingham Daily Post*'. The play was extolled in the sermon which had been preached at Liverpool by the Rev. Mr Lund who also printed his words as a pamphlet.

Earlier, in June, one of the matinées which were a feature of the period in London but which do not always warrant space here, was a strong melodrama called *Bess* by Mrs Beringer which she put on with her daughter Esmé, Geneviève Ward, Harry Esmond, Seymour Hicks and W. H. Vernon. (In the latter's Company Alec had made his début.)

1894

Tanqueray had opened the winter season and continued in all 225 times until the week ending 21st April, by which time Harry V. Esmond (Cayley Drummle), H. H. Vincent (Misquith), Bromley Davenport (Jayne), Laura Graves (Lady Orreyed), and Miss Granville (Mrs Cortelyon) were on the bill. The last named was understudy to Mrs Pat and had won favourable mention for her Paula when she took over during the winter. Ben Webster's young sister Lizzie had been Lady Orreyed and later Ellean for a while.

After a week for final rehearsals the doors reopened the following Saturday night for *The Masqueraders* by Henry Arthur Jones, main rival to Pinero. This was a melodramatic piece with Herbert Waring as wicked Sir Brice the husband of Mrs Pat as Dulcie. In a remarkable gambling scene between the former and Alec as the noble David Remon, the woman was played for and won by Remon who then found he had caught a tartar and so cleared off on a star-gazing expedition. The cast of twenty-two and many walkers-on included Irene Vanbrugh, Beryl Faber, W. G. Elliot, W. H. Day, H. V. Esmond, Vane Tempest in the best parts with Miss Granville, Mrs Edward Saker, Kinsey Peile, Ian Robertson, Arthur Royston, Ben Webster and Hollis. Frank(lin) Dyall—until the turn of the century without the euphonious first-name suffix—made his first appearance in the crowd as did Mabel Hackney. The latter subsequently took over from Beryl Faber whose brother Aubrey Smith was to join the company two years later.

The future King George and Queen Mary were in front on the first night. So too were Lord Randolph and Lady Churchill, parents of the future mighty Sir Winston.

The drama was successful. Even Scott praised it and all the company except for Mrs Pat who was slated for too dull and lifeless a performance. This time he was more justified but plot and dialogue, though heightened with bright spots, were so below the last play that she was almost justified herself in not giving her best. There was little sympathetic support from her manager for they were then at daggers drawn. Once whilst she was still Paula she had been up all night with her boy who was ill with suspected diphtheria. She arrived late to almost miss her cue and with the rush and worry her mind went blank as she made hurried entrance. Alec jumped to the wrong conclusion for as he grabbed the prompt book to pass to her she heard him mutter 'the woman's drunk!' She rallied and finished the act without further fault but her fury had been mounting and as soon as she got to her dressing-room she began to change. Maude Millett, however, rushed her a drink from The Golden Lion next door and persuaded her not to walk out. News that Beerbohm Tree was in front added weight to Maude's entreaties.

Tree arrived back-stage afterwards with the concrete congratulation of an offer of £60 a week to join him at The Haymarket. Next day she told Alec she had heard what he had mumbled, that she would honour her contract to the end of the season but that she would never speak to him off-stage again and that she was joining Tree at twice what he paid her.

Ridiculously they kept the quarrel running, the galling fact that it was Tree who had won her away, as he had tried to do with Elizabeth Robins four years earlier, not helping to soften Alec. The summer season of *The Masqueraders* was consequently not so happy for the two stars, and one night there was such a look of loathing on Alec's face just when he was saying endearing things to her that she burst out laughing! The stage manager arrived at her dressing-room after the show to say: 'Mr Alexander's compliments and will you please not laugh at him on the stage?' Her rejoinder did not make things smoother: 'My compliments to Mr Alexander and please tell him I never laugh at him until I get home!'

The twenty-eighth of July was the last night of the season and for the tour Evelyn Millard was engaged to follow Mrs Pat as Dulcie. Miss Granville was rewarded with Paula; Irene Vanbrugh was Ellean; both plays being toured. The former opened the winter on 10th November and drew until 22nd December when the doors closed for a short holiday prior to resumption of rehearsals of a play first announced twelve months before.

1895

The new play was *Guy Domville* which had been much publicised because its author was the Anglo-phile American novelist Henry James. All literary London gathered in front for this, his second play.

The curtain went up at twenty to eight on the night of Saturday 5th January for curtain-raiser *Too Happy By Half* by Julian Field, with H. V. Esmond, Arthur Royston, E. Benham and Evelyn Millard.

At twenty past it rose again on a garden scene in 1780. The set had been designed by H. P. Hall who also created the dark-panelled interior of elderly Mrs Domville's Richmond residence in Act II, and the white-panelled drawing-room of Mrs Peverel in Act III. Percy Anderson designed the costumes, which were a magnificent feature of the piece. Willy Clarkson, then thirty, created the wigs. Incidental music was composed by Walter Slaughter, still the musical director.

The action revolved around Guy Domville's determination to become a Roman Catholic priest, his subornation, and his ultimate rejection of carnal love for reawakened vocational call. In Act I Alec, as Guy in a Quakerish costume, was a puritanical Catholic tutor to the child of Mrs Peverel, a widow whom he did not realise was in love with him. Marion Terry, in grey shimmering silk adorned with black velvet ribbons, charmingly portrayed the widow who had had a half-welcome suitor in Herbert Waring as Frank Humber. W. G. Elliot played foppish old roué Lord Devenish, who arrived with the news that Guy's cousin had died and consequently Guy, as new head of the family, must renounce thoughts of priesthood in favour of marrying and subsequent fathering of lots of little Catholics instead.

In Act II Guy was a changed man, a gay spark about to marry Mary Brasier who was love-child of Devenish and Mrs Domville, the widow of the deceased cousin. Mrs Edward

Saker was that widow and Evelyn Millard was Mary Brasier
who had had to banish her lover Lieutenant George Round,
R.N. (H. V. Esmond). It was Devenish who had contrived the
proposed marriage by promising to marry Mary's mother if
she would marry Guy. The Lieutenant turned up in time to
allow Guy to back out of the marriage, whereupon Devenish
decided that Guy would have to marry Mrs Peverel. Guy then
remembered his original vocation and sidled off to be a priest
after all.

Frank(lin) Dyall was a servant, Blanche Wilmot and Lucy
Bertram (later replaced by Violet Lyster) were milliners,
Irene Vanbrugh was Fanny, Mrs Peverel's maid. Irene's delightful performance earned her especial mention by most of
the critics.

Though hailed then and later by many writers as a beautiful
and delightful work, the play uneasily holds attention and
hardly reads dramatically. Alec had committed himself long
before production, before even the writing was finished. James
had submitted three ideas from which the manager had made
his choice, but he must have had doubts during rehearsals.
Costs were certainly not stinted for all that.

Marion Terry in Act III appeared in a pale chocolate creation
in silk, gold satin-velvet and white silk muslin; Evelyn Millard
in white satin with forget-me-not blue trimmings. Mrs Saker
as widow Domville and befitting her elderliness was in an
earlier period of heavy black satin over an enormous hoop, all
striped with velvet and frilled with silken tassels, an apron of
white muslin and a bodice adorned with ruffles, frills and
velvet ribbons. Above her great curled wig was a mob-cap
crowned by a velvet hat adorned with a surround of nodding
ostrich plumes! Though only on in Act II, she had time during
it to change out of all this into a pink satin wedding gown so
trimmed with twirls, festoons and silver cords and tassels that
the fashion reporter of *The Sketch* said it was 'so fearfully and
wonderfully made that it absolutely baffles description!'

The opening act was well received, the second somewhat restively with laughter in the wrong places, the third began well but its reception deteriorated to finish to the accompaniment of loud derisive remarks. Elliot was perhaps miscast, for both G. B. Shaw and Scott said that he stressed a wrong comic note throughout. The latter suggested that Nutcombe Gould would have been far better in the part. Gould, however, was out of the company only because of failing sight. He died four years later, quite blind, when only fifty.

Poor Mrs Saker was unable to carry off her impossible costumes. Whether it was Percy Anderson's own idea to dress her in a much earlier period than the others, or whether he was inspired to do so by Henry James is to me unknown, but it was a mistake. As the gallery and pit regarded her they began to giggle. The titters increased her rather obvious embarrassment and set the tone before and behind the footlights for the rest of the night. A pointless scene between Guy and the Lieutenant, with both having to pretend to be drunker than the other, was cut after the first night. Towards the end of the last act Guy had to proclaim: 'I am the last, my lord, of the Domvilles!' A voice yelled out: 'It's a bloody good thing you are!' At the finale Guy had to make exit up-stage centre through a door. At the door he had to stop and turn around to address first Mrs Peverel and then her successful suitor Frank Humber: 'The Church takes me. Be kind to him. Be good to her. Be good to her!' The pit and gallery roared with laughter as the door closed on Alec's white unhappy face.

Mild applause allowed a couple of curtains and all would have been well if Vincent the stage manager had had his finger properly on the pulse of the audience. He had not and at cries for the author, instead of signalling 'The King' to the orchestra, he signed the curtain up again and Alec led on Henry James. Those who had queued that cold January night until the doors had opened at a quarter past seven for them to pay their half-crowns and shillings to sit on wooden benches for almost four hours felt themselves legitimately entitled to protest in the traditional manner. All undoubtedly would have been well had the curtain stayed down but the two lambs appeared, their friends applauded and the gallery and pit reacted with a ghastly outburst of boos and hisses.

At a cry of 'Speech!' James slipped out of Alec's grasp and disappeared. ''Tain't your fault Guv'nor. It's a rotten play!' was a shout as Alec stepped further forward. Alec said an apologetic word or two, there was a brief ovation, then the house dispersed.

With nothing untoward happening at subsequent performances there arose charges of anti-Americanism having inspired the disturbance, but James had been so long here and was so ultra English himself that such an allegation can be logically discounted. The critics were kinder than they might have been for all had something good to say and decried the bad reception. Clement Scott in some three thousand words said on the Monday that it was painful to see such men as Alec and James 'in the pillory', and he hoped the play would still be saved for a while for it was very beautiful despite its imperfections.

Henry James was an exceptionally sensitive person and, witness the accounts of many literary persons of the day, was much upset after the first night. Though success in the theatre was a strong ambition he never tried again to win it, even though he earned £250 this time and Alec lost that much plus five times more. When writing to his countrywoman Mary Anderson a letter of condolence at her loss of a child at birth he said how much he could feel for her, for after all had not he too just lost his first-born! She published that letter in her memoirs so must have taken it as he meant though sardonic laughter greets the story now.

The bonny girl Adrienne Dairolles had been in his *The American*. In December during rehearsals she was acting in New York, and James answered her good wishes thus from 34 De Vere Gardens on 7th December 1894. Being probably unpublished I quote in full:

SJT Q

Dear Miss Dairolles: I am much gratified at your note &
very glad to have news of you—you had so completely
vanished from our London horizon. I accept with pleasure
your good wishes for my play at the St James's—which is,
however, not to be produced till Jan. 5th. I have the
pleasantest recollection of those interesting weeks over the
American—which came to an end only too soon—& of
your accomplished performance of poor little Noemie. I
am also delighted to hear of your success in New York,
which is the city of my birth, though I haven't seen it for
years. Most truly, London is best & I congratulate you on
being homesick for our big black Babylon. Be very sure
that you have only to work, to be as clever & as patient as
you can, in order to come back here & take your place.
Pray for me on Saturday evening, Jan. 5th. & believe me
yours very truly—Henry James.

Guy Domville ran until Saturday 9th February and on the
following Thursday Oscar Wilde's final and finest play was
presented. *The Importance of Being Earnest* was written with
Hawtrey or Wyndham in mind for John Worthing, rather than
Alec who did however get the first offer. That happened from
knowledge of Wyndham's 'tightness' and Hawtrey's permanent
impecuniousness, not from any sense of loyalty on Wilde's part
to his first manager, who did not fit into his conception of
Worthing any more than into that of some of the critics when
later they saw Alec in 'a Hawtrey part'.

Although today it is difficult to conceive either of the two
playing the part with the panache of Alec, he may actually have
thought himself too old—as he erroneously did later in the case
of the Student Prince of *Old Heidelberg*. Anyway, Wyndham
apparently had the MS. at the time of the *Domville* fiasco but
relinquished his rights then to Alec. Hawtrey was to tell A. E.
Matthews and others that he could have had the play had he
had £50 when Oscar returned with it from Worthing where he

had written it in a month. Oscar had promised it to him before it was on paper as they sat at lunch in the Savoy—so he said. His annoyance at losing such a famous bargain, if he did, does not excuse the infamous dinner-party which he gave in association with the pompous snooper Charles Brookfield (rewarded with the post of Censor) to celebrate Oscar's downfall as the prison sentence began on 25th May.

The obnoxious Marquis of Queensberry had a seat for the first night, but Wilde got word from the Hon. Algernon Bourke that the madman intended to make a speech, so Shone was told to return his money with the explanation that the seat had been sold previously. The furious Marquis then bought an enormous bunch of carrots which he boasted he would present that night to the despoiler of his son Lord Alfred Douglas. The tradesman, so reported *The Sketch* on the 27th, sent warning to Alec about the 'novel bouquet' so the theatre, doubly warned, posted sufficient protectors to frustrate the Marquis. He then contented himself with giving the carrots to an attendant and accompanied by his pet bruiser, fumed about and shouted outside as the crowds went in.

George Alexander was of course John Worthing whose friend Algernon Moncrieffe was played by Allan Aynesworth. H. H. Vincent was Chasuble, Frank(lin) Dyall was the butler Merriman and Kinsey Peile the manservant Lane. Rose Leclercq played the formidable Lady Bracknell and Irene Vanbrugh was her daughter the Hon. Gwendolen. Evelyn Millard was Worthing's ward Cecily Cardew whose governess Miss Prism was played by Mrs George Canninge. The first two sets were by Hall and the other by Walter Hann; Willy Clarkson created the wigs and Mrs Alexander superintended the exquisite costuming executed by Jays of Oxford Circus.

The 'trivial comedy for serious people' is, and surely always will be, so well known that any discussion here may be dispensed with. The audience was enthusiastically delighted but the critics again more reservedly so. Bernard Shaw was quite out

of sympathy with it though 'it amused me of course'. *The
Sketch* doubted its securing 'success but for the prestige of the
theatre and name of the author, yet cannot deny that it contains many smart speeches' of which there were almost too
many. 'The quickness and alertness' of Alec's 'really comic
acting gave a valuable lesson to the others' whose style was not
sufficiently crisp and light, except for Rose Leclercq who was
ideal.

The unhappy climax to Queensberry's vendetta has also
been so exhaustively explored that I need only say that the
whole tragedy could have been avoided had Oscar's maso-
chistic Hibernian pig-headedness not kept him sitting waiting
all those hours of grace he was given by Fate through the
apparently purposefully slow-acting servants of the State on
5th April, when his stupid libel action against the Marquis
failed.

Feeling against Wilde ran so high during the trials that Alec
removed Wilde's name from the bills in a more or less vain
attempt to save the faces of the public. That was a sensible
thing to do though people have said stupidly harsh things about
him for doing so. Wilde then needed as much money as he
could get. On 8th May the play was withdrawn for by that time
the running expenses were not being covered.

On Saturday 11th May the house reopened for Henry
Arthur Jones's *The Triumph of the Philistines and how Mr Jorgan
preserved the Morals of Market Pewbury under very Trying
Circumstances*. This topically titled comedy would have gone
better as a farce and though not a satire upon the fall of his
friend, the guide he wrote for the make-up for Jorgan fairly
aptly aped the mad Marquis, who was also vaguely symphonic-
ised in the sub-title.

The play was strong, but not one of Jones's best. It was about
French tart Sally Lebrune (Juliette Nesville), the model for a
nude painting which shocked seven sanctimonious small-town
shopkeepers led by Jorgan (Herbert Waring), who evict Alma

(Elliott Page) from her art school to found an orphanage there instead. By so doing they throw Alma into the arms of their arch-enemy the wealthy young squire Sir Valentine (Alec). Lady Monckton played the other local aristocrat, Lady Beauboys, and H. V. Esmond was the artist who had painted the nude. Mark Paton was the butler Wheeler and the Jorgan supporters Pote, Blagg, Modlin, Skewett, Wapes, Corby were played by E. M. Robson, Ernest Hendrie, Arthur Royston, James Welch, H. H. Vincent and Duncan Tovey. Master Frank Saker was butcher-boy Thomas Blagg who was sent home to remove his trousers and await the cane for giggling at the painting. Blanche Wilmot completed the cast as ultra-religious Angela Soar. The three acts were set in one studio scene designed by William Morris & Co. and executed by H. P. Hall.

The comedy was booed but kept on for a month, when it was followed by revivals of *Tanqueray* with Evelyn Millard as Paula, and of *The Idler* from 4th July.

For a fortnight from 10th September, whilst the company were on tour, Elliot backed H. V. Esmond's *Bogey* in which they both played, with Eva Moore and others. The author acted a nice old gentleman whose body during a seance was taken possession of by the spirit of a crook whose thirst for whisky and desire to conclude unfinished diamond-mine schemes had kept him earth-bound. Clement Scott was not too kind about it but the gallery thought it amusing and exciting enough so they booed the critic for ten minutes when he next appeared (at The Strand).

In the autumn the Queen as usual was at Balmoral, her favourite residence. When Alec was playing Glasgow the Royal Command was received to travel north to perform *Liberty Hall* before her. Kinsey Peile tells delightful stories of them all on the way to and at the castle in his *Candied Peel*—especially about embarrassed E. M. Robson's quaint behaviour and the Queen's gracious and charming reception of him, even to the extent of laughingly calling him back when he scuttled too quickly out of sight after presentation, since she especially wanted to compliment him for his acting as the dear old bookseller Todman. She told him, too, that she still remembered with pleasure his famous uncle 'Little' Robson who had died so young thirty years before.

The only actors in the roles they originally created were Alec and Vincent. The elder sister Blanche was now played by Evelyn Millard and the younger Amy by Teresa Furtado Clarke whose father had been in the Seymour/Reade season. The others were Allan Aynesworth, Arthur Royston, Frank(lin) Dyall, Kinsey Peile, Master Jones, Winifred Dolan and, as Crafer, Miss Mouillot. (The pompous manager and actor Peile mentions were Shone and Vane-Tempest, the latter not on this tour.)

Souvenirs of the Queen's pleasure were later sent to all. Alec's silver cigar-box was engraved 'From V.R. George Alexander, Esq., Balmoral. Sept. 16. 1895.' For Florence there was a gold perfume bottle, set with diamonds. Aynesworth also received a silver cigar-box and the girls and men diamond tie-pins and brooches. Robson's was especially royal with emeralds and sapphires as well and young Dyall, who too had impressed Her Majesty, received a silver cigarette-box to the chagrin of the other juniors. That box is, as I write, a treasured possession of Mary Merrall, step-mother of Valentine Dyall who was a young stalwart of the London stage in the thirties until suborned by radio because of his remarkably evocative voice.

During the holidays before the winter reopening Alec had a most upsetting experience. They lived then at 57 Pont Street not far from the Scots Church. The impeccable Alec strolled out after dinner towards Cadogan Place intending there to call on a barrister friend, Alexander Wedderburn. 'An obviously poor, miserable, starved and half-clad woman' (Alec's words) accosted him on the way and then, dissatisfied with the half-crown given, kept up with him, asking for more. Alec's momentary relief turned to horrified amazement when policeman 284 B

Wilson appeared, for instead of chasing off the hag he arrested them both, saying, somewhat less delicately, that he had caught them in *flagrante delicto*! Protestations that his wife was in the house yonder and could verify he had just left her were ignored. The journey to Chelsea police station had to be made and a charge laid.

The Westminster magistrate, one de Rutzen, later proved himself to be as questionable a person as one could hope *not* to find amongst responsible public servants. However when Alec's Counsel Mr Dutton proved discrepancies between the evidence of the policeman and Station Inspector Burden, and after Pinero and others had testified, de Rutzen realised he would not be able to convict as he had shown throughout the case he intended to do. He gave in with impudent bad grace by saying that although the policeman had given his evidence 'in the most satisfactory manner' he would give the defendant the 'benefit of the doubt'. The policeman, it may be emphasised, had then just been proved by his own superior to have committed perjury!

The woman herself had earlier pled guilty, but as to that the responsible society weekly *The Sketch* had this to say:

Everybody familiar with the London streets knows that the word of an unfortunate creature, who is absolutely dependant upon the tolerance of the police, is utterly worthless. She simply dare not contradict a constable who is discharging what he is pleased to call his duty by making an accusation which, on the face of it, is too idiotic for belief. The magistrates are not yet alive to the fact that the public is getting restive under this constant assumption that a policeman *qua* policeman is a model of righteous discernment. In a case like Mr Alexander's, a man, however blameless, is at the mercy of a constable who may chance to be a fool or more zealous for promotion than for justice.

Procedure did not then allow defendants to give evidence on oath. Consequently Alec sent out a signed statement, giving a picture of the whole affair, which was published in most papers. De Rutzen was still going strong fifteen years later when at Bow Street, for instance, he ordered the destruction of 272 volumes of Balzac which had been seized by the police from a shop in Charing Cross Road, which the magistrate considered a 'foul and filthy black spot!' I had intended to discuss a number of other peculiar contemporary incidents to prove that this affair of Alec's was no isolated attempt to pervert justice by police and magistrates, but I must postpone doing so until another time.

The winter season opened on 7th November with *Liberty Hall* and the cast who had appeared at Balmoral. The ovation which greeted Alec on his entry amply indicated that public as well as Press were on his side. H. V. Esmond's *The Divided Way* and Godfrey's one-act *The Misogynist* replaced the revival but three weeks was the limit of attraction for these, so well before Christmas the theatre closed for holidays and rehearsals. Newcomers had been Ellis Jeffreys and W. H. Vernon.

1896

Anthony Hope's Ruritanian romance *The Prisoner of Zenda* had proved a best-seller when published in 1894. Edward Rose dramatised it but no London manager showed interest, probably because its prologue, four acts and large cast meant expense great even for those days. Edward Sothern, however, put it on with success in New York and Alec, suddenly in need, bought the English rights and presented it on 7th January. It ran 254 times.

Casting himself as Rudolph the Red Elphberg and doubling young Rassendyll, he made Evelyn Millard the Princess Flavia and Herbert Waring the Black Elphberg. C. Aubrey Smith and Julia Neilson later took over the last two parts. Colonel

Sapt was played by Alec's old manager Vernon, and Fritz by Arthur Royston. Mabel Hackney was the Countess in the prologue, Lily Hanbury was Mme de Mauban and Olga Brandon was Frau Teppich. Octogenarian Henry Loraine was Marshal Strakencz while his son Robert made his début as retainer Toni. Laurence Cautley played Captain Hentzau, W. H. Day being Detchard the other follower of Black Michael. Aynesworth was the young English artist Bertram, Dyall was Josef. Other named parts were played by Charles Glenney, Vincent Sternroyd, Henry Boyce, F. Featherstone, F. Lomnitz, George Hawtrey, George Bancroft making his début as Lord Topham, and I. Dawson. The stage was filled with a large crowd of courtiers, ambassadors, soldiers and others. All were magnificently costumed by Nathans and Savage & Purdue and bewigged by Clarkson. The sets were by Hall, Hann and W. Telbin. Slaughter composed the incidental music, the orchestra was augmented by Steadman's Choir.

The prologue could have been cut or even dispensed with since it was only to explain the likeness between the Red Rudolf and Rassendyll the Englishman who successfully took his place and defeated the wily cousin who drugged and captured the king just before the coronation. However, the audience were so delighted with everything that the company were rewarded with three or four curtain calls after every act and cheers greeted them and the author at the end.

The talented and beautiful American Fay Davis joined the company when they returned after touring to play Lily Hanbury's part and H. B. Irving then took over from Cautley. Others were Ellis Jeffreys, Kate Darvill, A. W. Munro and Richard Dalton. The theatre was lent for several Benefits in the summer. Alec this year had another company at the Dean Street Royalty in the autumn and a second company touring *Zenda*. Once Yorke Stephens and Gerald Godfrey took over from Alec and Glenney when the latter were wanted to entertain the Prince and Princess of Wales at Lord Londonderry's.

As You Like It was planned as winter attraction, so on Wednesday 2nd December Alec's first Shakespearian play was offered in five acts with eleven scenes, in seven sets variously by T. E. Ryan, Hall and Hann. The costumes were designed by Graham Robertson, and old Leon Espinosa, who was under contract to Sir Henry Irving, was engaged to devise a Masque of Hymen to music commissioned from Edward German.

Julia Neilson made a delightfully strong Rosalind, balanced beautifully by Fay Davis's Celia and Alec's virile yet charming Orlando. The other major roles were as well received. James Fernandez was the Duke and Aubrey Smith the Usurper; Bertram Wallis and W. H. Vernon were Amiens and Jaques; H. B. Irving was Oliver and Dorothea Baird was Phoebe. The last two had recently married; she was fresh from her great success as Trilby to Tree's Svengali. Kate Phillips was Audrey, H. V. Esmond was Touchstone and another American girl, Julie Opp, was Hymen and understudied Rosalind. The latter's husband-to-be Robert Loraine, as well as his father Henry, was also in it. Ellis Jeffreys later took over as Phoebe.

Four-year-old Phyllis Neilson-Terry unofficially joined for the first night for when her mother began the Cuckoo Song (traditionally introduced from *Love's Labour's Lost*) the child in a box joined in, and the louder Julia sang to drown the treble the more shrilly did the girl so they finished as a duet to the delight of the audience!

1897

The comedy ran 114 times to 20th March. There was a copyright matinée of Stoddart's *Tess of the d'Urbervilles* on the 2nd.

J. M. Barrie and Anthony Hope were in front on the 29th when a somewhat satirical sentimental comedy by Pinero called *The Princess and the Butterfly* was presented. The pressmen were not entirely friendly afterwards, perhaps because they had been kept from before eight until nearly midnight, though they had had four intervals amounting to almost fifty minutes to get most of their copy ready for the morning papers!

Julia Neilson as Princess Pannonia and Alec as Sir George Lamorant played middle-aged bewailers of lost youth who almost made a platonic marriage but declared a month's truce for one last fling, during which H. B. Irving's young passion as Edward Oriel rejuvenated the Princess, and Alec was captured by Fay Davis as Parisian gutter-snipe Fay Zuliani. There were five acts and as many scenes which were done by Hall, Hann and Telbin. No credit was given to designer of costumes which meant that Florence must have suggested and chosen these. When Julia wrote her memoirs forty years later she was to remember one of hers as the most beautiful she ever had to wear in a theatre: 'Very décolleté, in black satin with a two-yard train sparkling with thousands of black and silver sequins.'

Alec was as brilliant on the first night only. In Act 5 he made a reappearance in a change of suit which in Julia's memory was 'blood red and brick'. The audience didn't miss its cue for laughter when the Princess greeted him: 'Oh Sir George, you *are* looking better—more colour!'

As well as the four principals the cast of twenty-nine included Rose Leclercq, Mrs Cecil Raleigh, Julie Opp, Mabel Hackney, Miss Granville, H. V. Esmond, C. Aubrey Smith, George Bancroft and Robert Soutar.

Julia Neilson's husband Fred Terry joined for *The Tree of Knowledge* by R. C. Carton which opened the winter season on 25th October. The cast of eleven comprised, besides them and Alec, H. B. Irving and Carlotta Addison who had made her début when Irving's father Sir Henry had been here too in 1866. Another recruit was George Shelton who also had made his London début here long before. The others were Fay Davis, Winifred Dolan, H. V. Esmond, W. H. Vernon and H. Ives.

Julia played adventuress Belle who on the arm of her bridegroom Brian (Terry) met his old friend Nigel (Alec) who was a cast-off lover of hers. Nigel later failed to stop her running

off with wealthy villain Loftus Roupell (Irving) when she dis-
covered Brian was poor. Harry Esmond was pig-loving Major
Blencoe and further comic support was furnished by Miss
Dolan as bonny bucolic maidservant Deborah Sweadle with
Shelton as her poacher father.

Miss Addison was Nigel's mother, Mrs Stanyon, whose
adopted daughter Monica was played by Fay. Vernon was
Brian's father and Ives the latter's butler. The play was all
right as a popular piece and touched 116 performances. Dennis
Eadie starred in *The Idler* at a November matinée in aid of the
Walsham How Home for Training Lost and Wayward Girls,
for which Alec lent the theatre free as he did for any cause
with which he was in accord.

1898

Much Ado About Nothing followed for a month from 16th
February with Alec as a sometimes boisterous but generally
gentle and charming Benedict. Julia Neilson was Beatrice and
Fred Terry Don Pedro whose brother Don John the villain
was H. B. Irving. Hero was played by Fay Davis and for the
relatively static part of the Friar Alec kindly remembered the
now almost blind Nutcombe Gould. With Edward German
composing the overture and incidental music and Espinosa
again arranging the dances they made a delightful show and
were fairly well received.

They opened, perhaps just for luck, as a Wednesday matinée.
The costumes, which were quite magnificent in the Irving
tradition, were designed by Mr Karl and made by Nathans and
Mrs Evans. All the sets were designed by Arthur Melville and
Graham Robertson and painted by Ryan, Hall and Hann—except for the church scene of Act IV which was designed and
painted by Telbin, who was such an individualist that he
would not let anyone know even what his main colour scheme
was. The rest knew him well enough, however, to be sure it

would be rich red browns, which it was, so nothing clashed as it otherwise might have done.

Paul Potter (adapter of *Trilby*) had had his *The Conquerors* produced in New York in January but Alec's April presentation was not any better received and aroused as much controversy. It was about the occupation after the Franco-Prussian war and showed the Hun as his natural boorish self whilst in the ascendant, until the worst of them was softened by French charm.

Alec played Eric von Rodeck, a Uhlan billeted on Yvonne de Grandpré (Julia Neilson) who threw a glass of wine into his face when she entered to protest at noise and heard him declaring that everything in France, including the women, were rightful spoils of the German conquerors. Intent on ravishing her, he caught her alone later and chased her around a room until she fell on a chair and fainted, after declaring she could fight no more. The Hun then relented and left! An evil Frenchman was then about to take her but the Hun returned to fight and kill the second unsuccessful ravisher. As he fell Yvonne revived and decided that the Frenchman had died protecting her. In a later act Yvonne knifed Eric in the back. Then she learned the truth and fell in love with him and the curtain fell after they had promised to marry when he returned from a dangerous mission.

H. B. Irving was villain Bobeche Baudin. There was a large cast and crowd and numerous incidents involving others than the three mentioned. Constance Collier played Jeanne the wife of the French villain. She had intended to be the executioner of Eric and it was her knife Yvonne had grabbed to attempt to do the deed instead. The play folded after six weeks.

The young American novelist, Mrs Pearl Craigie, as 'John Oliver Hobbes', gave Alec a more pleasant role when he took the title part of her *The Ambassador* on 2nd June. Violet Vanbrugh appeared in it as Lady Beauvedere and Mary Jerrold made her first regular appearance on the stage though her actual début had been here at one of the charity matinées of

1896. There was nothing deep about the play, which Alec had originally intended only to try out as a matinée, but it was witty in a female Wildean way and served to the end of the season and for a long tour.

The Kendals returned to their old theatre for a successful run from 22nd September of a new comedy by Ernest Hendrie and Metcalf Wood called *The Elder Miss Blossom*. Madge played the title-role, that of an aunt who answered love letters from explorer Andrew Quick (W. H. Kendal) written to her from the wilds in mistake for her niece. He had purloined her handkerchief at a dance in London, not knowing it had just been borrowed from the aunt whose name was embroidered upon it.

The play was so delightfully written, and acted, especially with such beautiful charm by Madge Kendal, that the happy ending of the explorer's return and his initial bewilderment at his peculiar reception by aunt and niece appeared natural and entirely right. Nellie Campbell played the niece quite captivatingly. The others were Charles Groves, Frank Fenton, Rudge Harding, Rodney Edgecumbe, Percy Ames, G. P. Polson, Mrs Sennett and Mrs Tapping. Fifty years afterwards Harold Hobson recorded that his predecessor James Agate told him that Madge's performance in this role was the one of all others that he would choose not to have missed. In *Playgoer's Pilgrimage* A. E. Wilson records Agate making a similar remark to him.

The sub-season gave, after their tour, a winter break during which the Alexanders were on the Riviera. Oscar Wilde, eighteen months out of gaol, was there too, and Frank Harris tells (*The Life*, p. 341) how Oscar bemoaned that Alec turned his face away as he cycled past him sitting by the roadside. Now *The Letters* prove Frank to have been away for about a month from the end of December, so he heard the tale only after Oscar had had time to amplify and fabricate as was his habit. Frank was writing many years later and was prone to do the same thing anyway. Oscar, however, is convicted by his own letter to Robbie Ross (*The Letters*, p. 772) of 27th December 1898 when he says: 'Yesterday I was by the sea and suddenly George Alexander appeared on a bicycle. He gave me a crooked smile and hurried on without stopping.' Oscar was writing regularly to Ross so the incident is certain to have happened then and like that.

Alec's merely smiling and hurrying on cannot be held against him, for embarrassment would be a natural reaction at such *sudden* first sight of Oscar who after all had been imprisoned for offences quite repugnant to almost everyone. All the same Alec was later to express shame for being so brief and, as *The Letters* and A. E. W. Mason's book prove, he more than amply made up in money and visits any earlier slight.

1899

Alec reopened in the new year with *The Ambassador* and on 28th February added a one-act by Mrs Craigie called *A Repentance*. The overture and incidental music were conducted by their composer, Sir Hubert Parry, on the first night. It was a period piece about the Carlist Spanish rebellion and though praised for set and costumes proved too difficult for most to follow. One critic said, 'The one bright star of the play was Miss Julie Opp. . . .' She, incidentally, was playing with a gash in her forehead which she had sustained the previous afternoon against a door in the British Museum where she had been talking costumes with the famous dilettante Sir Sidney Colvin.

Edward Rose's costume drama of the Wars of the Roses, *In Days of Old*, followed at Easter. About a family of opportunists and double-dealers, it also proved difficult to follow and lasted sixty-one performances. In the cast were Esmé Beringer, Sydney Brough and Hartley Manners. When the doors closed on 23rd June the builders took over to begin extensive alterations which had been planned for some time.

CHAPTER 2

THE DAYS OF GEORGE ALEXANDER

PART 2: 1900-1918

ACQUIRED adjoining houses allowed many additions. The roof was raised, seats added and removed, offices added, stage extended to about 60 ft and raked, orchestra pit dropped, stalls lowered, a more pronounced rake made to give better aspect. A new entrance was made to the royal box on the left side and except for its counterpart all other boxes vanished. Percy Macquoid designed the decorations to a scheme of red, gold and green. Jackson and Walker were the architects. 'Ruritania' was chosen as a telegraphic address, perpetuating for some eighteen years the successful *Prisoner of Zenda*.

Pinero, in a long letter, refused to work with Alec again because he wanted his own way too much. So Alec passed the honour to Anthony Hope, who dramatised his own sequel to *Zenda* and that, as *Rupert of Hentzau*, on the first of February opened the playhouse rebuilt for the new century.

Great Canadian soprano Madame Albani sang the National Anthem in front of the curtain. Walter Slaughter conducted as he had at Alec's inaugural, though since the winter of '97 William Robins had been musical director. The cast was strong and large but the play much too melodramatic. Even so it might have given more satisfaction and run longer had it not closed to a mournful dirge-accompanied royal lying-in-state, the more upsetting since the Boer War was in progress.

Alec doubled the Ruritanian king with Rudolph Rassendyll,

Left
Brandon
Thomas

Right
John Hare

ud Tree

Julia
Neilson

Left
Irene Vanbrugh

Right
Fay Davis

17

Mrs Canninge and Alexander
in *The Importance of being Earnest*

E. M. Robson and Maude Millett
in *Liberty Hall*

W. G. Eliott and Mrs Saker
in *Guy Domville*

Evelyn Millard and Henry Ainley
in *Paolo and Francesca*

Charlotte Granville and Alexander
in *The Masqueraders*

The Kendals

Elizabeth Robins and Alexander in
Paolo and Francesca

Forbes-Robertson and Kate Rorke

19

Gerald du Maurier

H. V. Esmond

Herbert Waring

H. B. Irving

Franklin Dyall

George Barrett

Left
Florence Alexander

Right
Dorothea Baird
(Mrs H. B. Irving)
and Laurence
Irving (the 2nd)

Moira Lister

Gilbert Miller

Marie Lohr
and
adge Titheradge

A. E. Matthews and
Iugh McDermott in
r *the Grace of God*

Gladys Cooper

Left
Vivien Leigh
as Cleopatra

Right
Margaret
Leighton

Gwen
Cherrell

Mar
Hal

Left
Emlyn Williams
and
Barbara Couper in
The Wind of Heaven

Right
Henry Oscar

Donald Wolfit as Volpone

Angela Baddeley

Mary Morris

Nicholas Hannen, Kay Hammond, Charles Victor
and John Clements in *Pygmalion*

Reparation
Henry Ainley in the cen
Meggie Albanesi on th

Curtain Call for *Worse Things Happen At Sea*
Harry Andrews, Ena Burrill, Frank Lawton, Yvonne Arnaud,
Athole Stewart, Eileen Peel, Robert Flemyng

24

and Vernon again played the veteran Colonel Sapt. Fay Davis made a scarcely strong enough Flavia, Esmé Beringer was Helga and Julie Opp was Rosa Holf. Harry Irving played to the hilt the villainous Rupert. Harry Esmond was Fritz. Others were Kate Sargeantson, Mrs Maesmore Morris, Henrietta Leverett, George Hawtrey, Sydney Brough, Bassett Roe, Hartley Manners, Bonnin, Lawford, Fairclough, Hamilton, Leverett, Brown, Goddard and many extras.

The drama was in four acts and seven scenes but no credits were given to any designers. *Zenda* was run at twice-weekly matinées with Dennis Eadie and most of those in the sequel.

Alec had hoped to recruit as well as H. B. Irving the other son of his old chief, but his letter to Laurence suggesting this, having heard he was thinking of joining The Princess's, '... if you care to come to me, you would have to trust to my judgement as to whether it was suited to you. I am not often wrong in my casting...' did not bear fruit, for Laurence had other plans and in March appeared at The Adelphi instead, in his own *Bonnie Dundee*.

Walter Frith's *The Man of Forty* followed at the end of March to run 105 times to the end of the season. Alec played self-made millionaire M.P. and widower Fanshawe. H. B. Irving was again villain: no-account actor Lewis Dunster with more than one alias as well as being brother to the hero's secretary Roger, which part Irving doubled. Fanshawe's daughter Elsie (Fay Davis) had been made love to by Dunster on board ship from Cape Town. Julie Opp was Mrs Egerton, Dunster's grass widow, but she was kept in luxury by Fanshawe as both waited and hoped that the black but weak-hearted Dunster would die. At the end the two men fought and the heart did give out! The rest of the cast were Esmé Beringer, Carlotta Addison, Charlotte Granville, Mrs Maesmore Morris and C. Aubrey Smith, Dennis Eadie, Alfred Bonnin, R. E. Goddard. Their acting in many melodramatic scenes gave the play the run it otherwise hardly deserved.

SJT R

Sydney Grundy's *A Debt of Honour* opened the eleventh season on 1st September. In this Alec was selfish barrister Carlyon who rejected his loving, unselfish, ex-chorus girl

Alec's Letter to his Old Chief's Son

mistress Gipsy Floyd (Fay Davis) as soon as a seat in Parliament was offered by Holroyd (Vernon). The latter was an evil M.P. with pretty daughter Isabel (Julie Opp) to whom Carlyon was then married. Busybody Antrobus (Esmond) introduced the young wife to Gipsy (who had become a drug addict) just before she drank from a fatal phial. Isabel afterwards told her husband she would continue with him in name only as his wife but if he behaved himself in future then she would return to the conjugal bed.

It was Grundy's fortieth play but his characters were still too black or too white. The other villain was the Rev. Absalom Baxter who came to town to win money at billiards, and with viands and booze to make up for forced abstemious behaviour among his northern parishioners who thought him a tee-total and righteous vegetarian. All the politicians were Liberals and double-dealing contemptibles. Alec's political sentiments must have dimmed his perception. Marguerite Aubert, Lily Grundy, Marsh Allen, Manners and Goddard completed the cast.

More serious than the vulgarity was the charge of plagiarism which again was raised. A year before, Lady Randolph Churchill's *Anglo-Saxon Review* had published Mrs Clifford's play *The Likeness of the Night*. The Kendals had bought, rehearsed and booked it to open in October 1900 at Liverpool. No lawsuit resulted but comment in the papers was fairly prolific. In both plays the husband was a barrister before whom an ice-barrier was erected by his remaining woman, for in the one the ex-mistress commits suicide by poison and in the other the wife does so by drowning.

Grundy's effort earned a quota of groans and hisses and after a month was replaced by Pearl Craigie's *Wisdom of the Wise* which had been tried out the previous January in her homeland. It was preceded by *The Plot of the Story* by Mrs Beringer in which her daughter Esmé, H. B. Irving, Arthur Elwood and George Hawtrey put the early comers into a happy mood which was not to survive.

The main play was fairly well drawn with brightly acted characters, but it was plotless with many missed dramatic opportunities about a Duchess whose friends fail to upset her recent marriage. Margaret Halstan and A. E. Matthews were newcomers to the company, but the groans and boos which began when Alec led forth Mrs Craigie were not against the acting.

Alec was goaded this time to step forward to say 'I thank that portion of the audience which has shown appreciation of this play. As for the party of gentlemen who occupy a portion of the gallery on first nights, I can only say as an actor, as a manager, that as there is no rose without a thorn, so there seems to be no first-night without a boo.' Groans greeted his remarks but the house was preparing to leave as he spoke and no further demonstration occurred.

Scott castigated him for his speech but the resulting publicity, with his regulars and the novelist's admirers, kept the piece running for fifty-four performances.

1901

Queen Victoria died on 22nd January. All theatres closed and did not reopen until after the funeral on 4th February.

On the 6th Haddon Chambers entered the lists again with his *The Awakening*, a sort of comedy of modern manners presenting Alec as a marriageable bachelor together with A. E. Matthews, H. B. Irving, Vincent, Goddard and the Misses Granville, Kemmis, Talbot, Opp, Fay Davis and Gertrude Kingston. The latter sailed for South Africa, when the play folded after sixty performances, where she won mention as a nurse in the dispatches of Lord Roberts. Telbin did the garden and cottage interior for the middle acts; Hann the bachelor quarters of Acts I and IV from Percy Macquoid's designs. According to some of the critics it was almost 'killed by kissing', for Alec was chased and kissed by married, single, sophisticated and innocent in and out of turn!

The Wilderness followed from 11th April into July. This was a sentimental comedy by Harry Esmond, who did not take part though his wife Eva Moore was in it as Mabel, a flirtatious girl in love with love. Graham Browne, Aubrey Smith, Vincent,

Lennox Pawle and Edward Arthur supported Alec, with the Misses le Thiere, Roland, E. Saker, Talbot, Opp and Henrietta Cowen. A number of girls were named in the crowd and two children had relatively important parts. These were Phyllis Dare and Vyvian Thomas who owed their luck to having been with Eva Moore in Hans Andersen's *Ib and Little Cristina* the previous summer.

Phyllis tells the story, in her first book, of how she was waiting near the wings on the first night when Alec approached, stooped to pat her shoulder and said:

'Now little lady, you must not look so worried, for there's nothing for you to be nervous about.'

'But aren't you nervous?' asked Phyllis.

Alec smiled. 'Well, now I come to think of it, perhaps I am —just a little.'

'Then you mustn't be, for you've got nothing to be nervous about for I know the piece will be a success', said the long-haired eleven-year-old.

'Thank you, little woman, you've done me a lot of good!' murmured Alec as he picked her up and kissed her before slipping off to make his entrance.

Before the end of the run Cosmo Hamilton's one-act *Old Crimea* was added to the bill. Lilian Braithwaite made the first of many appearances in it.

The Kendals again took over for a sub-season from 16th September to the end of the year. At first they revived *The Elder Miss Blossom*. From 28th October they quite successfully presented *The Likeness of the Night* which had been the subject of contention with Grundy. They had already given it in London at The Fulham, counted then as a touring date as were many other theatres just outside the actual centre.

1902

Alec had meanwhile been touring the provinces with *The Idler* and Florence Warden's one-act *A Patched-up Affair* (matinée tried out here in May 1900) and, for the first time since the scandal, *The Importance of Being Earnest*. Oscar had been dead for a year but audience reaction was so problematical that Alec attributed the play to 'the author of *Lady Windermere's Fan*' and tested Londoners at the Bayswater Coronet for a week from 2nd December. Applause and no disturbance warranted St James's presentation, with the last-named curtain-raiser, from 7th January.

Only Alec had been in the original. Graham Browne played Algernon and Lyall Swete was Chasuble; Miss Talbot played Lady Bracknell and Bessie Page the old governess Miss Prism which on the tour had been acted by Mrs T. Laverton. Mabel Dubois, who was a regular member of the minor support, had played Gwendolen on tour. Margaret Halstan took that over in town. Lilian Braithwaite was Cecily and Dansey and Goddard the 'man' Lane and butler Merriman. Nothing sparkled quite as in 1895 but they proved that the merit of the farce was stronger than any hysterical emotion aroused by thought of the author. It ran fifty-five times with the help of matinées of *Liberty Hall* on Wednesdays and Saturdays and itself on Thursdays.

In the winter of 1899 John Lane had published *Paolo and Francesca* by Stephen Phillips, poet and Benson actor. Alec had commissioned the play and would have opened the century with it had casting difficulties not proved insurmountable. Now on 7th March it was at last ready. It was based on the thirteenth-century tragedy recounted in *The Inferno* by Dante who himself had known the real Francesca. Thirty-odd years after her death he still had felt the appeal of her charm and lovely personality, and because of that was not as objective as others, since accounts of the episode do differ. The lovers, however, were apparently affected by the story of the English parallel of Launcelot and Guinevere and this theme Phillips introduced into his drama.

Offsetting the young illicit lovers Paolo and Francesca, Phillips made Paolo's elder brother, her husband Giovanni Malatesta, fierce, deformed, a savage soldier; and their cousin Lucretia, mistress of the fortress home, widowed, barren and bitter. There too dwelt Angela, Giovanni's pensioned foster-mother, an ancient hag, blind and toothless, but a seer. Pulci, village apothecary of Rimini, and his daughter Tessa with various retainers completed the main character list which numbered forty-one plus chorus.

Title-role casting had proved difficult. Eventually Evelyn Millard was chosen for Francesca and Henry Ainley for Paolo. The latter was in his first professional engagement under Frank Benson whose company was playing to the south of London when Alec went down to watch Ainley in harness. A couple of years earlier the young actor, as a part-time super, had been in *The Masqueraders* at Leeds when Alec had advised him to join such a company as Benson's if he could surmount his father's displeasure at such a disreputable project. Since then he had made his town début under Benson at The Lyceum in 1900.

Stephen Phillips was a protégé of Sidney Colvin who went to immense trouble to advise Alec and everybody else about who, how, in what and with what; even to the extent of sending —according to Mason—Telbin and stage manager Reynolds to study for sets in Italy! However well meaning, he must have been an infernal nuisance.

The play was in four acts of seven scenes and hardly bears strict analysis. Briefly, it told of Paolo sent as proxy to bring the innocent Francesca to be bride of fierce Giovanni Malatesta, Tyrant of Rimini, who could not spare the time from wars to collect her for himself. Unwillingly the youngsters fell in love and though Paolo left to join his soldiers in attempt to put her from his mind, he found that that he could not do and so decided to purchase poison and then to see her once again for the final time.

Taking the fourteenth century as more theatrically suitable, Percy Macquoid designed the costumes and properties and Telbin the sets. The scenes were set in the hall of the castle of Rimini, a wayside inn, the drug-seller's shop, a lane outside the castle, an arbour in the gardens and a chamber within.

Incidental music was planned to be heard almost throughout the action and so was composed with particular care by Percy Pitt. For each chief character he created a theme which, recurring appropriately, was interrupted or followed by his themes of Fate and Doom. This was an amplification of the old melodrama custom which folk like Alec and Mrs Kendal, for example, never discouraged for they realised its value, when not abused, as do film-makers of the present.

Evelyn Millard and Henry Ainley were well matched in beauty of face and voice but they unfortunately had not the experience behind them to bring out the power and strength essential to make their love scenes pulsate. As Arthur Symons said afterwards in the *Star*, they seemed early Victorians instead of medieval Italians. Ada Ferrar was cast as the old blind Angela and she too had not the power to make credible the ancient doom-foretelling witch. Elizabeth Robins returned to her first London manager to play the melodramatic Lucretia, and though her beauty could hardly be hidden she played the harsh mistress of the dark domain with intelligence and remarkably movingly in the last scene when, too late, she tried to circumvent her jealous cousin Giovanni. Margaret Halstan was cast as Tessa the drug-seller's daughter and H. R. Hignett made his London début as her father Pulci. Lilian Braithwaite was Francesca's maid Nita and Beatrix de Burgh her kinswoman Costanza.

Carlo, servant to Giovanni, was played by Arthur Machen who too came from Frank Benson. Deserting acting for writing, he was to earn fame for his *The Great God Pan* and many strange works. He it was who, as a journalist, invented the curious story of the Angels of Mons which wishful thinking magnified to legend. Italia Conti, the founder of the famous school, played peasant girl Mirra whilst her sister, as well as Jean S. Mackinlay who married Harcourt Williams, May Saker and Mabel Dubois were others in the singing chorus.

Alec gave a notable performance which surprised all who only knew his work of the previous decade. Though scandal said he grew more and more like Irving's Richard III as the run progressed, the majestic tragic part was tremendously played with a strength and emotion Othello-like in its depth. Only Elizabeth Robins who, through Ibsen, had developed unsuspected power, rose to the majesty of his portrayal and heightened too much perhaps the Burne-Jones softness of the younger lovers.

The mood of doom was proclaimed in the opening when through a sun-bright doorway Paolo led Francesca into the gloomy sword-hung hall where Giovanni waited to greet his child-bride, token of peace between two warring tribes which was to make him, the victor, sheath his sword. Lucretia, displaying a more than cousinly feeling for Giovanni, at first resented the newcomer and warned the tyrant that 'Youth goes toward Youth!' Later she repented the seeds of suspicion she had helped to plant and would have saved the lovers had Giovanni not found them first and stabbed them both with one single blow. The lovers had had two major scenes, soldiers had had one outside an inn as they waited for Paolo; and Tessa served to indicate Pulci's trade when she sold love philtres to villagers prior to the arrival of Paolo desiring suicide poison—overheard by Giovanni who went there for a potion to make Francesca love him. Postponement of suicide for one farewell love-scene gave opportunity for fulfilment of the tragedy.

"'Tis not my blood!' the Tyrant coldly said when Lucretia pointed finger at his hand. Then he called for lights, and more lights, and then a priest to marry the dead lovers on their bier before burial in a single tomb.

Though the papers picked out many faults in the verse play,

there was enough beauty in the writing to allow the acting, music and decor carry it on 134 times until 5th July.

Another remarkable success began the new season when Justin McCarthy's *If I Were King* opened on 30th August. This (later reborn as the musical *Vagabond King*) had been dramatised by the author from his own novel and had already been successful in New York. The wild braggart poet Villon was played by Alec and the evil hunchback Louis XI by Charles Fulton. Julie Opp was the Lady Katherine and Lyall Swete the Grand Constable traitor spy of the Burgundians. Huguette, the poet's light o' love and leader of the whores, was played by Suzanne Sheldon, red-headed American beauty from Vermont who had been playing in London since 1898 but had returned to make her home début in this role the previous October. Jean Mackinlay, May Saker, Bessie Page and Auriol Lee were some of Huguette's companions. The latter, though English born, was a relative of the famous General Robert E. Lee. The large cast included Arthur Machen and Henry Ainley in minor roles though the latter understudied Villon.

Romance between Suzanne and Ainley blossomed to marriage during the run, but the union broke after a few years, mainly through long professional separations. By Ainley's second marriage, however, his golden voice was passed on to his son Richard whose tall, instinctively fine stage presence ceased to grace the London stage only because of severe war wounds which forced him to devote his talents to radio and teaching. His tenure as principal of the Bristol Old Vic School, for example, will not be forgotten by grateful pupils; whilst his daughter Pekoe is a remarkably interesting character actress.

The romantic drama opened on a 'thieves' kitchen' where the King, incognito, listened with growing anger to the hero singing the song of the title. With evil humour Villon was then created Constable for a week but with the scaffold as reward. Prowess against the enemy, however, made a grateful populace force the King to cancel this edict and all ended well with marriage to Katherine after the necessary death of Huguette as she intercepted a dagger thrust at Villon.

The four scenes were designed by Hann, Telbin and Percy Macquoid who also did the costumes. Robins composed the 'constant instrumental accompaniment' which tired the patience of J. T. Grein who had also seen The Garden Theatre production and preferred it as being 'less noisy and with clearer diction'. To Suzanne and Fulton he gave first honours, to Julie and Alec second, for the playing of the hero was just too earnest and lacked the leavening expression of humour.

1903

The historical inexactitudes which some of the critics objected to did not worry playgoers and the spectacular piece attracted 215 times until March.

Quite as successful was the next play which too, as *The Student Prince*, was to become a popular musical. This was Meyer-Forster's *Old Heidelberg*, adapted from the original, by Bleichmann, in five acts with scenery by Walter Hann. Alec played the princeling Karl who appeared first in his uncle's gloomy castle, then in the riotous university city where he loved the innkeeper's niece Kathie (Eva Moore and later Lilian Braithwaite) who had to be deserted when he was called to take up a ruler's reins and marry another for political reasons.

Delightful character studies were given by J. D. Beveridge as the Prince's old tutor Juttner, Lyall Swete as ultra-proud valet Lutz and Vivian Reynolds as the tippling old steward Kellermann. Others in the cast of thirty-one plus supers were Brydone, Hignett, Frances Wetherall, Elinor Aickin and Guy Pertwee.

After holidays, they went on a long provincial tour during which the theatre was let to the actor-manager E. S. Willard who commanded full houses wherever he played on both sides of the Atlantic. On 31st August he opened with Louis N. Parker's sixteenth-century drama of Rome, *The Cardinal*, which he had originally produced in the United States.

Willard played the title-role of Giovanni, the Medici who became Pope Leo X, in a mainly fictitious tale about Filiberta (Nina Lindsey), her lover the Cardinal's brother Giuliano (Homewood), their mother (Helen Ferrers) and a murderer-servant of Pope Julius II called Strozzi (Herbert Waring) who kills the girl's father (Frederick Volpé). Strozzi was given absolution when he confessed his crime to the Cardinal, who later contrived the killer's second confession when he could be overheard by others after Giuliano had been wrongly convicted instead.

Many supers augmented the cast of twenty who included Charles Fulton, Joseph Farjeon, Decima Brooke, Ada Webster, Alice Lonnon an American girl who was later promoted to play Filiberta, and W. Edmunds. The latter was making his London début after his American one. He was actually the manager's nephew and became the strong character actor of stage and screen under his own name of Edmund Willard. Particularly remembered will be his performance as the tall mad murderer opposite the short fat doctor one of Martin Miller in the *Arsenic and Old Lace* household of the mad family played by Lilian Braithwaite, Mary Jerrold and trumpet-tootling Frank Pettingell some forty years later at The Strand.

The name of Charles Dickens appeared at the theatre again when Dilley and Clifton's dramatisation from *Martin Chuzzlewit* called *Tom Pinch*, was put on for matinées from 5th September. Pecksniff and his daughters Charity and Mercy were played by Volpé, Joan Blair and Alice Lonnon. Edith Tombes was his servant Jane and his pupils Chuzzlewit, John Westlock and Tom Pinch were Homewood, H. C. Lonsdale and Mr Willard. Old Martin was played by J. G. Taylor and his ward Mary Graham by Maud Hoffman. Mrs Lupin and the ostler Mark Tapley of 'The Blue Dragon' were Mrs Russ Whytal and Ernest Stallard. Ada Webster was Ruth Pinch, 'W. Edmunds' the porter Murgatroyd and Decima Moore played the child Lizzie Poynter. The play was in three acts with sets by George Hemsley, the costumes by Simmons and the wigs by Clarkson. Carl Armbruster was back on the conductor's rostrum.

For the Christmas season *The Professor's Love Story* was revived from 7th December with Willard as Professor Good-willie which he had created in the original productions in the States and London. Willard's polished portrayal of the absent-minded old man's rejuvenation under the spell of love for his lovely secretary Lucy made the audience adore the early Barrie fantasy. Gracie Leigh was recruited from the musical comedy stage to play Lucy, but she did not earn commendations as did Volpé and Stallard as the comic Scots workers Pete and Henders. Helen Ferrers was the hero's spinster sister. The English accents of the others attempting the northern dialect would have otherwise ruined the general effect.

1904

Willard took his company on tour when his season ended on Saturday 23rd January, and Alec resumed the *Old Heidelberg* run from the Monday until 15th March. Changes of cast included Machen as the station-master instead of Brydone.

Love's Carnival, also by the previous adapter and from the German, lasted after that for five performances and the doors then stayed shut for a fortnight. They reopened with *Saturday to Monday*, a farce by Fenn and Pryce, to which was later added a one-act, by the same authors, called *'Op o' me Thumb*. Beatrice Forbes-Robertson, Hilda Trevelyan and H. Nye Chart were in the new company.

The winter season began with *The Garden of Lies* which Grundy had adapted from a story by Forman. Lilian Braith-waite, Fulton, Mark Kinghorne and Leslie Faber were in this which lasted six weeks though the bill was strengthened by Joshua Bates' one-act *The Decree Nisi*. The latter was kept on when from 19th November *Lady Windermere's Fan* was revived for the first time.

The dramatist's name this time was boldly billed, and though Alec did not take part, three others played roles they had created: Marion Terry as Mrs Erlynne, Fanny Coleman as the Duchess of Berwick and Vane-Tempest as Dumby. The rest of the cast was Ben Webster (Darlington), Sydney Brough (Augustus), Leslie Faber (Cecil Graham), Seymour (Hopper), Carrington (Parker). Lilian Braithwaite was Lady Windermere, Maud Harcourt was Rosalie and the Misses Pauline French, Eileen Lewis, Elinor Aickin and C. Hamilton the Ladies Plimdale, Cowper-Cowper, Jedburgh and Agatha Carlisle. Babara Hannay, who was in the one-act, took over as Lady Agatha for a while and Eric Lewis succeeded as Lord Augustus and Robert Horton as Graham.

The piece was reported by the *Daily Telegraph* to be as 'fresh and scintilating as ever' and that 'Marion Terry swept the whole house along with her by a performance as powerful, as convincing, as accomplished as anything this admirable artist has ever done'. The scenery was by Walter Hann.

1905

Netta Syrett's fairy play *White Magic* was the curtain-raiser from 10th January and then Sutro's *A Maker of Men* from the 27th. Marie Lohr, Australian-born daughter of Kate Bishop, was in the fairy piece as a princess and though only fifteen was already a delightfully experienced player on the road of charm she was to pursue for well over half a century.

Sutro's *Mollentrave on Women* replaced the Wilde on 13th February, and to his two pieces was added Bernard Shaw's playlet *How He Lied To Her Husband* on 21st March. This skit on Shaw's own *Candida* was a transfer from The Court with

Gertrude Kingston, Granville Barker and A. G. Poulton in the roles they had created three weeks earlier as Her, Her Lover, Her Husband. First performance had been in New York the previous September.

On May Day Alec returned as *John Chilcote, M.P.* by E. Temple Thurston. This adaptation, from a novel about mistaken identity by the dramatist's wife, did not transform well and lasted only six weeks. W. J. Thorold played Alec's double.

Simone le Bargy, with her delightful broken accent, was the most attractive thing about *The Man of the Moment* which followed from 13th June. In this adaptation from Capus and Arène's *L'Adversaire* she was wife to Alec in a marriage broken by the stupid machinations of Charlotte Granville as mother-in-law. George Giddens, Julian L'Estrange and Bella Pateman led the support.

At Hall Caine's express wish Alec now forsook his own theatre to play in *The Prodigal Son* at Drury Lane, the charm of the ancient theatre as much as £250 a week a bait impossible to ignore. Specially engaged also for that was Mrs John Wood. Nancy Price too was in the cast.

The Kendals consequently took over from 16th September with *Dick Hope* which they had presented at The Coronet in 1903. Next month they put on *The Housekeeper* by Metcalf Wood and Beatrice Heron-Maxwell, which had been tried out in Birmingham. With them were Hubert Harben and his wife Mary Jerrold who had joined the Kendals after her appearance in *The Ambassador*. Also in the company were Muriel Carmel, Jessie Moore, Elise Clarens, Bassett Roe, Hendrie, Wentworth, Wood, Tapping and Rutherfurd.

On 13th October, at Bradford, Sir Henry Irving died during his Farewell Tour. Laid to rest in Westminster Abbey, one of the countless wreaths was from his Queen, the good and ever beautiful Alexandra. A humble country lad, once a London office boy, he not only reached the top of his chosen most arduous profession but he raised it with himself into an honoured one and his knighthood, the first bestowed upon an actor, was accepted as a mark of honour to the profession as much as to himself. Norman Forbes (Robertson) and Alec were the joint honorary secretaries appointed by the funeral committee to make the many arrangements.

The Kendals finished before Christmas and two days after the festival William Mollison with Durward Lely took over to present Thomas and Macarthur's dramatisation of Ian Maclaren's famous novels. All first-night proceeds were given to the Queen's Unemployed Fund. *Beside the Bonnie Brier Bush* was not a very good play, and had too much lamenting from the dour old shepherd Lachlan (Mollison) and too little love-making between his cast-out daughter Flora (Lilian Braithwaite) and the laird's son Lord Hay (Henry Ainley). Londoners did not care for the mush garnered from the kailyard novelist who was in private life the Rev. John Watson. The Misses Lettice Fairfax, Woodward, Harvey, Stewart and Fitzgerald with Sydney Brough, Paget, Anderson, Charles Groves, Frank Cooper and Alec Thompson played the other more or less comic Highlanders well enough.

1906

As You Like It had been planned for matinées but from 9th January was run in the evenings also. Rosalind was acted by Lilian Braithwaite, Celia and Phoebe by Lettice Fairfax and Evelyn Macnay, Audrey by Clara Cowper. William Calvert was the exiled Duke and Mollison was Jaques with Ainley as Orlando. Charles Groves was Touchstone. Henry Worrall and Roy Cushing had minor roles. Hawes Craven and Joseph Harker did the scenery and Nathans the costumes. The great Sandow arranged the wrestling match.

Pinero's name went up again when Alec returned from 1st February with *His House In Order*. The dramatist had done

nothing since his *Wife Without A Smile* had flopped at Wyndham's in the autumn of 1904. In that the husband, hoping to
make his wife laugh, had hung a doll from the ceiling of the
summer-house in which the action was set. Every time a couple
in the attic above were left alone (unseen) the doll danced a
merry jig suggestive of connubial action somewhat more ad-
vanced than holding hands! Prudish protests had followed the
blushes which flushed the Ponds-creamed faces, though delighted giggles had emanated from the cheaper seats.

Pinero's subsequent 'retiral' encouraged Alec's successful
sealing the breach between them. The result was a year's run
without even the customary summer closing. Macquoid designed the scenery for Harker, the setting being the country
house of an M.P., meticulous Filmer Jesson.

Herbert Waring played the latter, whose second wife Nina
(Irene Vanbrugh) had been his boy's governess. Iris Hawkins
played the boy Derek, between whom and old friend of the
family Major Maurewarde (Dawson Milward) a strange friend-
ship existed. Jesson was completely under the thumbs of his
first wife's family, the extremely pompous Ridgeleys (Lyall
Swete and Bella Pateman) and their children Pryce and
Geraldine (C. M. Lowne and Beryl Faber). Nigel Playfair and
Vivian Reynolds played the local doctor and journalist and
Marcelle Chevalier the new governess, Horton, Fawcitt and
Jerome the secretary and servants. Alec was the hero Hilary,
Jesson's Ambassador brother on holiday. Without Hilary's
kindly friendship Nina's spirit would have been quite broken
by the obnoxiously domineering family who held up the dead
wife as a paragon of all the virtues.

Nina's discovery of a packet of love letters to her predecessor,
proving Derek to be an illicit child of the Major's, put an unexpected strengthening weapon into her hands. The noble
Hilary dissuaded her from throwing them in the faces of her
tormentors but he showed them to Jesson to make him give
the Ridgeleys their marching orders. Earlier he confronted the

SJT S

Major in a delightfully English tight-lipped manner. The Major replied:

'Something has been found?'

'Yes.'

'What?'

'Some letters.'

'Letters! Whose letters?'

'Yours. To Annabel. There's a train at 2.40.'

The father was allowed to say farewell to his unacknowledged son but Hilary spoke for him:

'Major Maurewarde has to go back to town, Derek.'

'Go back!'

'By the next train!'

The many dramatic scenes ended with Nina and Jesson left alone to begin their marriage anew, the house at last in order.

1907

The 430th performance on 27th February ended the remarkable run. Auriol Lee had played Nina for a while.

Alfred Sutro's exciting *John Glayde's Honour* followed from 8th March. Alec as Glayde played a very gentlemanly American magnate who followed his wife Muriel (Eva Moore) to Paris when he got a criptic cable from Lady Lerode saying her son Trevor was painting Muriel's portrait. Matheson Lang played the artist whose mother's interfering motive was not altruistic, since she wanted Trevor to marry an heiress.

The play opened just before Glayde and his rough but loyal secretary Shurmur (M. Sherbrooke) made their unheralded entrance, to the consternation of Muriel and her friends. Henrietta Watson was a princess (*née* Betsy Huggins), Norman Forbes was a cynical artist and Graham Browne a sensible Oxford graduate loved by Glayde's niece Dora (May Martyn). Vivian Reynolds played Glayde's elderly valet who peached on Muriel when she planned to run away with Trevor. Helen

Ferrers was Lady Lerode. Gwen Floyd, Cecil Bevan and Norman Trevor completed the cast. Virtue did not win, for after several excellent scenes Glayde rejected his wife who ran away after all with her lover.

A more successful compatriot of Mollison then took over for a season from 29th July when Edward Compton (father of Fay and Sir Compton Mackenzie—the family name) brought his famous Old English Comedy Company to town and opened with *The 18th Century*. This stylishly dressed fantasy he had first produced as *To-Morrow* (by Malyon and James) in Paisley on 12th February 1904. In it the ninth Earl of Laidlaw was transported back in time to become the fourth Earl, to kill in a duel his best friend, and after experiencing other chastening adventures to return to the twentieth century resolved to turn over a new leaf.

Though only fifty-four, Edward Compton had made his Company celebrated over two decades both at home and in America. He did not disdain juniors, but his leading roles were always filled by experienced and even brilliant players.

He presented *The School for Scandal* from 7th September with his daughter Viola as Lady Sneerwell, he himself being Charles Surface and Henry Ainley, Joseph. Lilian Braithwaite was Lady Teazle and Marie Hassell was Mrs Candour with Phyllis Relph as Maria and Mary Carnegy the maid. Eric Lewis was Sir Peter and Charles Groves the Sir Oliver. Moses was played by E. M. Robson. The others were H. Crocker, Wallace Johnston, Reginald Besant, P. Gordon, B. Butler, Charles Rose, Comberbach, Goldstein, Winton and Meade. Besides most of the foregoing, in the first play there had been Grace Lane, Marion Ashworth and Suzanne Sheldon. The latter had left to join a company at Wyndham's so for the last fortnight Viola had taken her place. Dolly Stamp had played a coloured page-boy. Nathan's had made most of the period costumes, the scenery for the first play was by Hann and for the Sheridan by Harker.

Alec took over again on 12th November with an adaptation by Lennox-Gordon from the French of Bernstein called *The Thief*. Both he and Irene Vanbrugh had strong parts as the Chelfords, guests in the country home of the Leytons (Sydney Valentine and Lilian Braithwaite) who had an impressionable son Harry (Reginald Owen). Lyall Swete played a detective in the guise of another guest because money had disappeared from Mrs Leyton's bureau. Harry fell in love with flighty empty-head Mrs Chelford and soon realised she was the thief. Consequently he took the blame when falsely accused. When Chelford found money in his wife's case she confessed she had stolen to pay her dress bill for she had wanted him to be proud of her before his wealthy friends. The husband was then torn between horror at her deed and fear that the boy was her lover, else why the confession to save her? Reconciliations, explanations and forgiveness all round followed the many dramatic scenes which sped the play to 186 performances.

1908

Ellen Terry, the Conan Doyles and W. S. Gilberts were on the committee of a Complimentary Matinée to Mrs Edward Saker on 20th February. Among the programme sellers was young actress Lilias Waldegrave who may have been related to the family of John Braham's daughter Fanny. Though there was actually a Waldegrave stage family.

Pinero was again the dramatist when *The Thunderbolt* appeared on 9th May. In theme and style this was much more like the work of Henry Arthur Jones, with most unpleasant characters wrangling over the effects of their late, almost unknown, brother who had apparently left no will. The heroine was the latter's illegitimate daughter Helen, played by Stella Campbell who was just back from touring America with her mother Mrs Pat. More upset that he had made no provision for her than about the actual money Helen became friendly with the only other nice relatives, music-master Thaddeus, his wife Phyllis and their children (Alec, Mabel Hackney, Mignon Clifford and Cyril Bruce). Other parts were played by Louis Calvert, Kate Bishop, Norman Forbes, Alice Beet, Wilfred Draycott, May Palfrey as other relatives and their spouses, with Arlton, Haigh, Gladys Dale, Sybil Maurisse, Vere Sinclair and Julian Royce. The last played a solicitor. So did J. D. Beveridge, an honest family one called Elkin who served to hold the play together with a well-drawn more normal character than the rest.

Dramatic quarrelling culminated eventually in Phyllis's confession that she had destroyed the will, and in the decision to divide the money equally except for the children getting their parent's share. The too ladylike Helen, who made no fight against the sordid, obnoxious relatives and their getting a share in the end, did not please audiences but the play lasted out the season. The scenery had been by W. Raphael.

Jerome K. Jerome's very moving morality play, *The Passing of the Third Floor Back*, opened the autumn on 1st September under Johnstone Forbes-Robertson with himself as The Passer-by in the Prologue, The Third Floor Back in the Play and A Friend in the Epilogue. The play was tried out in the provinces beginning at Harrogate. Now Jerome was famous as a humorist so the Yorkshire folk took their seats expecting to be amused. Nothing in the Prologue changed their minds as they enjoyed the exaggerated characters, so they laughed and continued to do so to the final curtain! This kind of success was dreadfully distressing but next week at Liverpool the audiences caught the correct mood and the reception was terrific.

The star's American wife Gertrude Elliott was 'Stasia the servant slut of the boarding house kept by the cheating Mrs Sharpe (Agnes Thomas). His brother Ian Robertson was the bully, retired Major Tompkins whose shrewish wife was played by Kate Carlyon. Haidee Wright was the too-painted spinster

Miss Kite and Kate Bishop the snobbish Mrs de Hooley. Marsh Allen was the cowardly artist Christopher Penny and Alice Crawford the Major's fairly nice daughter, Vivian, who instead of marrying the artist almost threw herself away on the bookmaker satyr Joey Knight (Ernest Hendrie). Edward Sass was the share-pushing rogue Jake Samuels and Wilfred Forster his caddish jackal Harry Larkcom. The song in the Epilogue was sung by young Cyril Derington-Turner. Walter Hann painted the scenery.

The Passer-by changed them all. As he made his final exit the no longer sluttish 'Stasia raised her arms outwards in a gesture of almost despairing farewell. In so doing she cast the shadow of a Cross on the wall against which he last had stood. All but one of the lights dimmed down until only the shadow of the Cross was visible. The curtains slowly closed. The silent house stayed hushed. On stage the players clenched their hands and held their breath as their gazes met. Tears filled the eyes of Mrs Jerome at the thought of failure as still not a sound came from the audience. Then with a great sigh the tense crowd relaxed and wild applause thundered out.

Ideal for the character were Forbes-Robertson's melodiously rich yet quiet and peaceful tones, his ascetic face and sad, kind eyes, tired as though they had too often been drowned in tears at the sorrows they had looked upon. The play became one of the greatest successes of his career and was revived and toured many times at home and abroad. He and Jerome directed the first productions of it. All were praised for their interpretations which could not have been bettered. They transferred to Terry's in the Strand after Saturday 7th November.

Alec reopened on the Wednesday with Sutro's *The Builder of Bridges* in which, as Thursfield, he was made love to by Irene Vanbrugh as Dorothy, to soften him because of defalcations by her brother Arnold (Dawson Milward). Dramatic complications lay in her prior betrothal to Harcourt Williams as Walter. William Farren, Vivian Reynolds, Florence Haydon,

Babara Hannay and Dora Sevening completed the cast. An unknown playgoer marked them all 'excellent' on his programme
—but of Alec he wrote: 'More offensive than usual, with a
horrible leery smile'!

King Edward commanded them to appear before his Christmas guests at Sandringham on 4th December, so on that Friday
night the doors were closed.

1909

Despite this cachet the play had to be replaced in less than
three months so *The Prisoner of Zenda* returned in the last
week of February with Stella Campbell as the Princess Flavia,
Alec in his old roles.

Mason's *Colonel Smith* lasted fifteen performances in April.
Ernest Thesiger made his début in it, arriving each day at the
stage door in a most magnificent fur-lined and collared overcoat
which almost hid his four-inch-high starched collar! *Heidelberg*
replaced the flop.

Caste was given at a complimentary matinée to Maud Robertson on 1st July. Alec played the Hon. George with which part
he was probably familiar because of his early time in her family
company. Fred Kerr played Hawtree, the Cyril Maudes were
Eccles and Esther, with Vivian Reynolds as Gerridge and
Bourchier as Dixon. Maud herself was the formidable Marquise
and Marie Tempest made a delightful Polly Eccles. Afterwards
Beerbohm Tree gave a monologue.

The new season began on Thursday 2nd September with
Pinero's *Mid-Channel*. The title signified that period in mar-
riage called less mellifluously in Americanese the seven-year-
itch. Lyn Harding was husband Theodore and Irene Vanbrugh
his wife Zoe. The others were Eric Maturin as Leonard Ferris,
C. M. Lowne as the Hon. Peter Mottram, A. E. Drinkwater,
Stuart Dennison and Sydney Hamilton as servants with Tommy
Weguelen and Owen Nares as upholsterers. The latter had

first appeared here in the summer revival and had been some
months in the touring company. Kate Serjeantson and Rosalie
Toller were Mrs and Ethel Pierpont, Nina Sevening was Mrs
Annerly, Ruth Maitland was Lena and Faith Celli a maid.
Raphael was again the scenarist.

The drama is a good 'actor's play' but very much a period
piece and though light and amusing in parts audiences were not
attracted. Those who were, left the theatre with the last scene
too vividly in mind: a room in a top flat of a high block, an
inner room up-stage with only one door which, opened, revealed the window pushed up—the curtains blowing in the
wind—the heroine Zoe no longer there.

The next play was even less successful for R. C. Carton's
Lorrimer Sabiston, Dramatist lasted only three weeks from 9th
November. Alec was a famous bearded writer who had penned
such a daring play that, rather than risk his reputation, he gave
it to unknown Noel Darcus. The latter rewarded him by
stealing his lover Lady Cheynley (Beryl Faber) whose cuckolded
husband Sir Henry was played by Ellen Terry's final husband
James Carew. Godfrey Tearle was Noel, having joined the
company for the previous tour. Others were Lewis, Lowne,
Reynolds, Pearse, Stirling, the Misses Toller and Faber.

On 30th November *The Importance of Being Earnest* was
revived for the second time. Alec and Allan Aynesworth played
their original roles, Stella Campbell was Gwendolen, Rosalie
Toller was Cecily and Alice Beet Miss Prism. Helen Rous was
Lady Bracknell. Vivian Reynolds played the Rev. Canon
Chasuble whilst Eric Stirling and Weguelin were Merriman
and Lane. Sutro's *A Maker of Men* was revived as curtain-
raiser when Duchesne's *Nursery Governess* flopped.

1910

Everyone present received a copy of the Wilde classic on the
night of 2nd February for that began the twenty-first year of

Alec's management counting from his Avenue days. There was now no need to hide Wilde's name which was boldly billed. The revival ran 324 times.

D'Arcy of the Guards by Louis E. Shipman began the winter on 27th September but this comedy of the War of Independence, set in Philadelphia, was withdrawn after forty-eight performances.

It was replaced on 19th November by a riotous farce called *Eccentric Lord Comberdene* by R. C. Carton. This skit on romantic novelettes ran to the 21st of the new year but really merited a longer run. It involved a gang of crooks, stolen jewels, secret dispatches, A Russian Grand Duchess, young and beautiful and incognito as a maid to a formidable Scots Marchioness, a suave and debonair English peer, rough old seasalts and Royal Navy matelots.

1910

The dramatist's wife, Kate Compton, was the Marchioness who was also incognito and once during the action had to be lowered from a seaside hotel window by sheets held by Alec and Rita Jolivet as Comberdene and the Duchess. Ashton Pearse was a crook disguised as the Rev. Alwyn Pilbrow and Lyston Lyle was his boss Radburn and Ruth Maitland their 'madame'. Marjorie Waterlow played Daphne the daughter of an M.P. (Fred Lewis), in reefer jacket on board the S.Y. *Morning Star*. J. H. Barnes was the crooked Captain Clamp whose assistants Grugger and Scoyle were played by Weguelin and Reynolds. Besides a large crowd nine others were named. All ended happily with the total defeat of the crooks and safe sailing away of the lovely Russian. Raphael did the scenery as usual, most of the costumes were by Simmons.

A matinée recital of *Paolo and Francesca* was given on 24th November, arranged by Princess Christian in aid of spectacles for poor London children.

At Stratford-upon-Avon in the summer Frank Benson had presented American Josephine Peabody's *The Piper* after it had won a prize offered by Otho Stuart for the most original play. It was given a London run on matinées from 21st December. Benson played the Piper of Hamelin who charmed the children of the burghers away to a cave after the latter had defaulted on their promised payment for the rat clearance. The large cast included Marion Terry and Violet Farebrother but though it opened merrily the last act dragged.

1911

Comberdene was withdrawn and *The Piper* put into the evening bill as well from the last week of January but it did not sufficiently attract.

A. E. W. Mason's *Witness for the Defence* was more successful than his previous effort for it ran 150 times from 1st February. Alec was Henry Thresk, an old lover of the wife of Ballantyne (Ethel Irving and Lyston Lyle) on a visit to them in their lonely tent in Rajputana. Thresk stopped her shooting herself in despair after her cad of a husband had tried to strangle her. When she killed him later in self-defence Thresk saved her by false evidence about an unknown robber. Two years afterwards, when she was about to marry Richard (Leslie Faber), Thresk turned up to persuade her to confess the past before the marriage. All went well.

This was the coronation year of King George and for his services to the stage and for his public work the name of Sir George Alexander was added to the roll of honour. Subsequently all titles were dropped from programmes except for actresses using their married name and for advance or production notices.

In May Ellen Terry at last appeared here when Alec gave the theatre for a couple of matinées in aid of the newly founded (feminist) Three Arts Club. She recited Wordsworth's 'Daffodils' and was followed by Edith Evans singing Antonia's Song from *The Tales of Hoffmann*. Other solo stars who sparkled were Marie Lloyd, Wilkie Bard and Phyllis Bedells.

The Importance was again revived on 11th June when Gladys Cooper played Cecily. It was virtually the golden-haired lovely girl's first appearance away from musical comedy and she found St James's back-stage decorum very different to the free and easy informality of Daly's. She was not subdued, however, even when rebuked for singing and running up the dressing-room stairs. When the militant Mrs Evans issued a stock dress Gladys did not like, she cut it to bits and bought a new one for herself. That misdemeanour nearly earned dismissal but she was just able to conjure up enough charm and spirit to disarm her new manager when sent for afterwards.

Henry Arthur Jones's *The Ogre* opened the new season on 11th September. This was a serious satire aimed at the Suffragettes in a sort of modern *Taming of the Shrew*, but it failed and Alec put up the notices after a couple of weeks. Then the company started quickening their pace and treating the play like a farce even though Alec was one of them. A. E. Matthews had rejoined to play Algernon in the summer, having played that part the year before in the New York production. Nearly fifty years later, both still in harness and quite as lively, 'Matty' and Gladys in the former's charming cottage at Bushey Heath, chuckled over tea cups as they told me about the company engineering fun from Jones's heavy satire.

Houses quickly improved as the news went round, but Alec persisted in his decision and took it off after thirty-seven performances. Only Nares, Roller and Dorothy Fane were re-engaged for the next piece. This was *Lady Windermere's Fan* on 15th November when Marion Terry played her original part as Mrs Erlynne. Thesiger was Dumby and Lilian Braithwaite Lady Windermere. The rest were Milward, Trevor, Eric Lewis, Weguelin, the Misses Kemmis, Powys, Chute, Macready, Chesney and Lascelles.

At last Mrs Patrick Campbell returned to the house where she had made her name. She was the evil heroine of the strong drama *Bella Donna* which J. B. Fagan had constructed from Hichens's novel of mystery and passion by the Nile. Alec was the Dr Isaacson who chased off the stupid Dr Hartley (Athol Stewart) so that he could save his friend Nigel (Charles Maude) who was being poisoned by his wicked wife (Mrs Pat). Trevor Roller was the latter's servant Mamza who stirred the poison powder into Nigel's coffee. Shiel Barry was Ibrahim, Alfred Harris was Hassan, Harold Holland was Monks and Charles Bryant the eastern villain Mamoud Baroudi, who first captivated the woman amongst the pyramids and then spurned her when the door had been shut in her face by her own people. Lydia Branscombe was Marie and Mary Grey was Mrs Marchmont.

1912

Critics were not entirely pleased with the drama but the public besieged the box-office all the same and it touched 253 performances. Norma Whalley, an Australian girl who had graduated from the chorus of The Gaiety, took over Mary Grey's part in the beginning of the year and then when Mrs Pat was injured in a taxi-smash she was promoted and played the intense role with great success. Happy event from the production was the marriage of Mary Grey to J. P. Fagan.

More murder and hate, passion and patriotism in a conglomeration from the French called *The Turning Point*, by Peter le Marchant after Kistemaeckers' *La Flambée*, managed 111 performances from 1st October. There were good parts in it for Ethel Irving and Alec.

1913

Alec now followed the fashion and adventured 'on the halls' in Max Beerbohm's one-act *A Social Success*. Meanwhile in association with the author he directed *Turandot* by Vollmoeller, English version by Bithell. The music was by Busoni and the scenery and costumes by Ernst Stern whose work in the original in Berlin had impressed Alec when he was there the previous summer. Stern's later London work was to include *Bitter Sweet* and *White Horse Inn*.

The story, of course, is of the Chinese princess whose suitors are beheaded when they fail to answer three questions. Evelyn D'Alroy and Godfrey Tearle were the Princess Turandot and lucky suitor Calaf. The others were Hilda Moore, Maire O'Neill, Margaret Yarde, Mary Clare, Margaret Chute, Susie Claughton and Stella Rho with J. H. Barnes, Edward Sass, Vivian Reynolds, Fred Lewis, Norman Forbes, James Berry, Austin Fehrman, Alfred Harris and W. E. Hall. The piece was produced with tremendous colour and most expensively with costumes by Baruch, but it was a hotch-potch of rubbish and lasted only twenty-seven times. Gwen Ffrangcon-Davies was in the crowd.

The Importance replaced the flop from 15th February, and then Mason's *Open Windows* began on 13th March with Pinero's curtain-raiser *Playgoers* added on the 31st. Mrs Pat and Alec played their original roles in *Tanqueray* from 4th June. Nigel Playfair was Cayley Drummle, Kate Bishop played Mrs Cortelyon and Rosalie Toller the daughter Ellean. Lettice Fairfax was Lady Orreyed and Mary Clare a servant, as was John Ridley. Reginald Malcolm was Captain Ardale whose early affair with Paula and then love for Ellean created the drama. Benedict, Reynolds and Bayly were Misquith, Jayne and Morse.

It was during either the Wilde or Pinero revival, in an interval when the curtain was down, that attendants had to rush to hustle outside a man who sprang up from his seat in the stalls to strip himself almost naked and shout aloud some crazy perverted protest. Hugh Walpole was there, as he says in *Above the Dark Circus*, and the story was whisperingly current among front-of-house staff into the twenties but otherwise it was hushed up as not in good form.

Their Majesties were present on 27th June at a matinée of *London Assurance* when over £1,000 was raised for King George's Pension Fund for Actors and Actresses. The cast was a roll-call of those already and to be famous in theatre annals.

The progressive Granville Barker and his wife Lillah McCarthy took over for four months from 1st September. They opened with *The Harlequinade* by Barker and Dion Calthrop, together with Shaw's *Androcles and the Lion*. The former was a satirical fantasy using the traditional characters of the title in many scenes covering 2,000 years. Cathleen Nesbitt was Alice Whistler and Arthur Whitby her Uncle Edward. Donald Calthrop, Sheila Hayes, Nigel Playfair and H. O. Nicholson were Harlequin, Columbine, Clown and Pantaloon. Leon Quartermaine, Herbert Hewetson and Ralph Hutton were A Hero, A Villain and A Philosopher. Victor Maclure painted the scenery the 'Decoration' of which was by Dion Calthrop. Barker directed.

Androcles did not prove entirely acceptable, for neither critics nor audiences could quite take Shaw's conception of Christian martyrs as ordinary light-hearted folk so different from Wilson Barrett's orthodox noble proletarians of the money-spinning *Sign of The Cross*. The first-night élite were, however, more amused than shocked and laughed more than Shaw relished.

Lillah McCarthy played the patrician Lavinia, and Alfred Brydone the simple-minded massive Ferrovius who found it so difficult to turn the other cheek and in the arena lost his temper and killed six gladiators before the Emperor stopped the slaughter with the salute. Leon Quartermaine was the Emperor, who pardoned the victims as reward for Ferrovius's valour, except for one, else the lions would have gone hungry. O. P. Heggie was animal-loving Androcles who volunteered but was saved by the lion from whose paw he had pulled the thorn in the opening scene. 'The Decoration of the Play' was by Albert Rothenstein, the scenery being painted by Maclure. Barker directed. Shaw took Lillah to the Zoo during rehearsals to study real lions' behaviour, but afterwards they admitted their journey unnecessary for Edward Sillward was the Lion and he had had almost twenty years experience playing panto-mime animals and needed no advice.

Ben Webster was the Captain in charge of the Christians and Hesketh Pearson and Donald Calthrop the patrician Metellus and Lentulus who were admonished for their vulgar behaviour outside the Colosseum. Allan Jeayes was gladiator Secutor ignominiously netted by J. P. Turnbull as Retiarius. Baliol Holloway was the Menagerie Keeper and Ralph Hutton the Slave Driver. J. F. Outram was cowardly Spintho, Clare Greet the shrewish wife Megaera. H. Hewetson was the Editor and Neville Gartside the Call Boy. The large crowd included Rose-mary Craig, Gladys Alwyn, Vera Tschaikowsky.

The mixture of fun-and-games with sacred history, of absurd but likeable little Androcles and the other well-drawn and acted characters was on the whole well received. Certainly all were deeply attentive throughout, whilst in the opening when Androcles and Megaera rest by the roadside 'as the wonderful panto lion, tawny whiskered and long-haired, crawled through the futurist forest and shook his mane' one young blood sitting near J. B. Booth screwed his monocle into his eye and muttered 'Gad! What have they got Hall Caine in it for?'

The double bill ran fifty-two times until 25th October. After a three-day break Masefield's *The Witch* was revived on the Wednesday. In Norway, Wiers-Jenssen's original had thrilled William Archer whose enthusiasm affected Lillah McCarthy. She failed to get Shaw to do a version for her and John Masefield too refused. Only her continual pressure made him relent and under his hand it became less harsh and evil even though the terrible power and intensity were retained. J. D. Beveridge was cast as the elderly pastor Absolon whose son Martin (Denis Neilson-Terry) becomes enthralled by his young step-mother Anne Pedersdotter (Lillah McCarthy).

Vera Tschaikowsky played Herlofs-Marte who is burnt at the stake off-stage, and Anne succumbs to the fearful realisation that she too has the horror-power and in it exults until in over-wrought ecstasy her cathedral confession condemns her to a similar fate. The four pastors were played by J. F. Outram, Nigel Playfair, Baliol Holloway and Arthur Whitby whilst Ralph Hutton was the Bishop. Janet Achurch was old Merete Beyer, Clare Greet (afterwards Mary Ross-Shore) and Rose-mary Craig were the servants Bente and Jorund. H. O. Nichol-son, Herbert Hewetson and Allan Jeayes were David, The Officer and a Guard. No credits were given so they probably used the sets and costumes of their 1911 Court production.

Many Londoners will remember the stark drama as it was produced at The Arts in 1944 when Mary Morris, Abraham Sofaer, Richard Wordsworth and Chris Castor were Peders-dotter, Absolon, Martin and Herlofs-Marte, and lucky provin-cial playgoers the earlier war-time Old Vic tour when Jean Forbes-Robertson was Anne.

Ibsen's *The Wild Duck*, Molière's *Le Mariage Forcé*, Mase-field's *Nan*, Maeterlinck and Sutro's *Death of Tintagiles*, Galsworthy's *Silver Box* and Shaw's *The Doctor's Dilemma* were later also offered and run in repertory.

They had first done the Shaw play at The Court in 1906 when Barker had been the brilliant but incorrigible artist Dubedat which Denis Neilson-Terry now played. Lillah McCarthy as Jennifer, Clare Greet as the ugly old bossy servant Emmy who treats the doctors as if she were their nanny, Ben Webster as Sir Colenso, Michael Sherbrooke as Schutzmacher who had made his fortune by guaranteeing cures, had all created their roles. Fresh to their parts were Nigel Playfair as surgeon Cutler Walpole, Beveridge as doyen Sir Patrick,

Quartermaine as poverty-stricken Blenkinsop who cured patients with greengages, Arthur Whitby as pompous Bloomington Bonnington and Turnbull, Gartside, Hesketh Pearson, G. Jerome and Ross Joynson supporting as Redpenny, The Newspaper Man, The Secretary, The Waiter and Minnie Tinwell.

Rothenstein designed Jennifer's fabulous Act IV dress. The famous Henry Tonks led the team who lent and arranged the pictures in the Epilogue.

For *The Death of Tintagiles* the music was composed by Vaughan Williams and the costumes designed by Charles Ricketts. Others in the company were Sydney Fairbrother, Irene Rooke, Esmé Beringer and Harcourt Williams.

1914

Alec took over again on the first day of the year with another adaptation after Bernstein, *The Attack*, which he replaced on 5th March with Sutro's *The Two Virtues* in which Athene Seyler, Henrietta Watson, George Bishop and Herbert Waring led, with himself and Martha Hedman, a Danish-American girl who had with Alec also been in *The Attack* in which she made her English début. Later Max Beerbohm's curtain-raiser *A Social Success* was added with Reginald Owen, Reynolds, Bishop, Dane, Elizabeth Chesney and Muriel Barnby.

To end the season *An Ideal Husband* was run seventy-seven times from 14th May to 24th July. Alec played Goring, Phyllis Neilson-Terry was Lady Chiltern, Amy Brandon-Thomas was Mabel Chiltern, Hilda Moore was Mrs Chevely, Henrietta Watson and Elizabeth Chesney were Lady Markby and the Countess of Basildon. Arthur Wontner was Sir Robert Chiltern and Alfred Bishop was the Earl of Caversham which he had created in Tree's original production.

The Great War began during the recess but on 19th September the theatre opened with *Those Who Sit In Judgement* by Michael Orme, the wife of J. T. Grein. This was a drama of finance and the Gold Coast in which one of the scenes was set. It lasted only twenty-one performances. In the large cast the most notable recruit was Nicholas Hannen in his first straight part in London after some time in the Glasgow Repertory Company. Before that he had been four years in musical comedy. *His House in Order* replaced the failure. Prices were reduced this autumn and all naval and military personnel in uniform admitted at half-price.

1915

Besier's *Kings and Queens* ran from 16th January to the end of March. As well as Alec the cast included Marie Lohr, Alma Murray, Marcelle Chevalier, Wontner, Webster and Pearson.

Twenty-five years of the Alexanders' management were celebrated on 4th February. The curtain rose to a stage empty except for three chairs and a table on which, covered by a green silk cloth, was a gold cup for Alec and a silver salver for Florence. On tripped Madge Kendal, finger to lips to stop applause. She exposed the gifts for a moment, then made exit to lead on the happy couple.

After a speech of summary and congratulation Madge called for three cheers, and then started off 'For He's a Jolly Good Fellow' before she presented the 1746 cup in which was a cheque for £200 for Alec's pet theatrical charities. As he rose to reply she waved him down. 'I haven't finished yet', she said and took Florence by the hand and made the remarkable speech of adulation mentioned in this section's opening. '. . . what your assistance and knowledge have accomplished for this theatre . . . by your marvellous art you have made short people tall, dark people fair, fat people thin . . . tenth wonder of the world. . . .'

The brilliant crowd in front included the Princess Victoria

and Earl of Kilmorey, Sir Charles Wyndham, Sir Squire and
Lady Bancroft, Sir Herbert and Lady Tree, du Maurier,
Anthony Hope, Marion Terry, Ben Webster and May Whitty,
Marie Lohr, H. V. Esmond and Eva Moore, Genevieve Ward
and many more.

The lovely Nina Boucicault, Madge Titheradge and Owen
Nares were in the unsuccessful comedy *Panorama of Youth*,
by Hartley Manners, which ran from 14th April to 8th May.
Laurette Taylor, wife of the latter, was with Godfrey Tearle
and Helen Ferrers at a theatre charity matinée of the Marchioness of Townsend's *The Monk and the King's Daughter* on
the 7th.

A spy drama, *The Day Before The Day*, ran nineteen times
only from 19th May, even though the cast was a strong one
including Lyn Harding, Nares, Pearson, Gerald Lawrence,
A. B. Imeson, Playfair and Edmund Gwenn, with the latter's
sister Elizabeth Chesney, Grace Lane, Clare Greet and Stella
Campbell. The author was Chester Fernald, father of John
Fernald who followed Sir Kenneth Barnes as director of
RADA.

Veteran Pinero's final play here, *The Big Drum*, opened the
winter season on 1st September and ran into December. This
time the programmes carried the caption 'The play produced
under the direction of the author'. Scenery was by G. Sackman
whose name had been on the bills for over a year.

Matheson Lang opened a month's season from 6th December
as Shylock with his wife Hutin Britton as Portia. The year
before they had played the same parts when with Estelle Stead
they had helped Lilian Baylis restart The Old Vic. Israel and
Louis Zangwill went back-stage for a long talk one day and
quite changed Lang's ideas for the early scenes. He had
created a cringing, fawning Jew instead of showing—through
outward signs of racial humility—a mind stronger and more
subtle than those of the Gentiles with whom he dealt. So, anyway, was how the Zangwills saw the character. They were

astonished when the Highlander denied any trace of Semitic blood, for Israel had seen all famous actors in the part and all, he thought, had some Jewish strain. 'But you', he said, 'seem more characteristically Jewish than any of them!'

1916

Alec returned on 6th January in Mrs Clifford Mills' *The Basker*, a comedy of high life in which he was a lazy descendant of an ancient house, roused eventually to a sense of responsibility by his valet's expatiation on past family glories. Genevieve Ward played his grandmother the Duchess.

After 112 performances it was followed by Horace Annesley Vachell's *The Pen* which lasted ten days to 13th May.

Alfred Butt filled the unexpected vacuum with Moya Mannering as *Peg O' My Heart*. It was directed by the author, Hartley Manners, but, after opening on 15th May, they had to transfer in a fortnight. Macqueen Pope was the business manager.

Alec had been rehearsing *Bella Donna* and presented it from 31st May to 15th July with Mrs Pat and himself in their original roles as were Athol Stewart and Alfred Harris. Leon Quartermaine was Nigel, Dawson Milward the villain Baroudi. Norma Whalley and five others supported.

In August Alec appeared at The Coliseum in a playlet.

Keneth Kent appeared as *Lucky Jim* sixty times from 19th October and then *Charley's Aunt* ran over Christmas from 14th December.

1917

The final play in which Alec was to act opened on 25th January. This was Louis N. Parker's *The Aristocrat*, an all mud and dirt versus colour and purity romance of the Revolution. Alec was the Duke of Chasttelfranc who scored off the lumpen proletariat in a trial scene and then, having been saved from the guillotine, proudly refused to civilise the rabble when asked to run a school for diplomats.

The play proved a good vehicle for a fine company headed by Genevieve Ward whom for the second time Alec had persuaded from retirement to play an attractive old duchess. The 27th March was her eightieth birthday so at a gathering on stage she was presented with an Address, illuminated by Percy Macquoid and signed by all the company. She was created a D.B.E. in 1921.

The cast-list ran: George Alexander, Mary Glynne, Helen Rous, Genevieve Ward, William Lugg, Lennox Pawle, Edward Combermere, Joyce Carey, Denis Neilson-Terry, Charles Glenney, William Stack, E. Rayson-Cousens, Miriam Lewes, E. Vivian Reymolds, Henry Oscar, W. R. Staveley, Hector Abbas, Sunday Wilshin, Phyllis Neal. Servants, Soldiers, Jury, Mob. Percy Macquoid, R.I., designed the costumes and scenery which was painted by Juan Sackman. Italia Conti trained the children in the crowd, Simmons made the costumes and Clarkson the wigs. The conductor was Albert Fox who had been musical director since William Robins retired in the summer of 1915. Vivian Reynolds was stage manager as he had been since he took over from Vincent for *Paolo* in 1902. Business manager was C. T. H. Helmsley who had been as loyal an aide to Alec for many years as he had been to their old master Irving for whom he had also acted as 'double'. He was married to Martin Harvey's sister.

Understudy William Stack had to take over when Alec dropped out because of illness. Until then the play had been running strongly but attendances fell so much that it was taken off after 2nd June, the 150th performance.

Alec was well enough to direct *Sheila*, a comedy by Githa Sowerby, which only ran from 7th to 23rd June. Fay Compton made her only appearance here, in the title-role. The others were Joyce Carey, Stella Campbell, Gwendolen Floyd, Helen Rous, Henrietta Leverett and C. Aubrey Smith, Henry Oscar,

William Home, Lance Lister, William Farren and W. Langley-Bill. Sackman did the scenery.

On 4th September the theatre reopened under Percy Hutchinson and Herbert Jay with *The Pacifists*, 'a parable in a farce' by Henry Arthur Jones. Ellis Jeffreys, Rita Otway, Arthur Chesney, Sam Livesey, Lennox Pawle, John M. East, Charles Glenny and J. S. Smith were in this, which had been tried out at Southport in August. It lasted twelve performances for neither Press nor public understood it.

A remark by one of the nastiest of the critics about the characters was copied by dear old Jones on to the flyleaf of his own copy: '. . . blind bastards begotten in the untimely old age of the Manchester bagman . . .' (Jones had originally been a commercial traveller). In another copy which he presented to 'My dear Mote' (his solicitor) was written: 'This is another of my great failures. I wrote it as a burlesque but the critics and the general body of playgoers took it for a realistic play. It was my own fault. I ought to have known them better—faithfully yours—Henry Arthur Jones.'

The same author's *The Liars* was then presented and followed by Ibsen's *Ghosts*. The two impresarios were successful in their venture because they had wanted to lose money for fear of excess profits taxes on productions elsewhere! *Loyalty* by Harold Owen ran twenty times until 8th December. The cast included Viola Tree, Aubrey Smith, Randle Ayrton, Sydney Paxton, Pawle, Sternroyd and Sam Livesey with his son Roger who was making his début.

From the 15th *Charley's Aunt* ran over the Christmas season into the new year. Edna Best made her London début as Ela Delahay whilst Amy Brandon-Thomas was Kitty in her late father's classic.

1918

Napoleon Lambelet offered his own comic opera *Valentine*

from 24th January to 12th April. Book was by Davenport and
Wibrow, the best known names in the company being Hayden
Coffin and Walter Passmore. Butt followed with *Peg O' My
Heart* again until 24th May.

In the early morning of 16th March Alec died in his Chorley
Wood country house. His motto had been 'Do thy duty, that
is best; Leave unto thy God the rest.' For him that had proved
worth while both spiritually and materially. Mourned by many
in and out of the theatre, who liked and honoured him for his
public and charitable work, he was to be long remembered with
affection by many friends. A modest man with no overweaning
sense of pride, he could laughingly call his company together
—including Kinsey Peile who recorded it—to point the moral
of being seated that day in 1895 at a luncheon party beside a
lady who had never heard of him!

At the Parliamentary Enquiry in 1909 he had upheld the
Censorship, his points including the fear that freedom could
allow opportunist vulgarians to debase the boards—as has
indeed been done since by clubs immune from the Censor. He
was, however, in favour of a tribunal to which appeals could
be made. He left some £90,000, bequeathed his rights in the
plays to Oscar Wilde's son, £250 to each of his head staff,
£100 to others of long service, £50 to those of five years and
£20 to those who had not been with him so long. Many stage
funds also benefited.

Book III

UNDER GILBERT MILLER

1918-1957

THE old Earl of Kilmorey had died in 1915 and was succeeded by his son who fought in France in the Life Guards throughout the war. Transfer of the lease was negotiated and thirty-four-year-old New Yorker Gilbert Miller took over in the autumn.

As a youth Miller had been in the Marines and then in the U.S. Naval Air Force, but since 1916 had been an impresario. His London-born father built the delightful Adam-style Henry Miller Theatre in New York, having made his début in Toronto where his father had immigrated. Gilbert's maternal grandmother was Mathilda Heron, who emigrated as a child with her mother from their Irish home as political refugees in the days of the Great Hunger when Ireland had been cleared of grain, potatoes and livestock by English Cromwellian relics, countenanced and encouraged by men like Sir Robert Peel who was however, as some said by the grace of God, killed in the end by an Irish horse in 1850. Gilbert's mother, Bijou Heron, became a well-known American actress like her mother Mathilda. The latter is particularly remembered as the first successful American Camille in her own genuine version of the Dumas classic.

Gilbert Miller in association with the Littlers was later to buy The St James's outright, and although it was often sub-let he remained ostensibly in control for almost forty years until the sell-out to the knackers.

His first tenant was another American, Gertrude Elliott (Lady Forbes-Robertson), whose husband, knighted in 1913, had now retired. Her brother-in-law Ian Robertson, besides playing a Yogi directed *Eyes of Youth* by Marcin and Guernon, a drama previously done in the States.

1919

They had opened on 2nd September, the King and Queen were in front in March and in August the play closed after 383 performances.

Miller joined with Henry Ainley to present on 26th September the Aylmer Maudes' translation of Tolstoy's *The Live Corpse* as *Reparation*. Stanley Bell directed. Décor was by J. A. Fraser after Moscow Art Theatre designs. Athene Seyler was Lisa Protasov and Ainley her husband Fedya. Marion Terry played Anna Karenin and Ion Swinley her son Victor. Others in the large cast were Meggie Albanesi, Claude Rains, Henry Morrell, Otho Stuart, Ernest Milton and Leonard Sickert. It ran 116 times into January.

1920

Julius Caesar was then presented eighty-three times from 9th January until 20th March. Ainley was Marcus Antonius to Basil Gill's Brutus with Clifton Boyne in the title-role. Esmé Beringer was Calpurnia and Lilian Braithwaite was Portia. Others included Milton Rosmer, Ernest Milton and Henry Oscar.

Douglas Murray's modern comedy about grumpy old millionaire *Uncle Ned* then ran from 27th March to 8th May with Ainley, Randle Ayrton, Rains, Alice Moffat, Edna Best, Irene Rooke, Phyllis McTavish, Ernest Digges and the veteran G. W. Anson, who died in August.

The active Ainley/Miller partnership now ceased and Daisy Markham presented herself in *The Mystery of the Yellow Room* by H. Bennett from the French. This ran ninety-three times from 26th May to 14th August with Nicholas Hannen, Franklin Dyall, Lewis Casson, Sybil Thorndike and others.

On 17th August happy-go-lucky light comedian Charles Hawtrey then appeared in *His Lady Friends* which was to run 135 times until 11th December. This was an American play after May Eginton's novel, with Hawtrey as a bookseller who somewhat miraculously started making money. Since Jessie Bateman as his wife was too used to economies to help him spend, he became 'rich uncle' to three different girls played by Mercia Swinburne, Joyce Gaymon and Madeline Seymour. When the girls all turned up at his home he was quickly swamped by trouble, for he pretended they were all victims of the trifling of his lawyer friend (James Carew) who entered too willingly into the charade and agreed with the wife that they ought to be well compensated with large cheques to mend their broken hearts.

Athene Seyler played the spendthrift wife of the lawyer and Joan Barry played a delightfully cheeky 'flapper'. Hawtrey was rapturously received by admirers for it was his return to the stage after a long illness.

Peter Pan arrived for the first time when five days before Christmas Edna Best crossed swords with Henry Ainley as Hook. George Shelton was Smee for the fifteenth time. Leslie Dwyer was one of the Wolves.

1921

Sarah Bernhardt was at The Prince's as *Daniel*. Though her voice and spirit were as golden almost as ever she was in her seventies and had lost a leg. The drama was specially written for her by Louis Verneuil, the husband-to-be of her grand-daughter, and consequently he conceived an enfeebled, ill, love-lorn drug-addict so that Sarah could play the part in a chair. Daniel's brother was elderly, fierce, tied to business, neglectful of his young wife who had a lover. Daniel pretended to be that lover so as to give the actual one more freedom.

Sybil Harris translated the piece and Miller presented it on 15th January with Claude Rains in the title-role. His task would have been easier had he not been tied to the original and therefore as static on the stage as Sarah. Alexandra Carlisle made a reappearance in London after a long sojourn in the United States, whither she later returned. She was the wife, Leslie Faber the lover and Lyn Harding the cuckolded husband. Also in it were Edith Evans and Henry Oscar.

Miller replaced the 'catchpenny' with another American play, *Polly with a Past* by Middleton and Bolton, 110 times from 2nd March to 3rd June. The cast was young Noël Coward, Henry Kendall, Donald Calthrop, Aubrey Smith, Claude Rains, Hatherton and Arthur with Edna Best, Helen Haye, Edith Evans, Alice Moffat and Nancye Kenyon.

Before the run ended May Palfrey presented a court-room comedy called *Emma*, by H. Thomas, which had been tried out in Bournemouth in 1918. From 16th May it was on for four matinées a week and then from 5th to 11th June in the evenings also. The company included Amy Brandon-Thomas and her brother Jevan as well as the author as a K.C. The others were Norfolk, Horton, Rae, Douglas, Littlejohns, Don, Greene and the Misses Hill, Frizell, Constable, Joan Swinstead, Karslake, Honor Bright, Ava, Drusilla Wills.

Now the Actor's Association, forerunner of Equity, was at this time well on the way to winning the fight for better conditions and a standard contract. Their heaviest opponent had been C. B. Cochran who capitulated in 1919. Though he had said he would not employ any member of the A.A. in any of his shows, he gave in when the 5,000-strong union passed a counter resolution and started a Fighting Fund which was headed by a donation from Madge Kendal of £50.

May Palfrey, the widow of Weedon Grossmith, was one of the minor managers still holding out. When *Emma* was put into the evening bill the cast naturally asked her manager for more money for ten shows a week, since they had been engaged for four a week only. Already there had been trouble over the small-part players not being paid anything for rehearsals. Nine of those in *Emma* were also rehearsing for a revival of her late husband's *Night of the Party*. Eventually Miss Palfrey refused to pay any extra at all and took *Emma* off after the Saturday performance of 11th June.

The posters went up for the revival to open on the Wednesday but meanwhile the A.A. issued an ultimatum to her saying that if she did not sign the Standard Contract Agreement their members, almost all the company, would not act. She stuck out until past the advertised opening time, the stage manager had to be prevented from ringing up the curtain on an empty stage, the company naturally all in a ferment of anxiety. To quote from a letter to me from Jevan Brandon-Thomas who was in both plays: 'It was an awful experience ... with the curtain held down while frantic negotiations were taking place. One girl was in hysterics. . . . Finally Miss Palfrey gave in rather ungraciously and flew in front of the curtain, saying to the audience that a pistol had been held to her head at the eleventh hour and that rather than disappoint she had been forced to sign. In that sort of atmosphere the curtain rose about twenty minutes late and it was an agonising first-night despite a very warmly sympathetic round of applause for the first person to make an entrance.'

Sydney Paxton was the only one who had been in the original production twenty years before. He played his old part of the Alderman and Lauri de Frece Weedon's part as the valet. Elsie Stranack was Lady Hampshire which Miss Palfrey had created. The others were Joan Swinstead, Frizell, Brooks, Newton and Bevan with the three men already indicated and Horton, Thomas, Rae, Geach, Greene, Raynor, Douglas,

Macrae, Littlejohns and Whittaker. They were all disbanded fifteen days later.

Lyn Harding then joined with Denys Grayson (later the baronet) in management to present a comedy called *Threads* by Frank Stayton. In the cast were Faith Celli, Dora Barton, Harding, Henry Kendall, Cyril Raymond, C. M. Lowne. The latter had been in charge of RADA during the war.

The author's programme note said it 'was written during snatched hours off duty in 1915' then published as a novel, 'but the war has been cut out owing to managerial prejudice'. It flopped in three weeks.

They then revived Conan Doyle's *The Speckled Band*, with Lyn Harding as the villain Rylott and H. A. Saintsbury as Sherlock Holmes which these two had originated in 1910 at The Adelphi. Mary Merrall was Enid and K. Rivington Dr Watson. Victor Pierpoint was the page-boy Billy which Charlie Chaplin had created. Except for trouble with the mechanical snake, which got stuck once on its poison journey, they were fairly successful and attracted ninety-two audiences before they transferred to The Royalty.

A strapping American wench called Joan Maclean then banged on the bedroom window as *Peter Pan* on 15th December. She romped through the part with little charm and no hint of feyness which was all the more a pity because Ernest Thesiger (to quote from an unidentified clipping) was a 'fascinating tuppence coloured' Captain Hook whose 'whimsical malignity of voice the younger generation' found 'alarming and delightful'.

1922

Peter finished on matinées only, on 28th January. Five days earlier Miller presented *The Bat* which ran until 4th November for this mystery thrilled Londoners as much as it had Americans with a missing banker, a secret room, viragoish fortune-teller

(Drusilla Wills) with her ouija-board, a scared Eurasian butler (Claude Rains), a sharp detective (Arthur Wontner), an 'unknown man' (Allan Jeayes) found lurking in the garden. Nora Swinburne, Eva Moore, George Relph, A. Scott-Gatty, Kershaw and Bolingbroke completed the cast who were directed by Collin Kemper.

Austin Page unsuccessfully presented his own *The Beating on the Door* for two weeks from 6th November with some of those in the last play as well as Mary Jerrold, Athole Stewart, Franklin Dyall and others. It was a Russian-set drama directed by R. Mamoulian with balalaikas accompanying the Makaroff Singers in Slav folk-songs.

Robert Loraine then presented himself with Miles Malleson, Fred Kerr, Jean Cadell and others including Adele Dixon in her second stage appearance though she was still at Italia Conti's school. They acted only twenty-nine times from 30th November in Ian Hay's early comedy *The Happy Ending*.

Lyn Harding was Hook to Edna Best's *Peter Pan* this time from 21st December to 27th January on matinées only. The First Twin was played by Ursula Moreton who was to be a strong support to Ninette de Valois in the founding of the Sadler's Wells Ballet. Nancy Price's daughter Joan Maude was Tootles and H. V. Esmond and Eva Moore's daughter Jill Esmond made her début as Nibs.

1923

If Winter Comes, the famous novel dramatised by its author A. S. M. Hutchinson with B. M. Hastings, was presented by Frank Curzon on the last day of January but ran only to 17th March. Grace Lane was Mrs Sabre, Frederick Volpé the Rev. Sebastian Fortune and Owen Nares the young Mark Sabre.

Isabel Jay was then starred in her own back-stage drama *The Inevitable* for only four nights. It was replaced by Horace Vachell's *Plus Fours* which was transferred from The Haymarket on 2nd April to finish 150 performances on 26th May. Peggy O'Neil, Una O'Connor, Denys Blakelock, Ronald Simpson, Aubrey Smith were among the cast.

Leon M. Lion directed Dorothy Brandon's *The Outsider* which he and Curzon presented 109 times from 30th May. The authoress was herself lame as was her heroine Lalage (Isobel Elsom) whose father (Dawson Milward), as a nerve specialist, completed her cure commenced by bone-setter Ragatzy (Leslie Faber).

George Moore returned to the theatre he had frequented in the days of Dick Mansell when Lion put on three matinées of his *The Coming of Gabrielle* in June. This revised version of the Stage Society 1913 production of *Elizabeth Cooper* had been held up for a long time until the availability of Athene Seyler and Leslie Faber. Moore had recently retired from France and settled in London. He harangued the cast at the first call but as rehearsals proceeded he sat dumb in the stalls as he followed every one of his golden words from the copy before him. Then he went home to compose long letters to Lion ordering complete restoration of all cuts and forbidding more.

The exciting *Green Goddess* began a year's run of 417 performances under Miller and Ames on 6th September. Purposely written as insurance against poverty in his old age, this play's unlikely author was the important critic, translator and advocate of Ibsen, William Archer. He died in his late sixties, three months after the end of the run. Few realised immediately that the melodrama was by him. One critic even scribbled on his first-night programme: 'Will run for 12 months at least. . . . Must know more of Archer. . . .'

The drama had already toured in America after two years at the New York Booth's following its try-out at the opening of the rebuilt Philadelphia Walnut. Ronald Colman then played a priest, and old friend Herbert Waring, in his third American engagement, was Major Crispin. Helen Nowell as an Ayah and George Arliss as the Raja were in both American and English productions. Arliss had not been home since Mrs Pat took him to New York to play Cayley Drummle in the winter of 1901 after her Royalty season. Now he played to perfection the suave, Cambridge-educated Raja of Rukh into whose remote state crash-landed an aeroplane with jingoish Major Crispin (Owen Roughwood), his wife Lucilla (Isobel Elsom) and her friend Dr Traherne (George Relph).

Over the border three of the Raja's half-brothers were about to be hanged by the English, so death was decreed for the visitors in retaliation but with three days grace during which they were treated as guests. The Raja owned a transmitting set which was in the charge of his valet Watkins. The latter, played by Arthur Hatherton, was an escaped Cockney murderer so it was morally quite correct for him to be thrown from a window down a precipice by the Major so that he could wireless a call for help. The Raja shot him dead as he did so; the doctor was pinioned preparatory to torture; Lucilla was reserved for the fate much worse than death since she had aroused the Raja's lascivious desires.

Rescue came with buzzing planes, a lieutenant who landed in the name of the King Emperor, bombs fell as warning. The Raja bowed to superior force with charming grace and as his guests departed he turned with a shrug to remark philosophically: 'Well, well. She'd probably have been a damned nuisance!'

There was a large crowd of priests and others. One of these was Raymond de la Motte, who told me that Queen Mary being present on the second night maybe so excited Isobel Elsom that she sprained her ankle and her understudy Helen Nowell had to take over whilst the wardrobe mistress played the Ayah. Amongst many Eastern potentates who enjoyed Arliss's portrayal was the Crown Prince of Kaputhala, as Arliss said in a letter in 1924 when he mentioned lunching at Claridges with the Raja and Rani of Sarawak. The Rani presented him with an ivory trophy as a 100th-night souvenir. Mary Merrall took over as the heroine in June.

1924

Charles Farrell and Mary Duncan were in the all-American company of *The Nervous Wreck* which ran ninety-three times from the middle of September. It was a farce of the Wild West which was followed by Catherine Cushing's *Pollyanna* (after Eleanor Porter's American classic) on 18th December. Joan Barry was the awful child who sees good in everybody. The others were Grace Lane, Mary Brough, Maire O'Neill, Elizabeth Watson and Alice Beet with Hugh Dempster, Athole Stewart, Lyn Harding and Tom Reynolds. The humour was lost in the Atlantic and the play was withdrawn on 3rd January.

1925

Saturday 10th January was the fifth and last night of *Meddlers* and curtain-raiser *Number 24*, which had Mimi Crawford, Honor Bright, John Wyse, Farren Soutar in the casts.

Grounds for Divorce by Guy Bolton from Vajda's Hungarian original then ran 118 times to 2nd May with Madge Titheradge, Owen Nares and others.

The Dancing Mothers transferred from The Queen's on 4th May until moved on to The Royalty after 1st June. Godfrey Tearle played the husband of Gertrude Elliott who ran away to Paris with Leslie Faber as the boy-friend of her stage daughter, played by her real-life one, Jean Forbes-Robertson.

The River, which was Sir Patrick Hastings' first play, ran from 2nd to 19th June. Clifford Mollison, Faber, Nares, Helen Ferrers and Jessie Winter were among those in this drama set on the Gold Coast which was transferred to The Lyric.

Seventeen performances were enough for Molnar's *The Guardsman*, translated by Colbron and Bartsch, with Seymour Hicks and his daughter Betty, Madge Titheradge, Margaret Yarde, etc. Last night was 4th July.

Ibsen's *The Wild Duck* arrived for fifty-three performances from the Hampstead Everyman on 15th July. Sybil Arundale was Gina Ekdal, Milton Rosmer her husband Hjalmar, Angela Baddeley their daughter Hedvig and Brember Wills was Old Ekdal. Harold Scott doubled Balle and Molvik, George Merritt was the merchant Werle and Ion Swinley his son Gegers. Sydney Bland played Dr Relling and directed.

Gerald du Maurier had been knighted in 1922. He and Gladys Cooper now joined in presenting Freddie Lonsdale's light and witty comedy *The Last of Mrs Cheyney* from 22nd September for fifteen months until 18th December 1926. Du Maurier played as well as directed. The others were Gladys Cooper, Ellis Jeffreys, May Whitty, Sealby, Gray and Camp-bell with Milward, Ronald Squire, Loder, Fletcher, Frank Lawton, Paterson and Steerman.

The long run was followed by *Charley's Aunt*, with Jevan Brandon-Thomas as Jack Chesney, from 21st December for a month.

1927

Miller had been sub-letting since *The Bat*, but he joined with du Maurier and Curzon to put on Pertwee and Dearden's *Interference* which ran 412 times from 29th January. Herbert Waring returned for this blackmail drama with Herbert Marshall, Frank Lawton, Moyna MacGill, Betty and Hilda Moore and others. Douglas Jeffries took over Sir Gerald's part later in the run.

Sir Johnstone Forbes-Robertson came out of retirement for two Clan Matinées of *Twelfth Night* on 17th and 20th May, when no fewer than fifteen of his family combined to help the Sadler's Wells Fund. The old star himself played the Priest and his famous daughter Jean was Viola, perhaps less of a love-lorn maiden of Illyria, some thought, than a deep-thinking woman of Ibsen but we'll let that pass. Her sisters Maxine,

Chloe and Diana were Olivia and two attendants. Jean's cousin Henry played her stage brother Sebastian, whilst his daughter Jill was an attendant and her grandfather Norman Forbes played Sir Andrew Aguecheek. The latter's sister-in-law, Gertrude Elliott, was the frolicsome maid Maria. Sir John-stone's brother Ian was Curio and his daughter Beatrice wrote and spoke the Chorus. Four others were attendants.

Recruits from outside the clan included Robert Atkins who directed and played his favourite part of Sir Toby, Esmond Knight as Valentine, Courtice Pounds as Feste the clown and Baliol Holloway as Malvolio. Rupert Harvey, Paul Cavanagh, St Barbe West and Andrew Leigh played the remaining roles. Programme sellers included Elissa Landi, Marie Ney and Gwynne Whitby. Du Maurier made an appeal in the interval.

1928

Sir Gerald and Miller presented Walter Ellis' *S.O.S.* on 11th February. Great publicity was gained when they recruited Gracie Fields at £100 a week to play a straight part in this. She was Lady Weir who arrived, expecting a passionate week-end, at the country inn of 'unco-guid' Cobb (Herbert Waring) at the invitation of Sir Gerald (who also directed) as Owen. He had only inveigled her there to extract a confession that she was guilty of stealing gems his late wife had been accused of taking some years earlier. Lady Weir died by suicide that night, so with a sub-plot of love between her child and Owen's there was sufficient excitement to keep the piece running to the end of July.

Herbert Marshall (later Roland Pertwee) was Sir Julian Weir. Others included George Curzon, Betty Stockfield and Grace Wilson. Gracie played her part strongly but she was really out of her element and wasted. Audiences also felt cheated for she was on only in the first act. Every night a car waited at the stage door after that to whisk her to The Coliseum where she was

top of the bill. Some other salaries may be mentioned. Sir
Gerald took £200 for his eight performances as well as a share
in the profits. Marshall got £67 10/-, but Waring, for all his
forty years experience, was paid a measly £25. Six of the
others actually got less than £10 each.

Arnold Bennett exploited Dr Voronoff's monkey glands,
which were sensational news about this time, when he wrote a
dull effort called *The Return Journey*. On 1st September du
Maurier played octogenarian Dr Fausting who was being rejuvenated by suavely sinister Satollyan (Henry Daniel) and
attempting seduction of the modern Marguerite (Grace
Wilson).

Michel Saint-Denis made his first English appearance on
29th November when with Jacques Copeau and the Compagnie
des Quinze they gave a short French season. Saint-Denis, as
Jacques Duchesne of the Free French Radio, was to do sterling
work in the Hitler war.

The gallery booed and Sir Gerald angrily rebuked them on
the first night of P. G. Wodehouse's *The Play's the Thing* (after
Molnar). Henry Forbes-Robertson and Ursula Jeans were in
this, which lasted from 4th to 15th December.

A. E. W. Mason's *No Other Tiger* started on Boxing Day and
flopped. Denis Neilson-Terry made the most of his strong part
in this melodrama of jealousy and revenge as he acted an ex-
Devil's Isle convict whose hate was directed at Mary Glynne,
who had not the vivacity to portray a Parisian cabaret dancer.
The play was enjoyed tremendously—for all the wrong
reasons!

1929

A. and W. Carten's *Fame* followed from 20th February. This
was an unintentionally funny, rubbishy and heavily drawn
drama of huntin' and fishin' folk. From their terrain flew Nora
Swinburne as Sonia into the arms of dago violinist Paolo (du

Maurier) who later lost the use of an arm. The pair avidly enjoyed many emotional opportunities which culminated in Sonia slapping his face—which revivified his arm. Nigel Bruce and Naomi Jacob (the writer) also enjoyed themselves as particularly snobbish 'county types'. The large cast also included Frank Vosper, Walter Fitzgerald, Scott-Gatty, Una Venning, Margery Clark, Dorothy Monkman, Mignon O'Doherty and, later in the run, Cathleen Nesbitt.

C. B. Cochran took over from 4th June to present the New York Theatre Guild's *Caprice* by Sil-vara and Moeller. Lynn Fontanne came home again in this and her husband Alfred Lunt made his first English appearance. Lily Cahill and Douglass Montgomery were also in this empty if brilliant vehicle.

Galsworthy's *The Skin Game* transferred from Wyndham's in the middle of September with Edmund Gwenn and Mabel Terry-Lewis. Leonard Sachs, later co-founder of the Players Theatre and famous television Chairman of Victorian Variety, had recently arrived from South Africa. He was assistant stage manager and since Gwenn's memory was failing him and he dreaded 'drying-up' more than anything, Leonard, as he told me years later, was made to sit not only within hearing but within Gwenn's sight throughout the action. The only suitable spot was the fireplace, so there he had to crouch and hide from the audience but stay in sight of the apprehensive star who a few years later decided to remain mostly in the safety of cinema studios.

Alec Rea then presented a drama of passion and jealousy in a far-flung outpost of Empire. This was *Heat Wave* by Pertwee from a story by Denise Robins which ran two months from 15th October. Walter Hackett directed Ann Todd, Phyllis Neilson-Terry, Herbert Marshall, Patric Curwen and others.

Jean Forbes-Robertson was *Peter Pan* for the third time for a month from 19th December. She was delightfully light-hearted yet virile opposite du Maurier as Hook and Darling, the parts he had created for Barrie twenty-five years before. Marie Lohr was Mrs Darling and Mary Casson was Wendy. George Shelton, who had made his London début here in 1876, was Smee for his twenty-third and final time; he was eighty when he died in 1932.

1930

The cast earned a tremendous reception on 1st February for A. A. Milne's *Michael and Mary*, which Charles Hopkins directed and presented with Miller. The moving love story showed a writer becoming successful as he lived with the runaway wife of a brutal husband who returned to attempt blackmail and die. The lovers were played by Herbert Marshall and Edna Best who added to their increasing prestige as one of the leading married couples of the London stage. Their portrayal covered twenty-five years. D. A. Clarke-Smith was the blackmailer who dropped dead with heart-failure when his demands were rejected. Elizabeth Allan and Frank Lawton were two young lovers, Reginald Bach was a comic policeman and Fisher White the parson father of the hero. Margaret Scudamore (mother of Sir Michael Redgrave) was a landlady and Torin Thatcher an Inspector. Seven others supported.

Five months later, 30th June, Miller was at last successful with a Hungarian adaptation, Molnar's *The Swan*, which he himself directed. It was a Ruritanian romance about a tutor (Colin Clive, Maurice Evans from October) in love with a princess (Edna Best) whose father was played by Herbert Marshall. Irene Vanbrugh, Henrietta Watson, Kinsey Peile, Basil Loder, A. B. Imeson, Bruce Belfrage, Basil Langton and Una Venning with Betty Turner and others supported.

Treasury sheets showed a loss of about £5,000 even though it ran 145 times. However, Miller as sole lessee collected a rent of £7,230 for the eighteen weeks. Apart from that the drain on the takings was not very heavy for eight of the minor players received £7 a week or less, and the box-office keeper who took all the money was only paid £8. Edna Best topped the salary list with £150 whilst her husband got £100. The play was later presented in New York.

Emlyn Williams then directed his own *A Murder Has Been Arranged* which was backed by Daniel Mayer. Margaretta Scott was Lady Jasper, Viola Compton her mother Mrs Arthur and J. H. Roberts was Sir Charles. Henry Kendall as Maurice Mullins with Ann Codrington, John Cheatle, Amy Veness, W. Humphreys and Veronica Turleigh as Miss Groze, Cavendish, Mrs Wragg, Jimmy North and A Woman completed the cast of this rather unsuccessful mystery set in the theatre in which it was staged.

1931

Alec Rea then on 17th February presented Emlyn Williams in the title-role of Wakefield's *Etienne* from Duval's French original. Nicholas Hannen directed this excellent vehicle about the precocious boy who stole his father's mistress. Mary Clare, Una O'Connor, Margaret Webster, Myno Burnet and David Horne were the chief support of the up-and-coming Welsh genius.

Miller took over on 4th May to lose money on *Payment Deferred* which Jeffrey Dell had dramatised from C. S. Forester's novel. The character of William Marble proved a tremendous part for lumbering Yorkshireman Charles Laughton, who transmitted the emotional stress he suffered so intensely that his wife later reported upon the unrestrained tears of audiences as they watched Laughton as an actual murderer and then innocent suspected one. Louise Hampton played the wife Annie Marble who committed suicide but for whom her husband was hanged. Jeanne de Casalis was the Frenchwoman to whom Marble made illicit love (Marlene Dietrich took the part in the film version). The star's real wife, Elsa Lanchester, played his twelve-year-old stage child. The others were Ernest

Jay, Edgar K. Bruce, Haines, Homewood, Longuet and McPherson. H. K. Ayliff directed. Only Laughton, his wife and Paul Longuet were in the company which opened at the New York Lyceum in September.

Sir Barry Jackson followed on 14th September with Sheridan's *A Trip to Scarborough* when he directed Ernest Thesiger as a delightful Lord Foppington, Harry Wilcoxon as Young Fashion and Gilian Lind as Amanda.

1932

The theatre was closed during the winter until Ernest Milton took it for a couple of months from 4th April, when he was Othello to Henry Oscar's Iago and Lydia Sherwood's Desdemona. Athene Seyler played Emilia, Flora Robson was Bianca, Harold Scott doubled a sailor and clown and Terence O'Brien was Montano.

On the 28th Milton was Shylock to Mary Newcombe's Portia when Lydia Sherwood was Jessica, Nicholas Hannen was Antonio and John Wyse, Horace Sequira and Ben Webster were Bassanio, Old Gobbo and the Duke. John Devine was Salanio.

Miller then backed Marie Tempest in Osborn's witty *Vinegar Tree* on 8th June. Her husband Graham Browne directed and took part with Celia Johnson, Louis Hayward, Henry Daniell, Barbara Hoffe and Frederick Moyes.

The lessee followed with two more successes. Van Druten's *Behold We Live* ran 158 times from 16th August. It opened with Ronald Ward as Tono being beastly and threatening to shoot his wife Sarah, who was interpreted with charm and sympathy by Gertrude Lawrence. Tono was one of the Mayfair 'smart set', as was frivolous flitterer Jewel (Eileen Peel) who had a dour husband Hector (Alexander Archdale). Tono rushed off to his latest affair in Cannes just after Sarah met leading barrister Gordon (du Maurier) who stopped her shooting herself, made her divorce Tono and start afresh with him. May Whitty was the understanding mother of Gordon whose wife refused him divorce so the lovers lived in sin though the scandal barred him from a coveted judgeship. After a year he died and Sarah was alone again. Everley Gregg and David Keir supported.

Auriol Lee, who had been here with Alec, directed the play with great insight. Gertrude Lawrence was exceptionally moving, both she and Sir Gerald making a deep impression with their well-conceived tragic parts. Though critics seemed disappointed with London's most promising dramatist of the day, this did not affect attendances.

1933

Ruth Draper in May gave a series of her remarkable solo interpretations quite in the tradition of Mr Love, and then on the 16th Emlyn Williams' *The Late Christopher Bean*, from the French of Fauchois, began a run of over a year.

Cedric Hardwicke made the most of his fine character part of provincial Dr Haggett who had lodged the then unacknowledged painter genius of the title. Louise Hampton was Mrs Haggett, Nadine Marsh and Lucille Lisle their daughters Ada and Susan. Edith Evans was their memorable silly old Welsh maid Gwennie. To their house in search of masterpieces came dealers and an honest critic played by Barry K. Barnes, Robert Holmes, Gilbert Davis (later Clarence Derwent) and Frederick Leister as Bruce Macrae, Tallant, Rosen and Davenport.

Except for some paintings that Gwennie had treasured and hidden, most of the now valuable canvases had been either burnt or used to stuff up rat-holes or mend broken windows, so the horror at what they had done and the bustle and search made excellent comedy. Eventually Gwennie's were found in her room but efforts to get them from her by hook or by crook all failed, and after she had reminded them that only she had treated the friendless artist with sympathy and kindness she flaunted her marriage ring before their flabbergasted faces and marched off with her little bundle and the paintings under her arms.

1934

Raymond Massey on 4th September directed his and Gladys Cooper's presentation of themselves in Keith Winter's *The Shining Hour*. This rather unpleasant piece of covetousness, adultery and suicide ran 213 times with brilliant acting, though it was far too stylishly dressed by Molyneux and lavishly set in a Mayfairish Yorkshire farmhouse designed by Aubrey Hammond.

The farm was the home of David (Massey), his wife Judy (Adrienne Allen), his housekeeper sister Hannah (Marjorie Fielding) and young brother Mickey (Derek Williams). On furlough arrived his elder brother Henry (Cyril Raymond) with glamorous wife Mariella played by Gladys Cooper. Mariella quite unwillingly disrupted the happy home, for her husband was an unseeing army type who refused to take her away when she realised the harm she fomented. David and Mickey fought over her and then Judy jumped to ghastly death amidst the flames of a blazing, lightning-struck barn so that her husband would be free to break his brother's marriage. After many histrionics that did occur.

1935

Gladys and Massey then backed the same author's *Worse Things Happen At Sea* from 26th March. Designed by Hammond and directed by Massey, this was set in sunny Sussex in the home of Lucy, pricelessly played by Yvonne Arnaud as the merry relict of an artist she had never encouraged. To make amends she took under her wing the ultra-modern unpublished novelist Ronald (Frank Lawton) and persuaded her stepson Edward (Robert Flemyng) to try to paint. Eileen Peel was her Ronald-struck naïve secretary Ellen and Harry Andrews her intellectual footman John. Athole Stewart was elderly amused Sir Maurice and Ena Burrill was Ronald's matter-of-fact sensible fiancée Laura.

Eventually, after games of tiddly-winks and croquet in the lounge, Bohemian modernity was rejected with much ripping up of manuscripts and Ronald disgustedly took the train to town.

From The Ambassador's on 15th May was transferred *The Mask of Virtue* by the accomplished and erudite husband of Madame Rambert, Ashley Dukes. With it came Vivien Leigh, an actress as capable and moving as beautiful, Frank Cellier, Jeanne de Casalis and, back after thirty-three years, Lady Tree.

The director of Alice Campbell's *Two Share A Dwelling* was the interesting South Africa-educated girl Leontine Sagan, who had later worked under Reinhardt in Berlin and won fame for her direction of the film *Mädchen in Uniform* and 1932 stage version of that at The Duchess. The drama was an Adler inspired affair, leavened with blackmail, about a split-personality wife played by Grete Mosheim. Among the cast were Wyndham Goldie, Helen Haye and Robert Eddison.

It was replaced by *The Two Mrs Carrolls* from The St Martin's, with Leslie Banks and Louise Hampton, on 4th November. The 200th performance of that coincided with the centenary of The St James's which Miller celebrated by installing a revolving stage.

1936

The transfer finished on 1st February and on the 27th Max Gordon joined Miller to put on Helen Jerome's *Pride and Prejudice* after Jane Austen. Miller directed this delightful effort which was designed by Rex Whistler with the scenery painted by Alick Johnstone and built by Loveday and Higson. The large cast included Celia Johnson as a surprisingly good Elizabeth Bennet, Dorothy Hyson as Jane, Leueen MacGrath (later Jacqueline Squire) as Lydia. Viola Lyel played Miss Bingley and Eva Moore the Lady Catherine. Hugh Williams was Darcy, Athole Stewart and Barbara Everest were Mr and Mrs Bennet and Frederick Moyes their butler Hill. Anthony Quayle (later Philip Morant) and Joan Harben were Mr Wickham and Charlotte Lucas.

William Mollison (Clifford's eldest brother), whose father had been here in 1905, then presented and directed an unfortunate Ben Travers comedy called *O Mistress Mine* on 3rd December. The large cast included Charles Lefeaux, Kathleen Harrison, Austin Trevor, Frederick Lloyd and Helen Haye in support of Parisian stars Yvonne Printemps and her husband Pierre Fresnay. Now the Prince of Wales had lately succeeded to the throne and West End gossip about his private life had suddenly just then become public and headline news. Consequently at Katherine Harrison's line 'Even the highest and mightiest must have their bit of fun at times', the house could not contain an immediate outburst of laughter!

1937

Henry Sherek was also unlucky when in his first essay as impresario he backed Hungarian Fodor's *The Orchard Walls* on 3rd February. Adapted by New Zealander Merton Hodge, the large cast included Sophie Stewart, Irene Vanbrugh, Valerie Taylor, Lola Duncan with Hugh Sinclair, Ronald Ward, Evelyn Roberts, Arthur Sinclair and, in the crowd, Jack Train. Massey directed.

Black Limelight, a success transferred from The Q Theatre, was then presented for a month by the Mayer company from 22nd April until moved on to The Duke of York's. Campbell Gullan directed this murder drama by Gordon Sherry. A year

before, Margaret Rawlings had startled playgoers in New York
and afterwards at the London Gate and then The New with
her playing of Kitty O'Shea in *Parnell*. Now she proved again
her dramatic quality as she acted the wife of a man hunted for
the murder of his mistress and made the police accept a moon-
maniac theory instead. Especially thrilling was a flashback
when she acted the swim-suited victim in a horror cameo as the
real murderer struck.

Yes, My Darling Daughter followed for another month only
from 3rd June although Jessica Tandy was delightful as the
charming blue-stocking Ellen who went off on a pre-marital
honeymoon with Alec Clunes as Douglas. Sybil Thorndike
played her mother who eventually agreed to the 'escapade'
when Ellen confronted her with her knowledge that she herself
had once been a suffragette who had lived 'in sin' with Leon
Quartermaine as a Chelsea poet. Margaret Bannerman, Ena
Moon and Evelyn Roberts played Aunt Connie, the maid, and
the father. Rodney Ackland had anglicised the comedy from
its American setting and original script by Mark Reed for the
New York Playhouse. Alfred de Liagre, jun. again directed it
here. This was a mistake because he was much too conscious
of the original production and audience reactions which he
expected would be identical with English ones. A fresh director
would not have been so bound, the players would have been
less inhibited, the comedy easier to find its own subtle level and
chance of longer run.

Keith Winter's Victorian period piece of love and trouble
called *Old Music* was presented by Miller on 18th August.
Directed by Margaret Webster in sets by Rex Whistler and
costumes by Benda, this did not attract though the cast was
excellent and included Greer Garson, Celia Johnson, Marjorie
Fielding, Hugh Williams, Giles Isham, Geoffrey Keen and
others. Leonard Sachs later took over from John Penrose as a
footman. A boy was played by young Robin Maule who, like
his sister Annabel, was more than showing promise. Unfortu-

nately, whilst still under seventeen, when with Ivor Novello
at Drury Lane in *Dancing Years*, he was killed as a Home
Guard dispatch rider. He was the son of Donovan Maule,
the creator of the remarkable Nairobi theatre bearing his
name.

The Silent Knight on 16th November was an unsuccessful
verse-play by Wolfe after Heltai's Hungarian original. Margaretta Scott, Freda Jackson, Diana Wynyard, Ralph Richardson,
Laidman Browne, Lyn Harding and Anthony Quayle were the
delightful if unlucky actors.

Nine days was enough for Pulitzer prize play *You Can't
Take It With You*, by Kaufman and Hart, which opened three
days before Christmas. It was the farcical comedy about a
crazy New York family who kept snakes, wrote plays, made fire-
works, played accordians and xylophones, printed Marxist
leaflets because they looked good, boiled candy and entertained
the normal boy-friend of one of them with his Wall Street
parents, who eventually fell for the mad charm and don't-worry
philosophy even after cellar explosions, a police raid and court
appearances! Under the direction of McFadden, the acting of
Hilda Trevelyan, Tristan Rawson and the rest of the mostly
British cast quite failed to put over the mad humour, though
the Hollywood film with Lionel Barrymore and Mischa Auer
was later more fully appreciated in this country.

1938

With O'Bryen and Dunfee, the charming and deservedly
popular London manager Bill Linnit, who most regrettably
died in 1956, produced *The Innocent Party* on 27th January.
Maurice Colbourne directed this comedy by Harwood and
Kirk which ran for five months almost surprisingly, for it was
certainly not type-cast. Cecil Parker was the charming husband
of his very bored Spanish wife, Mary Ellis, who was having an
affair with Basil Radford of all people as a dullish American.

Elizabeth Allan was a rather too Cockney secretary. Alison Pickard, Jack Lambert, Henry Thompson and Howell Davies completed the cast.

The same presenters then put on the Group Theatre's *Golden Boy* by Clifford Odets. Except for Lilian Emerson, who now played Lorna, most of the original previous November Belasco company played their old parts, including Luther Adler as the young hero Joe Bonaparte who rejected the concert violin platform for the boxing ring. Money, bitter fame and broken knuckles ended with Joe's death in the arms of Lorna at the wheel of his too fast car. Direction and sets were, as in New York, by Clurman and Gorelik.

Barry K. Barnes played rather a rotter of a hero in A. A. Milne's unsuccessful *Gentleman Unknown* which Colbourne directed for H. G. Stoker on 16th November. Others were Hilary Eaves, Ivy des Voeux, Ruth Dunning, Nora Nicholson, Betty Dorian, Rosamond Barnes and John Turnbull, Marcus Barron, Richard George, Kenneth Fraser and Harry Andrews.

Roy Limbert then transferred Shaw's *Geneva* from The Saville for some months. Ayliff directed this satire on the League of Nations, which had originated at Malvern, in sets by Paul Shelving. Alexander Knox was the Judge, but Donald Wolfit who had created the part took it over in January and relinquished it later to Clement McCallin.

The Latin dictators Bombardone and Flanco were played by Cecil Trouncer and Stuart Lindsell; Ernest Thesiger, H. R. Hignett and Cyril Gardner were Sir Orpheus, the Bishop and the Secretary; Donald Eccles as the Jew and Phillippa Gill as the Widow; all these had been at Malvern. The others were Walter Hudd as Battler, Alison Leggatt, Olive Milbourne and Tully Comber as Begonia, the Deaconess and the Betrothed; Tom Anstead, Arthur Ridley and Heilbronn as the Journalist, the Commissar and the Newcomer.

From Boxing Day 1938 a 'children's revue for grown-ups as well' called *Let's Pretend* ran over the holidays on matinées. In the cast were part-author Steve Geray, Magda Kun, Pat Taylor and twelve-year-old Peggy Cummins from the Dublin Gate making her London début and earning plaudits with star notices as a delightfully assured little colleen.

1939

Whether the dictators liked their portraits, as Shaw hoped they would, is unknown but audiences liked the play which eventually went back to The Saville to make way for Ackland's *Sixth Floor*, from the French of Gehri, which only lasted a week from 22nd May. It was a love and sorrow piece set in a Parisian garret with sensitive acting by James Mason, Joyce Barbour, Jeanne Stuart, Celia Johnson and Harold Scott.

The literary agent A. D. Peters took over from 21st June with Terence Rattigan's third play, *After The Dance*, which Michael Macowan directed in a set by Gower Parks. It was of an eternal triangle offset by ex-gay ones harping back to the twenties, and staider young forward-looking ones of the immediate pre-war days.

The cast was headed by Catherine Lacey and Robert Harris supported by Martin Walker, an actor better known then in the Dominions, Viola Lyell, Anne Firth, Hubert Gregg and others. Allan Davis, later the second director of the Bristol Old Vic, was stage manager. Making London début in the crowd was Dorothy Primrose, a girl who beat Mrs Kendal and all the French actresses mentioned in St James's early days for she had made her first appearance at the Edinburgh Lyceum when only three weeks old as the baby in *The Manxman*. She was to be a hit when she took over in *Salad Days* at The Vaudeville in 1955, have two long seasons charming Nairobi residents under Donovan Maule in Kenya as well as other successful engagements in London, notably under Clunes at The Arts. All that however followed years in the provinces as a child artiste in her father's (Frank Buckley) company or with others

SJT X

like Jimmy Lynton's Royal Repertory Players with whom she was Little Eva in *Uncle Tom's Cabin*.

War loomed with the autumn. Audiences dwindled. Then, except for variety houses, all theatres closed by order when war was finally declared in September. However, as initial shock dimmed with bombs failing to fall immediately, London's West End gradually returned to life despite the black-out of unlit streets and windows and curtained doorways. Official closure orders were relaxed.

William Mollison reopened The St James's on 12th December with *Ladies in Retirement* by Edward Percy and Reginald Denham which the latter directed. This sombre dramatisation of a nineteenth-century crime was suitably set in a lonely Thames marsh house by Sidney Gausden. Mary Clare was Ellen Creed, the housekeeper of raddled ex-chorus girl Miss Fiske (Mary Merrall) whose murder began the drama. Richard Newton was Albert Feather, Ellen's blackmailing spiv of a nephew, and Margaret Watson and Phyllis Morris her two crazy sisters Louisa and Emily. Joan Kemp-Welch was Lucy Gilham and Olga Slade was the nun, Sister Theresa.

The strongly evocative mystery was just what Press and public needed to help them forget the war, which still only throbbed preparatory to violent explosion. Tried out at Richmond, the drama ran 174 times before going out on tour.

1941

For some nine months the dust-covers remained in place. Then on 10th March Tennents moved Yvonne Arnaud in Margery Sharp's *The Nutmeg Tree* from The Lyric where it had been running since October. Una Venning, Helen Haye and many others were in it as well as the variety act The Balatons, and Naomi Jacob returned temporarily to the stage. The Australian Mignon O'Doherty later took over Maire O'Neill's part.

Jan Cobel's Anglo-Polish Ballet began a short season on Boxing Day. They produced three new ballets, *Polonia*, *Pan Twardowski* and a *Bolero* to Ravel music. Formed mainly from refugees whose leaders were Konarski, Alicja Halama and Maria Sanina, the company was strengthened by the South African girl Florence Read and by Alexis Rassine.

1942

Donald Wolfit, not yet knighted for his Shakespearian services but already established in the great tradition as an actor-manager, moved in from The Strand in February to lead in *The Merry Wives of Windsor*, *The Merchant of Venice*, *Richard III* and Ben Jonson's *Volpone*. His company included his future wife Rosalind Iden, Bryan Johnson, Peggy Livesey and Clare Harris.

Noël Coward arrived from The Piccadilly in the summer with *Blythe Spirit* prior to touring it in September. In the final weeks here he himself took over the part of Charles which Cecil Parker had created for him.

Patrick Hamilton's strong *The Duke in Darkness* was presented by Linnit and Dunfee on 8th October. The set was by Ernest Stern who had been brought from Berlin by Alec for *Turandot*. Michael Redgrave directed, and played the servant Gribaud who went mad after fifteen years incarceration in a sixteenth-century Spanish castle where he had voluntarily accompanied his master the Duke. Leslie Banks was the latter, who feigned blindness as part of an escape plan, and Walter Fitzgerald was the enemy in whose power they were. Hugh Burden played Voulain who arranged the eventual escape but with the sacrifice of Gribaud. All gave remarkable performances. Richmond Nairne, as chief gaoler d'Aublaye, acted 'shuddersomely well' to quote James Agate. The idiom of the dialogue was perhaps a little mixed but the powerful emotions displayed by the team attracted audiences for two months. Alan Bush composed the music. R. Lancelyn Green (*Peter Pan* historian) was assistant stage manager.

Beverley Baxter, Canadian, critic and M.P., was author of *It Happened in September* produced 10th December. Leon M. Lion directed it for Jack Hylton. Eva Moore, Joan Kemp-Welch and Anne Firth were in this analytical piece upon the reactions of a true-blue pompous father, his children and a young Nazi guest to the happenings and chances of the four Septembers from 1937 to 1940. Audiences found it impossible to be sufficiently objective about the recorded speeches, bomb explosions and siren noises. It was soon withdrawn.

On 29th December Wolfit returned in the title-role of Constance Cox's *Romance of David Garrick*, adapted from the early Victorian play. Rosalind Iden was Ada Ingot, Iris Russell was Kitty Clive, Worrall-Thompson was Macklin, Eric Maxon was James Quin and Patrick Crean was Farren. Much alteration and addition was at Wolfit's suggestion.

1943

Wolfit's season continued with *King Lear*, one of his most successful roles; and *Twelfth Night*, when he was Malvolio to Rosalind's Viola. Ann Casson, Peter Copley, Brian Rix and Roy Dean were in the company. Most of Wolfit's sets were by Ernest Stern who had been with him to their mutual advantage since the Shakespearian's famous Strand Season in 1940.

Emlyn Williams then directed his own adaptation of Turgenev's *Month in the Country* with Redgrave and Valerie Taylor as Rakitin and Natalia. Michael Shepley, Ronald Squire and Tom Gill were Yslaef, the Doctor and the tutor Beliaev. Isolde Denham, Winifred Hindle, Jacqueline Clarke and Annie Esmond were Vera, Lizaveta, Katia and Anna. Schiller, Baxter, Gill, Blakelock and Ruddock completed the cast; all gave delightful performances.

A matinée of Knoblock's *Bird of Passage* was presented at the end of May, and in June six were given in aid of stage charities of Ashley Duke's *Parisienne* with Sonia Dresdel and Michael Redgrave.

The Russian play ran 313 times and was followed on 17th November by Agatha Christie's *Ten Little Niggers* which reached 260. The programme emphasised this as being after 'her famous best seller'. Irene Hentschel directed. The acting of Allan Jeayes and Henrietta Watson proved an object lesson in gesture and inflection to the others. They played Sir Lawrence and Emily Brent. Rogers, Narracot, Mrs Rogers and Vera were played by William Murray, R. Barlow, Hilda Bruce-Potter and Linden Travers; Marston, Blore and the General by Michael Blake, Percy Walsh and Eric Cowley. Gwynn Nicholls was Dr Armstrong.

1944

A sex-flop by Gordon Sherry called *Felicity Jasmine* opened and closed in September. However, in it the South African girl Moira Lister made a good impression on her way to the top, which really started the following year under Robert Atkins at Stratford-upon-Avon where she proved herself a capable and moving actress opposite the delightful American Claire Luce.

Jay Pomeroy backed the next piece also. This was a boarding-house comedy, *Residents Only* by Gordon and Pratt, which lasted ten days from 8th November with veteran Ada Reeve, Anna Turner, Martin Walker and others.

Robert Donat took over on 22nd December with the Farjeons' *Glass Slipper*, a 'fairy tale with music' and delightful harlequinade. Choreography was by Andrée Howard, score by Clifton Parker, decor and lighting by Hugh Stevenson and Hamish Wilson. William Armstrong directed and Ernest Irving conducted. Audrey Hesketh was Cinderella whose father was John Ruddock and stepmother Elliot Mason. Megs Jenkins and Doris Gilmore were the Ugly Sisters. Most of the company

were recruited from the Ballet Rambert whose stars Walter
Gore and Sally Gilmour were enchanting as Harlequin and
Columbine. Paula Hinton, John Kerslake, Nina Shelley and
Betty Baskcomb were some of the others.

1945

Anna Neagle starred in the title-role of Gordon Glennon's
version of Jane Austen's *Emma* from 7th February, in a beautifully dressed set by Gladys Calthrop. The company, directed
by Jack Minster, included Gillian Lind, Margaret Vines, Cecil
Ramage, Ambrosine Phillpotts and H. R. Hignett, seventy-five
years old and making his last appearance. It was all quite delightful even though it only ran a month.

Emlyn Williams then directed himself in his own *Wind of
Heaven* from 12th April in 268 performances. He was ably
supported by Diana Wynyard as Dilys (from August by Valerie
Taylor), Megs Jenkins as Bet (later Meg Maxwell), Arthur
Hambling as Pitter, Herbert Lomas as Evan Howell and
Dorothy Edwards, Clifford Huxley and Barbara Couper as
Menna, Gwyn and Mrs Lake.

King George VI was present in August for this charming
mystic play about a Christ-child saviour in a cholera-struck
Welsh village in 1856, and of how flashy showman Ambrose
Ellis (Emlyn Williams), who had sold his soul, did eventually
regain it.

For the Christmas season a fresh *Glass Slipper* was directed
by Stephen Thomas and Robert Donat. Choreography was
again in the charmingly capable hands of Andrée Howard. Except for Geoffrey Dunn, Lulu Dukes and Michael Holmes the
cast was new. Sara Gregory, a happy little Australian girl, was
Cinderella whose father and stepmother were Lawrence Hanray
and Elsie French and Ugly Sisters Joan Sterndale Bennett and
Olga May. Harlequin and Columbine were Frank Staff and
Annette Chapell. Others included Helen Cherry, Patricia

Dainton, Sara Luzita, Elizabeth Schooling and Ann Lascelles.

The last-named delightful character ballerina was, like some of the others, recruited from the Sadler's Wells Ballet. She danced the Spirit of Earth, the Maid, and, as one of the Three Graces, Truth in the Harlequinade. The romantic charm of the old theatre aroused such enquiring interest in her that to Ann Lascelles can really be attributed the stimulation and nascence of this history.

1946

The war over, Gilbert Miller returned with Krasna's American comedy *Dear Ruth* from the end of February until 6th April. Margaret Barton, Dulcie Gray, Betty Warren and Evelyn Roberts were among the players. For a month afterwards Menzie's *Astonished Ostrich* was revived, with Basil Radford delightful as the middle-aged bachelor doing his utmost to impress his suddenly discovered adolescent son.

On 12th May the curtain rose on a fresh brave venture unfortunately prematurely doomed through the illness of a principal. Actor-manager John Clements had, in the thirties, founded and progressively run north London's Intimate Theatre. During the war he had entertained the Forces in the most inaccessible places and now since the beginning of the year he had been rehearsing a company, many of them still in uniform.

Clements opened with Margaret Luce's *The Kingmaker*, himself in the title-role of Warwick. The many sets were designed and painted by Harald Melvill who, like many of the others, had been at The Intimate. Costumes were by Elizabeth Haffenden. Leslie Bridgewater composed the music. The action covered ten years of the Wars of the Roses and ranged up and down the country, to a ship at sea, to France, back to London and finally to the battlefield of Barnet.

It was all rather too tremendous, especially for the critics, for the intrigues and machinations of the opposing sides required more concentration and knowledge than could be expected of the average reporter. The players, however, acquitted themselves admirably even if few had the chance to build a character except for Clements who also directed, Robert Eddison as Edward of York, Irene Vanbrugh as Lady Rivers the mother of Edward's wife Elizabeth who was played by Kay Hammond; and other leads. Warwick's daughters Isabel and Anne were Moira Lister and Mary Stone. During the season the latter married Peter Noble the film publicist and historian. Afterwards, amplifying her name to Marianne, she rejected stage for screen and soon began to progress in character roles.

The large cast included Brian Hayes, Charles Lloyd Pack, Howieson Culff, David Peel, David Bird.

It was intended to run plays in repertory so at the end of July Dryden's stylised comedy *Marriage à la Mode* was introduced. Laurence Irving followed in the steps of his father and grandfather Sir Henry, but as designer, not actor.

Appropriate to the title, another happy event was the marriage of John Clements to his leading lady Kay Hammond. Most unfortunately in the beginning of August Kay became ill, plans for extension of the repertory were abandoned and the theatre was relinquished.

Freddie Lonsdale's *But For The Grace Of God* was presented by Peter Daubeny and Miller 201 times from 3rd September. An admirable cast saved this from earlier extinction. Leslie Armstrong directed them in a Scottish mansion at which arrived two English detectives (J. H. Roberts and Cyril Smith), quite out of jurisdiction, investigating embezzlement. Michael Gough played most delightfully and revoltingly the suspect Gerard, caddish son of Stuart Lindsell as Sir William. Gerard's demands for money to save the family name were rejected in a stage-English tight-lipped manner by his father's enquiry as to how long, therefore, he would expect to be 'away'.

Gerard then attempted to blackmail his sister-in-law Mary,

who was as charmingly played as the part permitted by Yvonne
Owen, who had been in the long running *Acacia Avenue* at
The Vaudeville and was married to Alan Badel then in the
Parachute Regiment. Mary had been more than flirting with
Hugh McDermott as American guest Geoffrey. Robert Douglas
played her naval husband Richard who appeared later, dressed,
incidentally, in the actor's own active-service uniform.

Act I ended with Gerard's death in a tremendous fight with
Geoffrey, so real that before long fingers, wrists and ribs had
been fractured, Michael Gough being the worst sufferer, since
the script called for his death after being hurled over the back
of a couch. Eventually the management called in two old pro's,
Ernie Rice and Vince Hawkins to teach the actors how to fake
the fight without so much damage to themselves! The second
act would have proved too tedious without Michael Gough's
villainous characterisations had it not been for the inimitable
fooling and 'ad-libbing' of A. E. Matthews, back here after
forty years, who made it sparkle with the aid of another veteran,
Mary Jerrold. The others were Marian Manisty, H. G. Stoker,
Leigh, Forwood and Gordon.

1947

Roland Young, home after nearly forty years in America,
earned star notices in Parish's *Truant in Park Lane*. Sherek
presented this weak comedy which was withdrawn after two
weeks on 5th April. It was about an Earl, killed in an accident,
who returned to his family in the body of a tradesman following
a seance. Lilian Braithwaite, Faith Brook, Gladys Henson and
others did their best but the idea had been better exploited here
fifty years earlier by Harry Esmond.

The next backer was Emile Littler with a queer piece by
Clemence Dane, *Call Home The Heart*, directed by Charles
Hickman. Valerie White played quite beautifully a war-torn
wife who had to endure the return from the same prisoner-of-

war camp, of her husband and her lover. Sybil Thorndike, Leon Quartermaine, William Fox and Bryan Coleman were the chief support but the public were not attracted.

Their place was taken on 19th May by Clive Brook, the strong actor who had recently returned to the stage after twenty years in films, in Molnar's *The Play's The Thing* which had been on tour. He played the du Maurier part of Sandor with Irene Worth, Michael Shepley, Ian Lubbock, Geoffrey Dunn and others.

On 14th August Dearsley's *Fly Away Peter* was transferred from the Hammersmith King's by Peter Saunders. Margaret Barton, J. H. Roberts and Peter Hammond were the leads.

Backed by the Arts Council, the British Theatre Group took over in the autumn for a year. In charge was Basil Dean whose early years had been under Miss Horniman in Manchester; then between the wars he had earned renown with Alec Rea who was his deputy as director of ENSA.

Geoffrey Kerr's *The Man in the Street* was the opening production on 9th October. This comedy would have had some chance as a farce. Bobby Howes played a little bank clerk chosen by a Press Lord to be his paper's stunt-guest for a week. It concluded with a sacked announcer broadcasting a debunking of Press and BBC. Kynaston Reeves and Mary Martlew were in the large cast.

Dean then directed fiery Ulsterman St John Ervine's *Private Enterprise*, a polemical tirade pro and con a closed-shop strike. It ended with moral triumph but financial ruin for the mill-owners, led by Nicholas Hannen and André Morell as his strong elder son, who was off-set by the younger contrasting Hector Ross and William Fox. The women-folk of the last two were played by Elizabeth Gray and Elizabeth Allan. C. Lloyd Pack was the local vicar, Meadows White an old-time loyal worker and Russell Waters a class-conscious strike leader. Eileen Peel, Nigel Neilson, Julien Mitchell and Ella Atkinson completed the cast.

1948

Ervine's play ran for two months, its successor even less—from 6th to 28th February. This was Jack Alldridge's *All This Is Ended*, a war play set in 1944 Italy. Despite the author's sincerity and his emphasis that most characters were based on fellow-soldiers, many of whom had been killed in action, it was again too polemical with insufficient movement and no women. The cast however was well chosen with six from the last play and Gordon Bell, Halfpenny, Walton, Raglan, Marischka. For the first time since *Ladies in Retirement* the programme was illustrated. So were the subsequent Group productions but the example was rarely followed in the future.

Because of the failure a bright little revue from The Bolton's was transferred here from 9th March to 17th April. Headed by Billy Milton, Daphne Anderson, Shiela Mathews, Patricia Dainton, Richard Gilbert and Reg Barney, they entertained accompanied by pianos and drum in sets by Geoffrey Ghin.

Margaret (*Constant Nymph*) Kennedy then saw her *Happy With Either* last only a month from 22nd April, her subject one for farce, not comedy. Her hero was Wilfred Hyde White as a bigamist back from gaol to find Angela Baddeley and Valerie Taylor as his two 'wives' living together. Constance Cummings played their foreign cook who also fell for his charm, which, however, was not too evident. Cyril Raymond was a neighbour and two daughters of the first marriage offset the elder women as well as themselves, Sheelagh Macalpine as the more sophisticated contrasting with the lively tom-boy of her fellow-Celt, the flaming redhead Adrienne Corri. Basil Dean, who directed all the productions, had picked both the girls at the RADA annual public matinée which had been here on 2nd March.

A successful and interesting experiment ensued with the bringing to town of four major repertory companies. Each

presented a play for two weeks, in sets made in their own work-
shops. The Liverpool Rep. opened on 1st June in a charmingly
nostalgic *Cherry Orchard* in sets designed by Paul Mayo and
made by Douglas Moss and Penelope Sparling. The large cast
included Gladys Boot and Cyril Luckham as Mme Ranevskaya
and her brother Gayev; Nancie Jackson as Varya and Catherine
Bogle as Anya; Eric Berry as Lopahin the merchant and David
Phethean the student Trophimov. John Fernald directed. Enchanting the audience with her presence as she always did,
Queen Mary sat in the royal box on the last night and obviously
enjoyed the performance.

Sheffield Rep. followed on the 15th with Alfred Sangster's
The Brontës which Geoffrey Ost, who designed the sets,
directed. Charles Sewell was the gloomy father, Sheila Mullin,
Micheline Patton and José Trevelyan the sisters Charlotte,
Emily and Anne. John Rutland was Branwell. Wilson, Beckett
and Wearing played Thackeray, G. H. Lewes and the curate
Nicholls in love with Charlotte. Patrick McGoohan was the
other curate. The play had been first done in 1933 at The
Royalty and might have been tightened a little, but the players
evoked the period and people very well.

Sir Barry Jackson's Birmingham company awoke the town
on the 29th with an almost too fast and vigorous modern dress
The Rivals, complete with telephone box, bicycles, Salvation
Army lasses and sailors; the sets so constructed by Paul
Shelving and Nevil Dickin that they could be whirled around
into positions by the cast as warranted. The repeated shocks
to traditionalists by director Willard Stoker were, however,
compensated for by the speed and novelty; certainly by the enthusiasm displayed. Gwen Cherrell made a most appealing and
eminently kissable Lydia Languish; Dorothy Wheatley and
Patricia Russell were charming also as Julia and Lucy whilst
Rosamond Burne was a credible Mrs Malaprop. Good also
were the men, led by Robin Bailey as Faulkland, Alan Mac-
naughton as Bob Acres, John Phillips as O'Trigger, Ninian

Brodie and Malcolm Farquhar as Sir Anthony and Captain Absolute.

The Bristol Old Vic brought up the rear in a very pedestrian *Hamlet* in sets and costumes by Alan Barlow. They were directed by Hugh Hunt (brother of the mountaineer) who, after some years in Australia, was given the first chair of drama in Manchester. Robert Eddison was a very weak and willowy Prince whereas Donald Sinden and Stephen Kaye as Rosencrantz and Guildenstern were so robust one felt they must have been products of Sir Frank Benson, who chose his companies as much for their prowess on the cricket field as on the boards. Jane Wenham was quite a sexy wench of an Ophelia; William Devlin was strong and regal as King and Ghost, Catherine Lacey maybe too intelligent and sharp sometimes as Gertrude. Paul Rogers was old Polonius, Allan Cuthbertson and Rolf Lefebvre were Laertes and Horatio.

The Group's next production was Ted Willis's *No Trees in the Street* which on 7th August ended their activity after a fortnight's run. It had toured the four cities whilst the Reps were in town and doubtless confirmed many parental opinions about sinful London, for it was a most melodramatic travesty about East End slums, a Tract to prove Environment the Cause of Wicked Immorality!

Basil Dean and his company enjoyed themselves maybe more than their audiences who could not take the too strongly conceived characters (Clement Scott must have turned in his grave in futile fury). Beatrix Lehmann was Jess Gold, a ghastly gin-soaked harridan who filled with booze the lovely Charmian Eyre, as Hetty her innocent virgin daughter. Arthur Lane was Wilkie, one-time bed-mate of Jess who bribed the latter with a couple of bottles so that as soon as Hetty was fuddled she could be picked up by Wilkie and raped in the back room off-stage. Harry Herbert, himself an old-timer of fifty years experience, played neighbour Kipper, an old performer with a heart of gold. Others who appeared in the sleazy set designed by Cyril Denny were Hilda Fenemore, Russell Waters, John Stratton, Duncan Lamont and Diana Hely-Hutchinson.

The lurid drama, acted though it was with gusto and abandon, was not supported by the public any more than the pre-Rep. productions had been. They therefore had to close down even though plans had been made for *The School for Scandal* and *Hassan*. Dean did the former however in Bath, and the latter later in South Africa and in town.

Alec L. Rea, Dean's pre-war and wartime partner who like him earned the C.B.E. for his ENSA work, then took over from 2nd September with E. P. Clift to put on *Don't Listen, Ladies!* This piece of French froth by Sacha Guitry, adapted by Powys and Bolton, crossed the Channel lightly and attracted 219 audiences. William Armstrong directed in an excellent set by Leon Davey.

The company were remarkably bright. Francis Lister was a husband torn between the machinations of his present and ex-wife who were Constance Cummings and Betty Marsden. Ada Reeve, veteran of the Edwardian halls herself, was a perfect cameo as an ancient relic of Lautrec. Ferdy Mayne, Denholm Elliott, Pamela Bevan, D. A. Mehan, Tom Webster and Peter Franklin, especially the first-named, gave varyingly interesting characterisations. Jack Buchanan, one-time top star of musical comedy who had played the part in New York, took over in January when Lister went sick. He certainly made his two marriages seem as if they had been fomented by love rather than just money!

1949

Paul Scofield starred as Alexander the Great in *Adventure Story* by Terence Rattigan which Tennents presented in the spring. Peter Glenville directed in sets by Georges Wakhevitch which Alick Johnstone painted and Brunskill and Loveday built. The costumes by Simmons were also evocative. About a dozen years of the conqueror's life were covered. The cast, large and strong, included Joy Parker, Hazel Terry, Gwen Ffrangcon-Davies, Veronica Turleigh, Robert Flemyng, William Devlin, Cecil Trouncer, Nicholas Hannen, Stanley Baker and John van Eyssen. Music was specially composed by Benjamin Frankel.

From 8th June the theatre stayed shut until on the 28th the American Cornelia Otis Skinner took over for a fortnight with her impersonations of a compatriot in Paris packing for home, Mom helping junior's homework, etc. and then Henry VIII's wives, one after the other.

Eric Linklater, Orcadian novelist, saw his *Love in Albania* transferred from the Hammersmith Lyric on 12th July. A leading part was taken by Peter Ustinov, who also directed and got the best out of his company, though, perhaps afraid of parrot-cries about the centre of the stage, the action was always too far up-stage in one corner or the other.

Into the 1944 London flat of primly respectable Robert (Robin Bailey) and flighty young wife Susan (a delightfully roguish Brenda Bruce) there arrived Peter Jones as loquacious poet Ramilees, fresh from adventures as a partisan in Albania. He was quickly followed by Ustinov as a most rumbustious ex-gangster become a mixed-up, punch-drunkish, maudlin but very formidable United States Army police sergeant Dohda, complete with white helmet and full American trappings. Dohda was bent on proving the guilt or innocence of the poet over the death of a girl partisan. The girl had been the poet's lover, her father had been Dohda before his emigration to Chicago.

The comedy was perfectly played, for Ustinov lived his part so authentically and with such tremendous gusto that illusion was quite complete with the others reacting just as realistically to their author's creations. Molly Urquhart as Flora McIver completed the cast as a gem of a stage Scots maid. The 142nd and last night was 12th November.

Four days later Tchekov's *The Seagull* moved in from the

same theatre to run on into the new year. Irene Hentschel directed in sets by Sheriff and costumes by Chappell. This Calderon version of the distinguished play was beautifully acted by Mai Zetterling as Nina; Nuna Davey as Pauline with Hazel Terry as her daughter Masha and Richard Caldicot her husband Shamrayef; Isabel Jeans as Mme Arkadina the actress with Paul Scofield her son Treplef and Philip Stainton her brother Sorin; Nicholas Hannen the doctor Dorn, Ian Hunter the writer Trigorin; Adrian Cairns, John Kidd and Anne Woodward as Yakof, Medvedenko and the maid.

1950

Expectant hope hummed through theatre circles when news broke that Sir Laurence Olivier had joined Gilbert Miller. A reborn Lyceum failed, however, to materialise and the association did not continue more than a couple of years, for the materialistic owner and visionary actor-knight proved rather that physical and spiritual opposites do not always make good unions. Though the rent was lowered to three-quarters of the figure last mentioned, few of the other requirements of the actor were so easy to fulfil. Whether a longer management would have resulted had he been partnered only by his brilliant and practical as well as lovely wife, Vivien Leigh, may only be guessed at since it was not hazarded.

Dramatic poet of the day was Christopher Fry and his *Venus Observed* opened the new management on 18th January. Olivier directed in sets by Roger Furse with incidental music by Herbert Menges. The star himself played the Duke of Altair, an old roué of an amateur astronomer who decided to settle down. So to a house-party he invited three old flames and then told his son Edgar (Denholm Elliott) to pick his stepmother! The plan was upset by Heather Stannard as Perpetua, the fascinating daughter of the Duke's land-agent Reedbeck who was made a delightful character by George Relph.

Father and son competed for Perpetua's favours but when Valerie Taylor as Rosabel burnt down the observatory the Duke decided that she was the one for him after all. The other prospective wives were Rachel Kempson and Brenda de Banzie as Hilda and Jessie. Robert Beaumont was the agent's son Dominic, Fred Johnson the butler and Tom Heathcote (later H. Goodwin) the footman.

On 9th August the programme was changed to Dennis Cannan's *Captain Carvallo*. Tanya Moiseiwitsch, daughter of the pianist, designed the set of this delightful comedy, a farm-house kitchen of perhaps the Balkans. She was then of course by no mean unknown, but Olivier had worked with her in their New Theatre/Old Vic days. The farm was a home of the Re-sistance where Carvallo, captain of the other side, billeted him-self. The Captain was played with remarkable charm by James Donald who had reached stardom not long before with his compatriot Eileen Herlie in *The Eagle Has Two Heads*, adapted by Ronald Duncan from Cocteau.

Like the Captain, his batman Gross (Tom Heathcote) had been a great philanderer but they met their match in Diana Wynyard as Smilja their hostess and Jill Bennett, an enchanting rogue of a character actress, as her cheeky maid Anni. Peter Finch and Richard Goolden were Professor Winke and Caspar, especially delightful when ordered by their chief the Baron (Anthony Pelly) to destroy the enemy couple. They had been so charmed by the latter that they blew up an outhouse instead. Between the love-making and other farcical situations the whole thing was superb. Two months later a transfer was arranged to The Garrick.

An extraordinary play by famous Ulsterman Tyrone Guthrie opened on 9th October. *Top of the Ladder*, directed by Guthrie himself, was played on a strange set dominated by the symbolic ladder of life which stretched up out of sight behind the action. Roger Ramsdell designed.

Bertie, whose life was portrayed from birth to death as a

mental case, was acted by John Mills. He had to be on stage throughout and it not only tested his powers but proved them. In a series of flashbacks the play proceeded with Mills ably supported by Alison Leggatt, Rachel Kempson, Mary Kerridge, Esme Church (as his old nurse also on stage throughout), Miles Malleson and Toke Townley. Eleven others completed the cast.

1951

Bernard Delfont followed as sub-tenant on 15th February for the Guthrie play did not draw. He presented *The Madwoman of Chaillot*, a queer riot by Giraudoux, adapted by Valency and directed by Robert Speaight in sets and costumes by Christian Bérard. Set in Paris where it originated, it came via New York where it had been a success. The cast deserved a longer run than the two months it lasted in London.

Martita Hunt was the heroine, as fantastic as her costume, who held 'court' on a café terrace and then in her subterranean 'palace'. The characters were a nightmare of disorderly persons, essence of a year's sweepings of the cells of Bow Street and cellars of Soho cocktailed with their opposite numbers from the sewers of Paris. Three companion madwomen were acted by Angela Baddeley, Jane Grahame and Veronica Turleigh. Marius Goring was a ragpicker, Martin Miller a prospector for oil in the sewers, Brian Hayes a deaf mute, Bill Shine a sewerman. Meadows White was a policeman and Joe Astor a juggler. The latter was a recruit from the halls whose act later became known as Joe Ruggles and Rene. Among many others were Catherine Salkeld and Ann Heffernan.

Meanwhile the Oliviers were preparing their contribution to the Festival of Britain for this the centenary year of the Crystal Palace Exhibition. They exploited brilliantly the bold idea to offer alternately Shaw's *Caesar and Cleopatra* with Shakespeare's *Antony and Cleopatra*, opening with the Shaw on 10th May and on the night after with the Shakespeare. Costumes were by Audrey Cruddas in sets by Roger Furse. Michael Benthall directed. Music was by Herbert Menges.

Preliminary publicity blare proved fully justified. The company was as brilliant as it was enormous. Both Olivier and Vivien Leigh were magnificent, first as the weary Caesar and teen-age Queen and then as the sensual worn-out Italian and the maturer woman as conceived by the Irish and English dramatists. Robert Helpmann was Appollodorus in the Shaw and then Octavius Caesar; Henry Oscar was Pothinus, then Philo Canidius; Esmond Knight Belzanor, then Menas; Richard Goolden Theodotus, then Lepidus; Norman Wooland Lucius, then Enobarbus. Wilfred Hyde White was Britannus and then the soothsayer Lemprius, Peter Cushing later took over the first and Timothy Bateson the other. Nial MacGinnis was Rufio and then Pompey.

Most striking female support was that of Ftatateeta, Shaw's nurse to Cleopatra: Elspeth March opened and later in the run Pat Nye took over. Maxine Audley was Charmian in both plays and Jill Bennett was Iris. Some of the others in more or less important roles were Elizabeth Kentish, Ronald Adam, Clifford Williams and Lyndon Brook.

With Arts Council backing, money was spent almost as if Irving himself had returned, and certainly the brilliance of the productions and the acting showed what could still be done in the English theatre. Running three weeks into September they then broke for a rest. After much further polishing they moved to New York where the reception and success were equal if not greater than in London.

On 25th September Jean-Louis Barrault, Olivier's opposite number in Paris, opened a short season with his wife Madeleine Renaud and, as guest star, Edwige Feuillere. They quite scintillated. In the repertoire were *Partage de Midi*, *Amphitryon*, *Oedipe*, *Les Fourberies de Scapin*, *Les Fausses Confidences* and *Baptiste*.

A one-time child prodigy, the much publicised Orson
Welles, arrived from America to play *Othello* from 18th October
to 15th December. He himself directed his own version for, to
quote Ivor Brown in the *Observer*, he 'treated the text as a
script to work on rather than as a document to be revered'. His
own costume might have been inspired by the funny tire-man
of Michelin advertisements, for the tall and robust star,
teutonic shaven skull emphasising his leaden-coloured bullet
head, wore a velvet jumper so excessively muscle-padded with
great lumps of kapok that he even reminded some onlookers of
moronic mountains of the all-in wrestling ring. Corks beneath
his heels raised his natural height still further above his company, perhaps to bolster up an inferiority complex strongly
suggested in a monotoned production where a lower-keyed
Iago was for ever slimy and a Desdemona maidenly insipid.

On the third night the padding slipped to give him seeming
dropsy in peculiar places, and any illusion there might have
been was further killed by careless stage-hands—perhaps un-
greased—for scenery swung skywards before the curtains
closed the gap, and once a strange great honeycomb grill,
which for some moments had divided the stage, suddenly too
went sailing upwards as though the stage manager had just
changed her mind and felt it out of joint!

Supporting players, spoken favourably of by local papers on
the preceding tour, included Peter Finch and Gudrun Ure as
Iago and Desdemona and Maxine Audley as Emilia. The
interpretations by these three, it must be said, pleased the
erudite Stephen Williams in the *Evening News*, who said of
Welles that 'he missed tremendous chances, misquoted or threw
away some of the most sonorous lines in the language'. Most
of the other critics, however, accepted the extrovert visitor's
own estimation of himself without much qualification.

Michael Warre and John van Eyssen were Montano and
Cassio, Basil Lord and Keith Pyott were Roderigo and Brab-
antio, Dianne Foster was Bianca. It was a sad production on

the whole for material was there in company and star but a
separate guiding hand was lacking to unify, and especially to
control the overweaning giant-desire which broke illusion and
stopped the blending of light and scene, sound and action.

The scene-shifters may have improved before the end of
Othello but they were up to their tricks again for the opening
of the Christmas show on 20th December—*Snow White and
the Seven Dwarfs*. Even the orchestra was almost as poor as
that 1874 one, and though the conductor didn't throw down
his baton he was certainly heard too loudly admonishing some
of his band! This was a pity for the enchanting music was from
the film from which the piece was adapted. However the
children in the audience enjoyed the humour of unrehearsed
effects, exposures of half-set scenery and such-like accidents
so perhaps little harm was done. Kay Osborne successfully kept
her charm and composure throughout like a good trouper.
So did the seven who were mostly old circus pro's: Chapman,
Heritage, Whitaker, Phillips, Pattison, Price and Bennett;
though they hadn't been picked for their voices. Denis Martin
was the Prince, Joy Robins and Bernard Ansell the Queen and
King; Nora Chapman was the Bear, Henderson the Astrologer,
Owen the Huntsman and Gay Cameron the Storyteller. Additional lyrics were by Dennis Arundell who directed.

1952

A Tchekovian-American-French farce, Samuel Taylor's *The
Happy Time*, was presented on 30th January after Broadway
success. George Devine directed in sets by Vivienne Kernot
with costumes by Motley. It was a delightful inconsequential
piece about the mad household of a French-Canadian (Peter
Finch) with a Scots wife (Rachel Kempson) and young son
(Andrew Ray). Various philandering and drunken relatives
were led by Ronald Squire as a wonderful old rogue of a grandfather. Genevieve Page, like the boy making London début, was
an enchanting maid but G. Bayldon had to be an exaggerated

caricature of a rather unethical doctor. Patricia Fryer was the daughter whose teetotal fiancé (M. Redington) was soon made tipsy. Ann Wilton, George Devine, Peter Dyneley and Aubrey Dexter all helped to keep the ball mostly in the air. Accents certainly tended to wax and wane but everything went with gusto, not forgetting a remarkable piano upon which the boy was brilliantly and merrily playing as the curtain fell at one point, for the melody continued into the following scene a whole afternoon later!

Another American success, Clifford Odets' *Winter Journey*, was backed by Sherek and Wanamaker on 3rd April. The latter directed in excellent sets by Anthony Holland which the old family Harkers painted and Brunskill & Loveday built. Michael Redgrave was masterly as Frank, alcoholic once-great emotional actor, being given a come-back chance by a dreadfully uncouth all-American dynamic stage director called Bernie. Sam Wanamaker was also remarkable as Bernie, even if scandal was right in saying he was merely being himself.

Googie Withers brought tears to the eyes of many by her beautiful performance as Georgie, the still lovely but almost defeated wife in the struggle against Frank's weakness and the unjustified animosity of the boorish director, who accepted his hero Frank's lie that she was the real drunkard and original cause of the slide from fame to the 'sticks'. The note of pathos in the finale was well conceived, the eventual mutual understanding and attraction between Bernie and Georgie and her rejection of any future in such a situation, when her husband was heard off-stage reaching his old heights to a clamouring audience. Guy Kingsley Poynter, Hazel Penwarden, Perceval, Hill and Main supported.

A tremendous storm broke over London on the night of 6th August, and as Act II opened the roof above the prompt corner was struck by lightning and rain poured down upon the stage. Lights fused and voices were so drowned in the noise that the performance had to be abandoned. The run ended in

November, before which Constance Cummings and Alexander
Knox took over from Googie and Redgrave.

On Guy Fawkes Night a somewhat farcical melodrama, *Dead
Secret*, was presented by Rosen of California and Hugh Wakefield, who himself played a wonderfully besotted drunken
blackmailer wanting no more than a happy home and money
for booze as price for secrets. Ian Hunter and Sophie Stewart
were the guilty couple Miles and Ruth, who lived near a handy
cliff-top over which their guest Charles would have been
pushed had he not turned virtuous and lined up with Ruth and
her friend Diana (Joyce Heron) against Miles.

The author was the young writer Michael Clayton Hutton.
Already he had had a couple of plays produced and showed
signs of brilliancy, but a few months later he decided that this
world was not for him.

An American husband and wife team, Mary Orr and Reginald
Denham, next saw their *Sweet Peril* run five weeks from 3rd
December until withdrawn because of alleged libel upheld by
the courts some months later. Norman Marshall directed in a
country cottage set by Laurence Irving. Daniel Mayer presented
Michael Dennison and his wife Dulcie Gray as the occupiers
with Marie Lohr as mother-in-law. Two charming Americans,
Margot Stevenson and her husband Ron Randell, played a
visiting couple and George Woodbridge and Brian Harding
supported.

1953

Roger Macdougall's delightful *Escapade* followed on the 20th
of the new year with the backing of Henry Sherek. Hutchinson
Scott designed the sets and John Fernald directed. The dramatist was being hailed as the new James Bridie and this play
certainly did not detract from his rising reputation. Sherek
picked an excellent company.

Nigel Patrick was vital as John Hampden, a writer bitten by

the Peace Movement 'bug' who was ever ready with militant fists and banging shut of doors to emphasise his ideals. In her first stage part for some years, Phyllis Calvert charmingly supported him as Stella, his almost downtrodden but increasingly exasperated and eventually rebellious wife. Phyllis, however, sometimes seemed perhaps too blond and beautiful quite to fit the harrassed mother, so when she later left the cast and her auburn-haired understudy Patricia Marmont took over to play even more realistically opposite the neurotic husband, Henry Sherek rightly confirmed Pat's new status so her name went up in lights to the end of the run here and at The Strand.

Off-stage were set the adventures of their offspring at boarding school. A master was shot with a pistol made in their 'useful work' period; an aeroplane was stolen and flown off to a European Conference with the school's Peace Manifesto! Ernest Clark's character study of Headmaster Dr Skillingworth earned him an annual award for the best supporting role. Lance Secretan and Alec McCowen as schoolboys Paton and Daventry gave long, finished, most promising performances during questioning by the Head in his study, to the accompaniment of fuming noises from Hampden.

Hugh Griffiths rounded off the play perfectly in his droll Welsh way as local reporter Deeson. Edith Sharpe was Hampden's mother and Michael Aldridge was Peter, side-issue in love with Stella. Michael Logan was a pompous pacifist. Other parts were played by David March, John Carew, Dorothy Turner and Sheila Taylor.

Escapade was transferred to The Strand because Olivier had earlier booked Italy's doyen Ruggero Ruggeri, who appeared from 20th April to 2nd May. Pirandello's strange *Enrico IV* and his *Tutto Per Bene* were presented, the main support being Andreina Pagnani, Margherita Bagni, Lea Padovani and among the men Sergio Tofani and Sandro Ruffini.

The Comédie-Française followed for three weeks. They offered *Tartuffe*, Racine's *Britannicus* and Marivaux' *Jeu de l'Amour* with Musset's one-act *On ne saurait penser à tout*. M. Ledoux was Tartuffe and M. Roland Alexandre Britannicus when Mme Marie Bell was Agrippine. Both foreign companies were well received and fairly well supported by the public, certainly by the fashionable on opening nights.

John Mills returned at the end of May in an unlucky play by his wife Mary Hayley Bell. He was *The Uninvited Guest*, a young man back from an unjustified sojourn in an asylum to the home of his resentful mother (Cathleen Nesbitt). Joan Greenwood very movingly played the mother's secretary who was the daughter of the man accidentally killed long ago by the newcomer, who soon was in love with her and a rival therefore to his younger brother played by Lyndon Brook. Clive Morton was the family doctor. Nothing was wrong with acting or play but it lasted only three weeks.

Whether Anna Broun was the last Czar's daughter or an imposter was the subject of *Anastasia* which Guy Bolton had adapted from the French of Marcelle Maurette. The MS. had been rejected by most London managements, maybe—for action descriptions are anathema—because Prince Bounine has to *describe* saving Anastasia from suicide. Of course a known author can get past a management with such a scene as Lonsdale for example, did in a little cameo for the detectives in *But for the Grace of God* here in 1946, when Cyril Smith and J. H. Roberts earned a round of applause.

Anyway, John Counsell of the Windsor Theatre Royal was the eventual sagacious manager. His May production was afterwards presented on television when Vivien Leigh saw it and then got busy so that her husband's company presented most of the original cast here on 5th August. Anthony Ireland played the leader of the crooks, the boorish and insensitive Prince Bounine, who saved the girl Anna from suicide only to fob her off as Anastasia in an attempt to share the late Czar's millions.

Mary Kerridge most intelligently and movingly interpreted Anna, who gradually awakened as the play unfolded to make it more than possible that she could be the Grand Duchess after all. Helen Haye as the Czar's mother earned acclaim for her regal and sensitive study of the old Dowager whose reserve slowly faded as realisation dawned that it *was* a grandchild before her. The sympathy created by Mary Kerridge as she evolved from a half-drowned waif to a possible princess was essential to that emotion-rousing scene and its finale as she in the end rejected acceptance and walked out on the ball arranged in her honour.

An unnecessary character, Sergei (M. Malnick), introduced in the last act to throw doubt on the girl's identity, ought to have been cut for the part was vulgar and grated, and upset the mood created. It had no point since Anna must have had some existence somewhere between escape and present. Otherwise the play went well except where the director's hand seemed very evident in the movements of minor players and their facial expressions, especially with the crooks in Act I whose reactions were mostly psychologically misconceived.

The others in the cast list were Susan Richards, Ruth Goddard, Verina Kimmins and Messrs Payne, Illing, Tyrrell, Godfrey, Michael. Hal Henshaw did the sets and Michael Ellis the costumes; John Counsell himself directed. During the run the seventy-ninth birthday of Helen Haye was celebrated with the gift of a motor-car from her fans in and out of the profession.

Pygmalion arrived on 19th November, some forty years after Shaw had discussed its genesis with Alexander, though Tree of course was eventually the first Higgins.

The actor-manager this time was John Clements, whose interpretation was certainly not what Alec's would have been for he was brittle and almost brash as the boorish Professor Higgins with the hidden heart of gold. Nicholas Hannen offset him delightfully as the kindly, gentlemanly soldier Colonel Pickering. Athene Seyler as the Professor's understanding mother could not of course have been bettered. Nor could Nuna Davey as the bossy housekeeper Mrs Pearce. Susan

Richmond was Mrs Eynsford Hill, Clare Bradley her 'yes mamma' daughter Clara and Robert Beaumont her son Freddy. Charles Victor was a good but perhaps too refined dustman Doolittle.

To the surprise of many, Kay Hammond completely dropped her famous drawl and made one of the most genuinely Cockney Elizas for a long time. She delightfully fitted the changing girl with a gradual charm which seemed very true. Elizabeth Haffenden designed the costumes and Penny Colman assisted Laurence Irving who designed the sets. Unfortunately John Clements, who also directed, did not realise that Irving was paying too little attention to his grandfather's famous injunction that the boy at the back of the gallery was entitled to see and hear, for in the sitting-room set he had designed an alcove so up-stage o.p. that even a quarter of the stalls could not see into it. Otherwise the whole ensemble and the acting were charmingly evocative and admirably started off with a vintage taxi which trundled on to the opening scene and shared publicity with the genuine phonograph introduced later on. In the silence after the famous 'not bloody likely', one elderly spinster turned to her companion in the stalls, as Clements reported in a radio interview, with 'Now are you satisfied, Hester?'

1954

Googie Withers returned, this time with her husband John McCallum, when Olivier's company presented them in Ronald Miller's *Waiting for Gillian* on 21st April. It was based on Nigel Balchin's novel *A Way through the Wood*. Googie was frivolous Jill Manning who would have hidden her accidental killing of a pedestrian had her husband James (McCallum) not attempted to pin the blame on the man next door, the Hon. William, played by Frank Lawton. James eventually dragged the truth out of her. Noel Howlett as Doctor Frewen with Anna Turner as Elsie Pearce led the other support in Kathleen

Boutall, Catherine Campbell, Heathcote and Pierce. The play ran 101 times until 17th July.

On the 22nd, transferred from The Arts, came Pirandello's strange drama *Six Characters in search of an Author*. The version was by Frederick May, the equally able direction by Royston Morley, sets by Ronald Brown.

The lights went up on a company at rehearsal. Suddenly the six trooped in to interrupt for they were born of an author of the past who found fear and failed to finish his fiction, thus leaving them with life without end, no existence other than their past but with a search without rest until they find a theatre where the drama of themselves may be enacted. By the power of their own earnestness they at last succeed for the director of the rehearsal succumbs to their empassioned pleadings and bit by bit they demonstrate their lives so that the professional actors may learn their parts. But these shallow mirrors distort too ludicrously the vivid drama they do not have the depth of mind to comprehend, and so the characters themselves take command of the stage to play out their sordid near-incestuous crazy existence, until Death can claim the half and then Oblivion the rest.

A child who drowns; another who stands watching and then shoots himself, a son who waits and hates; a poor torn mother who sobs but quivers sometimes suddenly to life when stung by grief and shame; a deserting father, pathetic and pitiful in shambling weakness ever explaining actions of his past; a vivid stepdaughter pushed to prostitution by a seventh character—a milliner-brothel beldame brought to existence on the spot by the intensity of remembrance. Doris Rogers played Mme Pace, this apparition from a Zola brothel.

Marda Vanne was the Mother whose occasional comfort-seeking outbursts emphasised her normal dulled-by-pain quiescence. Diane Cook and Alan Stebbings were the two children and Roger Gage the Son. Diana Blackwood was the Leading Lady and Bruno Barnabe the Leading Actor who

deliciously leered as he parodied the father in the brothel scene.
Gordon Bell was the Stage Manager, Barbara Lynne and Anne
Jenkins his delightfully harassed Assistants.

Reginald Tate was excellent as the Director holding the
balance and driven almost frantic by the argumentive interplay
of the squabbling factions, the temperamental players con-
tinually suffering interjection and rejection as the Characters
interrupted. Cyril Luckham had been cast as the Father, but
other commitments gave the part to Ralph Michael who was
excellent as the hesitant, diffident, yet eternally chattering
Father, quivering under the dominating disdain and ever
threatening scorn of Mary Morris as the Stepdaughter who
interspersed vivid cameos of her past with sudden moments of
sullen shame at the recollections.

The Celtic Morris, who had recently won acclaim for her
moving interpretation for over a year of *The Young Elizabeth*,
was ideal for the part, her quality that of Rachel without the
cold icyness of the Jewess, for in her too was the deep velvet
of the Italian Duse. Now, passionate wide nostrils trembling
beneath dark large expressive eyes crowned by black unruly
wind-swept tresses, her rich contralto tones sang vibrantly out
so that at the end, as the lights dimmed down and her weird
demonic laughter peeled round the auditorium, the listeners
sat in chilled awed silence until they could shake themselves
back to life and vent applause in thunder from all parts of the
ancient theatre.

Hardly a piece for the average playgoer who anyway could
have seen a television preliminary showing of it, it ran for a
month only, though with full houses when news circulated that
it was being withdrawn. Arrangements to replace it with Rhys
Davies' touring *No Escape* broke down when his star, Flora
Robson, suddenly revolted against being a dark murderess.
The famous Welsh novelist modestly shrugged off disappoint-
ment with the remark that if Pirandello could only last a month
what chance had he?

So Terence Rattigan's double bill of *Separate Tables* was presented by Stephen Mitchell on 22nd September and beat all records here with 726 performances. Both one-acts were set in the same seaside boarding house and provided sufficient self-identificational or other parts to please most onlookers, which must have accounted partly for the long run. Margaret Leighton followed excellently in the footsteps of her Victorian predecessors by playing two quite diverse roles each night, a faded at-the-end-of-her-tether ex-model and a dowdy unhappy girl brow-beaten by her mother who was played by Phyllis Neilson-Terry. Priscilla Morgan, making her West End début, gave an interesting character study as the maid Doreen. In fact the dramatist gave all the cast some chance to interpret his well delineated characters. The others were Patricia Raine, Marion Fawcett, Jane Eccles, May Hallatt, Beryl Measor and Aubrey Mather, Eric Portman, Basil Henson. Peter Glenville directed.

1956

Ruth Draper followed the long run for a month from 2nd July 1956. She was an astonishing impersonator in the Mr Love tradition and peopled the stage inimitably with her *Opening a Bazaar*, *A Railway Station*, *Three Women and Mr Clifford*, *Love in the Balkans*, etc. *The Times* enthused: '. . . vigorous homely woman, in love with the fireman, whose business was to look after the railway staff. The first part of the scene was a relaxed affair in which she chatted with people who breezed in and out; a telephone call then revealed that 30 people injured in a crash were to be brought to the station. Miss Draper made plans to receive them all—getting in touch with the doctor, asking neighbours to bring bedding and bottles of whisky. Everyone began to arrive and Miss Draper gave them all personal attention—offering coffee and towels, taking a boy from an injured woman, reasoning, issuing orders. . . .'

Leslie Storm's *The Long Echo* then ran for a month from

1st August. A newspaper sensation of the day was about two intellectuals of the Foreign Office who cleared out to Moscow having decided to live under Communism. This play was based on a like affair and displayed the reactions of friends and the women left behind. Murray Macdonald directed for Laurier Lister in a London flat set by R. Weaver. Denholm Elliott was go-between Alex, and Joyce Redman the wife Fay Edwards, whose mother-in-law was played by Marjorie Fielding, a sterling actress especially in sensible no-nonsense parts, greatly missed since her early death not long afterwards. Moira Lister was domineering sister-in-law Kate; Philippa Gill and David Hutcheson supported.

Macdonald also directed the next two plays, the first being a Peter Saunders production of Agatha Christie's *Towards Zero* which her fans kept running from September to March. Despite the valiant efforts of William Kendall, Cyril Raymond, Frederick Leister, George Baker and the two charming girls Gwen Cherrell and Mary Law with Gillian Lind, Janet Borrow, Michael Scott, Brimmell and Nightingale, some of the gallery actually walked out before the end but others stayed to boo!

Milton Shulman in the *Evening Standard* justifiably revealed the name of the murderer, so using as he said 'the critic's ultimate weapon in desperation' against a dramatist 'immune from ordinary criticism'. In the *Evening News* Stephen Williams wrote '. . . the second act, in which William Kendall as the Superintendant brilliantly conducts his enquiry, is easily the best. The first is tediously occupied . . . the third turns the play upside down and inside out . . . to such absurdity.' The late Stephen Williams is another great loss to the theatre as indeed is A. E. Wilson of the *Star* who too handed in his checks at about the same time. Both were shrewd though kindly lovers of the art they criticised, the former, a tall Grimaldi-faced Lancastrian rarely seen without papers and books under his arm but the author of only one; vulnerable therefore to the crack of the stocky practical Wilson, with half-a-dozen to his credit, that the bundle under Williams' arm was a fixture glued together only for effect!

1957

Another mystery ran six weeks only from 3rd March when Richard Attenborough played a dual role of twins in *Double Image* by Macdougall and Allan after a story by Roy Vickers. The veteran Zena Dare was in this with Raymond Huntley, Ernest Clark, Sheila Sim, Rudling, Stevens, Pelley.

An early piece by Anouilh, translated by Lucienne Hill, *Restless Heart*, attracted for three weeks for Stephen Mitchell, who passed the direction to William Chappell and decor to Peter Rice. The three best roles went to Donald Pleasance as a scruffy old dissolute leader of a café orchestra, Betty Warren as his wife Madame Tarde, and Mai Zetterling as his effervescent though often guilt-laden violinist daughter Thérèse. George Baker was handsome, wealthy hero Florent France. Annabel Maule played Jeanette, another girl in the orchestra. John Bennett, Peter Bull and many others supported.

Final presentation of all was put on by Toby Rowland from 12th June to 29th July. Noel Willman directed this mystery *It's The Geography That Counts*, by Raymond Bowers, in a living-room set by Hutchinson Scott. Chief suspect was played by the strong and interesting John Gregson making an all too infrequent flit from screen to stage. He was well supported by John Stratton as his brother, another suspect, and by Liam Redmond as a richly Irish but hardly true to life Scotland Yard detective. Jane Griffiths was excellent as a hard little charmer. Michael Duffield and Jack Hedley completed the company.

The play would have run longer had it not been really only a stopgap until certain money-barons and others could arrange their signatures on the death-warrant of the theatre.

At the final curtain on the Saturday night of 29th July John

Gregson stepped forward to say: 'In this historic, beautiful theatre, the scene of so many great successes, you share the awful distinction of being in at the death. The talk has now become a grim reality. It should never have been allowed to happen. I want you to make a resolution in your hearts that such a thing shall never happen again.'

The house was full, but subdued. They went away as from a funeral.

Towards the end of 1954 a speculator had obtained London County Council sanction to demolish the theatre and build an office block on the site. News of this circulated in January 1955 but public protests and Parliamentary questions ceased when the owners—'S. J. & L. Ltd.'—denied all knowledge. Managing directors were Gilbert Miller and Prince Littler. The latter had held the licence since 1943, the company having been the lessees since 1937. Negotiations, however, were conducted by somebody and in June 1957 secrecy was no longer necessary and announcement made that the theatre would be demolished.

National and London journals devoted leading articles to the matter and printed countless readers' letters almost unanimously against destruction. Sir Winston Churchill offered £500 to start a fund to save the theatre, and then American Huntington Hartford said he would give seven times that amount. Exquisite Vivien Leigh and burly *News Chronicle* critic Alan Dent actually paraded the streets with protest placards; as indeed did veteran Athene Seyler whose first appearance at the doomed theatre had been almost fifty years before.

Then Vivien Leigh, spontaneously or not, certainly with courage, sprang to her feet in the august House of Lords on 11th July to call out: 'My Lords! I wish to protest against The St James's Theatre being demolished!'

Actors Equity, with the support of the Variety Artistes Federation and the Concert Artistes Association, organised units from the London theatres in a march from the theatre to

SJT Z

a meeting behind St Martin's in-the-Fields on 20th July when Felix Aylmer, Sir Laurence and Vivien Leigh who had led the march, with other notabilities, spoke and resolutions were passed. The matter was several times raised in Parliament and on 30th July Lord Silkin's motion to the effect that their Lordships were against demolition was carried against the Government. All to no avail.

Fittingly for a theatre which had welcomed so many foreign artistes, the last on her boards were visiting touring continentals, the 'Lyrica Italiana'. In August they rehearsed to unshrouded empty crimson stalls. During a break between arias the Anglo-Polish actor Francis Stanislaw spoke Hamlet's lines, as from the theatre herself to the players and playgoers she had known:

> What is the reason that you use me thus?
> I loved you ever. But it is no matter;
> Let Hercules himself do what he may,
> The cat will mew. And dog will have his day.

APPENDICES

THE MAIN MANAGEMENTS

1835-41 Braham family management

	Director or tenant (T)	details
Dec. 1835-April 1836	William Mitchell	
April-Aug. 1836	Jenny Vertpré (T)	French co.
Sept. 1836-May 1837	J. P. Harley	
Sept. 1837-April 1838	J. P. Harley	
April-June 1838	J. Hooper	
Feb.-May 1839	J. Hooper (T)	Menagerie
Nov.-Dec. 1839	A. Bunn (T)	
April-July 1840	A. Bunn	German op. co.
Aug. 1840		French co.
Nov.-Dec. 1840	M. & J. Barnett (T)	English op. co.
1841	concerts and amateurs	

1842-54 Lessee and Impresario: John Mitchell. His directrice for
French companies: Mlle Forgeot

Feb.-July 1842	French co.
April-Aug.	Dobler (magic)
Jan.-July 1843	French
Nov.	Les Enfants Castelli
Jan.-July 1844	French
April-July	Dobler
July	Charles Kemble Readings
Jan.-July 1845	French
June-July	Philippe (magic)
Nov. 1845-Aug. 1846	French
Feb.-Aug. 1846	Ethiopian Serenaders
Nov. 1846-July 1847	French
Dec. 1846-July 1847	Ethiopian Serenaders
Dec. 1847-July 1848	French
May-Aug. 1848	Robert-Houdin (magic)
Dec. 1848-Jan. 1849	Dumbolton's Serenaders
Dec. 1848-April 1849	Robert-Houdin
Jan.-June 1849	French comic opera
Jan.-March 1850	French comic opera
March 1850	Alfred Bunn (lectures)
March-July 1850	French dramatic co.

July-Aug. 1850	Fanny Kemble Readings
Feb.-March 1851	Mr Love (vent.)
March	Tyrolese Singers
March-April	Fanny Kemble
April-May	J. H. Anderson (magic)
April-Aug.	French
June	Fanny Kemble (matinées)
Aug.-Oct.	Barnum (Bateman children)
Feb.-April 1852	Fanny Kemble (matinées only in March)
Feb.-July	French
March	Hungarian concerts
April and Sept.	Tyrolese Singers
June	German dramatic co.
Oct.	Organophonic Band
Nov.-Dec.	Henry Smith (lectures)
Dec. 1852-Jan. 1853	Marionettes
Jan.-June 1853	French
April-	Robert-Houdin
July-	German dramatic co.
Oct.	English op. co.
April-Aug. 1854	French dram. Fr. lyric
Oct. 1854-March 1855	Reade/Seymour
June 1855	Levassor/Tessiere entertainments
Aug. 1855	Felix French co. (Rachel's last)
Spring 1856	concerts
Winter	German co.
March-April 1857	Emery/ Sir Wm. Don
May-June	Offenbach co.
Aug.	Rayner's Christy Minstrels
Nov.-Dec.	Ronzani Italian op. buffa
Dec. 1857-May 1858	Frikell (magic)
May	Andreoletti (magic)
June-July	Ristori It. dram. co.
Dec. 1858-Feb. 1859	Remusat Fr. lyric co.
June-July	Augustus Braham op. co.
Oct. 1859-April 1860	F. B. Chatterton (Miss Wyndham, directrice)
April-May	Talexy Fr. co.
Aug.-Sept.	Chatterton (cont.)
Oct. 1860-May 1861	Alfred Wigan (Mrs Wigan, directrice)
Oct.-Dec. 1861	Wigan (cont.) (French in summer)
Dec. 1861-Sept. 1862	George Vining
Dec. 1862-July 1863	Frank Matthews (George Ellis, director)
Dec. 1863-Aug. 1864	Ben Webster (Fred Webster, director)
Sept.-Dec. 1864	Webster (cont.)

Dec. 1864-May 1868	Miss Herbert (summer breaks)
June-Aug. 1867	Felix Fr. co.
May-June 1868	Felix
June-July	Offenbach co.
Aug.	'Don Edgardo Colona'
Dec. 1868-Feb. 1869	Mlle de la Ferte/W. S. Emden
April-July	Felix co.
Oct. 1869-May 1877	Mrs John Wood and sub-tenants:
Sept. 1871	Royal Nat. Op. Co.
Nov. 1871-July 1872	Felix
Nov. 1872-Feb. 1873	Mansell
May 1873	Humbert Belgian co.
May-July 1874	Francis Fairlie (*Vert-Vert*)
July	Marye Fr. co.
Oct.-Dec.	Stephen Fiske
March-June 1875	Marie Litton
Jan.-April 1876	Horace Wigan
April 1876-May 1877	Mrs John Wood (with summer break)
June-July 1876	French co.
Dec. 1877-June 1878	Sam Hayes
Oct. 1879-July 1888	Hare and Kendal
Oct.-Dec. 1888	Barrington
Feb.-July 1890	Mrs Langtry
Nov.-Dec. 1890	French co.
1891-1918	George Alexander (occasional sub-tenants)
1918-1957	Gilbert Miller (numerous sub-tenants and associations)

SOME WEST-END DÉBUTS AT THE ST JAMES'S
(Foreign-speaking productions normally excepted)

Addison, Carlotta	6.10.1866	Lady F. Touch-wood	(*Belle's Stratagem*)
Adler, Luther	21.6.1938	Joe	(*Golden Boy*)
Alleyne, Bessie	12.1.1865	Mrs Woodcock	(*Woodcock's Little Game*)
Ashley, Henry	29.10.1860	Greenway	(*Up at the Hills*)
Aynesworth, Allan	5.11.1887	Friedrich	(*The Witch*)
Bancroft, George	7.1.1896	Lord Topham	(*Prisoner of Zenda*)
Bateman, Ellen	25.8.1851	Richard	(*Richard III*)
Bateman, Kate	25.8.1851	Richmond	(*Richard III*)
Beaumont, Diana	15.12.1921	a child	(*Peter Pan*)
Best, Edna	15.12.1917	Ela	(*Charley's Aunt*)
Bohnen, Roman	21.6.1938	Tom Moody	(*Golden Boy*)
Bourchier, Arthur	24.2.1890	Jaques	(*As you like it*)
Boyne, Leonard	2.5.1871	John Fern	(*Progress*)
Bridgeford, T. W.	16.12.1865	Snake	(*School for Scandal*)
Brook, Lyndon	10.5.1954	a guard	(*Caesar and Cleopatra*)
Brough, Fanny	15.10.1870	Fernande	(*Fernande*)
Bufton, Eleanor	30.10.1854	Vanette	(*Honour before Titles*)
Cahill, Lily	4.6.1929	Amelia	(*Caprice*)
Calhern, Louis	22.8.1938	Tom Moody	(*Golden Boy*)
Chambers, Emma	6.5.1871	Harry	(*Poll and Partner Joe*)
Clarke, John S.	16.10.1867	de Boots	(*A Widow Hunt*)
Clarke, Teresa F.	7.11.1895	Amy	(*Liberty Hall*)
Clayton, John	27.2.1866	Hastings	(*She Stoops to Conquer*)
Collette, Mary	1888	Suzanne	(*Ironmaster*)
Copeau, Jaques	29.11.1928	in *L'Illusion*	
Corri, Adrienne	22.4.1948	Kitty	(*Happy with Either*)
Cummins, Peggy	26.12.1938	Maryann	(*Let's Pretend*)
Devine, George	28.4.1932	Salanio	(*Merchant of Venice*)
Dewar, F. C.	29.10.1860	Tunstall	(*Up at the Hills*)
Dickens, C. S.	23.1.1932	Richard	(*The Bat*)
Dodd, Alice	22.2.1873	Gertrude	(*Loan of a Lover*)
Dryden, John	6.12.1849	Duke	(*The Honeymoon*)
Duncan, Emily	25.2.1873	The Ragged Boy	(*Rabagas*)

Dyall, Frank(lin)	28.4.1894	crowd	(*Masqueraders*)
Eadie, Dennis	7.2.1900	Glyn	(*Prisoner of Zenda*)
Eden, Louisa	31.10.1865	Susan	(*St James's Ladies Club*)
Emerson, Lillian	21.6.1938	Lorna	(*Golden Boy*)
Esmond, Jill	21.12.1922	Nibs	(*Peter Pan*)
Fairman, Austin	1.10.1912	Orderly	(*Turning Point*)
Fechter, Charles	6.12.1847	French season	
Field, Kate	12.3.1877	Maude	(*Extremes Meet*)
Fielding, Marjorie	4.9.1934	Hannah	(*Shining Hour*)
Flockton, Charles	26.12.1868	Holdsworth	(*Glitter*)
Galer, Elliot	29.10.1853	Elvino	(*Sonnambula*)
Gordon, H.	4.10.1871	Arthur	(*Lucy of Lammermoor*)
Groves, Fred	26.4.1899	Target	(*In Days of Old*)
Hackney, Mabel	28.4.1894	crowd	(*Masqueraders*)
Harcourt, Charles	30.3.1863	Robert Audley	(*Lady Audley's Secret*)
Harland, Ada	8.3.1862	Theodore	(*Friends or Foes*)
Hedman, Martha	1.1.1914	Renée	(*The Attack*)
Hersee, Clive	4.10.1871	Henry Ashton	(*Lammermoor*)
Hignett, H. R.	6.3.1902	Pulci	(*Paolo and Francesca*)
Hill, Barton	16.10.1869	Marlow	(*She Stoops to Conquer*)
Holles, Antony	14.12.1916	Charley	(*Charley's Aunt*)
Holman, William	1.1.1868	M'Haughty	(*The Needful*)
Jerrold, Mary	14.4.1896	Prudence	(*Mary Pennington*)
Kazan, Elia	21.6.1938	Eddie Fuselli	(*Golden Boy*)
Lancia, Florence	31.9.1871	opera season	
Lea, Marion	24.1.1885	Audrey	(*As you like it*)
Lewis, Martin	24.5.1909	student	(*Heidelberg*)
Linden, Eric	22.8.1938	Joe	(*Golden Boy*)
Lister, Lance	7.6.1917	Geoffrey	(*Shiela*)
Livesey, Roger	21.11.1917	office boy	(*Loyalty*)
Lorraine, Robert	7.1.1896	Toni	(*Prisoner of Zenda*)
Lunt, Alfred	4.6.1929	von Echardt	(*Caprice*)
Macalpine, Sheelagh	22.4.1948	Helena Benson	(*Happy with Either*)
McDonnell, Ellen	5.5.1866	Harriet	(*Rear Admiral*)
Macrae, Arthur	15.12.1921	third wolf	(*Peter Pan*)
Maybrick, Mr	1.10.1871	Count Arnheim	(*Bohemian Girl*)
Mervin, Frederick	16.1.1871	Oscar	(*War*)
Millward, Jessie	27.10.1881	Mary Preston	(*The Cape Mail*)
Minster, Jack	31.1.1923	Harold	(*If Winter Comes*)
Montgomery, Douglass	4.6.1929	Robert	(*Caprice*)
Moore, Nelly	29.10.1859	Winifred	(*Cupid's Ladder*)
Morgan, Priscilla	22.9.1954	Doreen	(*Separate Tables*)
Mosjeim, Greta	8.10.1935	Lilia	(*Two Share a Dwelling*)
Mowbray, Thomas	4.4.1848	Evelyn	(*Money*)
Neilson, Julia	27.11.1888	Ruth	(*Brantingham Hall*)
Nelson, Carry	5.5.1862	Prince Amabel	(*Prince Amabel*)

Nelson, Sarah	5.5.1862	Princess Violet	(*Prince Amabel*)
Nertann, Henri	16.1.1871	Colonel	(*War*)
Nordblom, Mr	1.10.1871	Thaddeus	(*Bohemian Girl*)
Opp, Julie	2.12.1896	Hymen	(*As you like it*)
Page, Genevieve	30.1.1952	Mignonette	(*The Happy Time*)
Parry, John	29.9.1836	The Prince	(*The Sham Prince*)
Primrose, Dorothy	21.6.1939	crowd	(*After the Dance*)
Rainforth, Elizabeth	27.10.1836	Mandane	(*Artaxerxes*)
Randell, Ron	3.12.1952	Chester Ames	(*Sweet Peril*)
Ray, Andrew	30.1.1952	Bibi	(*The Happy Time*)
Robson, Fred, jun.	17.4.1865	Ulysses	(*Ulysses*)
Saint-Denis, Michel	29.11.1928	Lucas	(*Le Médicin Malgré Lui*)
Sangster, Alfred	1911	crowd	(*Eccentric Lord Comberdene*)
Schneider, Hortense	22.6.1868	Duchesse	(*Grande Duchesse de Gérolstein*)
Shelton, George	17.4.1876	Lord Chamberlain	(*Sultan of Mocha*)
Sheridan, Amy	1861	Blanche	(*Game of Romps*)
Skinner, Cornelia Otis	6.1929	Impersonations	
Smith, Julia	29.9.1836	Mary Wilson	(*Strange Gentleman*)
Smith, Kitty	29.9.1836	Fanny Wilson	(*Strange Gentleman*)
Stanley, Frances	29.9.1836	Nina	(*Monsieur Jacques*)
Stephens, W. H.	18.1.1862	The Marquis	(*Self-Made*)
Stevenson, Margot	3.12.1952	Marianne Ames	(*Sweet Peril*)
Stirling, Arthur	3.1.1863	Philip Austin	(*Dark Cloud*)
Stratton, John	27.7.1948	Tommy Gold	(*No Trees in the Street*)
Swinstead, Joan	16.5.1921	Miss Adair	(*Emma*)
Tapley, Joseph	24.1.1885	Amiens	(*As you like it*)
Thesiger, Ernest	23.4.1909	James Raleigh	(*Colonel Smith*)
Toole, J. L.	2.10.1854	Pepys	(*King's Rival*)
Wakefield, Hugh	26.4.1899	a child	(*In Days of Old*)
Wallis, Bertram	2.12.1896	Amiens	(*As you like it*)
Waring, Herbert	17.9.1883	Col. Macdonald	(*Impulse*)
Waters, Russell	25.11.1947	Bert	(*Private Enterprise*)
Webster, Annie	20.10.1883	Esmeralda	(*Young Folks Ways*)
Webster, Ben	3.3.1887	Lord Woodstcok	(*Lady Clancarty*)
Willard, Edmund	31.8.1903	Luigi	(*The Cardinal*)
Williams, Arthur	26.12.1868	Thomas	(*Secret Panel*)
Wright, Edward	29.9.1837	Splash	(*Young Widow*)
Young, A. W.	16.10.1869	Diggory	(*She Stoops to Conquer*)

APPENDIX 3

RUNS OF 100 AND OVER

Title	Author	Opened	Perf's.
Adventure Story	Rattigan	17.3.1949	108
The Ambassador	Hobbs	2.6.1898	163
Anastasia	Maurette/Bolton	5.8.1953	117
The Aristocrat	Parker	25.1.1917	150
As you like it	Shakespeare	2.12.1896	114
The Basker	Mills	6.1.1916	112
The Bat	Rhinehart & Hopwood	23.1.1922	327
Behold we live	van Druten	16.8.1932	158
Bella Donna	Fagan	9.12.1911	253
La Belle Sauvage	Brougham	27.11.1869	200
The Big Drum	Pinero	1.9.1915	111
Black Limelight	Sherry	22.4.1937	414
But for the Grace of God	Lonsdale	3.9.1946	201
The Cardinal	Parker	31.8.1903	105
Don't Listen Ladies	Guitry/Powys	2.9.1948	219
The Elder Miss Blossom	Hendrie & Wood	22.9.1898	106
The Eyes of Youth	Marcin & Guerin	2.9.1918	384
Fame	A. & W. Carten	20.2.1929	108
Glass Slipper (rvl)	H. &. E. Fargeon	20.12.1945	101
Golden Boy	Odets	21.6.1938	109
Green Goddess	Archer	6.9.1923	416
Grounds for Divorce	Bolton	21.1.1925	118
His House in Order	Pinero	1.2.1906	430
His Lady Friends	Nyitray & Mandel	17.8.1920	135
The Hobby Horse	Pinero	23.10.1886	109
The Idler	Chambers	26.2.1891	176
If I were King	McCarthy	30.8.1902	215
Importance of being Earnest (rvl)	Wilde	30.11.1909	324
Impulse	Stephenson	9.12.1882	224
Interference	Pertwee & Dearden	29.1.1927	412
The Ironmaster	Pinero	17.4.1884	200
John Glayde's Honour	Sutro	8.3.1907	138
Ladies in Retirement	Percy & Denham	12.12.1939	174
Lady Audley's Secret	Roberts	28.2.1863	104
Lady Clancarty (rvl)	Taylor	3.3.1887	160

Lady Windermere's Fan	Wilde	20.2.1892	156
The Last of Mrs Cheyney	Lonsdale	22.9.1925	514
The Late Christopher Bean	Williams	16.5.1933	488
Liberty Hall	Carton	3.12.1892	183
Love in Albania	Ustinov	12.8.1949	142
Magic Entertainment	Frekell	9.12.1857	200
Magic Toys	Oxenford	5.10.1859	103
Man of Forty	Frith	28.3.1900	105
The Masqueraders	Jones	28.4.1894	139
Michael and Mary	Milne	1.2.1930	159
The Money Spinner	Pinero	8.1.1881	105
Month in the Country	Williams	11.2.1943	313
Old Heidelberg	Bleichmann	19.3.1903	189
The Outsider	Brandon	31.5.1923	107
Paolo and Francesca	Phillips	14.3.1902	136
Passing of the Third Floor Back	Jerome	1.9.1908	186
Polly with a Past	Middleton & Bolton	2.3.1921	110
Pride and Prejudice	H. Jerome	27.2.1936	316
Prisoner of Zenda	Rose	7.1.1896	254
The Queen's Shilling	Godfrey	4.10.1879	135
Reparation	Tolstoy	26.9.1916	114
Saturday to Monday	Fenn & Price	14.4.1904	100
A Scrap of Paper	Simpson	20.12.1883	120
Second Mrs Tanqueray	Pinero	27.5.1893	225
Separate Tables	Rattigan	22.9.1954	726
She Stoops to Conquer (rvl)	Goldsmith	16.10.1869	160
The Shining Hour	Winter	4.9.1934	213
S.O.S.	Ellis	11.2.1928	188
The Speckled Band (rvl)	Conan Doyle	22.9.1921	124
The Squire	Pinero	29.12.1881	170
The Swan	Molnar	30.6.1930	140
Ten Little Niggers	Christie	17.11.1943	260
The Thief	Gordon-Lennox	12.11.1907	186
Tree of Knowledge	Carton	25.10.1897	116
The Turning Point	Marchant	1.10.1912	111
Venus Observed	Fry	18.1.1950	230
The Wilderness	Esmond	11.4.1901	118
Wind of Heaven	Williams	12.4.1945	268
Winter Journey	Odets	30.4.1952	243
Witness for the Defence	Mason	1.2.1911	150

CHRONOLOGY OF FIRST WEST-END PERFORMANCES

Foreign productions, revivals, transfers, special matinees are not normally listed. Name in brackets = composer unless last when it means real name of author. Translator or adaptor/originator. sc = scene; a = act; br = burlesque; c = comedy; co = comic opera; e = entertainment; ext = extravaganza; f = farce; m = musical. Absence of cue = drama or play, except for some up to the sixties, mostly one-acts, with details undetermined.

1835	Dec.	14	*Agnes Sorel* co, 2a	(Mary A.) and Gilbert A. à Beckett
			A Clear Case f, 1a	à Beckett
			The French Company f, 1a	à Beckett
		26	*Rasselas or The Happy Valley* m, 1a	(Stansbury) à Beckett
1836	Jan.	4	*A House Divided* c, 2a	J. T. Haines
		12	*Monsieur Jacques* m, 1a	(John) and Morris Barnett
		18	*Brown's Horse* br	à Beckett
		23	*My Wife and Child* 1a	anon
	Feb.	1	*The Mendicant* 2a	à Beckett
			A Rough Diamond	anon
		25	*Rejected Addresses*	(Stansbury) J. Lunn
		26	*Thalia's Scrapbook* e	C. Selby
	March	10	*Can Love Kill?* 1a	anon
	Sept.	29	*The Strange Gentleman* f, 2a	Boz (C. Dickens)
			The Sham Prince f	anon
			The Tradesmen's Ball f	à Beckett
	Oct.	13	*Harmony Hall*	J. Lunn
	Nov.	1	*The Miniature*	anon
		24	*Delicate Attentions* f	Poole
	Dec.	6	*Village Coquettes* co	(Hullah) Dickens
		26	*Bletchington House*	anon
			The Enchanted Horn (*Oberon*) m	à Beckett
			The Parish Revolution f	à Beckett

1837	Jan.	5	*Love is Blind*	à Beckett
			The Wager f	Tom Parry
		11	*Misfortunes of Poor Simpkins*	anon
	Feb.	9	*Pedrillo or Castle of Andalusia*	anon
			Mayor of Garratt	anon
		20	*The French Refugee*	Mrs S. C. Hall
	March	6	*Is She His Wife?* f, 1a	Boz
		13	*The Postilion* o, 3a	à Beckett
			Pickwick e	Boz
		27	*Mabel's Curse* 2a	Mrs Hall
	April	19	*Wags of Windsor*	anon
	May	5	*Eagle's Haunt* o	(Glaeser) Fitzball
		?12	*Jack Brag* c, 2a	à Beckett
	Sept.	29	*Assignation* br, 2a	à Beckett
			Methinks I see my Father c, 1a	à Beckett
	Oct.	4	*The Cornet*	à Beckett
		14	*King John* br	à Beckett
		26	*Natural Magic*	Selby
	Nov.	11	*Temptation or Vale of Sarnem*	à Beckett
		27	*Angeline de Lis* 1a	J. T. Haines
	Dec.	6	*Wanted a Brigand* f, 1a	à Beckett
		26	*Pascal Bruno* 2a	à Beckett
1838	Jan.	3	*The Culprit* f, 1a	Bayly
		17	*Musician of Venice*	(Pilati) M. Barnett
		29	*The Black Domino* 3a	à Beckett
	Feb.	6	*Tis She, or The Maid, The Wife and The Widow* f, 1a	T. E. Wilks
		10	*Spitalfields Weaver* 1a	T. H. Bayly
		24	*The Fatal Secret*	anon
	March	1	*Jenny Jones* co, 1a	(Sloman and Harroway) Fox Cooper
		4	*The Ambassadress* o, 3a	(Stansbury/Auber) à Beckett
		27	*Oliver Twist* 2a	à Beckett
		29	*Valet de Sham* f, 1a	Selby
			Munich Huntsman	anon
	April	16	*My Album* 1a	Bayly
			The Brothers 1a	Wilks
			Hero and Leander ext, 1a	Leman Rede
	May	3	*Love and Charity* 1a	Mark Lemon
			Cosimo co	anon
		7	*The British Legion* 1a	Bayly
1839	Feb.	11	*The Young Sculptor*	H. Mayhew
			Friends and Neighbours	Bayly
			A Troublesome Lodger	Mayhew and Baylis
		25	*Take your Choice*	Lunn

1839	March	4	*The Rear Admiral* f, 1a	W. S. Emden
	April	8	*A Day's Training*	anon
		22	*The Jealous Husband*	Raymond
	Nov.	5	*Hainault Forest* e	Bunn
		9	*Lefevre or The Lost Likeness* 2a	Barnett
		25	*A Close Seige*	G. Dance
		30	*A Pupil of da Vinci*	Lemon
1840	Nov.	26	*Fridolin* o	(Romer) Lemon
			The Sergeant's Wedding f, 1a	Wilks
1843	Nov.	9	*Clementine*	anon
1847	April	24	*Hernani*	anon
1852	Jan.	23	*Crotchet Hall*	anon
	Dec.	6	*Appeal to the Audience* (puppets)	A. Brown
		27	*Harlequin Ali Baba* (puppets)	Hugo Vamp
1853	Nov.	5	*Pierre*	Duggan
1854	Oct.	2	*The King's Rival* 5a	C. Reade
			My Friend the Major f, 1a	Selby
		18	*The Spanish Dancers* br	Selby
		20	*An Artist's Wife*	anon
		30	*Honour before Titles*	Reade
	Nov.		*Perigrine Pickle*	Reade
		13	*Beauties of the Harem*	anon
	Dec.	9	*Love and Chastity*	anon
		26	*Abon Hassan* ext, 8sc	Talfourd
1855	Jan.	15	*Alcestis* m, 3a	(Guernsey/Gluck)
				H. Spicer
	Feb.	17	*Clarisse or The Foster Sister*	anon
			Art (revised)	Reade
	March	5	*The Dancing Scotchman*	anon
1857	Jan.	23	*The Libertine's Bet*	Reade
	March	23	*The Belle and the Boor*	anon
1858	May	31	*Miss Prudentia Single's Soiree*	anon
1859	June	11	*The Pearl of Spain*	anon
			The Feast of Saragossa	anon
			Raymond and Agnes o	Fitzball
		27	*Patchwork*	H. Paul
			Tobin and Nanette	anon
	July	4	*The Mountaineer's Dance*	anon
	Oct.	1	*The Widow's Wedding* c, 1a	Fitzball
			Virginius br, 6sc	Buckingham
		5	*Magic Toys* ballet f, 1a	Oxenford
		29	*Cupid's Ladder* c, 2a	Buckingham
	Nov.	9	*London Pride* c	J. Kenney
		16	*Swan and Edgar* ext	Edwards and Kenney
		21	*All to Astonish the Browns*	anon
		24	*The Three Winterbottoms*	anon

1859	Nov.	30	*The Chatterbox*	B. Jerrold
	Dec.	24	*Garibaldi's Englishmen*	Lemon
			The Household Fairy	Talfourd
			Punch and Judy panto	J. C. Collins
1860	Jan.	18	*My Name is Norval* br	Oxenford
			Parents and Guardians	anon
	Feb.	11	*Dido* br, 1a, 6sc	Burnand
		13	*First Affections* c, 1a	P. Simpson
			I will if you will f, 1a	J. Bruton
	March	5	*Number Forty-Nine* f, 1a	F. Lawrence
	April	9	*Lucrezia Borgia* br	Buckingham
			A Change of System	Howard Paul
		23	*A Friend in Need* c, 2a	French and Sorrell
	June	12	*Furnished Apartments* (?Ben.)	Hay
	Oct.	29	*Up at the Hills*	T. Taylor
	Nov.	19	*Next Door* (revised)	A. Wigan
		26	*Smack for a Smack*	P. Simpson
	Dec.	26	*Isle of St Tropez* 4a	Burnand and Williams
			Endymion ext	W. Brough
1861	April	15	*Pasha of Pimlico*	M. Morton
		22	*A Scrap of Paper*	P. Simpson
	Nov.	14	*The Poor Nobleman* c, 2a	Selby
	Dec.	26	*Perseus and Andromeda* ext	W. Brough
1862	Jan.	18	*Self-made*	George Vining
	March	8	*Friends or Foes* c, 4a	Horace Wigan
		24	*Under the Rose* f, 1a	Geo. Roberts
	May	5	*Prince Amabel* ext, 1a	W. Brough
	June	2	*Forty Winks*	Roberts
		21	*His Last Victory* c, 2a	Watts Phillips
	July	19	*Captain of the Watch*	anon
	Aug.	11	*Bristol Diamonds* f, 1a	Oxenford
			Return Ticket to the International	
			Exhibition f, 1a	James and Spencer
	Sept.	6	*She would and He wouldn't* c, 2a	J. M. Morton
	Dec.	26	*Golden Hair the Good* ext	H. J. Byron
			Carte de Visite f, 1a	Williams and Burnand
1863	Jan.	3	*The Dark Cloud* 2a	Arthur Sketchley
				(Rose)
		19	*Smiths at Norwood* f, 1a	anon
		31	*The Merry Widow* c, 2a	Buckingham
	Feb.	28	*Lady Audley's Secret* 2a	Roberts
	April	6	*The Great Sensation Trial* br	W. Brough
	May	4	*The Little Sentinel* c. 1a	T. J. Williams
	July	29	*The Embarrassed Man* f, 1a	Mrs E. Thomas
	Dec.	26	*1863 or Sensations of the Past*	
			Season ext	H. J. Byron

1864	Jan.	30	*The Silver Lining* c, 3a	Buckingham
	May	11	*The Fox Chase* c, 5a	Boucicault
	July	9	*Faust and Marguerite* br, 5sc	Burnand
	Aug.	12	*How will they get out of it?* c, 3a	Sketchley
	Oct.	6	*Woodcock's Little Game* f, 2a	J. M. Morton
		29	*Sybilla* c, 3a	P. Simpson
	Nov.	7	*Baronet Abroad and the Rustic Prima Donna* m, 1a	L. Horne
	Dec.	22	*A Lesson in Love* c, 3a	Cheltnam
		26	*Hercules and Omphale* ext	W. Brough
1865	Feb.	25	*Faces on the Fire* c, 3a	Buckingham
	March	13	*The Three Furies* c	G. Roberts
	April	17	*Ulysses* br	Burnand
	May	29	*Eleanor's Victory* 4a	Oxenford
	June	19	*Pouter's Wedding* f	J. M. Morton
	Oct.	14	*Caught in the Toils* 3a	J. Brougham
		30	*The St James's Ladies Club* c, 1a	Lemon
	Dec.	26	*Please to remember* (revue)	(Musgrave) Oxenford
1866	June	11	*Jack in a Box* c, 1a	Simpson
	Oct.	6	*Professor of what?* f, 1a	Oxenford
	Nov.	2	*Newington Butts* f, 1a	J. M. Morton
		5	*Hunted Down* 3a	Boucicault
	Dec.	29	*Dulcamara* br	(van Hamme) W. S. Gilbert
1867	March	2	*A Rapid Thaw* c, 2a	T. W. Robertson
	April	22	*Idalia* 3a	G. Roberts
	Oct.	16	*A Widow Hunt* c, 3a	J. S. Coyne
	Nov.	4	*Story of Procida* 1a	anon
1868	Jan.	1	*The Needful* c, 1a	H. T. Craven
	March	2	*A Happy Pair* c, 1a	S. T. Smith
	Dec.	26	*Secret Panel* f, 1a	anon
			Glitter c, 2a	à Beckett
			Sleeping Beauty (revised) ext	Planche
1869	Jan.	30	*Red Hands* 3a	à Beckett
	Nov.	27	*La Belle Sauvage* br, 5sc	Brougham
1870	April	14	*Frou Frou* c, 5a	B. Webster/ Meilhac and Halevy
	June	25	*Frou Frou* c, 5a	A. Daly
	Oct.	15	*Fernande* 4a	Edwards/Sardou
	Nov.	21	*Christmas Eve* f	Cheltnam
1871	Jan.	16	*War* 3a	T. W. Robertson
	Feb.	9	*Vesta* br	H. B. Farnie
	March	4	*The Two Thorns* c	J. Albery
	April	8	*The Rival Romeos* f, 1a	Farnie
			Actress by Daylight	Cowell or Reade
	May	6	*Poll and Partner Joe* br, 4sc	Burnand

1872	Nov.	18	*Bridge of Sighs* co	(Offenbach) Leigh
1873	Feb.	25	*Robert Rabagas*	S. Fiske
	Dec.	19	*Conrad Converted* br	A. W. Allan
		20	*Caught at Last* c, 1a	anon
1874	May	2	*Vert Vert* co, 3a	(Offenbach) Herman and Mansell
	Oct.	24	*Guardian Angel* c, 1a	Oxenford and Hatton
			Black Prince co	Farnie
	Dec.	8	*Eclipsing the Sun* f	Hartrop
1875	April	24	*Tom Cobb* f, 3a	W. S. Gilbert
	June	5	*The Zoo* m, 1a	(Sullivan) B. Rowe
1876	Jan.	8	*Pretty Poll* c, 1a	R. Reece
	April	17	*Sultan of Mocha* co, 3a	A. Celier
	July	3	*Les Danicheff* (French) 4a	Newsky
	Oct.	14	*Three Millions of Money* c, 4a	Lyster and Mackay
	Nov.	20	*The Virginian* c, 5a	B. Campbell
		22	*Nillson or Nothing* br	anon
1877	Jan.	6	*The Danicheffs* 4a	Newry/Newsky
	March	12	*Extremes Meet* c, 1a	Kate Field
1878	March	9	*The Scar on the Wrist* 3a	Simpson and Templar
	April	20	*Such is the Law* 3a	T. Taylor and Merritt
	May	17	*Bold Dick Turpin* m	(Leslie) P. Simpson
1879	Oct.	4	*Monsieur le Duc* 1a	Val Prinsep
	Dec.	18	*The Falcon* 1a	Tennyson
1880	March	6	*Old Cronies* c, 1a	Theyre Smith
	Oct.	9	*William and Susan* 3a	W. G. Wills/Jerrold
	Dec.	4	*Good Fortune* c, 3a	C. F. Coghlan/Feuillet
1881	Jan.	8	*The Money Spinner* c, 2a	A. W. Pinero
	May	28	*Coralie* 4a	G. W. Godfrey/Delpit
	Oct.	27	*The Cape Mail* c, 1a	Clement Scott
	Dec.	29	*The Squire* 3a	Pinero
1882	March	6	*Medusa* c, 1a	F. W. Hayes
	Dec.	9	*Impulse*	B. C. Stephenson
1883	Oct.	20	*Young Folk's Ways* c, 4a	Mrs Burnett and W. H. Gillette
	Dec.	20	*Case for Eviction* c, 1a	T. Smith
1884	April	17	*The Ironmaster* 4a	Pinero/Ohnet
1885	June	10	*The Castaways* 1a	T. Smith
	Oct.	31	*Mayfair* 5a	Pinero/Sardou
1886	Feb.	13	*Antoinette Rigaud* c, 3a	E. Warren/Deslandes
	April	1	*A Private Detective* (mat.) c, 1a	Leigh and Pemberton
	May	25	*The Wife's Sacrifice* 5a	Grundy and Edwards
		31	*In the Old Time* (mat.) 4a	Walter Frith
	Oct.	23	*The Hobby Horse* c, 3a	Pinero
1887	Nov.	5	*The Witch* 4a	C. W. Rae
1888	Oct.	13	*The Dean's Daughter* 4a	Grundy and Philips

1888	Oct.	17	*A Patron Saint* c, 1a	C. Thomas
	Nov.	27	*Brantingham Hall* 4a	W. S. Gilbert
1889	May	14	*Well Matched* (mat.)	P. Havard
1890	May	3	*The Tiger* o, 1a	(Soloman) Burnand
			Esther Sandraz	Grundy
	June	26	*Your Wife* (mat.) f, 3a	J. McCarthy
			Old Friends 1a	Lady V. Greville
1891	Jan.	30	*Gay Lothario* c, 1a	A. C. Calmour
	Feb.	26	*The Idler* 4a	C. H. Chambers
	July	17	*Moliere* 1a	W. Frith
	Nov.	7	*Lord Anerley* 4a	Quinton and Hamilton
	Dec.	30	*Forgiveness* c, 4a	Comyns Carr
1892	Feb.	20	*Lady Windermere's Fan* 3a	Oscar Wilde
	March	30	*Midsummer Day* 1a	W. Frith
	Oct.	31	*Kit Marlowe* 1a	W. L. Courtney
	Dec.	3	*Liberty Hall* c, 4a	R. C. Carton
1893	May	27	*The Second Mrs Tanqueray* 4a	Pinero
	June	12	*Bess* (mat.)	Mrs Berenger
1894	April	28	*The Masqueraders* 4a	H. A. Jones
1895	Jan.	5	*Too Happy by Half* 1a	J. Field
			Guy Domville 3a	Henry James
	Feb.	14	*In the Season* 1a	L. E. Mitchell
			The Importance of Being Earnest c, 3a	Wilde
	May	11	*Triumph of the Philistines* c, 3a	Jones
	Sept.	10	*Bogey* 3a	H. V. Esmond
	Nov.	23	*The Misogynist* 1a	G. W. Godfrey
			The Divided Way 3a	Esmond
1896	Jan.	7	*The Prisoner of Zenda*	E. Rose
	April	14	*Mary Pennington, Spinster* c, 4a	Wilkes
1897	March	2	*Tess* (mat.)	Stoddard
		29	*The Princess and the Butterfly* c, 5a	Pinero
	Oct.	25	*The Tree of Knowledge* 4a	R. C. Carton
1898	April	14	*The Conquerors* 4a	P. M. Potter
	June	2	*The Ambassador* c, 4a	J. O. Hobbs (Mrs Craigie)
	Sept.	22	*The Elder Miss Blossom* 3a	Hendrie and Wood
1899	Feb.	28	*A Repentance* 1a	J. O. Hobbs
	April	26	*In Days of Old* 4a	E. Rose
1900	Feb.	1	*Rupert of Hentzau* 4a	Anthony Hope
	March	28	*The Man of Forty* 4a	W. Frith
	Sept.	1	*A Debt of Honour* 5a	Grundy
	Nov.	22	*The Plot of His Story* 1a	Mrs Berenger
			The Wisdom of the Wise 3a	J. O. Hobbs
1901	Feb.	6	*The Awakening* 4a	C. H. Chambers

1901	April	11	*The Wilderness* c, 3a	H. V. Esmond
	July	?2	*Old Crimea* 1a	C. Hamilton
1902	March	6	*Paolo and Francesca* 4a	S. Phillips
	May	8	*Finding of Nancy* (mat.)	Netta Syrett
	Aug.	30	*If I were King* 4a	J. McCarthy
1903	March	19	*Old Heidelberg* 5a	Bleichmann/Forster
	Aug.	31	*The Cardinal* 4a	L. N. Parker
1904	March	17	*Love's Carnival* 5a	Bleichmann/Hartleben
	April	14	*Saturday to Monday* c, 3a	Fenn and Pryce
		25	*'Op o' me Thumb* 1a	Fenn and Pryce
	Sept.	3	*The Garden of Lies* 4a	Grundy
	Oct.	18	*The Decree Nisi* 1a	J. Bates
1905	Jan.	10	*White Magic* 1a	Syrett
		27	*A Maker of Men* 1a	A. Sutro
	Feb.	13	*Mollentrave on Women* 3a	Sutro
	March	21	*How He Lied To Her Husband* (Court, Feb. 28) 1a	G. B. Shaw
	May	1	*John Chilcote, M.P.* 4a	Thurston
	June	13	*The Man of the Moment* 4a	Melvill
	Oct.	12	*The Housekeeper* f, 3a	Wood and Maxwell
	Dec.	27	*Beside the Bonnie Briar Bush* 4a	Macarthur
1906	Feb.	1	*His House in Order* c, 4a	Pinero
1907	March	8	*John Glayde's Honour* 4a	Sutro
	July	29	*The 18th Century* 3a	*after* Malyon and James
	Nov.	12	*The Thief* 3a	Gordon-Lennox
1908	May	9	*The Thunderbolt* 4a	Pinero
	Sept.	1	*Third Floor Back* 3a	J. K. Jerome
	Nov.	11	*Builder of Bridges* 4a	Sutro
1909	April	9	*Colonel Smith* c, 4a	A. E. W. Mason
	May	3	*The Nursery Governess* 1a	Duchesne
	Sept.	2	*Mid-Channel* 4a	Pinero
	Nov.	9	*Lorimer Sabiston* 5a	Carton
1910	Sept.	27	*D'Arcy of the Guards* c, 4a	Shipman
	Nov.	19	*Eccentric Lord Comberdene* 3a	Carton
	Dec.	21	*The Piper* 4a	J. P. Peabody
1911	Feb.	1	*The Witness for the Defence* 4a	A. E. W. Mason
	Sept.	11	*The Ogre* 3a	H. A. Jones
		22	*The Miniature* 1a	W. Frith
	Dec.	9	*Bella Donna* 5a	J. B. Fagan
1912	Oct.	1	*The Turning Point* 3a	le Marchant
1913	Jan.	18	*Turandot* m, 3a	(Busoni) Bithell/ Vollmoeller
	March	11	*Open Windows* 3a	A. E. W. Mason
		31	*Playgoers* 1a	Pinero
	Sept.	1	*The Harlequinade* m	(Stephenson) Calthrop and Barker

1913	Sept.	1	*Androcles and the Lion* pro and 2a	G. B. Shaw
	Oct.	29	*The Witch* (Court, 1911) 4a	Masefield/Wiers-Jenssen
	Dec.	2	*Le Mariage Forcé* (in English) 1a	Molière
		9	*The Doctor's Dilemma* (Court, 1906) 4a and ep	G. B. Shaw
1914	Jan.	1	*The Attack* 3a	Egerton/Bernstein
	March	5	*The Two Virtues* c, 4a	Sutro
	Sept.	19	*Those Who Sit In Judgement* 4a	Michael Orme
1915	Jan.	16	*Kings and Queens* 3a	R. Besier
	April	14	*Panorama of Youth* c, 4a	J. H. Manners
	May	19	*The Day Before The Day* 4a	C. B. Fernald
	Sept.	1	*The Big Drum* c, 4a	Pinero
1916	Jan.	6	*The Basker* c, 4a	Mrs Clifford Mills
	May	3	*The Pen* c, 3a	H. A. Vachell
	Oct.	19	*Lucky Jim* 3a	Seton
1917	Jan.	25	*The Aristocrat* 3a	L. N. Parker
	April	3	*Michael* (RADA mat.)	Miles Malleson
	June	7	*Sheila* c, 3a	Githa Sowerby
	Sept.	4	*The Pacifists* 3a	H. A. Jones
	Nov.	21	*Loyalty* 4a	H. Owen
1918	Jan.	24	*Valentine* co, 2a	(Lambelet) Davenport and Wibrow
	Sept.	2	*Eyes of Youth* 3a	Marcin and Guernon
	Dec.	3	*The Great Moment* (mat.) 1a	Gwen Lally
			The Proposal 1a	West/Tchekof
1919	Sept.	26	*Reparation* 3a	Maudes/Tolstoy
	March	27	*Uncle Ned* c, 4a	D. Murray
	May	26	*Mystery of the Yellow Room*	H. Bennett
	Aug.	17	*His Lady Friends* c, 3a	Nyitray and Mandel
1921	Jan.	15	*Daniel* 4a	Harris/Verneuil
	March	2	*Polly with a Past* 3a	Middleton and Bolton
	May	16	*Emma* c, 3a	H. Thomas
	Aug.	23	*Threads* c, 3a	F. Stayton
1922	Jan.	23	*The Bat* 3a	Rinehart and Hopwood
	Nov.	4	*The Beating on the Door* 3a	A. Page
	Nov.	30	*The Happy Ending* c, 3a	Ian Hay
1923	Jan.	31	*If Winter Comes* 4a	Hutchinson and Hastings
	March	21	*The Inevitable* 3a	Isabel Jay
	May	30	*The Outsider* 3a	Dorothy Brandon
	June	17	*Coming of Gabrielle* (mat.)	George Moore
	Sept.	6	*The Green Goddess* 4a	William Archer
1924	Sept.	17	*The Nervous Wreck* f, 3a	Owen Davis

1924	Dec.	18	*Pollyanna* c, 4a	Cath. Cushing
1925	Jan.	6	*Meddlers* f, 3a	Pugh and Platt
		21	*Grounds for Divorce* 3a	Bolton/Vajda
	June	2	*The River* 3a	Patrick Hastings
		20	*The Guardsman* 3a	Colbron and Bartsch/ Molnar
	Sept.	22	*The Last of Mrs Cheyney* 3a	F. Lonsdale
1927	Jan.	29	*Interference* 3a	Pertwee and Dearden
1928	Feb.	11	*S.O.S.* 3a	W. Ellis
	Sept.	1	*The Return Journey* pro and 3a	Arnold Bennett
	Dec.	4	*The Play's the Thing* c, 2a	P. G. Wodehouse/ Molnar
		26	*No Other Tiger*	A. E. W. Mason
1929	Feb.	20	*Fame* 3a	A. and W. Carten
	June	4	*Caprice* 3a	Moeller/Sil-vara
	Oct.	15	*Heat Wave* 3a	Pertwee
1930	Feb.	1	*Michael and Mary* 3a	A. A. Milne
	June	30	*The Swan* c, 3a	Molnar
	Nov.	26	*A Murder has been arranged* 3a	Emlyn Williams
1931	Feb.	17	*Etienne* c, 3a	Wakefield/Deval
	May	4	*Payment Deferred* pro, 3a and ep	J. Dell
1932	June	8	*The Vinegar Tree* c, 3a	P. Osborne
	Aug.	16	*Behold We Live* 3a	van Druten
1933	May	16	*The Late Christopher Bean* c, 3a	Williams/Fauchois
1934	Sept.	4	*The Shining Hour* 3a	K. Winter
1935	March	26	*Worse Things Happen At Sea* c, 3a	Winter
	Oct.	8	*Two Share A Dwelling* 3a	Alice Campbell
1936	Feb.	27	*Pride and Prejudice* 3a	Helen Jerome
	Dec.	3	*O Mistress Mine* 3a	Ben Travers
1937	Feb.	3	*The Orchard Walls* 2a	Hodge/Fodor
	April	18	*Strange Rhythm* (mat.)	Bolton and Vagliano
		22	*Black Limelight* 3a	Gordon Sherry
	June	3	*Yes, My Darling Daughter* c, 3a	Rodney Ackland/Reed
	Aug.	18	*Old Music* pro, 3a and ep	Winter
	Nov.	16	*The Silent Knight* c, 3a	Wolfe/Heltai
	Dec.	22	*You Can't Take It With You* f, 3a	Kauffman and Hart
1938	Jan.	27	*The Innocent Party* c, 2a	Harwood and Kirk
	June	21	*Golden Boy* 3a	Clifford Odets
	Nov.	16	*Gentleman Unknown* 2a	A. A. Milne
	Dec.	26	*Let's Pretend* (revue)	Geray and others
1939	May	22	*Sixth Floor* 3a	Ackland/Gehri
	June	21	*After The Dance* 3a	T. Rattigan
	Dec.	12	*Ladies in Retirement* 3a	Percy and Denham
1942	Oct.	8	*The Duke in Darkness* 3a	P. Hamilton

1942	Dec.	10	*It Happened In September* 3a	Beverley Baxter
		29	*Romance of David Garrick*	C. Cox
1943	May	31	*Bird of Passage*	Knoblock
	Nov.	17	*Ten Little Niggers* 3a	A. Christie
1944	Sept.	20	*Felicity Jasmine* f, 3a	G. Sherry
	Nov.	8	*Residents Only* c, 3a	Gordon and Pratt
	Dec.	22	*The Glass Slipper* m	H. and E. Farjeon
1945	Feb.	7	*Emma* 3a	G. Glennon
	April	12	*The Wind of Heaven* 2a	E. Williams
1946	Feb.	28	*Dear Ruth* c, 2a	N. Krasna
	May	14	*The Kingmaker* 3a	M. Luce
	Sept.	3	*But for the Grace of God* 2a	F. Lonsdale
1947	March	5	*Truant in Park Lane* 3a	J. Parish
	April	10	*Call Home The Heart* 2a	C. Dane
	Aug.	14	*Fly Away Peter* c, 3a	Dearsley
	Oct.	9	*The Man in the Street* 3a	G. Kerr
	Nov.	25	*Private Enterprise* 3a	St John Ervine
1948	Feb.	6	*All This Is Ended* 3a	J. Alldridge
	April	22	*Happy With Either* 3a	M. Kennedy
	July	27	*No Trees in the Street* 3a	T. Willis
	Sept.	2	*Don't Listen, Ladies* 2a	Powys and Bolton/ S. Guitry
1949	March	17	*Adventure Story* 2a	Rattigan
	July	12	*Love in Albania* c, 3a	E. Linklater
1950	Jan.	18	*Venus Observed* 3a	C. Fry
	Aug.	9	*Captain Carvallo* c, 3a	D. Cannan
	Oct.	11	*Top of the Ladder* 3a	Tyrone Guthrie
1951	Feb.	15	*Madwoman of Chaillot* 2a	Valency/Giradoux
1952	Jan.	30	*The Happy Time* 3a	S. Taylor
	April	3	*Winter Journey* 2a	C. Odets
	Nov.	5	*Dead Secret* 3a	M. C. Hutton
	Dec.	3	*Sweet Peril* 3a	Orr and Denham
1953	Jan.	20	*Escapade* 3a	R. Macdougall
	May	27	*The Uninvited Guest* 3a	M. Hayley Bell
	Aug.	5	*Anastasia* 3a	Bolton/Maurette
1954	April	21	*Waiting for Gillian* 3a	R. Millar
	Sept.	22	*Separate Tables* 2 × 1a	Rattigan
1956	Aug.	1	*The Long Echo* 3a	Lesley Storm
	Sept.	4	*Towards Zero* 3a	A. Christie
1957	March	3	*Double Image* 3a	Macdougall and Allan
	May	8	*Restless Heart* 3a	Hill/Anouilh
	June	12	*It's The Geography That Counts* 2a	R. Bowers

ÍNDEXES

1. Theatres. 2. Some Productions. 3. Various. 4. Persons

Appendices and plates are not indexed but the List of Illustrations
gives the names of those who appear in the plates

THEATRES

SOME PRODUCTIONS

VARIOUS

PERSONS

ERRATA

P. 7, para. 1. Reid should be Reed.

P. 179, para. 4. Maude Milton (who later dropped the final 'e') may have made her town début elsewhere earlier.

P. 200, para. 1. Phoebe ought to be Phebe, for the Kendals used the more archaic form which got changed, without my noticing in time, to the modern Phoebe which both Mrs Langtry and Alexander used.

Pp. 209, para. 2, and 371, line 2. In Gilbert's play *Brantinghame Hall* I missed out the final 'e'.

Pp. 264, para. 3, and 361, line 19. H. R. Hignett did not make his town début here but in The Lyceum 1900 season of classics with Benson's brilliant company including Henry Ainley, Oscar Asche, Graham Browne, Alfred Brydone, O. B. Clarence, Leslie Faber, Matheson Lang, H. O. Nicholson, B. Iden Payne (father of Rosalind Iden), Lyall Swete, Arthur Whitby (father of Gwynne Whitby), Harcourt Williams and Lily Brayton, Ada Ferrar, Kitty Loftus, Nancy Price, &c.

P. 276, para. 1. Lennox-Gordon should be Gordon-Lennox.

Pp. 277, para. 3, and 307, para. 5. There should be no final 'e' in Sir Johnston.

P. 302, para. 4. I seem to imply that 'Master Charles Chaplin' created the part of Billy in *The Speckled Band* at The Adelphi. He created a Billy but at The Duke of York's in 1905 in Gillette's skit *The Painful Predicament of Sherlock Holmes.*

P. 310, para. 1. The names of Cathleen Nesbitt and Margery Clark should be transposed.

P. 313, para. 2. H. K. Ayliff directed, not Sir Barry Jackson.

P. 314, para. 4. The names of Gilbert Davis and Clarence Derwent should be transposed.

Pp. 351, para, 2, and 375, line 38. Gerald Verner collaborated with Agatha Christie in *Towards Zero.*

Pp. 352, para. 2, and 375, line 40. Double Image was not a first but a transfer from The Savoy.

I regret a few more errors in spelling names, but the index will be correct: names sometimes changed and newspapers and programmes do not always concur, whilst accents and hyphens sometimes appeared later or were omitted in publicity.

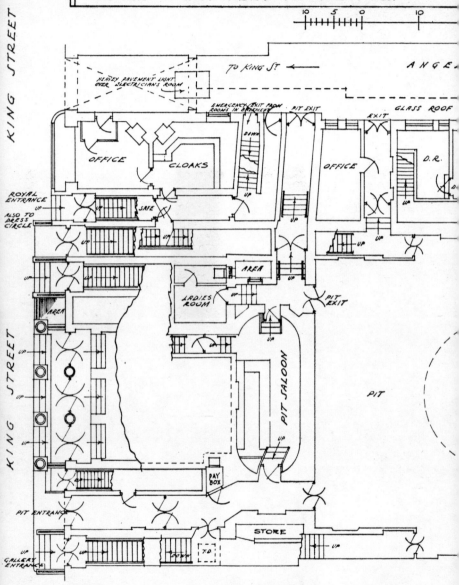

· ST JAMES'S THEATRE

· KING STREET · S·W·1 ·

· SCALE: EIGHT FEET TO ONE INCH ·

10 5 0 10

KING STREET

TO KING ST ←

ANGEL

HEAVY PAVEMENT LIGHT
OVER ELECTRICIANS ROOM

EMERGENCY EXIT FROM
ROOMS IN BASEMENT

PIT EXIT

EXIT

GLASS ROOF

DOWN

OFFICE

CLOAKS

OFFICE

D.R.

UP

ROYAL
ENTRANCE

UP

ALSO TO
DRESS
CIRCLE

UP

SAFE

UP

UP

UP

UP

UP

AREA

AREA

LADIES
ROOM

UP

PIT
EXIT

KING STREET

UP

AREA

UP

PIT SALOON

PIT

UP

UP

UP

UP

PAY
BOX

PIT ENTRANCE

STORE

UP

UP

GALLERY
ENTRANCE

DOWN

T.D.